£10

TWO CHEERS
FOR
DEMOCRACY

BY THE SAME AUTHOR

 WHERE ANGELS FEAR TO TREAD

 A ROOM WITH A VIEW

 THE LONGEST JOURNEY

 HOWARDS END

 A PASSAGE TO INDIA

 ASPECTS OF THE NOVEL

 GOLDSWORTHY LOWES DICKINSON

 ABINGER HARVEST

TWO CHEERS FOR DEMOCRACY

BY

E. M. FORSTER

LONDON

EDWARD ARNOLD & CO.

PRINTED IN GREAT BRITAIN BY
BUTLER AND TANNER LTD., FROME AND LONDON

To

JACK SPROTT

*of the University of Nottingham
England*

and to

BILL ROEHRICH

*of Lost Farm   Tyringham
Massachusetts*

PREFATORY NOTE

These essays, articles, broadcasts, etc., were nearly all of them composed after the publication of *Abinger Harvest*, that is to say after 1936. A title for the collection has been difficult to find. One of my younger friends suggested *Two Cheers for Democracy* as a joke, and I have decided to adopt it seriously.

Arrangement has been still more difficult. A chronological arrangement would have been simplest. But I was anxious to produce a book rather than a time-string, and to impose some sort of order upon the occupations and preoccupations, the appointments and disappointments of the past fifteen years. Division into two sections proved helpful. The opening section, 'The Second Darkness,' concentrates on the war which began for Great Britain in 1939, though earlier elsewhere, and which is still going on. Subjects such as Anti-Semitism, the Nazis, Liberty, the Censorship are here discussed. The climate is political, and the conclusion suggested is that, though we cannot expect to love one another, we must learn to put up with one another. Otherwise we shall all of us perish.

The second section, 'What I Believe,' covers the same period as the first and sometimes the same subjects, but its climate is ethical and aesthetic. It opens with an essay which may be regarded as a key to the book. Then come the arts. I have found by experience that the arts act as an antidote against our present troubles and also as a support to our common humanity, and I am glad to emphasise this at a time when they are being belittled and starved. Theories of art are followed by the arts in action—literature particularly : Skelton and Shakespeare to Forrest Reid, Voltaire to Proust and Iqbal, together with items less easily accommodated, such as Mrs. Miniver, the Duke of Portland, my own grandfather, and my own library. Then places : in them also I believe. Beginning with the Pelew Islands, which I have only visited vicariously, I flit via India and South Africa to the United States, to Europe, to England, and finally spiral down upon Abinger, the village in Surrey which was for many years my home.

7

That ends the miscellany. I hope it may reveal some unity of outlook, for it certainly lacks unity of atmosphere ; some of the items being expository in tone and others allusive. The broadcasts have been troublesome. There is something cajoling and ingratiating about them which cannot be exorcised by editing, and they have been the devil to reproduce. I have not been consistent over broadcasts. In some cases I have taken the microphone by the horns and printed the script as it stood. Elsewhere I have attempted concealments which the reader will probably detect.

Until livelier counsels prevailed ' The Last of Abinger ' was to have been the book's general title. But I do not really want to record the last of anything and am glad to change. Human life is still active, still carrying about with it unexplored riches and unused methods of release. The darkness that troubles us and tries to degrade us may thin out. We may still contrive to raise three cheers for democracy, although at present she only deserves two.

Cambridge,
England,
1951

ACKNOWLEDGMENTS

My thanks for permission kindly given to reprint previously published material are due, in the first place, to the Syndics of the Cambridge University Press for *Virginia Woolf*; the University Board of the University of Glasgow for *English Prose between 1918 and 1939*—and for the quotations within it from T. E. Lawrence's *Seven Pillars of Wisdom* (Jonathan Cape Ltd.) and Lytton Strachey's *Queen Victoria* (Chatto and Windus) to the respective authors' executors and publishers; the Harvard University Press for *The Raison d'Être of Criticism in the Arts*; and the Hogarth Press for *Anonymity* and *A Letter to Madan Blanchard*.

Also to the following : the *Abinger Chronicle*, the British Broadcasting Corporation (and more particularly the *Listener*), *Horizon*, *Reynold's Weekly*, the *New Statesman and Nation*, *New Writing*, the *Spectator*, *Time and Tide*, and *Anjuman-e-Tarrqi Urdu*.

The essays on Crabbe and on Skelton have not been published before ; nor has the meditation with which the miscellany closes.

CONTENTS

PAGE

PART I. THE SECOND DARKNESS

THE LAST PARADE 15
THE MENACE TO FREEDOM 21
JEW-CONSCIOUSNESS 24
OUR DEPUTATION 27
RACIAL EXERCISE 29
POST-MUNICH 33
GERALD HEARD 37
THEY HOLD THEIR TONGUES 40
THREE ANTI-NAZI BROADCASTS :
    1. CULTURE AND FREEDOM 43
    2. WHAT HAS GERMANY DONE TO THE GERMANS ? . . . 47
    3. WHAT WOULD GERMANY DO TO US ? 50
TOLERANCE 55
RONALD KIDD 59
THE TERCENTENARY OF THE ' AREOPAGITICA ' 62
THE CHALLENGE OF OUR TIME 67
GEORGE ORWELL 72

PART II. WHAT I BELIEVE

WHAT I BELIEVE 77

Art in General

ANONYMITY : AN ENQUIRY 87
ART FOR ART'S SAKE 98
THE DUTY OF SOCIETY TO THE ARTIST 105
DOES CULTURE MATTER ? 110
THE RAISON D'ÊTRE OF CRITICISM IN THE ARTS 117
THE C MINOR OF THAT LIFE 132
NOT LISTENING TO MUSIC 136
NOT LOOKING AT PICTURES 140

The Arts in Action

JOHN SKELTON 145
JULIUS CAESAR 162
THE STRATFORD JUBILEE OF 1769 166
GIBBON AND HIS AUTOBIOGRAPHY 169
VOLTAIRE AND FREDERICK THE GREAT 174

PAGE

GEORGE CRABBE AND PETER GRIMES 178
BISHOP JEBB'S BOOK 193
HENRY THORNTON 197
WILLIAM ARNOLD 202
'SNOW' WEDGWOOD 207
WILLIAM BARNES 209
THREE STORIES BY TOLSTOY 213
EDWARD CARPENTER 217
WEBB AND WEBB 220
A BOOK THAT INFLUENCED ME 224
OUR SECOND GREATEST NOVEL? 229
GIDE AND GEORGE 233
GIDE'S DEATH 236
ROMAIN ROLLAND AND THE HERO 238
A WHIFF OF D'ANNUNZIO 242
THE COMPLETE POEMS OF C. P. CAVAFY 246
VIRGINIA WOOLF 251
TWO BOOKS BY T. S. ELIOT 267
THE ASCENT OF F.6 271
THE ENCHAFÈD FLOOD 274
FORREST REID 277
ENGLISH PROSE BETWEEN 1918 AND 1939 280
AN OUTSIDER ON POETRY 292
MOHAMMED IQBAL 296
SYED ROSS MASOOD 299
A DUKE REMEMBERS 302
MRS. MINIVER 305
IN MY LIBRARY 309
THE LONDON LIBRARY 313

Places

A LETTER TO MADAN BLANCHARD 317
INDIA AGAIN 327
LUNCHEON AT PRETORIA 336
THE UNITED STATES 339
MOUNT LEBANON 344
FERNEY 348
CLOUDS HILL 352
CAMBRIDGE 356
LONDON IS A MUDDLE 361
THE LAST OF ABINGER 366

PART I
THE SECOND DARKNESS

The Last Parade

Paris Exhibition, 1937 : Palace of Discovery, Astronomical Section : model of the Earth in space. Yes, here is a model of this intimate object. It is a tidy size—so large that Europe or even France should be visible on it—and it revolves at a suitable rate. It does not take twenty-four hours to go round as in fact, nor does it whizz as in poetry. It considers the convenience of the observer, as an exhibit should. Staged in a solemn alcove, against a background of lamp-super-black, it preens its contours eternally, that is to say from opening to closing time, and allows us to see our home as others would see it, were there others who could see. Its colouring, its general appearance, accord with the latest deductions. The result is surprising. For not France, not even Europe, is visible. There are great marks on the surface of the model, but they represent clouds and snows, not continents and seas. No doubt the skilled observer could detect some underlying fussiness, and infer our civilisation, but the average voyager through space would only notice our clouds and our snows ; they strike the eye best. Natural boundaries, guns in action, beautiful women, pipe-lines—at a little distance they all wear the same veil. Sir Malcolm Campbell beats his own records till he sees his own back, Mr. Jack Hulbert cracks still cleaner jokes, forty thousand monkeys are born in Brazil and fifty thousand Italians in Abyssinia, the Palace of the Soviets rises even higher than had been planned, Lord Baden-Powell holds a yet larger jamboree, but all these exercises and the areas where they occur remain hidden away under an external shimmer. The moon—she shows her face. Throned in an adjacent room, the moon exhibits her pockmarks nakedly. But the Earth, because she still has atmosphere and life, is a blur.

Paris Exhibition : the Spanish Pavilion, the Italian Pavilion. The other pavilions. The Palaces of Glass and of Peace. The Eiffel Tower. The last named occasionally sings. Moved by an emission of Roman Candles from its flanks, it will break of

15

an evening into a dulcet and commanding melody. When this happens the pavilions fold their hands to listen, and are steeped for a little in shadow, so that the aniline fountains may play more brightly in the Seine. The melody swells, inciting the fireworks as they the melody, and both of them swell the crowd. O synchronisation ! O splendour unequalled ! Splendour ever to be surpassed ? Probably never to be surpassed. The German and Russian Pavilions, the Chinese and Japanese Pavilions, the British and Italian Pavilions, any and all of the pavilions, will see to that. The Eiffel Tower sings louder, a scientific swan. Rosy chemicals stimulate her spine, she can scarcely bear the voltage, the joy, the pain. . . . The emotion goes to her tiny head, it turns crimson and vomits fiery serpents. All Paris sees them. They astonish the Pantheon and Montmartre. Even the Institut de France notices, heavy browed, dreaming of cardinals, laurels, and réclame in the past. O inspired giraffe ! Whatever will the old thing turn into next ? Listen and see. The crisis is coming. The melody rises by slight and sure gradations, à la César Franck, spiralling easily upward upon the celestial round-about. Bell pop popple crack, is the crisis, bell pop popple crack, the senses reel, music and light, lusic and might, the Eiffel Tower becomes a plesiosauros, flings out her arms in flame, and brings them back smartly to her vibrating sides, as one who should say ' là ! ' Bell pop crack pop popple bell. The carillon dies away, the rockets fall, the senses disentangle. There is silence, there are various types of silences, and during one of them the Angel of the Laboratory speaks. ' Au revoir, mes enfants,' she says. ' I hope you have enjoyed yourselves. We shall meet again shortly, and in different conditions.' The children applaud these well-chosen words. The German Pavilion, the Russian Pavilion, confront one another again, and a small star shines out on the top of the Column of Peace.

Paris Exhibition : Van Gogh. When the day breaks, Van Gogh can be found if wanted. He is housed in the corner of another palace between maps of Paris and intellectual hopes for the future, and the space suffices him. Well content with his half-dozen rooms, he displays his oddness and his misery to tired feet. ' Sorrow is better than joy,' he writes up upon the white walls of his cell. Here are pictures of potatoes and of miners who have eaten potatoes until their faces are tuberous and dented and their skins grimed and unpeeled. They are hopeless and humble, so he loves them. He has his little say, and he understands what he is saying, and he cuts off his own ear with a knife. The gaily painted boats of Saintes Maries sail away into the Mediterranean at last, and the Alpilles rise over St. Rémy for ever, but nevertheless ' Sorrow is better than joy,' for Van Gogh. What would the Eiffel Tower make of such a conclusion? Spinning in its alcove for millions of years, the earth brings a great artist to this. Is he just dotty, or is he failing to put across what is in his mind? Neither, if we may accept historical parallels. Every now and then people have preferred sorrow to joy, and asserted that wisdom and creation can only result from suffering. Half a mile off, Picasso has done a terrifying fresco in the Spanish Pavilion, a huge black and white thing called ' Guernica.' Bombs split bull's skull, woman's trunk, man's shins. The fresco is indignant, and so it is less disquieting than the potato-feeders of Van Gogh. Picasso is grotesquely angry, and those who are angry still hope. He is not yet wise, and perhaps he is not yet a creator. Nevertheless, he too succeeds in saying something about injustice and pain. Can one look through pain or get round it? And can anything be done against money? On the subject of money, Van Gogh becomes comprehensible and sound. He has got round money because he has sought suffering and renounced happiness. In the sizzle surrounding him, his voice stays uncommercial, unscientific, pure. He sees the colour ' blue,' observes that the colour ' yellow ' always occurs in it, and writes this preposterous postulate up upon the white walls. He has a home beyond comfort and common sense with the saints, and perhaps he sees God.

The Soviet Pavilion. This, bold and gleaming, hopes to solve such problems for the ordinary man. And for the ordinary woman too, who, of enormous size, leans forward on the roof beside her gigantic mate. Seen from the side, they and the building upon which they stand describe a hyperbola. They shoot into space, following their hammer and sickle, and followed by the worker's world state. The conception is satisfying, but a hyperbola is a mathematical line, not necessarily an aesthetic one, and the solid and ardent pair do not group well when viewed from the banks of the bourgeois Seine. Challenging injustice, they ignore good taste, indeed they declare in their sterner moments that injustice and good taste are inseparable. Their aims are moral, their methods disciplinary. Passing beneath their sealed-up petticoats and trousers, we enter a realm which is earnest, cheerful, instructive, constructive and consistent, but which has had to blunt some of the vagrant sensibilities of mankind and is consequently not wholly alive. Statistics, maps and graphs preach a numerical triumph, but the art-stuff on the walls might just as well hang on the walls of the German Pavilion opposite : the incidents and the uniforms in the pictures are different but the mentality of the artists is the same, and is as tame. Only after a little thinking does one get over one's disappointment and see the matter in perspective. For the Soviet Pavilion is a nudge to the blind. It is trying, like Van Gogh, to dodge money and to wipe away the film of coins and notes which keeps forming on the human retina. One of the evils of money is that it tempts us to look at it rather than at the things that it buys. They are dimmed because of the metal and the paper through which we receive them. That is the fundamental deceitfulness of riches, which kept worrying Christ. That is the treachery of the purse, the wallet and the bank-balance, even from the capitalist point of view. They were invented as a convenience to the flesh, they have become a chain for the spirit. Surely they can be cut out, like some sorts of pain. Though deprived of them the human mind might surely still keep its delicacy unimpaired, and the human body eat, drink and make love. And that is why every bourgeois ought to reverence the Soviet Pavilion. Even if he is scared at Marxism he ought to realise that Russia has tried to put men into touch with things. She has come along with a handkerchief and wiped. And she has wiped close to the exhibition turnstiles and amid the chaos and carnage of international finance.

Park of Attractions. I did enjoy myself here, I must say. That is the difficulty of considering the Exhibition : it is in so many pieces and so is oneself. After seeing the German Pavilion, which presents Valhalla as a telephone box, and the Belgian Pavilion, which is very lovely, and many other sacred and serious objects, I sought the Park of Attractions and went up to space in a pretence-balloon. A crane lifted me into the void while another crane lowered another balloon which filled with people when my balloon was up. Then my balloon came down and the other balloon went up. So I got out and walked over the surface of the earth to the Dervish Theatre. Then I watched other people play a game called 'Deshabillez vos vedettes.' I thought a vedette was a boat. Here it was a tin lady, naked except for a cincture of green feathers which the entrants tried to shoot off. Then I went to a booth advertising ' Perversités. Images Troublantes.' The entrance fee was a franc, which helped me to keep my head. Inside were some distorting mirrors, a little black savage who kept lashing herself or himself with a bunch of boot-laces, and some holes through which improper photographs should have been seen, but I got muddled and missed them. Oh, the French, the French ! Well pleased, I came out. It was a lovely evening. The moon, which had been trying various styles from Neon to Pantheon, now imitated a pretence-balloon. The Park of Attractions, which is extremely clever and pretty, was girt with a scenic railway, and at intervals the shrieks of voyagers through space rent the night. There was plenty to spend money on. Money, money, money ! The crowd was what journalists call ' good humoured ' ; and I, a journalist, was part of it. Tunisians and Moroccans strolled about and sometimes kissed one another. Oh the French ! Why are they so good at organizing these lighter happinesses ? The English admire them, and themselves produce the suety dreariness, the puffed pretentiousness, of Wembley.

Satan. Unexpected but unmistakable, he appears in the great entrance court of the Italian Pavilion, amongst the fragments of the lovely Italian past. These fragments are bent to his service —Garibaldi, St. Francis, Ravenna mosaics, Pompeian doves. He is to the left as one comes in, clothed all in black, and he dominates a large feeble picture of carnage. He is weakness triumphant —that is his rôle in the modern world. He presses a button and a bull bursts. He sprays savages with scent. He tilts his head back till his chin sticks out like a tongue and his eyeballs stare into his brain. Decent people take no notice of him or make fun of him, but presently something goes wrong with their lives ; certain islands are inaccessible, a letter is unanswered, bonds confiscated, a friend takes a trip over the frontier and never returns. Elsewhere in this same pavilion are his instruments : things easily let off. He has only one remark to make : ' I, I, I.' He uses the symbols of the sacred and solemn past, but they only mean ' I.' Here, among superficial splendours of marble, he holds his court, and no one can withstand him except Van Gogh, and Van Gogh has nothing to lose. The rest of us are vulnerable, science is doing us in, the Angel of the Laboratory switches off the fireworks, and burns up the crowd without flame.

Meanwhile, and all the while, the Earth revolves in her alcove, veiled in wool. She has sent samples of her hopes and lusts to Paris ; that they will again be collected there, or anywhere, is unlikely, but she herself will look much the same as soon as one stands a little back in space. Even if the Mediterranean empties into the Sahara it will not make much difference. It is our clouds and our snows that show.

[1937]

The Menace to Freedom

The menace to freedom is usually conceived in terms of political or social interference—Communism, Fascism, Grundyism, bureaucratic encroachment, censorship, conscription and so forth. And it is usually personified as a tyrant who has escaped from the bottomless pit, his proper home, and is stalking the earth by some mysterious dispensation, in order to persecute God's elect, the electorate. But this is too lively a view of our present troubles, and too shallow a one. We must peer deeper if we want to understand them, deep into the abyss of our own characters. For politics are based on human nature ; even a tyrant is a man, and our freedom is really menaced to-day because a million years ago Man was born in chains.

That unfortunate event lies too far back for retrospective legislation ; no declarations of independence touch it ; no League of Nations can abolish it. Man grew out of other forms of life ; he has evolved among taboos ; he has been a coward for centuries, afraid of the universe outside him and of the herd wherein he took refuge. So he cannot, even if he wishes it, be free to-day. In recent centuries—Greece saw the first attempt—he tried to become an individual, an entity which thinks for itself, says what it thinks, and acts according to its own considered standards ; and there has been much applause for this attempt in art and literature, but it is abortive morally because of those primaeval chains. The ghosts of chains, the chains of ghosts, but they are strong enough, literally stronger than death, generation after generation hands them on. More recently still, Man has dallied with the idea of a social conscience, and has disguised the fear of the herd as loyalty towards the group, and has persuaded himself that when he sacrifices himself to the State he is accomplishing a deed far more satisfying than anything which can be accomplished alone. Alone ? As if he had ever been alone ! He has never had the opportunity. Only Heaven knows what Man might accomplish alone ! The service that is perfect freedom, perhaps. As things are, the poor creature presents a sorry spectacle to the philosopher—or, rather, he would do so if

philosophers existed, but we have realised since the days of
Voltaire and Rousseau that they do not exist. There is no
such person as a philosopher ; no one is detached ; the observer,
like the observed, is in chains.

To the best minds of the eighteenth and nineteenth centuries
freedom appeared as a blessing which had to be recovered.
They believed that a little energy and intelligence would accomplish this. The chains had only to be broken violently, the
conventions patiently unloosed, and either by revolutionary or by
constitutional methods Man would re-enter his heritage and the
tyrant sink back into his pit. The twentieth century knows
more history than that and more psychology, and has suffered
more ; its disillusion over peace in 1914 has been swiftly followed
by its disillusion over democracy to-day. The tyrant no longer
appears as a freak from the pit, he is becoming the norm, country
after country throws him up, he springs from any class of society
with an ease which once seemed admirable ; requiring only
opportunity and ruthlessness, he supersedes parliaments and kings.
And consequently many people do not believe in freedom any
more, and the few who do regard it as something that must
be discovered, not recovered. They think that it is a blessing
which we have never possessed up to now. They hope for a
revelation in the human make-up which will allow it to emerge.
And there is this to be said for such optimism : the human make-
up is certainly changing ; we alter ourselves merely by knowing
more about ourselves, and we know more about ourselves yearly.
Perhaps, under the inrush of scientific inventions, the change will
proceed still quicker. Perhaps, after the storms have swept by
and the aeroplanes crashed into one another and wireless jammed
wireless, a new creature may appear on this globe, a creature
who, we pretend, is here already : the individual.

How the globe would get on, if entirely peopled with
individuals, it is impossible to foresee. However, Man has
another wish, besides the wish to be free, and that is the wish
to love, and perhaps something may be born from the union
of the two. Love sometimes leads to an obedience which is
not servile—the obedience referred to in the Christian epigram
above quoted. Love, after a dreadful period of inflation, is
perhaps coming back to its proper level and may steady civilisation ; up-to-date social workers believe in it. It is difficult not
to get mushy as soon as one mentions love, but it is a tendency

that must be reckoned with, and it takes as many forms as fear. The desire to devote oneself to another person or persons seems to be as innate as the desire for personal liberty. If the two desires could combine, the menace to freedom from within, the fundamental menace, might disappear, and the political evils now filling all the foreground of our lives would be deprived of the poison which nourishes them. They will not wilt in our time, we can hope for no immediate relief. But it is a good thing, once in a way, to speculate on the remoter future. It is a good thing, when freedom is discussed, not always to be wondering what ought to be done about Hitler, or whether the decisions of the Milk Marketing Board are unduly arbitrary. There is the Beloved Republic to dream about and to work for through our dreams ; the better polity which once seemed to be approaching on greased wheels ; the City of God.

[1935]

Jew-Consciousness

Long, long ago, while Queen Victoria reigned, I attended two preparatory schools. At the first of these, it was held to be a disgrace to have a sister. Any little boy who possessed one was liable to get teased. The word would go round : ' Oh, you men, have you seen the Picktoes' sister ? ' The men would then reel about with sideway motions, uttering cries of ' sucks ' and pretending to faint with horror, while the Picktoes, who had hitherto held their own socially in spite of their name, found themselves banished into the wilderness, where they mourned, Major with Minor, in common shame. Naturally anyone who had a sister hid her as far as possible, and forbade her to sit with him at a Prizegiving or to speak to him except in passing and in a very formal manner. Public opinion was not bitter on the point, but it was quite definite. Sisters were disgraceful. I got through all right myself, because my conscience was clear, and though charges were brought against me from time to time they always fell through.

It was a very different story at my second school. Here, sisters were negligible, but it was a disgrace to have a mother. Crabbe's mother, Gob's mother, eeugh ! No words were too strong, no sounds too shrill. And since mothers at that time of life are commoner than sisters, and also less biddable, the atmosphere of this school was less pleasant, and the sense of guilt stronger. Nearly every little boy had a mother in a cupboard, and dreadful revelations occurred. A boy would fall ill and a mother would swoop and drive him away in a cab. A parcel would arrive with ' From Mummy for her darling ' branded upon it. Many tried to divert suspicion by being aggressive and fastening female parents upon the weak. One or two, who were good at games and had a large popularity-surplus, took up a really heroic line, acknowledged their mother brazenly, and would even be seen walking with her across the playing-field, like King Carol with Madame Lupescu. We admired such boys and envied them, but durst not imitate them. The margin of safety was too narrow. The convention was established that a mother spelt disgrace, and no individual triumph could reverse this.

Those preparatory schools prepared me for life better than I realised, for having passed through two imbecile societies, a sister-conscious and a mother-conscious, I am now invited to enter a third. I am asked to consider whether the people I meet and talk about are or are not Jews, and to form no opinion on them until this fundamental point has been settled. What revolting tosh ! Neither science nor religion nor common sense has one word to say in its favour. All the same, Jew-consciousness is in the air, and it remains to be seen how far it will succeed in poisoning it. I don't think we shall ever reintroduce ghettoes into England ; I wouldn't say for certain, since no one knows what wickedness may not develop in his country or in himself if circumstances change. I don't think we shall go savage. But I do think we shall go silly. Many people have gone so already. To-day, the average man suspects the people he dislikes of being Jews, and is surprised when the people he likes are Jews. Having been a Gentile at my first preparatory school and a Jew at my second, I know what I am talking about. I know how the poison works, and I know too that if the average man is anyone in particular he is a preparatory school boy. On the surface, things do not look too bad. Labour and Liberalism behave with their expected decency and denounce persecution, and respectability generally follows suit. But beneath the surface things are not so good, and anyone who keeps his ears open in railway carriages or pubs or country lanes can hear a very different story. A nasty side of our nation's character has been scratched up—the sniggering side. People who would not ill-treat Jews themselves, or even be rude to them, enjoy tittering over their misfortunes ; they giggle when pogroms are instituted by someone else and synagogues defiled vicariously. ' Serve them right really, Jews.' This makes unpleasant reading, but anyone who cares to move out of his own enlightened little corner will discover that it is true. The grand Nordic argument, ' He's a bloody capitalist so he must be a Jew, and as he's a Jew he must be a Red,' has already taken root in our filling-stations and farms. Men employ it more frequently than women, and young men more frequently than old ones. The best way of confuting it is to say sneeringly ' That's propaganda.' When ' That's propaganda ' has been repeated several times, the sniggering stops, for no goose likes to think that he has been got at. There is another reply which is more intellectual but which requires more courage. It is to say, ' Are you sure you're not a Jew yourself ? Do you know who your eight great-grand-parents were ? Can you swear that all the eight are Aryan ? ' Cool reasonableness would be best of all, of course, but it does not work in the world of to-day any better than in my preparatory schools. The only effective check to silliness is silliness of a cleverer type.

Jew-mania was the one evil which no one foretold at the close of the last war. All sorts of troubles were discerned and discernable—nationalism, class-warfare, the split between the haves and the have-nots, the general lowering of cultural values. But no prophet, so far as I know, had foreseen this anti-Jew horror, whereas to-day no one can see the end of it. There had been warnings, of course, but they seemed no more ominous than a poem by Hilaire Belloc. Back in India, in 1921, a Colonel lent me the Protocols of the Elders of Zion, and it was such an obvious fake that I did not worry. I had forgotten my preparatory schools, and did not see that they were about to come into their own. To me, anti-Semitism is now the most shocking of all things. It is destroying much more than the Jews ; it is assailing the human mind at its source, and inviting it to create false categories before exercising judgment. I am sure we shall win through. But it will take a long time. Perhaps a hundred years must pass before men can think back to the mentality of 1918, or can say with the Prophet Malachi, ' Have we not all one father ? Hath not one God created us ? ' For the moment, all that we can do is to dig in our heels, and prevent silliness from sliding into insanity.

[1939]

Our Deputation

Our deputation straggled across Whitehall in the sleet, harried by taxis upon either flank. It jumped a bank of slush, slid upon the pavement, caught hands, upsa! and finally entered the Government Office of its choice. We took off our hats in the vestibule, then realised that we had done so too soon and were being despised by the commissionaires, so we put them on again. Dinginess and warmth surrounded us; it was like being in the belly of a not very healthy monster. At the top of a huge and enormous stairway (both adjectives are needed to describe the architecture) stretched the huge and enormous room where the Minister had consented to receive us and to hear our prayer. Away at the end of it loomed the picture of some statesman or royalty, huge and enormous, and only partially visible through the spume. Our hats came off for good now. Having hung them and our great-coats and mufflers upon the branches of a metallic tree, we placed ourselves at a table which may justly be called gigantic. The chairs seemed miles apart. Honoured but isolated, we could no longer hold one another's hands. After a minute or two, which were spent in dreamily looking at papers, a door near the picture opened, and the Minister popped in.

All rose to their feet. The Minister recoiled as if horror-struck by the commotion he had created. ' Sit sit down, do please sit sit sit,' he said. We obeyed. The Minister sat too, supported on either side by important permanencies belonging to his department. . . . He heard our prayer, which was tersely phrased so as not to waste his time. He thanked us and announced that even now he was attempting to grant it, and to find a statutory form in which to embody our wishes and his own. This sounded splendid. But he was finding it difficult to do this, he went on, very, very difficult difficult. His manner now became bewildered and almost childlike; he seemed baffled by the intricacies of drafting and began to hint that the task of doing as he liked might prove to be beyond his power. ' If you can can can help me,' he pleaded, ' if you can can can can . . . ' and before we knew where we were, he was giving us a good dressing-down.   He said that if we—not that he meant us personally or any of the organisations that we represented—still if we could check certain undesirable tendencies and ensure that certain contraventions of the law were not repeated in the future we should greatly facilitate his task.   The deputation bowed its head like a flower in a frost, and, gazing at my particular bit of the table, I reflected upon the technique which is employed by those in high authority when they desire to administer a snub.   They carry on like this : they begin a sentence deeply, gruffly, gently ; it moves along like a large friendly animal ; then it twitters, turns acid and thin and passes right overhead with a sort of whistling sound.   An awed pause followed.   However, one of the deputation pulled himself together and gave, I thought, an excellent performance in the same key.   We entirely agreed with the Minister, he said, his voice still deep.   We felt exactly as the Minister felt.   No one could deplore more than we did the tendencies, the manifestations that had been mentioned.   But (and here his voice grew thinner) there was surely an Act of Parliament already in existence which dealt with such matters, and this being so (voice now well overhead) the deputation did not quite appreciate why they should be raised here.   There was now a pause at the ministerial end of the table, and it was conveyed to us, by shiftings of pince-nez and bleakness of cheeks, that our champion had not contributed anything constructive. Next, one of the important permanencies spoke, and his voice too went up in the air at the end in a bitter whistle.   Was the interview going to be an unfriendly one ?   No, no, nothing as definite as that.   Civilities were re-exchanged, time was up, we thanked and were counter-thanked, our opinions were to be given their full weight, and performing a final can-can, the Minister slipped from the room.   He had performed his duty, and we ours.   We went to the tree which had all the time supported our great-coats, we unwound our mufflers from its branches and placed our hats upon our heads, and we passed down the stairway back into the snow and the dirt outside, and resolved into our component parts.

[1939]

Racial Exercise

Let us do some easy exercises in Racial Purity.

And let me offer myself for dissection-purposes.

If I go the right way about it, I come of an old English family, but the right way is unfortunately a crooked one. It is far from easy going in the branches of my genealogical tree. I have to proceed via my father to his mother, thence to her mother, and thence to her father. If I follow this zigzag course I arrive in the satisfactory bosom of a family called Sykes, and have a clear run back through several centuries. The Sykes' go right away ever so far, right back to a certain Richard of Sykes Dyke who flourished somewhere about the year 1400. Whether inside their dyke, which lay in Cumberland, or outside it, which was Yorkshire, this family never did anything earth-shaking, still they did keep going in the documentary sense, they made money and married into it, they became mayors of Pontefract or Hull, they employed Miss Anna Seward as a governess, and, in the seventeenth century, one of them, a Quaker, was imprisoned on account of his opinions in York Castle, and died there. I come of an old English family, and am proud of it.

Unfortunately in other directions the prospect is less extensive. If I take a wrong turning and miss the Sykes', darkness descends on my origins almost at once. Mrs. James is a case in point, and a very mortifying one. Mrs. James was a widow who not so very long ago married one of my great-grandfathers. I am directly descended from her, know nothing whatever about her, and should like at all events to discover her maiden name. Vain quest. She disappears in the mists of antiquity, like Richard of Sykes Dyke, but much too soon. She might be anyone, she may not even have been Aryan. When her shadow crosses my mind, I do not feel to belong to an old family at all.

After that dissection, let us proceed to do our easy Racial Exercise.

It is this : Can you give the names of your eight great-grandparents ?

The betting is at least eight to one against. The Royal

Family could, some aristocrats could, and so could a few yeomen who have lived undisturbed in a quiet corner of England for a couple of hundred years. But most of the people I know (and probably most of the people who read these words) will fail. We can often get six or seven, seldom the whole eight. And the human mind is so dishonest and so snobby, that we instinctively reject the eighth as not mattering, and as playing no part in our biological make-up. As each of us looks back into his or her past, doors open upon darkness. Two doors at first— the father and the mother—through each of these two more, then the eight great-grandparents, the sixteen great-greats, then thirty-two ancestors . . . sixty-four . . . one hundred and twenty-eight . . . until the researcher reels. Even if the stocks producing us interbred, and so reduced the total of our progenitors by using some of them up on us twice, even if they practised the strict domestic economy of the Ptolemies, the total soon becomes enormous, and the Sykes' in it are nothing beside the Mrs. James'. On such a shady past as this—our common past—do we erect the ridiculous doctrine of Racial Purity.

In the future the situation will be slightly less ridiculous. Registers of marriage and birth will be kept more carefully, bastardy more cunningly detected, so that in a couple of hundred years millions of people will belong to Old Families. This should be a great comfort to them. It may also be a convenience, if governments continue to impose racial tests. Citizens will be in a position to point to an Aryan ancestry if their government is Aryan, to a Cretinist ancestry if it is Cretin, and so on, and if they cannot point in the direction required, they will be sterilised. This should be a great discomfort to them. Nor will the sterilisation help, for the mischief has already been done in our own day, the mess has been made, miscegenation has already taken place. Whether there ever was such an entity as a 'pure race' is debatable, but there certainly is not one in Europe to-day—the internationalisms of the Roman Empire and of the Middle Ages have seen to that. Consequently there never can be a pure race in the future. Europe is mongrel for ever, and so is America.

How extraordinary it is that governments which claim to be realistic should try to base themselves on anything so shadowy and romantic as race ! A common language, a common religion, a common culture all belong to the present, evidence

about them is available, they can be tested. But race belongs
to the unknown and unknowable past. It depends upon who
went to bed with whom in the year 1400, not to mention Mrs.
James, and what historian will ever discover that ? Community
of race is an illusion. Yet belief in race is a growing psychological force, and we must reckon with it. People like to feel
that they are all of a piece, and one of the ways of inducing that
feeling is to tell them that they come of pure stock. That explains
the ease with which the dictators are putting their pseudo-science
across. No doubt they are not cynical about it, and take themselves in by what they say. But they have very cleverly hit on
a weak spot in the human equipment—the desire to feel a hundred
per cent., no matter what the percentage is in.

A German Professor was holding forth the other day on the
subject of the origins of the German people. His attitude was
that the purity of the Nordic stock is not yet proved and should
not be spoken of as proved. But it should be spoken of as a
fact, because it is one, and the proofs of its existence will be
forthcoming as soon as scholars are sufficiently energetic and
brave. He spoke of ' courage ' in research. According to his
own lights, he was a disinterested researcher, for he refused to
support what he knew to be true by arguments which he held
to be false. The truth, being *a priori*, could afford to wait on
its mountain top until the right path to it was found : the truth
of Nordic purity which every German holds by instinct in his
blood. In India I had friends who said they were descended
from the Sun and looked down on those who merely came
from the Moon, but they were not tense about it and seemed
to forget about it between times, nor did they make it a basis
for political violence and cruelty ; it takes the west to do that.

Behind our problem of the eight great-grandparents stands
the civilising figure of Mendel. I wish that Mendel's name was
mentioned in current journalism as often as Freud's or Einstein's.
He embodies a salutary principle, and even when we are superficial about him, he helps to impress it in our minds. He suggests
that no stock is pure, and that it may at any moment throw up
forms which are unexpected, and which it inherits from the past.
His best-known experiments were with the seeds of the pea.
It is impossible that human beings can be studied as precisely
as peas—too many factors are involved. But they too keep
throwing up recessive characteristics, and cause us to question

the creed of racial purity. Mendel did not want to prove anything. He was not a 'courageous' researcher, he was merely a researcher. Yet he has unwittingly put a valuable weapon into the hands of civilised people. We don't know what our ancestors were like or what our descendants will be like. We only know that we are all of us mongrels, dark haired and light haired, who must learn not to bite one another. Thanks to Mendel and to a few simple exercises we can see comparatively clearly into the problem of race, if we choose to look, and can do a little to combat the pompous and pernicious rubbish that is at present being prescribed in the high places of the earth.

[1939]

Post-Munich

During the present decade thousands and thousands of innocent people have been killed, robbed, mutilated, insulted, imprisoned. We, the fortunate exceptions, learn of this from the newspapers and from refugees, we realise that it may be our turn next, and we know that all these private miseries may be the prelude to an incalculable catastrophe, in which the whole of western civilisation and half oriental civilisation may go down. Perhaps history will point to these years as the moment when man's inventiveness finally outbalanced his moral growth, and toppled him downhill.

The decade being tragic, should not our way of living correspond? How can we justify trivialities and hesitations? Ought we not to rise to the great dramatic conception which we see developing around us? The situation is tremendous; it has never been equalled because the world has never before been so closely interlocked. The pillars of the twenty-thousand-year-old house are crumbling, the human experiment totters, other forms of life watch. Ought we not, at such a moment, to act as Wagnerian heroes and heroines, who are raised above themselves by the conviction that all is lost or that all can be saved, and stride singing into the flames?

To ask such a question is to answer it. No one who debates whether he shall behave tragically can possibly be a tragic character. He may have a just sense of the stage; he may discern the scene darkening and the powers of evil marching and the ravens gathering; he may feel the first breath of the tempest as it lifts him off his feet and whirls him backwards. But he is not properly cast as an actor; there will be something petty in him—perhaps something recalcitrant—which mars the aesthetic unity. He will not even pay the tribute of unalloyed terror. He will be half-frightened and half-thinking about something else on the very steps of the altar, and when the sacrificial knife falls he will perish an unworthy victim, a blemished and inferior lamb, of little esteem at the banquet of the gods.

The state of being half-frightened and half-thinking about

something else at the same time is the state of many English people
to-day. It is worth examining, partly because it is interesting,
partly because, like all mixed states, it can be improved by
thought. Only Heaven and Hell are stable. It is a 1939 state.
In 1938 we were fresher and less complex. War was promised
or threatened us for a certainty; we went inspired or demented
according to our quality, and our actions bore some relation to
the Zeitgeist's. Exalted in contrary directions, some of us rose
above ourselves and others committed suicide. One elderly
gentleman, for instance, described in the newspaper as having
a great many friends, exclaimed to his housekeeper, ' Oh Agnes,
Agnes, what will become of us all now ? ' and jumped out of
a top-storey window in his pyjamas. He saw what he could
do and he did it, and his conduct when analysed shows parallels
with Brünnhilde's. Others saw something else they could do
and, like Siegmund, prepared to fight—with what weapons and
against what they did not stay to consider. These certainties and
heroisms came to their end when Mr. Chamberlain paid his first
call upon Herr Hitler. I was in London that dark Wednesday
night when the news of an agreement between them seeped
through. It was good news, and it ought to have brought
great joy ; it did bring joy to the House of Commons. But
unimportant and unpractical people often foresee the future more
clearly than do those who are engaged in shaping it, and I knew
at once that the news was only good in patches. Peace flapped
from the posters, and not upon the wings of angels. I trailed
about reading the notices, some of which had already fallen into
the gutter. On the Thursday I returned to the country, and
found satisfaction there in a chicken run which I had helped
build earlier in the week.

This post-Munich world may not last long, but we are living
in it now, and we have not any other life. We have to make
the best of an unexplored and equivocal state, and we are more
likely to succeed if we give up any hope of simplicity. ' Prepare,
prepare ! ' does not do for a slogan. No more does ' Business
as usual.' Both of them are untrue to the spirit of 1939, the
spirit which is half-afraid and half-thinking about something else.
We are urged, by bishops and captains of industry, to face facts,
and we ought to. But we can only face them by being double-
faced. The facts lie in opposite directions, and no exhortation
will group them into a single field. No slogan works. All is

lost if the totalitarians destroy us. But all is equally lost if we have nothing left to lose. And the imperfect and blemished lamb, as he stands at the foot of the altar, is partly atremble because of the oncoming knife, and partly thinking of other things—of the meadows he has walked in, of the games he has played, of the books he has read, of the friends he has made. Perhaps he will decide to be a brave lamb and not to fear death, and if he does this, death will certainly become painless for him, and mutilation painless until it occurs. It is common sense to be brave. But bravery and cowardice are only different sides of the same small shield. They do not cover the whole complexity. Apart from them exist the ' other things ' which riddle the little creature's mind, and make him now stronger and now weaker, now the heir of all of the ages, and now a contemptible failure : the ' other things,' which are summed up as civilisation.

These mixed states are terrible for the nerves. That is the real drawback in them. They give us no chance to feel solid. What with the bravery-cowardice factor, and what with the civilisation factor, we are assailed right and left. Sensitive people are having a particularly humiliating time just now. Looking at the international scene, they see, with a clearness denied to politicians, that if Fascism wins we are done for, and that we must become Fascist to win. There seems no escape from this hideous dilemma, and those who face it most honestly often go jumpy. They are vexed by messages from contradictory worlds, so that whatever they do appears to them as a betrayal of something good ; they feel that nothing is worth attempting, they drop their hands, break off in the middle with a shriek, smash physical or spiritual crockery. If they could sell themselves, they would find peace ; they could, on the one hand, go out hammer and tongs for National Service, pacifism, suicide, etc. ; or on the other hand, they could shut themselves up with their culture and try to hatch something out in isolation, as Remy de Gourmont did in the last war and as Jean Giono hopes to do in the next one. But they are too fine to sell themselves ; that is their glory and their trouble. They see through all the slogans. Their grasp on reality paralyses them. Paradoxically, they become more and more negative and ineffective, until leadership passes to their inferiors.

It is not easy to help such people ; they are too highly developed to be saved by anyone but themselves. One little tip does occur to me, but it is only applicable to such of them as still have money. Those of them who have money should start spending it at once—spending quiets the nerves—and should spend it as if civilisation is permanent ; buy books, go to concerts and plays. It is childish to save ; thrift was only a virtue so long as it paid, which it has ceased to do. And it is fantastic to spend too much on charity ; all the money in England could not stay the world's misery now, or even solve the refugee problem. Spending on art has this advantage, apart from the pleasure to be gained from it ; it does maintain an artistic framework which may come in useful in the future ; it is connected with a positive hope.

This decade has lasted long enough, and the Crisis in particular has become a habit, indeed almost a joke. Emotions are no longer deeply stirred by it, and when Germany or Italy destroys an extra country we are upset for a shorter period each time. We are worried rather than frantic. But worry is terribly insidious ; besides taking the joy out of life, it prevents the victim from being detached and from observing what is happening to the human experiment. It tempts him to simplify, since through simplification he may find peace. Nagging and stinging night and day, it is the undying worm, the worst of our foes. The only satisfactory release is to be found in the direction of complexity. The world won't work out, and the person who can realise this, and not just say it and lament it, has done as well as can be expected of him in the present year.

[1939]

Gerald Heard

While the noise of the conflict grows nearer, it is curious to listen to another sound, which bids us hope. Curious, and disturbing ; for we are reluctant to hope when we have once settled comfortably down to despair. Some spiritual retreat seems the best that remains for a decent person at this moment of general collapse, this moment when the governments kill and the churches have nothing to say. Spiritual ! Such a comfortable word ! Mr. Gerald Heard would agree that salvation lies in its direction, but, differing from the rest of our monitors, he would say that the spirit is not a dug-out but a bomb. It explodes. It attacks by leaping forward inside the individual. Such leaps have occurred in the past, and much of his latest book, *Pain, Sex and Time*, is engaged in examining them. They have been made unconsciously ; to-day man is conscious of himself, and must advance consciously. He has to learn how to let himself off. Where is the trigger ? And how shall he pull it ?

Of these two questions, the first is easier to answer than the second. Mr. Heard can point—and most people will agree with him—to unused energy inside the human animal. Man has not specialised ; he did not go in for wings like the birds, or armour-plating like the crocodiles. He kept himself free, with the result that he has created aeroplanes and tanks, and with the still more important result that he is free to develop psychologically. Man's physical evolution is at an end ; his evolution through the psyche can, if he chooses, continue. His capacity for pain and his capacity for sex (in both of which he surpasses his fellow-animals) are both symptoms of unused energy. If he can detonate his powers, he will blow away the economic and political horrors now surrounding him—horrors which do not merely destroy his body but work inward and destroy his power to understand.

We have here the old doctrine of the Change of Heart but in a violent and earthly form. Mr. Heard dislikes other-worldliness ; he thinks it is one of the three mistakes that the human race must rectify, the other two mistakes being belief in an anthropomorphic god, and belief in reason. He dislikes the Quaker ineffectiveness which, after a quiet sit, goes back to money-making and meals, and opposes Armageddon with philanthropy. A Change of Heart in the explosive sense does, however, appeal to him, and if any tricks, gadgets or drugs are likely to induce it, he is willing to try them. They have been practised in the past—the Fakirs and the Shakti-Yogins have both tried, by experimenting with pain and with sex, to enhance normal consciousness. And though we need not, and probably should not, copy the past, we can learn from it.

Now one of these gadgets has been the Group. He has always invested heavily in the Group. The Group could, in his judgment, pull the trigger and detonate the bomb. 'When two or three are gathered together' an accession of power is felt. He thinks that all who believe in Man's unused powers, should gather into what he calls 'Colleges.' We should there train scientifically the development of our consciousness, which has hitherto been allowed to sprout haphazard. And the Colleges would contain three grades of inmates, roughly corresponding to the three first grades of the Hindu caste-system. The highest grade, the 'Neo-Brahmin,' would be indifferent to amusement and to possessions, and so have the authority and the integrity out of which an International Police Force could be created.

Here we come up against the third, and the most difficult, of his problems. Find the trigger—that is not difficult ; most of us can find it ; most of us know that there are unexplored forces in the human heart, which could be used for good. Pull the trigger and release the bomb—that is more difficult, still it may be possible ; it may be possible, through group work and scientific technique, to produce the Neo-Brahmin. But hit the mark ? Ah, that is more difficult still ! In other words : Would the least notice be taken, by any existing political authority, of Mr. Heard's Colleges ?

He faces this, he faces everything. His International Police Force is, of course, psychological ; it would not work by scolding people into good behaviour but by helping them to understand themselves. It would, in particular, have a Mission to Dictators. But how would they receive such a mission ? Here, as always, his analysis is admirable. He draws a convincing picture of the Dictator's misery, and we can endorse it. Our horror and disgust at Hitler are mixed up with pity for a fellow-creature who has so completely missed the boat.   Never, to his dying day, can such a man enjoy the joys of which he deprives others.   He has cut himself off for ever from the beauty and the glory of the civilised world.   Mr. Heard would, however, argue that, at certain moments, a Hitler can be 'got at' by the Neo-Brahmin, the trained psychologist, and be brought round ; he *can* be made to catch the boat.   And he quotes a few examples from history.   But the examples are unconvincing and meagre.   Tyrants have seldom listened to sages for more than a minute or two, and they have seldom done more than listen. The bomb of the spirit can explode, but its direct action seems no stronger than a paper-bag's.   Mr. Heard's analysis works. His remedy would fail.

[1939]

They Hold their Tongues

Some day, some intellectual day, when Satire revisits our madhouse, an entertaining book could be written around this war. Its title might be *They Hold Their Tongues*, and it would be a ballet rather than a book. The scene will be laid in the Ministry of Decontamination, in the Announcer's Parlour, and at the signs of the Walls Have Ears and the No Bird Sings. The enemy will also be shown, listening to us listening to him listening to us listening to him in an infinite series of sandbags, and the strain will become so great that the military mind will collapse and be unable to distinguish objective from base. Truth and falsehood will be disintegrated into particles which are so small as to be equally useless, and action will become so indirect as to be indirigible. Armies march in the correct direction in order to deceive their generals, airmen drop lethal messages wrapped round dud bombs, clergymen pray for evil lest their congregations be led into it, donkeys bark, dogs mew, cats mew too because cats are subtler than dogs. Enter the experts, for the military mind is conscious to-day of the existence of the mind. Enter the Science of Psychology. Officially installed in a cellar, it abolishes the art of knowing what people are like, and ensures that they are incomprehensible to themselves as well as to others. Frankness is as fatal as kindness, so all hold their tongues. Yes— it might be an amusing entertainment. But it will not be a genial one, and it will not end with an all-round laugh and a kindly apotheosis of the average man. It will have a touch of the rancid flatness which is a part of true satire—for Satire does not merely bite the victim, it lets down the reader too. A few grim survivors, aristocrats, may appreciate it. Swift might contribute. Blake even :

> I was buried near this dyke
> That my friends may weep as much as they like.

Dante too. Dante ·the fantasist—how wickedly he would have described the folk who have held their tongues so well that their tongues come off in their hands. There, beyond

40

Phlegethon, he would place them, and at the base of each tongue would nestle an atrophied brain. Their enormous ears are sewn against their scalps, so that they listen in with a vengeance. Virgil points at the horrible posies, gathers his mantle around him, and registers historical disgust. ' Here,' says Virgil, ' is the recompense of those who have gagged their countrymen for their country's sake, instead of praising their God. Here are the chiefs of police and the card-indexers, and the takers of finger-prints, and Creon, King of Thebes, who issued the fatal edict, and the silencers of Lorca. Look at them, take warning from those dribbling gullets and, while speech is yours, speak.' Far away, beyond the other bank of the river, in Paradise, Beatrice, who is the divine wisdom, echoes the secular warning : ' Speak, speak,' she cries, ' for in the beginning was the Word.'

The light shineth in the darkness, and the light comprehendeth not the darkness. It was the true light, which lighteth every man that cometh into the world, but it has had to be put out. There is no place in a modern war for spontaneity, and never before has the spirit of man been so menaced and insulted. The cloud of his inventions has thickened, descended upon him, blacked him out. He is dazed by darkness. Night is right, and if he holds up so much as a candle to the naughty world, the airwarden reports him for beckoning to death. One natural gesture, and he may destroy himself and his friends. If indeed he still has any friends. Old intimacies may survive the censor-ship, but what new ones can grow up under it ? In this scientific mist, this skilful and deliberate disintegration, what place can be found for the camaraderie and love that have sweetened wars in the past ? Blood used to get warm before it was shed. Now—coldness, depression, suspicion, loneliness. Courage—abundance of courage, but it is the courage that dares not be neighbourly, lest the enemy smell out the place. ' When two or three are gathered together . . .' As if by the intervention of Satan, all the old religious and moral tags work out wrong. When two or three are gathered together, they are more readily detected by hostile aircraft, so they must be prohibited.

Those of us who were brought up in the old order, when Fate advanced slowly, and tragedies were manageable, and human dignity possible, know that that order has vanished from the earth. We are not so foolish as to suppose that fragments of it can be salvaged on some desert island. But since it is the best thing we knew or are capable of knowing, it has become a habit which no facts can alter, it has gone underground like the subterranean Nile in the Book of the Dead. Love, peace, speech, light—these four are the columns of the Temple of Osiris, which no longer stands upon earth. Descending with Dante and the old Egyptians, we seek subterranean streams, we adjust in some spiritual region the balance which has been upset for ever here, we rejoin our friends, we punish our victorious foes, and—most important of all—we see face to face, and know even as we are known. This is sometimes called faith. The honester word for it is habit. It is no more than remembering a tune, it is carrying a rhythm in one's head after the instruments have stopped.

We hope of course that a new tune, inaudible to ourselves, is now being played to the young, and that one day it will re-echo and give them the strength which certainly keeps us going now. But on that point we can get no evidence, and never shall get any. We do expect though that those who chronicle this age and its silliness, and look back from their intellectual day upon us, the tongue-holders, will accord us not only pity, which we fully deserve, but disdain.

[1939]

Three Anti-Nazi Broadcasts

I

CULTURE AND FREEDOM

By profession, I am a writer. I know nothing about economics or politics, but I am deeply interested in what is conveniently called culture, and I want it to prosper all over the world. My belief is that if the Nazis won, culture would be destroyed in England and the Empire. In the Kaiser's war, Germany was just a hostile country. She and England were enemies, but they both belonged to the same civilisation. In Hitler's war Germany is not a hostile country, she is a hostile principle. She stands for a new and a bad way of life and, if she won, would be bound to destroy our ways. There is not room in the same world for Nazi Germany and for people who don't think as she does. She says so herself, and if any Nazi should honour me by listening to my remarks, I do not think he will disagree with them.

Now, Germany is not against culture. She does believe in literature and art. But she has made a disastrous mistake ; she has allowed her culture to become governmental, and from this mistake proceed all kinds of evils. In England our culture is not governmental. It is national : it springs naturally out of our way of looking at things, and out of the way we have looked at things in the past. It has developed slowly, easily, lazily ; the English love of freedom, the English countryside, English prudishness and hypocrisy, English freakishness, our mild idealism and good-humoured reasonableness have all combined to make something which is certainly not perfect, but which may claim to be unusual. Our great achievement has been in literature : here we rank high, both as regards prose and verse. We have not done much in painting or music, and patriots who pretend that we have only make us look silly. We have made a respectable, though not a sublime, contribution to philosophy. That—so far as it can be summed up in a few words—is the English achievement.

But before going on to the German achievement, which was

also an important one, I want to say something about freedom, because, to my mind, freedom is bound up with the whole question of culture. The Nazis condemn it, in practice and theory, and assert that civilisation will flourish without it. Individualists like myself believe that it is necessary. As a writer, I have three reasons for believing in freedom.

Firstly the writer himself must feel free, or he may find it difficult to fall into the creative mood and do good work. If he feels free, sure of himself, unafraid, easy inside, he is in a favourable condition for the act of creation.

The second reason also concerns the writer—and indeed the artist generally. It is not enough to feel free ; that is only the start. To feel free may be enough for the mystic, who can function alone and concentrate even in a concentration camp. The writer, the artist, needs something more—namely freedom to tell other people what he is feeling. Otherwise, he is bottled up and what is inside him may go bad. And here is where the trouble starts. The Nazis step forward and say, ' One moment, please. Allow me, the government, first to hear what you are wanting to say. If I decide it is convenient, you may say it, but not otherwise.' The Nazis do not and cannot prevent freedom to think and to feel—though they would no doubt condemn it from the National-Socialist point of view as a selfish waste of time. They cannot interfere there, but they can and do prevent freedom to communicate. They do step in and say, ' Before you publish your book, before you show your picture, before you sing your song, I must read, I must look, I must listen.' And the knowledge that they can do this reacts disastrously upon the artist. He is not like the mystic ; he cannot function in a vacuum, he cannot spin tales in his head or paint pictures in the air, or hum tunes under his breath. He must have an audience, he must express his feelings, and if he knows he may be forbidden to express himself, he becomes afraid to feel. Officials, even when they are well-meaning, do not realise this. Their make-up is so different. They assume that when a book is censored only the book in question is affected. They do not realise that they may have impaired the creative machinery of the writer's mind, and prevented him from writing good books in the future.

So here are two of my reasons for believing that freedom is necessary for culture. The third reason concerns the general public. The public, on its side, must be free to read, to listen, to look. If it is prevented from receiving the communications which the artist sends it, it becomes inhibited, like him, though in a different way : it remains immature. And immaturity is a great characteristic of the public in Nazi Germany. If you look at a photograph of our enemies they may strike you as able and brave and formidable, even heroic. But they will not strike you as grown up. They have not been allowed to hear, to listen, or to look. Only people who have been allowed to practise freedom can have the grown-up look in their eyes.

I do not want to exaggerate the claims of freedom. It does not guarantee the production of masterpieces, and masterpieces have been produced under conditions far from free—the *Aeneid*, for instance, or the plays of Racine. Freedom is only a favour- able step—or, let us say, three little steps. When writers (and artists generally) feel easy, when they can express themselves openly, when their public is allowed to receive their communica- tions, there is a chance of the general level of civilisation rising. Before the war, it was rising a little in England, it was rising a great deal in France, it was rising in Czechoslovakia, Scandinavia, the Netherlands. In Germany it was falling. During the last ten years her achievements in art, in literature, in speculation, in unapplied science, were contemptible. But she was perfecting her instruments of destruction and she now hopes by their aid to reduce neighbouring cultures to the same level as her own.

When a culture is genuinely national, it is capable, when the hour strikes, of becoming super-national, and contributing to the general good of humanity. It gives and takes. It wants to give and take. It has generosity and modesty, it is not confined by political and geographic boundaries, it does not fidget about purity of race or worry about survival, but, living in the present and sustained by the desire to create, it expands wherever human beings are to be found. Our civilisation was ready to do this when the hour struck, and the civilisation of France, our lost leader, was ready, too. We did not want England to be England for ever ; it seemed to us a meagre destiny. We hoped for a world to which, when it had been made one by science, England could contribute. Science has duly unified the world. The hour has struck. We cannot contribute. And why ?

The historian of the future, and he alone, will be able to answer this question authoritatively. He will see the true perspective of this 1940 crisis, and it may appear as small to him as the crisis of 1914 already appears to us. Our present troubles may be the prelude to a vast upheaval which we cannot hope to understand. We have to answer out of our ignorance, and as well as we can. And to my limited outlook, Hitler's Germany is the villain, it is she who, when the hour struck, ruined the golden moment and ordered an age of bloodshed.

Germany also has had a great national culture. She was supreme in music, eminent in philosophy, weak (like England) in the visual arts, and highly gifted though not supremely gifted in literature. That, put in a sentence, was her achievement, and all the world was wanting to share it with her, and to profit by it, and to give and take. The Nazis willed otherwise. A national culture did not suit them. It had to be governmental. It can therefore never become super-national or contribute to the general good of humanity. Germany is to be German for ever, and more German with each generation. ' What is to be German?' asked Hitler, in a speech he made a few years ago at Munich, and he replied : ' The best answer to this question does not define : it lays down a law.' Did you ever hear such an extraordinary reply? To be German is—to be German. Thus labelled, Germany presses on to a goal which can be described in exalted language, but which is the goal of a fool. For all the time she shouts and bullies her neighbours, the clock of the world moves on, and science makes the world one. ' Gangsterdom for ever ' is a possibility and the democracies are fighting against it. ' Germany for ever ' is an uneducated official's dream.

When a national culture becomes governmental, it is always falsified. For it never quite suits the official book. The words and the images that have come down to us through the centuries are often contradictory, they represent a bewildering wealth of human experience, which it is our privilege to enjoy, to examine and to build on. A free country allows its citizens this privilege. A totalitarian country cannot because it fears diversity of opinion. The heritage of the past has to be overhauled so that the output of the present may be standardised, and the output of the present has to be standardised or Germany would cease to be German. Nothing could be more logical than the dreary blind-alley down which the Nazis advance, and down which they want to herd the whole human family. It leads nowhere, not even into Germany. They have got into it because they have worshipped the State. And they cannot feel safe until the rest of the world is in it too. Wherever they see variety, spontaneity, anything different from themselves, they are doomed to attack it. Germany's very gifts, her own high cultural achievement, must be recompounded and turned to poison, so that the achievements of others may perish.

2

WHAT HAS GERMANY DONE TO THE GERMANS?

It is most important to remember that Germany had to make war on her own people before she could attack Europe. So much has been happening lately that we sometimes forget that during the past seven years she robbed and tortured and interned and expelled and killed thousands and thousands of her own citizens. When she had got rid of them, and not until then, she was in a position to transfer operations, and start against France and England. The 1914 war was not preceded by all this cruelty inside Germany, nor by these floods of unhappy and innocent refugees.

So here are a few instances of Germany's treatment of Germans. I shall not be so much concerned with physical bullying as with the attempts of the Nazis to bully and twist the mind. They are no fools—it is a great mistake to keep on making fun of them—and a good deal of what they say sounds at first sensible and even noble. For instance, they say that instinct is superior to reason, and character better than book-learning. I agree. Baldur von Schirach, who was until lately one of their youth-leaders, says : ' The Nazi revolution is and always has been a revolution of the soul. It reveals that power which the intellectual will deny, since it is as inconceivable to him as is the God who gave it : the power of the soul and sentiment.'

This sounds all right, but why does the soul always require a machine-gun ? Why can the character only cope with the intellect when it has got it inside a concentration camp, and is armed with a whip ? Why does the instinct instinctively persecute ? Why does sentiment mean insensitiveness ? On the surface, the Nazi creed seems not too bad ; scratch the surface, and you will find intolerance and cruelty. I cannot go through the list of German writers and painters and sculptors and architects and musicians and philosophers and scientists and theologians who have been persecuted by Germany in the past seven years. It would take too long. But think of Einstein, the greatest scientist living, who gave us a new view of the universe : he is in exile. Think of Freud, the psychologist : he has died in exile. Think of Thomas Mann : he only wanted to write his novels and live in peace, but he had to write them in his own way, he had to be independent, and he is in exile. Think of the smaller people, friends of my own : I know a writer who escaped from Vienna, a charming fellow, whose crime it was to be a Jew, and another writer, a pure-blooded Aryan from Berlin, whose crime it was to think. I see my own sort of person being downed and insulted, and when I am told that the Nazi revolution is a revolution of the soul—well, I wonder.

Not long ago, at Munich, Hitler made a speech about art. He began by complaining that the Jews, with their so-called artistic criticism, had muddled the public, and put art on the level of fashion, which changes yearly. Art, he said, was not fashionable, not international, but eternal, like the national spirit of Germany, and the artist must set up a monument to his country, not to himself. You may not object to this ; indeed when Hitler distinguishes art from fashion, you may quite well agree. But he goes on : ' As for the degenerate artists, I forbid them to force their so-called experiences upon the public. If they do see fields blue, they are deranged, and should go to an asylum. If they only pretend to see them blue, they are criminals, and should go to prison. I will purge the nation of them, and let no one take part in their corruption—his day of punishment will come.'

Just as the scientist may not settle what experiments to make, so the artist may not settle how to express himself. In both cases an official intervenes. The official has never seen a field blue, and that decides for all time the colour of fields. The speech ends with the crack of a whip ; the audience has been transported from the art-gallery to the concentration camp, where it will remain unless it mends its ways and enjoys what Hitler says is beautiful. This threat of a purge runs through all Nazi culture : the idea that one person may like one thing and another another is intolerable to it ; it cannot be happy unless it bullies. I do not myself see fields blue, but I do not get upset about it, and when a great artist like Van Gogh does see them blue, I am thankful to look for a moment through his eyes.

Now for literature. Let me recall that famous burning of the books, for it illustrates better than any single event can the way in which Germany has been behaving to Germans. The Nazis wished it to symbolise their cultural outlook, and it will. It took place on May 13, 1933. That night twenty-five thousand volumes were destroyed outside the University of Berlin, in the presence of forty thousand people. Most people enjoy a blaze, and we are told that the applause was tremendous. Some of the books were by Jews, others communist, others liberal, others ' unscientific,' and all of them were ' un-German.' It was for the government to decide what was un-German. There was an elaborate ritual. Nine heralds came forward in turn, and consigned an author with incantations to the flames. For example, the fourth herald said : ' Concerning the corrosion of the soul by the exaggeration of the dangers of war ! Upholding the nobility of the human spirit, I consign to the flames the writings of Sigmund Freud.' The seventh herald said : ' Concerning the literary betrayal of the World War Soldier ! Upholding the education of our people in the spirit of reality, I consign to the flames the writings of Erich Marie Remarque,' the author of the novel *All Quiet on the Western Front.* There were holocausts in the provinces too, and students were instructed to erect ' pillars of infamy ' outside their universities ; the pillar should be ' a thick tree-trunk, somewhat above the height of a man,' to which were to be nailed ' the utterances of those who, by their participation in activities defamatory of character, have forfeited their membership in the German nation.' Note the reference to ' character,' it is significant. ' Character,' like the ' soul,' is always an opportunity for brutality. The Burning of the Books was followed by a systematic control of literature. A bureau was created to look after public libraries, second-hand shops were purged, books may not be published without licence, and a licence is also required for commenting.

Unfortunately for the Nazis, not all books are modern books. Germany has had a great literature in the past, and they have had to do something about that. They have been especially troubled

by Goethe and Heine.   Over Heine they have taken a strong
line, since he was a Jew ;   they have denounced him as ' the
most baneful fellow that has ever passed through German life,
soul-devastating, soul-poisoning ' (notice again the ' soul '), and
have banned his works.   Goethe had to be treated with more
respect—so far as I know, they have not banned Goethe.   But
they rightly consider him their arch-enemy.   For Goethe
believed in toleration, he was the nationalist who is ripe for
super-nationalism, he was the German who was wanting Germany's genius to enrich the whole world.   His spirit will re-arise
when this madness and cruelty have passed.

I could give more examples, but I have said enough to show
how Germany has behaved to her own people.   When she had
finished with them, she turned against us.   It is all part of
a single movement, which has as its aim the fettering of the
writer, the scientist, the artist and the general public all over the
world.

3

WHAT WOULD GERMANY DO TO US?

What would the Nazis do to civilisation in these islands and
in the Empire if they won ?

I don't suggest that conditions over here are perfect.   During
the present century, the writer and the artist generally have
worked under growing disabilities ;   the law of libel hits them
unfairly, so does the dramatic censorship.   And since last Septem-
ber, things have got worse, owing to regulations necessary for
the Defence of the Realm ;   publishers and printers are frightened
of handling anything which may be thought disloyal, with the
result that much original work and valuable comment are being
stifled.   This cannot be helped ;   a war is on so it is no use
whining.   But it is as well to remember that as soon as the war
is won people who care about civilisation in England will have
to begin another war, for the restoration and extension of cultural
freedom.

But although cultural conditions are not perfect in this country,
(and it would be cant to pretend that they are) they are paradise

compared with the conditions in Germany, and heaven compared with the conditions which Germany would impose on us if she beat us. I want to describe what she would do to us if she got the chance.

You may say : ' Oh, but how do you know ? No doubt the Nazis would impose appalling peace terms on us if they won, but why should they interfere with our culture ? ' My answer to that is : ' I do know, because I have the record of what they have done to other countries, particularly to Czechoslovakia and to Poland.' Destruction of national culture is part of their programme of conquest. In Czechoslovakia, for instance, they have barred the operas of Smetana and the plays of Capek. They have revised school books, falsified Czech history, forbidden the singing of Czech national songs, and subsidised German educational institutions, for which the Czechs have to pay. In Poland the fate of culture has been still more tragic, since Poland is a conquered country : their conduct in Poland is the model which the Nazis would follow if they got over here. Listen, for instance, how they have treated the University of Cracow—and then put for ' Cracow ' ' Oxford ' or any other university which you know. Last November, one hundred and seventy professors and teachers at Cracow were summoned by the chief of the Gestapo to the hall of the university and placed under arrest on the grounds that they were continuing their work without Nazi permission. They were sent straight off to concentration camps in Germany, where sixteen of them died, and their places were filled by Nazi nominees. I know Cracow. I have had friends in the university there of whom I can get no news. They have welcomed me to their charming little flat overlooking the green boulevards : they have shown me their noble city with its great Catholic churches and its marvellous fortress. Owing to their kindness and hospitality, it has happened that Cracow has become for me a symbol of Nazi bullying on the continent, and I can hardly see its name without trembling with rage. I mention it now—that lost and lovely place—because one needs to visualise in these terrible times. It does not convey much if I say ' The Nazis would reorganise and re-staff our educational system.' It does convey something if I say ' They would treat Oxford as they have treated Cracow.' They are stamping out culture everywhere in Poland, so far as they can. They consider it their mission to do so, on the ground that the Poles are naturally inferior to Germans. ' A Pole is a Pole,' writes a Nazi journalist, ' and any attempt at familiarity must be rebuffed.'

Let us now consider the effect of a Nazi victory upon our civilisation.

Our press, our publishing and printing trades, our universities and the rest of our educational system would be instantly controlled. So would theatres, cinemas, and the wireless. The British Government (assuming that one remained) would be held responsible for their conduct, and have to punish them if they did anything which annoyed Berlin. There would be complete remodelling. In these respects, the methods adopted in Czechoslovakia and Poland would be followed, and with the maximum of brutality ; the joy of baiting Englishmen in England would be intoxicating. Germanisation would probably not be attempted. But the Gestapo and the rest of the occupying force would, of course, import such Nazi culture as was necessary for their spiritual sustenance, and we should have to pay for German libraries and German schools, into which, as members of an inferior race, we should not be allowed to go.

What about our literature ? The fate of individual writers would be hard. Those of any eminence would probably be interned and shot. This, however painful to themselves, would not, it is true, be a great blow to literature, for by the time writers have become eminent they have usually done their best work. What would matter, what would be disastrous, is the intimidation of our younger writers—men and women in their twenties and thirties, who have not yet had the chance to express themselves. The invaders would take good care to frighten or cajole them. Forbidden to criticise their conquerors, forbidden to recall the past glories of their country, or to indulge that free movement of the mind which is necessary to the creative art, they would be confined to trivialities, or to spreading their masters' opinions. A bureau would be established, and licences to create or to comment would be issued, as in Germany by Dr. Goebbels, and withdrawn if independence were shown. Rebelliousness might mean death. I don't think this is a fancy picture. It is only what is happening in Europe, and why should we get special terms ? And I am not accusing our enemies of any general hatred of culture. They like culture. They are human beings, who enjoy reading books or going to plays and films, just as we

do. They too want to be happy. The Germans don't hate
culture, but they are doomed to oppose it because it is mixed
up with thought and action, because it is mixed up with the
individual ; just as it is their doom to oppose science and religion.
Would they try to burn English books too ? I don't think so.
It would mean too big a blaze. We should probably be left
with our existing libraries and allowed to read our classics in
such spare time as we possessed. I do think though that a
different interpretation of English literature would be attempted
in our schools. They would put it to our young people that
our best writers were Nazis at heart, and so try to warp their
minds. It is interesting, in this connection, to read what Nazi
critics have been saying lately about Shakespeare and Carlyle.
They have not got a bad case over Carlyle—he had something
of the Nazi about him : he despised individualism and liberty
and worshipped the dictator-hero. However, Carlyle also said
' Thought is stronger than artillery-parks,' and this side of him
the Nazis don't mention. The case of Shakespeare is more complicated. The Germans have, for several generations, invested
so heavily in Shakespeare that they dare not, even under the
present regime, sell out ; and they are worried because we like
Shakespeare too—we even maintain that he was an Englishman.
So they have had to make him into ' the special case of a poet
who is not affected by a war with England,' and they brandish
him at us for our castigation, and to our shame. You may
think this foolish, but it shows their mentality ; it shows how
they twist things and how they would twist our minds through
our own national literature if they got into our country.

Those seem to me the chief cultural points in a Nazi conquest
—and you will remember that I am keeping to this particular
aspect, and not talking about politics and economics. They
want our land, it is true ; they want our money—sure. But
they also want to alter our civilisation until it is in line with their
own. If my view of them is right, they cannot *help* doing this :
it is, so to speak, their fate. They have identified civilisation
with the state, and the National Socialist state cannot be secure
until no civilisation exists except the particular one which it
approves.

This being so, I think we have got to go on with this hideous
fight. I cannot see how we are to make terms with Hitler, much
as I long for peace. For one thing, he never keeps his word ;

for another, he tolerates no way of looking at life except his own way. A peace which was the result of a Nazi victory would surely not differ much from a Nazi war. Germans would no longer be killed, but they would go on killing others until no one survived to criticise them. In the end, they might achieve world-domination and institute a culture. But what sort of culture would it be? What would they have to work with? For you cannot go on destroying lives and living processes without destroying your own life. If you continue to be greedy and dense, if you make power and not understanding your aim, if, as a French friend of mine puts it, you erect ' a pyramid of appetites on a foundation of stupidity,' you kill the impulse to create. Creation is disinterested. Creation means passionate understanding. Creation lies at the heart of civilisation like fire in the heart of the earth. Around it are gathered its cooler allies, criticism, the calm use of the intellect, informing the mass and moulding it into shape. The intellect is not everything—the Nazis are quite right there. But no one can insult the intellect as they do without becoming sterile and cruel. We know their cruelty. We should see their sterility if this orgy of destruction were to stop, and they turned at their Fuehrer's command to the production of masterpieces.

In this difficult day when so many of us are afraid : in this day when so many brave plans have gone wrong and so many devices have jammed, it is a comfort to remember that violence has so far never worked. Even when it seems to conquer, it fails in the long run. This failure may be due to the Divine Will. It can also be ascribed to the strange nature of Man, who refuses to live by bread alone, and is the only animal who has attempted to understand his surroundings.

[1940]

Tolerance

Everybody is talking about reconstruction. Our enemies have their schemes for a new order in Europe, maintained by their secret police, and we on our side talk of rebuilding London or England, or western civilisation, and we make plans how this is to be done. Which is all very well, but when I hear such talk, and see the architects sharpening their pencils and the contractors getting out their estimates, and the statesmen marking out their spheres of influence, and everyone getting down to the job, a very famous text occurs to me : ' Except the Lord build the house they labour in vain who build it.' Beneath the poetic imagery of these words lies a hard scientific truth, namely, unless you have a sound attitude of mind, a right psychology, you cannot construct or reconstruct anything that will endure. The text is true, not only for religious people, but for workers whatever their outlook, and it is significant that one of our historians, Dr. Arnold Toynbee, should have chosen it to preface his great study of the growth and decay of civilisations. Surely the only sound foundation for a civilisation is a sound state of mind. Architects, contractors, international commissioners, marketing boards, broadcasting corporations will never, by themselves, build a new world. They must be inspired by the proper spirit, and there must be the proper spirit in the people for whom they are working. For instance, we shall never have a beautiful new London until people refuse to live in ugly houses. At present, they don't mind ; they demand comfort, but are indifferent to civic beauty ; indeed they have no taste. I live myself in a hideous block of flats, but I can't say it worries me, and until we are worried, all schemes for reconstructing London beautifully must automatically fail.

What though is the proper spirit ? We agree that the basic problem is psychological, that the Lord must build if the work is to stand, that there must be a sound state of mind before diplomacy or economics or trade-conferences can function. But what state of mind is sound ? Here we may differ. Most people, when asked what spiritual quality is needed to rebuild civilisation, will reply 'Love.' Men must love one another, they say; nations must do likewise, and then the series of cataclysms which is threatening to destroy us will be checked.

Respectfully but firmly, I disagree. Love is a great force in private life; it is indeed the greatest of all things: but love in public affairs does not work. It has been tried again and again: by the Christian civilisations of the Middle Ages, and also by the French Revolution, a secular movement which reasserted the Brotherhood of Man. And it has always failed. The idea that nations should love one another, or that business concerns or marketing boards should love one another, or that a man in Portugal should love a man in Peru of whom he has never heard —it is absurd, unreal, dangerous. It leads us into perilous and vague sentimentalism. 'Love is what is needed,' we chant, and then sit back and the world goes on as before. The fact is we can only love what we know personally. And we cannot know much. In public affairs, in the rebuilding of civilisation, something much less dramatic and emotional is needed, namely, tolerance. Tolerance is a very dull virtue. It is boring. Unlike love, it has always had a bad press. It is negative. It merely means putting up with people, being able to stand things. No one has ever written an ode to tolerance, or raised a statue to her. Yet this is the quality which will be most needed after the war. This is the sound state of mind which we are looking for. This is the only force which will enable different races and classes and interests to settle down together to the work of reconstruction.

The world is very full of people—appallingly full; it has never been so full before, and they are all tumbling over each other. Most of these people one doesn't know and some of them one doesn't like; doesn't like the colour of their skins, say, or the shapes of their noses, or the way they blow them or don't blow them, or the way they talk, or their smell, or their clothes, or their fondness for jazz or their dislike of jazz, and so on. Well, what is one to do? There are two solutions. One of them is the Nazi solution. If you don't like people, kill them, banish them, segregate them, and then strut up and down proclaiming that you are the salt of the earth. The other way is much less thrilling, but it is on the whole the way of the democracies, and I prefer it. If you don't like people, put up with them as well as you can. Don't try to love them: you can't, you'll only strain yourself. But try to tolerate them. On the basis of that tolerance a civilised future may be built. Certainly I can see no other foundation for the post-war world.

For what it will most need is the negative virtues : not being huffy, touchy, irritable, revengeful. I have lost all faith in positive militant ideals ; they can so seldom be carried out without thousands of human beings getting maimed or imprisoned. Phrases like ' I will purge this nation,' ' I will clean up this city,' terrify and disgust me. They might not have mattered when the world was emptier : they are horrifying now, when one nation is mixed up with another, when one city cannot be organically separated from its neighbours. And, another point : reconstruction is unlikely to be rapid. I do not believe that we are psychologically fit for it, plan the architects never so wisely. In the long run, yes, perhaps : the history of our race justifies that hope. But civilisation has its mysterious regressions, and it seems to me that we are fated now to be in one of them, and must recognise this and behave accordingly. Tolerance, I believe, will be imperative after the establishment of peace. It's always useful to take a concrete instance : and I have been asking myself how I should behave if, after peace was signed, I met Germans who had been fighting against us. I shouldn't try to love them : I shouldn't feel inclined. They have broken a window in my little ugly flat for one thing. But I shall try to tolerate them, because it is common sense, because in the post-war world we shall have to live with Germans. We can't exterminate them, any more than they have succeeded in exterminating the Jews. We shall have to put up with them, not for any lofty reason, but because it is the next thing that will have to be done.

I don't then regard tolerance as a great eternally established divine principle, though I might perhaps quote ' In My Father's House are many mansions ' in support of such a view. It is just a makeshift, suitable for an overcrowded and overheated planet. It carries on when love gives out, and love generally gives out as soon as we move away from our home and our friends and stand among strangers in a queue for potatoes. Tolerance is wanted in the queue ; otherwise we think, ' Why will people be so slow ? ' ; it is wanted in the tube, or ' Why will people be so fat ? ' ; it is wanted at the telephone, or ' Why are they so deaf ? ' or conversely, ' Why do they mumble ? ' It is wanted in the street, in the office, at the factory, and it is wanted above all between classes, races, and nations. It's dull. And yet it entails imagination. For you have all the time to be putting yourself in someone else's place. Which is a desirable spiritual exercise.

This ceaseless effort to put up with other people seems tame, almost ignoble, so that it sometimes repels generous natures, and I don't recall many great men who have recommended tolerance. St. Paul certainly did not. Nor did Dante. However, a few names occur. Going back over two thousand years, and to India, there is the great Buddhist Emperor Asoka, who set up inscriptions recording not his own exploits but the need for mercy and mutual understanding and peace. Going back about four hundred years, to Holland, there is the Dutch scholar Erasmus, who stood apart from the religious fanaticism of the Reformation and was abused by both parties in consequence. In the same century there was the Frenchman Montaigne, subtle, intelligent, witty, who lived in his quiet country house and wrote essays which still delight and confirm the civilised. And England : there was John Locke, the philosopher ; there was Sydney Smith, the Liberal and liberalising divine ; there was Lowes Dickinson, writer of *A Modern Symposium*, which might be called the Bible of Tolerance. And Germany—yes, Germany : there was Goethe. All these men testify to the creed which I have been trying to express : a negative creed, but necessary for the salvation of this crowded jostling modern world.

Two more remarks. First it is very easy to see fanaticism in other people, but difficult to spot in oneself. Take the evil of racial prejudice. We can easily detect it in the Nazis ; their conduct has been infamous ever since they rose to power. But we ourselves—are we guiltless ? We are far less guilty than they are. Yet is there no racial prejudice in the British Empire ? Is there no colour question ? I ask you to consider that, those of you to whom tolerance is more than a pious word. My other remark is to forestall a criticism. Tolerance is not the same as weakness. Putting up with people does not mean giving in to them. This complicates the problem. But the rebuilding of civilisation is bound to be complicated. I only feel certain that unless the Lord builds the house, they will labour in vain who build it. Perhaps, when the house is completed, love will enter it, and the greatest force in our private lives will also rule in public life.

[1941]

Ronald Kidd

An address delivered at his funeral
'Und eine Freiheit macht uns alle frei.'

In the past few months the Council for Civil Liberties has lost
both its President, Henry Nevinson, and its first secretary. It is
the President who should be speaking now, but as he is no longer
with us I have been asked to give a short address. I do so
reluctantly ; but I see that an address is necessary, for Ronald
Kidd was a public figure, and it is seemly that there should be
some public discourse here, however inadequate.

Those who knew him best, better than I did, will agree with
me, I think, that the public side in him, the civic side, the side
that serves humanity, was superbly developed. Of course he
had his personal life, like the rest of us, but it is this altruistic
activity that so impressed, this service of the elusive principle
which we call liberty ; which we can none of us define, but in
which we all believe. I suppose he must have had an enthusiasm
for liberty all his life, but it became noticeable in 1934, when he
called together a few others who shared his hopes and his
anxieties, and founded this Council. I was not one of the original
group, but I joined soon afterwards, and I well remember our
original offices. They were in a mews. The staircase was so
narrow that one could scarcely get up it, and the room at the
top was so small that one could scarcely turn round. There was
no organisation and no staff. And from that room Kidd hired
a great hall down in Westminster, and convened there the great
meeting of protest against the Sedition Bill which first brought
our Council into general notice. From that moment he never
looked back; he moved from enterprise to enterprise, and he not
only achieved himself : he left foundations upon which others
are building and will build. The little room has become a suite
of offices, the reaching out of individual to individual has become
a great national organisation with branches and affiliations all
over the British Isles, and indeed outside them. That Sedition
Bill I mentioned—the B.B.C. would not report it, but when

59

Ronald Kidd died this week accounts of his life and work were broadcast over the Continent and the Empire as well as at home.

That is fame. That is success. But there is something more to remember. He gave to that work all his strength, and he did, literally, die that we might be free. If he had cared for our freedom less, if he had worked less, if he had nursed his health and considered his own comfort, he could have been alive now, though it could not have been a life he valued. I know the political and philosophical difficulties inherent in this idea of freedom : freedom for what : freedom to do what : freedom at whose expense, and so on. As a conception it is negative : but as a faith it is positive, and Ronald Kidd upheld it till his dying day.

When during his last illness I went down to see him in his private residence and later in the hospital, I found him still concentrated on the Council and its work, on our annual general meeting which he could not attend, on his pamphlet *The Fight for a Free Press*, which has just appeared. He knew he was ill and he could discuss his symptoms, but they never held the first rank, as they do with ordinary invalids.

This is not the place nor have I the ability to discuss his outlook, or to illustrate the various methods through which he worked ; pamphlets, speeches, interviews with Cabinet Ministers, visits to police stations and police courts, street watchings—all played their part. One thing strikes me, though, and that is why I quoted that line from Schiller : he knew that freedom is not the perquisite of any one section of the community : neither the employing classes nor the working classes nor the artistic and literary classes can be truly free unless all are free. That— unformulated perhaps—was his belief, and perhaps that was why such contradictory judgments were passed on him by those who had not worked with him. I have heard him accused in different quarters of being a Communist, a Gladstonian Liberal, a secret agent, the wrong sort of Irishman and a hopeless John Bull. Happy the man who is accused of so much, for it proves that his mind is alive. Kidd was active, whenever he saw the possibility of promoting and extending civil liberty. He was tethered to no other formula.

When a man dies, he becomes part of history and one thinks of historical parallels, and it occurs to me to-day—I don't know whether you will agree—that there was in our friend something of the Ancient Roman, the Tribune of the People, who contends that the *Res Publica* should be the possession of all. Even in his outward habit I see something of this ; in his gravity, his courtesy, his eloquence. I see it still more in his selflessness, his stubborn courage, his loyalty, his refusal to admit defeat, his adherence to principles. There is here something that suggests the grandeur and the sternness of certain heroes of the ancient world, and their strife for an individual liberty compatible with civic righteousness. May his example remain with us! May we continue the fight that is never done!

[1942]

The Tercentenary of the 'Areopagitica'

Milton's *Areopagitica* was published exactly three hundred years ago. The Parliament was fighting the King. Milton upheld Parliament, but it had just given him a very unpleasant shock. It had passed a defence regulation for the control of literature, and had placed all printed matter under a censorship. 'No book etc. shall from henceforward be printed or exposed for sale unless the same be first approved of and licensed by such persons' as Parliament shall appoint.

There are usually two motives behind any censorship—good, and bad. The good motive is the desire of the authorities to safeguard and strengthen the community, particularly in times of stress. The bad motive is the desire of the authorities to suppress criticism, particularly of themselves. Both these motives existed in 1644, as they do in 1944, and, in Milton's judgment, the bad then predominated over the good. He was profoundly shocked that Parliament, which fought for liberty, should be suppressing it, and he issued his *Areopagitica* as a protest. It is the most famous of his prose works—partly because it is well written, but mainly because it strikes a blow for British freedom. It has been much praised, and sometimes by people who do not realise what they are praising and what they are letting themselves in for. In celebrating its tercentenary let us do so with open eyes.

To begin with one of Milton's smaller points : the inconvenience of a censorship to a creative or scholarly writer. All that he says here is true, though not of prime importance. It is intolerable, he exclaims, that 'serious and elaborate writings, as if they were the theme of a grammar lad, must not be uttered without the eyes of a temporising and extemporising licenser'. It is being treated like a schoolboy after one is grown up. The censor is probably some overworked and dim little official who knows nothing about literature and is scared of anything new. Yet the writer has to 'trudge' to him to get his script passed, and if he makes any alteration afterwards, he must make application again. 'I hate a pupil teacher, I endure not an instructor,' proud Milton cries, and when he is reminded that the censor does after all represent the State, he hits back fiercely with ' The State shall be my governors but not my critics.' All this is very much what a scholar or a creative artist might charge against a censor to-day : the big mind having to apply for permission to the fidgety small mind, and the small mind being supported by the authority of the State. It is all quite true ; though why should not distinguished writers be put to trouble if it is to the general good ? Why should they not submit to censorship if the national welfare requires it ?

But there is much more to the problem, and the bulk of the *Areopagitica* is occupied with larger questions. Censorship means —uniformity and monotony : and they mean spiritual death. ' Where there is much desire to learn, there of necessity will be much arguing, much writing, and many opinions : for opinion in good men is but knowledge in the making.' And he apostrophises London at war in words we might gladly use to-day :

Behold now this vast City : a city of refuge, the mansion house of liberty ; encompassed and surrounded with God's protection ; the shop of war hath not there more anvils and hammers working . . . than there be pens and heads there, sitting by their studious lamps, musing, searching, revolving new notions and ideas . . . others as fast reading, trying all things, assenting to the force of reason and convincement.

All this free writing and reading will pass with the institution of the censorship, and its disappearance means the spiritual impoverishment of us all, whether we write and study or not. Intellectuals, in Milton's opinion, are not and cannot be apart from the community, and are essential to its health.

And then he tackles the problem of bad or harmful books. Might it not be well to prohibit them ? He answers, No. It is preferable that bad books should be published rather than that all books should be submitted before publication to a government official. What is bad will be forgotten, and free choice in reading is as important as it is in action. ' Truth is a perpetual progression.' Also who is to settle what is bad ? Who indeed ! I recall in this connection an argument I had with an acquaintance during the first war. He was for prohibiting bad books, and when I asked him which books he answered

'Conrad's novels.' He did not care for them. He was an able public-spirited fellow, and later on he became an M.P.

If there is no censorship, is the writer or the newspaper editor to be above the law? Not at all. That is not Milton's position. If a book or pamphlet or newspaper is illegal it can, after publication, be prosecuted. The grounds of prosecution in his day were two—blasphemy and libel—and they hold good in our day, prosecutions for blasphemy now being very rare and prosecutions for libel very frequent. Milton did not set writers above the law. He did insist on punishment afterwards rather than censorship beforehand. Let a man say what he likes and then suffer if it is illegal. This seems to me the only course appropriate to a democracy. It is for the courts, and for no one else, to decide whether a book shall be suppressed.

Milton, would'st thou be living at this hour? 'Yes and No,' Milton would answer. He would certainly be heart and soul with us in our fight against Germany and Japan, for they stand for all that he most detested. And he would note with approval that there is no direct censorship of books. But he would disapprove of the indirect censorship operating on them through the paper control. At the present moment, most of the paper available goes to government departments, the publication of new books gets cut down, and most of our great English classics have gone out of print. Nor would he have approved of any attempt of publishers to combine and decide what books should be published. Would he have liked the wireless? Yes and No. He would have been enthusiastic over the possibilities of broadcasting, and have endorsed much it does, but he would not approve of the 'agreed script' from which broadcasters are obliged to read for security reasons. He believed in free expression and in punishment afterwards if the expression turned out to be illegal: but never, never supervision beforehand, and whether the supervision was called censorship or licensing or 'agreed script' would have made no difference to him. You can argue that the present supervision of broadcasters is necessary and reasonable, and that a silly or cranky speaker might do endless harm on the air. But if you feel like that, you must modify your approval of the *Areopagitica*. You cannot have it both ways. And do not say 'Oh it's different to-day—there's a war on.' There was equally a war on in 1644. The fact is we are willing enough to praise freedom when she is safely tucked away in the past and cannot be a nuisance. In the present, amidst dangers whose outcome we cannot foresee, we get nervous about her, and admit censorship. Yet the past was once the present, the seventeenth century was once 'now,' with an unknown future, and Milton, who lived in his 'now' as we do in ours, believed in taking risks.

In places, then, the *Areopagitica* is a disturbance to our self-complacency. But in other places it is an encouragement, for Milton exalts our national character in splendid words. He was intensely patriotic—on the grounds that when France was a tyranny and Germany a muddle, we were insisting on freedom of speech and being admired for it by European scholars. He had travelled on the Continent before the civil war, and sat among her learned men, 'and,' he goes on,

> I bin counted happy to be born in such a place of philosophic freedom as they supposed England was, while they themselves did nothing but bemoan the servile condition into which learning amongst them was brought. . . . I tooke it as a pledge of future happiness that other nations were so persuaded of her liberty.

And he is proud—and how justly—of the variety of opinion incidental to our democracy of ' this flowering crop of knowledge and new light' as opposed to ' that dark conjealment of wood and hay and stubble' engendered by the pressure of totalitarianism. Our enemies, he notes, mistake our variety for weakness—exactly the mistakes the Germans were to make about us both in 1914 and in 1939.

> The adversary applauds and waits the hour : ' When they have branched themselves out,' saith he, ' small enough into parties and partitions, then will be our time.' Fool ! he sees not the firm root of which we all grow, though into branches, nor will beware until he see our small divided maniples cutting through at every angle of his ill-united and unwieldy brigade.

'Ill-united and unwieldy brigade'—could there be a phrase more prophetic of the Axis ? But we must not dwell on the phrase too much, for the subject of the *Areopagitica* is not tyranny abroad but the need, even in wartime, of liberty at home. Not the beam in Dr. Goebbel's eye, but the mote in our own eye. Can we take it out? Is there as much freedom of expression and publication in this country as there might be? That is the question which, on its tercentenary, this explosive little pamphlet propounds.

[1944]

The Challenge of our Time [1]

Temperamentally, I am an individualist. Professionally I am a writer, and my books emphasise the importance of personal relationships and the private life, for I believe in them. What can a man with such an equipment, and with no technical knowledge, say about the Challenge of our Time? Like everyone else, I can see that our world is in a terrible mess, and having been to India last winter I know that starvation and frustration can reach proportions unknown to these islands. Wherever I look, I can see, in the striking phrase of Robert Bridges, 'the almighty cosmic Will fidgeting in a trap.' But who set the trap, and how was it sprung? If I knew, I might be able to unfasten it. I do not know. How can I answer a challenge which I cannot interpret? It is like shouting defiance at a big black cloud. Some of the other speakers share my diffidence here, I think. Professor Bernal does not. He perceives very precisely what the Challenge of our Time is and what is the answer to it. Professor Bernal's perceptions are probably stronger than mine. They are certainly more selective, and many things which interest or upset me do not enter his mind at all—or enter it in the form of cards to be filed for future use.

I belong to the fag-end of Victorian liberalism, and can look back to an age whose challenges were moderate in their tone, and the cloud on whose horizon was no bigger than a man's hand. In many ways it was an admirable age. It practised benevolence and philanthropy, was humane and intellectually curious, upheld free speech, had little colour-prejudice, believed that individuals are and should be different, and entertained a sincere faith in the progress of society. The world was to become better and better, chiefly through the spread of parliamentary institutions. The education I received in those far-off and fantastic days made me soft and I am very glad it did, for I have seen plenty of hardness since, and I know it does not even pay. Think of the end of Mussolini—the hard man, hanging

[1] From a broadcast series; Professor Bernal had been one of the previous speakers.

67

upside-down like a turkey, with his dead mistress swinging beside him. But though the education was humane it was imperfect, inasmuch as we none of us realised our economic position. In came the nice fat dividends, up rose the lofty thoughts, and we did not realise that all the time we were exploiting the poor of our own country and the backward races abroad, and getting bigger profits from our investments than we should. We refused to face this unpalatable truth. I remember being told as a small boy, ' Dear, don't talk about money, it's ugly '—a good example that of Victorian defence mechanism.

All that has changed in the present century. The dividends have shrunk to decent proportions and have in some cases disappeared. The poor have kicked. The backward races are kicking—and more power to their boots. Which means that life has become less comfortable for the Victorian liberal, and that our outlook, which seems to me admirable, has lost the basis of golden sovereigns upon which it originally rose, and now hangs over the abyss. I indulge in these reminiscences because they lead to the point I want to make.

If we are to answer the Challenge of our Time successfully, we must manage to combine the new economy and the old morality. The doctrine of *laisser-faire* will not work in the material world. It has led to the black market and the capitalist jungle. We must have planning and ration books and controls, or millions of people will have nowhere to live and nothing to eat. On the other hand, the doctrine of *laisser-faire* is the only one that seems to work in the world of the spirit ; if you plan and control men's minds you stunt them, you get the censorship, the secret police, the road to serfdom, the community of slaves. Our economic planners sometimes laugh at us when we are afraid of totalitarian tyranny resulting from their efforts—or rather they sneer at us, for there is some deep connection between planning and sneering which psychologists should explore. But the danger they brush aside is a real one. They assure us that the new economy will evolve an appropriate morality, and that when all people are properly fed and housed, they will have an outlook which will be right, because they are the people. I cannot swallow that. I have no mystic faith in the people. I have in the individual. He seems to me a divine achievement and I mistrust any view which belittles him. If anyone calls you a wretched little individual—and I've been called that—don't you take it lying down. You are important because everyone else is an individual too—including the person who criticises you. In asserting your personality you are playing for your side.

That then is the slogan with which I would answer, or partially answer, the Challenge of our Time. We want the New Economy with the Old Morality. We want planning for the body and not for the spirit. But the difficulty is this : where does the body stop and the spirit start ? In the Middle Ages a hard and fast line was drawn between them, and according to the mediaeval theory of the Holy Roman Empire men rendered their bodies to Caesar and their souls to God. But the theory did not work. The Emperor, who represented Caesar, collided in practice with the Pope, who represented Christ. And we find ourselves in a similar dilemma to-day. Suppose you are planning the world-distribution of food. You can't do that without planning world population. You can't do that without regulating the number of births and interfering with family life. You must supervise parenthood. You are meddling with the realms of the spirit, of personal relationship, although you may not have intended to do so. And you are brought back again to that inescapable arbiter, your own temperament. When there is a collision of principles would you favour the individual at the expense of the community as I would ? Or would you prefer economic justice for all at the expense of personal freedom ?

In a time of upheaval like the present, this collision of principles, this split in one's loyalties, is always occurring. It has just occurred in my own life. I was brought up as a boy in one of the home counties, in a district which I still think the loveliest in England. There is nothing special about it—it is agricultural land, and could not be described in terms of beauty spots. It must always have looked much the same. I have kept in touch with it, going back to it as to an abiding city and still visiting the house which was once my home, for it is occupied by friends. A farm is through the hedge, and when the farmer there was eight years old and I was nine, we used to jump up and down on his grandfather's straw ricks and spoil them. To-day he is a grandfather himself, so that I have the sense of five generations continuing in one place. Life went on there as usual until this spring. Then someone who was applying for a permit to lay a water pipe was casually informed that it would not be granted since the whole area had been commandeered. Commandeered for what ? Had not the war ended ? Appropriate officials of the Ministry of Town and Country Planning now arrived from London and announced that a satellite town for 60,000 people is to be built. The people now living and working there are doomed ; it is death in life for them and they move in a nightmare. The best agricultural land has been taken, they assert ; the poor land down by the railway has been left ; compensation is inadequate. Anyhow, the satellite town has finished them off as completely as it will obliterate the ancient and delicate scenery. Meteorite town would be a better name. It has fallen out of a blue sky.

' Well,' says the voice of planning and progress, ' why this sentimentality ? People must have houses.' They must, and I think of working-class friends in north London who have to bring up four children in two rooms, and many are even worse off than that. But I cannot equate the problem. It is a collision of loyalties. I cannot free myself from the conviction that something irreplaceable has been destroyed, and that a little piece of England has died as surely as if a bomb had hit it. I wonder what compensation there is in the world of the spirit, for the destruction of the life here, the life of tradition.

These are personal reminiscences and I am really supposed to be speaking from the standpoint of the creative artist. But you will gather what a writer, who also cares for men and women and for the countryside, must be feeling in the world to-day. Uncomfortable, of course. Sometimes miserable and indignant. But convinced that a planned change must take place if the world is not to disintegrate, and hopeful that in the new economy there may be a sphere both for human relationships, and for the despised activity known as art. What ought the writer, the artist, to do when faced by the Challenge of our Time ? Briefly, he ought to express what he wants and not what he is told to express by the planning authorities. He ought to impose a discipline on himself rather than accept one from outside. And that discipline may be aesthetic, rather than social or moral ; he may wish to practise art for art's sake. That phrase has been foolishly used and often raises a giggle. But it is a profound phrase. It indicates that art is a self-contained harmony. Art is valuable not because it is educational (though it may be), not because it is recreative (though it may be), not because everyone enjoys it (for everybody does not), not even because it has to do with beauty. It is valuable because it has to do with order, and creates little worlds of its own, possessing internal harmony, in the bosom of this disordered planet. It is needed at once and now. It is needed before it is appreciated and independent of appreciation. The idea that it should not be permitted until it receives communal acclaim and unless it is for all, is perfectly absurd. It is the activity which brought man out of original darkness and differentiates him from the beasts, and we must continue to practise and respect it through the darkness of to-day.

I am speaking like an intellectual, but the intellectual, to my mind, is more in touch with humanity than is the confident scientist, who patronises the past, over-simplifies the present, and envisages a future where his leadership will be accepted. Owing to the political needs of the moment, the scientist occupies an abnormal position, which he tends to forget. He is subsidised by the terrified governments who need his aid, pampered and sheltered as long as he is obedient, and prosecuted under Official Secrets Acts when he has been naughty. All this separates him from ordinary men and women and makes him unfit to enter into their feelings. It is high time he came out of his ivory laboratory. We want him to plan for our bodies. We do not want him to plan for our minds, and we cannot accept, so far, his assurance that he will not.

[1946]

George Orwell

George Orwell's originality has been recognised in this country ; his peculiar blend of gaiety and grimness has been appreciated, but there is still a tendency to shy away from him. This appeared in our reception of his most ambitious work, *1984*. America clasped it to her uneasy heart, but we, less anxious or less prescient, have eluded it for a variety of reasons. It is too bourgeois, we say, or too much to the left, or it has taken the wrong left turn, it is neither a novel nor a treatise, and so negligible, it is negligible because the author was tuberculous, like Keats ; anyhow, we can't bear it. This last reason is certainly a respectable one. We all of us have the right to shirk unpleasant-ness, and we must sometimes exercise it. It may be our only defence against the right to nag. And that Orwell was a bit of a nagger cannot be denied. He found much to discomfort him in his world and desired to transmit it, and in *1984* he extended discomfort into agony. There is not a monster in that hateful apocalypse which does not exist in embryo to-day. Behind the United Nations lurks Oceania, one of his three world-states. Behind Stalin lurks Big Brother, which seems appropriate, but Big Brother also lurks behind Churchill, Truman, Gandhi, and any leader whom propaganda utilises or invents. Behind the North Koreans, who are so wicked, and the South Koreans, who are such heroes, lurk the wicked South Koreans and the heroic North Koreans, into which, at a turn of the kaleidoscope, they may be transformed. Orwell spent his life in foreseeing trans-formations and in stamping upon embryos. His strength went that way. *1984* crowned his work, and it is understandably a crown of thorns.

While he stamped he looked around him, and tried to amelior-ate a world which is bound to be unhappy. A true liberal, he hoped to help through small things. Programmes mean pogroms. Look to the rose or the toad or, if you think them more significant, look to art or literature. There, in the useless, lies our scrap of salvation.

If a man cannot enjoy the return of spring, why should he

be happy in a Labour-saving Utopia ? . . . By retaining one's childhood love of such things as trees, fishes, butterflies and toads, one makes a peaceful and decent future a little more probable. By preaching the doctrine that nothing is to be admired except steel and concrete, one merely makes it a little surer that human beings will have no outlet for their surplus energy except in hatred and hero worship.

The above is a quotation from *Shooting an Elephant*, his posthumous volume of essays. Here is another quotation from it :

If you wanted to add to the vast fund of ill-will existing in the world at this moment, you could hardly do it better than by a series of football matches between Jews and Arabs, Germans and Czechs, &c., &c. . . . each match to be watched by a mixed audience of 100,000 spectators.

Games are harmless, even when played unfairly, provided they are played privately. It is international sport that helps to kick the world downhill. Started by foolish athletes, who thought it would promote ' understanding,' it is supported to-day by the desire for political prestige and by the interests involved in the gate-moneys. It is completely harmful. And elsewhere he considers the problem of Nationalism generally. British imperialism, bad as he found it in Burma, is better than the newer imperialisms that are ousting it. All nations are odious but some are less odious than others, and by this stony, unlovely path he reaches patriotism. To some of us, this seems the cleanest way to reach it. We believe in the roses and the toads and the arts, and know that salvation, or a scrap of it, is to be found only in them. In the world of politics we see no salvation, we are not to be diddled, but we prefer the less bad to the more bad, and so become patriots, while keeping our brains and hearts intact.

This is an uneasy solution, and no one can embrace Orwell's works who hopes for ease. Just as one is nestling against them, they prickle. They encourage no slovenly trust in a future where all will come right, dear comrades, though we shall not be there to see. They do not even provide a mystic vision. No wonder that he could not hit it off with H. G. Wells. What he does provide, what does commend him to some temperaments, is his belief in little immediate things and in kindness, good-temper and accuracy. He also believes in ' the people,' who, with their beefy arms akimbo and their cabbage-stalk soup, may survive when higher growths are cut down. He does not explain how ' the people ' are to make good, and perhaps he is here confusing belief with compassion.

He was passionate over the purity of prose, and in another essay he tears to bits some passages of contemporary writing. It is a dangerous game—the contemporaries can always retort—but it ought to be played, for if prose decays, thought decays and all the finer roads of communication are broken. Liberty, he argues, is connected with prose, and bureaucrats who want to destroy liberty tend to write and speak badly, and to use pompous or woolly or portmanteau phrases in which their true meaning or any meaning disappears. It is the duty of the citizen, and particularly of the practising journalist, to be on the lookout for such phrases or words and to rend them to pieces. This was successfully done a few years ago in the case of ' bottle-neck.' After ' a vicious circle of interdependent bottle-necks ' had been smashed in *The Times*, no bottle-neck has dared to lift its head again. Many critics besides Orwell are fighting for the purity of prose and deriding officialese, but they usually do so in a joking off-hand way, and from the aesthetic standpoint. He is unique in being immensely serious, and in connecting good prose with liberty. Like most of us, he does not define liberty, but being a liberal he thinks that there is more of it here than in Stalin's Russia or Franco's Spain, and that we need still more of it, rather than even less, if our national tradition is to continue. If we write and speak clearly, we are likelier to think clearly and to remain comparatively free. He gives six rules for clear writing, and they are not bad ones.

Posthumous sweepings seldom cohere, and *Shooting an Elephant* is really a collection of foot-notes to Orwell's other work. Readers can trace in it affinities with *Animal Farm* or *1984* or *The Road to Wigan Pier* or *Burmese Days*. They can also trace his development. The earlier writing (e.g. the title-essay) is forceful but flat. There are no reverberations. In the later work —despite his preoccupation with politics—more imaginative notes are sounded. We part company with a man who has been determined to see what he can of this contradictory and dis-quieting world and to follow its implications into the unseen— or anyhow to follow them round the corner.

[1950]

PART II

WHAT I BELIEVE

What I Believe

What I Believe

I do not believe in Belief. But this is an age of faith, and there are so many militant creeds that, in self-defence, one has to formulate a creed of one's own. Tolerance, good temper and sympathy are no longer enough in a world which is rent by religious and racial persecution, in a world where ignorance rules, and science, who ought to have ruled, plays the subservient pimp. Tolerance, good temper and sympathy—they are what matter really, and if the human race is not to collapse they must come to the front before long. But for the moment they are not enough, their action is no stronger than a flower, battered beneath a military jack-boot. They want stiffening, even if the process coarsens them. Faith, to my mind, is a stiffening process, a sort of mental starch, which ought to be applied as sparingly as possible. I dislike the stuff. I do not believe in it, for its own sake, at all. Herein I probably differ from most people, who believe in Belief, and are only sorry they cannot swallow even more than they do. My law-givers are Erasmus and Montaigne, not Moses and St. Paul. My temple stands not upon Mount Moriah but in that Elysian Field where even the immoral are admitted. My motto is: 'Lord, I disbelieve—help thou my unbelief.'

I have, however, to live in an Age of Faith—the sort of epoch I used to hear praised when I was a boy. It is extremely unpleasant really. It is bloody in every sense of the word. And I have to keep my end up in it. Where do I start?

With personal relationships. Here is something comparatively solid in a world full of violence and cruelty. Not absolutely solid, for Psychology has split and shattered the idea of a 'Person,' and has shown that there is something incalculable in each of us, which may at any moment rise to the surface and destroy our normal balance. We don't know what we are like. We can't know what other people are like. How, then, can we put any trust in personal relationships, or cling to them in the gathering political storm? In theory we cannot. But in practice we can and do. Though A is not unchangeably A or B unchangeably B, there can still be love and loyalty between the two.

For the purpose of living one has to assume that the personality is solid, and the 'self' is an entity, and to ignore all contrary evidence. And since to ignore evidence is one of the characteristics of faith, I certainly can proclaim that I believe in personal relationships.

Starting from them, I get a little order into the contemporary chaos. One must be fond of people and trust them if one is not to make a mess of life, and it is therefore essential that they should not let one down. They often do. The moral of which is that I must, myself, be as reliable as possible, and this I try to be. But reliability is not a matter of contract—that is the main difference between the world of personal relationships and the world of business relationships. It is a matter for the heart, which signs no documents. In other words, reliability is impossible unless there is a natural warmth. Most men possess this warmth, though they often have bad luck and get chilled. Most of them, even when they are politicians, *want* to keep faith. And one can, at all events, show one's own little light here, one's own poor little trembling flame, with the knowledge that it is not the only light that is shining in the darkness, and not the only one which the darkness does not comprehend. Personal relations are despised to-day. They are regarded as bourgeois luxuries, as products of a time of fair weather which is now past, and we are urged to get rid of them, and to dedicate ourselves to some movement or cause instead. I hate the idea of causes, and if I had to choose between betraying my country and betraying my friend, I hope I should have the guts to betray my country. Such a choice may scandalise the modern reader, and he may stretch out his patriotic hand to the telephone at once and ring up the police. It would not have shocked Dante, though. Dante places Brutus and Cassius in the lowest circle of Hell because they had chosen to betray their friend Julius Caesar rather than their country Rome. Probably one will not be asked to make such an agonising choice. Still, there lies at the back of every creed something terrible and hard for which the worshipper may one day be required to suffer, and there is even a terror and a hardness in this creed of personal relationships, urbane and mild though it sounds. Love and loyalty to an individual can run counter to the claims of the State. When they do—down with the State, say I, which means that the State would down me.

This brings me along to Democracy, ' even Love, the Beloved Republic, which feeds upon Freedom and lives.' Democracy is not a Beloved Republic really, and never will be. But it is less hateful than other contemporary forms of government, and to that extent it deserves our support. It does start from the assumption that the individual is important, and that all types are needed to make a civilisation. It does not divide its citizens into the bossers and the bossed—as an efficiency-regime tends to do. The people I admire most are those who are sensitive and want to create something or discover something, and do not see life in terms of power, and such people get more of a chance under a democracy than elsewhere. They found religions, great or small, or they produce literature and art, or they do disinterested scientific research, or they may be what is called ' ordinary people,' who are creative in their private lives, bring up their children decently, for instance, or help their neighbours. All these people need to express themselves ; they cannot do so unless society allows them liberty to do so, and the society which allows them most liberty is a democracy.

Democracy has another merit. It allows criticism, and if there is not public criticism there are bound to be hushed-up scandals. That is why I believe in the Press, despite all its lies and vulgarity, and why I believe in Parliament. Parliament is often sneered at because it is a Talking Shop. I believe in it *because* it is a talking shop. I believe in the Private Member who makes himself a nuisance. He gets snubbed and is told that he is cranky or ill-informed, but he does expose abuses which would otherwise never have been mentioned, and very often an abuse gets put right just by being mentioned. Occasionally, too, a well-meaning public official starts losing his head in the cause of efficiency, and thinks himself God Almighty. Such officials are particularly frequent in the Home Office. Well, there will be questions about them in Parliament sooner or later, and then they will have to mind their steps. Whether Parliament is either a representative body or an efficient one is questionable, but I value it because it criticises and talks, and because its chatter gets widely reported.

So Two cheers for Democracy : one because it admits variety and two because it permits criticism. Two cheers are quite enough : there is no occasion to give three. Only Love the Beloved Republic deserves that.

What about Force, though ? While we are trying to be

sensitive and advanced and affectionate and tolerant, an unpleasant question pops up : does not all society rest upon force ? If a government cannot count upon the police and the army, how can it hope to rule ? And if an individual gets knocked on the head or sent to a labour camp, of what significance are his opinions ?

This dilemma does not worry me as much as it does some. I realise that all society rests upon force. But all the great creative actions, all the decent human relations, occur during the intervals when force has not managed to come to the front. These intervals are what matter. I want them to be as frequent and as lengthy as possible, and I call them ' civilisation.' Some people idealise force and pull it into the foreground and worship it, instead of keeping it in the background as long as possible. I think they make a mistake, and I think that their opposites, the mystics, err even more when they declare that force does not exist. I believe that it exists, and that one of our jobs is to prevent it from getting out of its box. It gets out sooner or later, and then it destroys us and all the lovely things which we have made. But it is not out all the time, for the fortunate reason that the strong are so stupid. Consider their conduct for a moment in the Niebelung's Ring. The giants there have the guns, or in other words the gold ; but they do nothing with it, they do not realise that they are all-powerful, with the result that the catastrophe is delayed and the castle of Walhalla, insecure but glorious, fronts the storms. Fafnir, coiled round his hoard, grumbles and grunts ; we can hear him under Europe to-day ; the leaves of the wood already tremble, and the Bird calls its warnings uselessly. Fafnir will destroy us, but by a blessed dispensation he is stupid and slow, and creation goes on just outside the poisonous blast of his breath. The Nietzschean would hurry the monster up, the mystic would say he did not exist, but Wotan, wiser than either, hastens to create warriors before doom declares itself. The Valkyries are symbols not only of courage but of intelligence ; they represent the human spirit snatching its opportunity while the going is good, and one of them even finds time to love. Brünnhilde's last song hymns the recurrence of love, and since it is the privilege of art to exaggerate, she goes even further, and proclaims the love which is eternally triumphant and feeds upon freedom, and lives.

So that is what I feel about force and violence. It is, alas !

the ultimate reality on this earth, but it does not always get to the front. Some people call its absences ' decadence ' ; I call them ' civilisation ' and find in such interludes the chief justification for the human experiment. I look the other way until fate strikes me. Whether this is due to courage or to cowardice in my own case I cannot be sure. But I know that if men had not looked the other way in the past, nothing of any value would survive. The people I respect most behave as if they were immortal and as if society was eternal. Both assumptions are false : both of them must be accepted as true if we are to go on eating and working and loving, and are to keep open a few breathing holes for the human spirit. No millennium seems likely to descend upon humanity ; no better and stronger League of Nations will be instituted ; no form of Christianity and no alternative to Christianity will bring peace to the world or integrity to the individual ; no ' change of heart ' will occur. And yet we need not despair, indeed, we cannot despair ; the evidence of history shows us that men have always insisted on behaving creatively under the shadow of the sword ; that they have done their artistic and scientific and domestic stuff for the sake of doing it, and that we had better follow their example under the shadow of the aeroplanes. Others, with more vision or courage than myself, see the salvation of humanity ahead, and will dismiss my conception of civilisation as paltry, a sort of tip-and-run game. Certainly it is presumptuous to say that we *cannot* improve, and that Man, who has only been in power for a few thousand years, will never learn to make use of his power. All I mean is that, if people continue to kill one another as they do, the world cannot get better than it is, and that since there are more people than formerly, and their means for destroying one another superior, the world may well get worse. What is good in people—and consequently in the world—is their insistence on creation, their belief in friendship and loyalty for their own sakes ; and though Violence remains and is, indeed, the major partner in this muddled establishment, I believe that creativeness remains too, and will always assume direction when violence sleeps. So, though I am not an optimist, I cannot agree with Sophocles that it were better never to have been born. And although, like Horace, I see no evidence that each batch of births is superior to the last, I leave the field open for the more complacent view. This is such a difficult moment to live

in, one cannot help getting gloomy and also a bit rattled, and
perhaps short-sighted.

In search of a refuge, we may perhaps turn to hero-worship.
But here we shall get no help, in my opinion. Hero-worship
is a dangerous vice, and one of the minor merits of a democracy
is that it does not encourage it, or produce that unmanageable
type of citizen known as the Great Man. It produces instead
different kinds of small men—a much finer achievement. But
people who cannot get interested in the variety of life, and
cannot make up their own minds, get discontented over this,
and they long for a hero to bow down before and to follow
blindly. It is significant that a hero is an integral part of the
authoritarian stock-in-trade to-day. An efficiency-regime cannot
be run without a few heroes stuck about it to carry off the dullness—much as plums have to be put into a bad pudding to make
it palatable. One hero at the top and a smaller one each side of
him is a favourite arrangement, and the timid and the bored are
comforted by the trinity, and, bowing down, feel exalted and
strengthened.

No, I distrust Great Men. They produce a desert of uniformity
around them and often a pool of blood too, and I always feel a
little man's pleasure when they come a cropper. Every now and
then one reads in the newspapers some such statement as : ' The
coup d'état appears to have failed, and Admiral Toma's whereabouts is at present unknown.' Admiral Toma had probably
every qualification for being a Great Man—an iron will, personal
magnetism, dash, flair, sexlessness—but fate was against him, so
he retires to unknown whereabouts instead of parading history
with his peers. He fails with a completeness which no artist and
no lover can experience, because with them the process of creation
is itself an achievement, whereas with him the only possible
achievement is success.

I believe in aristocracy, though—if that is the right word, and
if a democrat may use it. Not an aristocracy of power, based
upon rank and influence, but an aristocracy of the sensitive, the
considerate and the plucky. Its members are to be found in all
nations and classes, and all through the ages, and there is a secret
understanding between them when they meet. They represent
the true human tradition, the one permanent victory of our queer
race over cruelty and chaos. Thousands of them perish in
obscurity, a few are great names. They are sensitive for others

as well as for themselves, they are considerate without being fussy, their pluck is not swankiness but the power to endure, and they can take a joke. I give no examples—it is risky to do that—but the reader may as well consider whether this is the type of person he would like to meet and to be, and whether (going farther with me) he would prefer that this type should *not* be an ascetic one. I am against asceticism myself. I am with the old Scotsman who wanted less chastity and more delicacy. I do not feel that my aristocrats are a real aristocracy if they thwart their bodies, since bodies are the instruments through which we register and enjoy the world. Still, I do not insist. This is not a major point. It is clearly possible to be sensitive, considerate and plucky and yet be an ascetic too, and if anyone possesses the first three qualities, I will let him in ! On they go —an invincible army, yet not a victorious one. The aristocrats, the elect, the chosen, the Best People—all the words that describe them are false, and all attempts to organise them fail. Again and again Authority, seeing their value, has tried to net them and to utilise them as the Egyptian Priesthood or the Christian Church or the Chinese Civil Service or the Group Movement, or some other worthy stunt. But they slip through the net and are gone ; when the door is shut, they are no longer in the room ; their temple, as one of them remarked, is the Holiness of the Heart's Affection, and their kingdom, though they never possess it, is the wide-open world.

With this type of person knocking about, and constantly crossing one's path if one has eyes to see or hands to feel, the experiment of earthly life cannot be dismissed as a failure. But it may well be hailed as a tragedy, the tragedy being that no device has been found by which these private decencies can be transmitted to public affairs. As soon as people have power they go crooked and sometimes dotty as well, because the possession of power lifts them into a region where normal honesty never pays. For instance, the man who is selling newspapers outside the Houses of Parliament can safely leave his papers to go for a drink and his cap beside them : anyone who takes a paper is sure to drop a copper into the cap. But the men who are inside the Houses of Parliament—they cannot trust one another like that, still less can the Government they compose trust other governments. No caps upon the pavement here, but suspicion, treachery and armaments. The more highly public life is organised the lower does its morality sink ; the nations of to-day behave to each other worse than they ever did in the past, they cheat, rob, bully and bluff, make war without notice, and kill as many women and children as possible ; whereas primitive tribes were at all events restrained by taboos. It is a humiliating outlook—though the greater the darkness, the brighter shine the little lights, reassuring one another, signalling : ' Well, at all events, I'm still here. I don't like it very much, but how are you ? ' Unquenchable lights of my aristocracy ! Signals of the invincible army ! ' Come along—anyway, let's have a good time while we can.' I think they signal that too.

The Saviour of the future—if ever he comes—will not preach a new Gospel. He will merely utilise my aristocracy, he will make effective the good will and the good temper which are already existing. In other words, he will introduce a new technique. In economics, we are told that if there was a new technique of distribution, there need be no poverty, and people would not starve in one place while crops were being ploughed under in another. A similar change is needed in the sphere of morals and politics. The desire for it is by no means new ; it was expressed, for example, in theological terms by Jacopone da Todi over six hundred years ago. ' Ordina questo amore, O tu che m'ami,' he said ; ' O thou who lovest me—set this love in order.' His prayer was not granted, and I do not myself believe that it ever will be, but here, and not through a change of heart, is our probable route. Not by becoming better, but by ordering and distributing his native goodness, will Man shut up Force into its box, and so gain time to explore the universe and to set his mark upon it worthily. At present he only explores it at odd moments, when Force is looking the other way, and his divine creativeness appears as a trivial by-product, to be scrapped as soon as the drums beat and the bombers hum.

Such a change, claim the orthodox, can only be made by Christianity, and will be made by it in God's good time : man always has failed and always will fail to organise his own good-ness, and it is presumptuous of him to try. This claim—solemn as it is—leaves me cold. I cannot believe that Christianity will ever cope with the present world-wide mess, and I think that such influence as it retains in modern society is due to the money behind it, rather than to its spiritual appeal. It was a spiritual force once, but the indwelling spirit will have to be restated if it is to calm the waters again, and probably restated in a non-Christian form. Naturally a lot of people, and people who are not only good but able and intelligent, will disagree here ; they will vehemently deny that Christianity has failed, or they will argue that its failure proceeds from the wickedness of men, and really proves its ultimate success. They have Faith, with a large F. My faith has a very small one, and I only intrude it because these are strenuous and serious days, and one likes to say what one thinks while speech is comparatively free : it may not be free much longer.

The above are the reflections of an individualist and a liberal who has found liberalism crumbling beneath him and at first felt ashamed. Then, looking around, he decided there was no special reason for shame, since other people, whatever they felt, were equally insecure. And as for individualism—there seems no way of getting off this, even if one wanted to. The dictator-hero can grind down his citizens till they are all alike, but he cannot melt them into a single man. That is beyond his power. He can order them to merge, he can incite them to mass-antics, but they are obliged to be born separately, and to die separately, and, owing to these unavoidable termini, will always be running off the totalitarian rails. The memory of birth and the expectation of death always lurk within the human being, making him separate from his fellows and consequently capable of intercourse with them. Naked I came into the world, naked I shall go out of it ! And a very good thing too, for it reminds me that I am naked under my shirt, whatever its colour.

[1939]

ART IN GENERAL

Anonymity: An Enquiry

Do you like to know who a book's by?

The question is more profound than may appear. A poem for example : do we gain more or less pleasure from it when we know the name of the poet? The *Ballad of Sir Patrick Spens*, for example. No one knows who wrote *Sir Patrick Spens*. It comes to us out of the northern void like a breath of ice. Set beside it another ballad whose author is known—*The Rime of the Ancient Mariner*. That, too, contains a tragic voyage and the breath of ice, but it is signed Samuel Taylor Coleridge, and we know a certain amount about this Coleridge. Coleridge signed other poems and knew other poets ; he ran away from Cambridge ; he enlisted as a Dragoon under the name of Trooper Comberback, but fell so constantly from his horse that it had to be withdrawn from beneath him permanently ; he was employed instead upon matters relating to sanitation ; he married Southey's sister, and gave lectures ; he became stout, pious and dishonest, took opium and died. With such information in our heads, we speak of the *Ancient Mariner* as ' a poem by Coleridge,' but of *Sir Patrick Spens* as ' a poem.' What difference, if any, does this difference between them make upon our minds? And in the case of novels and plays—does ignorance or knowledge of their authorship signify? And newspaper articles—do they impress more when they are signed or unsigned? Thus—rather vaguely —let us begin our quest.

Books are composed of words, and words have two functions to perform : they give information or they create an atmosphere. Often they do both, for the two functions are not incompatible, but our enquiry shall keep them distinct. Let us turn for our next example to Public Notices. There is a word that is sometimes hung up at the edge of a tramline : the word ' Stop.' Written on a metal label by the side of the line, it means that a tram should stop here presently. It is an example of pure information. It creates no atmosphere—at least, not in my mind. I stand close to the label and wait and wait for the tram.

If the tram comes, the information is correct ; if it doesn't come, the information is incorrect ; but in either case it remains information, and the notice is an excellent instance of one of the uses of words.

Compare it with another public notice which is sometimes exhibited in the darker cities of England : ' Beware of pick-pockets, male and female.' Here, again, there is information. A pickpocket may come along presently, just like a tram, and we take our measures accordingly. But there is something else besides. Atmosphere is created. Who can see those words without a slight sinking feeling at the heart ? All the people around look so honest and nice, but they are not, some of them are pickpockets, male or female. They hustle old gentlemen, the old gentleman glances down, his watch is gone. They steal up behind an old lady and cut out the back breadth of her beautiful sealskin jacket with sharp and noiseless pairs of scissors. Observe that happy little child running to buy sweets. Why does he suddenly burst into tears. A pickpocket, male or female, has jerked his halfpenny out of his hand. All this, and perhaps much more, occurs to us when we read the notice in question. We suspect our fellows of dishonesty, we observe them suspecting us. We have been reminded of several disquieting truths, of the general insecurity of life, human frailty, the violence of the poor, and the fatuous trustfulness of the rich, who always expect to be popular without having done anything to deserve it. It is a sort of *memento mori*, set up in the midst of Vanity Fair. By taking the form of a warning it has made us afraid, although nothing is gained by fear ; all we need to do is to protect our precious purses, and fear will not help us to do this. Besides conveying information it has created an atmosphere, and to that extent is literature. ' Beware of pickpockets, male and female,' is not good literature, and it is unconscious. But the words are performing two functions, whereas the word ' Stop ' only per-formed one, and this is an important difference, and the first step in our journey.

Next step. Let us now collect together all the printed matter of the world into a single heap ; poetry books, exercise books, plays, newspapers, advertisements, street notices, everything. Let us arrange the contents of the heap into a line, with the works that convey pure information at one end, and the works that create pure atmosphere at the other end, and the works that do both in their intermediate positions, the whole line being graded so that we pass from one attitude to another. We shall find that at the end of the pure information stands the tramway notice ' Stop,' and that at the extreme other end is lyric poetry. Lyric poetry is absolutely no use. It is the exact antithesis of a street notice, for it conveys no information of any kind. What's the use of ' A slumber did my spirit seal ' or ' Whether on Ida's snowy brow ' or ' So we'll go no more a roving ' or ' Far in a western brookland ' ? They do not tell us where the tram will stop or even whether it exists. And, passing from lyric poetry to ballad, we are still deprived of information. It is true that the *Ancient Mariner* describes an antarctic expedition, but in such a muddled way that it is no real help to the explorer, the accounts of the polar currents and winds being hopelessly inaccurate It is true that the *Ballad of Sir Patrick Spens* refers to the bringing home of the Maid of Norway in the year 1285, but the reference is so vague and confused that the historians turn from it in despair. Lyric poetry is absolutely no use, and poetry generally is almost no use.

But when, proceeding down the line, we leave poetry behind and arrive at the drama, and particularly at those plays that purport to contain normal human beings, we find a change. Uselessness still predominates, but we begin to get information as well. *Julius Caesar* contains some reliable information about Rome. And when we pass from the drama to the novel, the change is still more marked. Information abounds. What a lot we learn from *Tom Jones* about the west countryside ! And from *Northanger Abbey* about the same countryside fifty years later ! In psychology too the novelist teaches us much. How carefully has Henry James explored certain selected recesses of the human mind ! What an analysis of a country rectory in *The Way of All Flesh* ! The instincts of Emily Brontë—they illuminate passion. And Proust—how amazingly does Proust describe not only French Society, not only the working of his characters, but the personal equipment of the reader, so that one keeps stopping with a gasp to say ' Oh ! how did he find that out about me ? I didn't even know it myself until he informed me, but it is so ! ' The novel, whatever else it may be, is partly a notice-board. And that is why many men who do not care for poetry or even for the drama enjoy novels and are well qualified to criticise them.

Beyond the novel we come to works whose avowed aim is information, works of learning, history, sociology, philosophy, psychology, science, etc. Uselessness is now subsidiary, though it still may persist as it does in the *Decline and Fall* or the *Stones of Venice*. And next come those works that give, or profess to give, us information about contemporary events : the newspapers. (Newspapers are so important and so peculiar that I shall return to them later, but mention them here in their place in the procession of printed matter.) And then come advertisements, time tables, the price list inside a taxi, and public notices : the notice warning us against pickpockets, which incidentally produced an atmosphere, though its aim was information, and the pure information contained in the announcement ' Stop.' It is a long journey from lyric poetry to a placard beside a tramline, but it is a journey in which there are no breaks. Words are all of one family, and do not become different because some are printed in a book and others on a metal disc. It is their functions that differentiate them. They have two functions, and the combination of those functions is infinite. If there is on earth a house with many mansions, it is the house of words.

Looking at this line of printed matter, let us again ask ourselves : Do I want to know who wrote that ? Ought it to be signed or not ? The question is becoming more interesting. Clearly, in so far as words convey information, they ought to be signed. Information is supposed to be true. That is its only reason for existing, and the man who gives it ought to sign his name, so that he may be called to account if he has told a lie. When I have waited for several hours beneath the notice ' Stop,' I have the right to suggest that it be taken down, and I cannot do this unless I know who put it up. Make your statement, sign your name. That's common sense. But as we approach the other function of words—the creation of atmosphere —the question of signature surely loses its importance. It does not matter who wrote ' A slumber did my spirit steal' because the poem itself does not matter. Ascribe it to Ella Wheeler Wilcox and the trams will run as usual. It does not matter much who wrote *Julius Caesar* and *Tom Jones*. They contain descriptions of ancient Rome and eighteenth century England, and to that extent we wish them signed, for we can judge from the author's name whether the description is likely to be reliable ; but beyond that, the guarantee of Shakespeare or Fielding might just as well be Charles Garvice's. So we come to the conclusion, firstly, that what is information ought to be signed ; and, secondly, that what is not information need not be signed.

The question can now be carried a step further.

What is this element in words that is not information ? I have called it ' atmosphere,' but it requires stricter definition than that. It resides not in any particular word, but in the order in which words are arranged—that is to say, in style. It is the power that words have to raise our emotions or quicken our blood. It is also something else, and to define that other thing would be to explain the secret of the universe. This ' something else ' in words is undefinable. It is their power to create not only atmosphere, but a world, which, while it lasts, seems more real and solid than this daily existence of pickpockets and trams. Before we begin to read the *Ancient Mariner* we know that the Polar Seas are not inhabited by spirits, and that if a man shoots an albatross he is not a criminal but a sportsman, and that if he stuffs the albatross afterwards he becomes a naturalist also. All this is common knowledge. But when we are reading the *Ancient Mariner*, or remembering it intensely, common knowledge disappears and uncommon knowledge takes its place. We have entered a universe that only answers to its own laws, supports itself, internally coheres, and has a new standard of truth. Information is true if it is accurate. A poem is true if it hangs together. Information points to something else. A poem points to nothing but itself. Information is relative. A poem is absolute. The world created by words exists neither in space nor time though it has semblances of both, it is eternal and indestructible, and yet its action is no stronger than a flower : it is adamant, yet it is also what one of its practitioners thought it to be, namely, the shadow of a shadow. We can best define it by negations. It is not this world, its laws are not the laws of science or logic, its conclusions not those of common sense. And it causes us to suspend our ordinary judgments.

Now comes the crucial point. While we are reading *The Ancient Mariner* we forget our astronomy and geography and daily ethics. Do we not also forget the author ? Does not Samuel Taylor Coleridge, lecturer, opium eater, and dragoon, disappear with the rest of the world of information ? We remember him before we begin the poem and after we finish it, but during the poem nothing exists but the poem. Consequently while we read *The Ancient Mariner* a change takes place in it. It becomes anonymous, like the *Ballad of Sir Patrick Spens*. And here is the point I would support : that all literature tends towards a condition of anonymity, and that, so far as words are creative, a signature merely distracts us from their true significance. I do not say literature ' ought ' not to be signed, because literature is alive, and consequently ' ought ' is the wrong word to use. It wants not to be signed. That puts my point. It is always tugging in that direction and saying in effect : ' I, not my author, exist really.' So do the trees, flowers and human beings say ' I really exist, not God,' and continue to say so despite the admonitions to the contrary addressed to them by clergymen and scientists. To forget its Creator is one of the functions of a Creation. To remember him is to forget the days of one's youth. Literature does not want to remember. It is alive—not in a vague complementary sense—but alive tenaciously, and it is always covering up the tracks that connect it with the laboratory.

It may here be objected that literature expresses personality, that it is the result of the author's individual outlook, that we are right in asking for his name. It is his property—he ought to have the credit.

An important objection ; also a modern one, for in the past neither writers nor readers attached the high importance to personality that they do to-day. It did not trouble Homer or the various people who were Homer. It did not trouble the writers in the Greek Anthology, who would write and re-write the same poem in almost identical language, their notion being that the poem, not the poet, is the important thing, and that by continuous rehandling the perfect expression natural to the poem may be attained. It did not trouble the mediaeval balladists, who, like the Cathedral builders, left their works unsigned. It troubled neither the composers nor the translators of the Bible. The Book of Genesis to-day contains at least three different elements—Jahvist, Elohist and Priestley—which were combined into a single account by a committee who lived under King Josiah at Jerusalem and translated into English by another committee who lived under King James I at London. And yet the Book of Genesis is literature. These earlier writers and readers knew that the words a man writes express him, but they did not make a cult of expression as we do to-day. Surely they were right, and modern critics go too far in their insistence on personality.

They go too far because they do not reflect what personality is. Just as words have two functions—information and creation —so each human mind has two personalities, one on the surface, one deeper down. The upper personality has a name. It is called S. T. Coleridge, or William Shakespeare, or Mrs. Humphry Ward. It is conscious and alert, it does things like dining out, answering letters, etc., and it differs vividly and amusingly from other personalities. The lower personality is a very queer affair. In many ways it is a perfect fool, but without it there is no litera- ture, because unless a man dips a bucket down into it occasionally he cannot produce first-class work. There is something general about it. Although it is inside S. T. Coleridge, it cannot be labelled with his name. It has something in common with all other deeper personalities, and the mystic will assert that the common quality is God, and that here, in the obscure recesses of our being, we near the gates of the Divine. It is in any case the force that makes for anonymity. As it came from the depths, so it soars to the heights, out of local questionings ; as it is general to all men, so the works it inspires have something general about them, namely beauty. The poet wrote the poem no doubt, but he forgot himself while he wrote it, and we forget him while we read. What is so wonderful about great literature is that it trans- forms the man who reads it towards the condition of the man who wrote, and brings to birth in us also the creative impulse. Lost in the beauty where he was lost, we find more than we ever threw away, we reach what seems to be our spiritual home, and remember that it was not the speaker who was in the beginning but the Word.

If we glance at one or two writers who are not first class this point will be illustrated. Charles Lamb and R. L. Stevenson will serve. Here are two gifted, sensitive, fanciful, tolerant, humorous fellows, but they always write with their surface- personalities and never let down buckets into their underworld. Lamb did not try : bbbbuckets, he would have said, are bbeyond me, and he is the pleasanter writer in consequence. Stevenson was always trying oh ever so hard, but the bucket either stuck or else came up again full of the R.L.S. who let it down, full of the mannerisms, the self-consciousness, the sentimentality, the quaintness which he was hoping to avoid. He and Lamb append

their names in full to every sentence they write. They pursue
us page after page, always to the exclusion of higher joy. They
are letter writers, not creative artists, and it is no coincidence
that each of them did write charming letters. A letter comes
off the surface : it deals with the events of the day or with plans :
it is naturally signed. Literature tries to be unsigned. And the
proof is that, whereas we are always exclaiming ' How like
Lamb ! ' or ' How typical of Stevenson ! ' we never say ' How
like Shakespeare ! ' or ' How typical of Dante ! ' We are conscious only of the world they have created, and we are in a sense
co-partners in it. Coleridge, in his smaller domain, makes us
co-partners too. We forget for ten minutes his name and our
own, and I contend that this temporary forgetfulness, this
momentary and mutual anonymity, is sure evidence of good
stuff. The demand that literature should express personality
is far too insistent in these days, and I look back with longing to
the earlier modes of criticism where a poem was not an expression
but a discovery, and was sometimes supposed to have been shown
to the poet by God.

The personality of a writer does become important after we
have read his book and begin to study it. When the glamour
of creation ceases, when the leaves of the divine tree are silent,
when the co-partnership is over, then a book changes its nature,
and we can ask ourselves questions about it such as ' What is
the author's name ? ' ' Where did he live ? ' ' Was he married ? ' and ' Which was his favourite flower ? ' Then we are
no longer reading the book, we are studying it and making it
subserve our desire for information. ' Study ' has a very solemn
sound. ' I am studying Dante ' sounds much more than ' I am
reading Dante.' It is really much less. Study is only a serious
form of gossip. It teaches us everything about the book except
the central thing, and between that and us it raises a circular
barrier which only the wings of the spirit can cross. The study
of science, history, etc., is necessary and proper, for they are
subjects that belong to the domain of information, but a creative
subject like literature—to study that is excessively dangerous, and
should never be attempted by the immature. Modern education
promotes the unmitigated study of literature and concentrates
our attention on the relation between a writer's life—his surface
life—and his work. That is one reason why it is such a curse.
There are no questions to be asked about literature while we

read it because ' la paix succède à la pensée,' in the words of Paul Claudel. An examination paper could not be set on the *Ancient Mariner* as it speaks to the heart of the reader, and it was to speak to the heart that it was written, and otherwise it would not have been written. Questions only occur when we cease to realise what it was about and become inquisitive and methodical.

A word in conclusion on the newspapers—for they raise an interesting contributory issue. We have already defined a newspaper as something which conveys, or is supposed to convey, information about passing events. It is true, not to itself like a poem, but to the facts it purports to relate—like the tram notice. When the morning paper arrives it lies upon the breakfast table simply steaming with truth in regard to something else. Truth, truth, and nothing but truth. Unsated by the banquet, we sally forth in the afternoon to buy an evening paper, which is published at midday as the name implies, and feast anew. At the end of the week we buy a weekly, or a Sunday paper, which as the name implies has been written on the Saturday, and at the end of the month we buy a monthly. Thus do we keep in touch with the world of events as practical men should.

And who is keeping us in touch ? Who gives us this information upon which our judgments depend, and which must ultimately influence our characters ? Curious to relate, we seldom know. Newspapers are for the most part anonymous. Statements are made and no signature appended. Suppose we read in a paper that the Emperor of Guatemala is dead. Our first feeling is one of mild consternation ; out of snobbery we regret what has happened, although the Emperor didn't play much part in our lives, and if ladies we say to one another ' I feel so sorry for the poor Empress.' But presently we learn that the Emperor cannot have died, because Guatemala is a Republic, and the Empress cannot be a widow, because she does not exist. If the statement was signed, and we know the name of the goose who made it, we shall discount anything he tells us in the future. If—which is more probable—it is unsigned or signed ' Our Special Correspondent '—we remain defenceless against future misstatements. The Guatemala lad may be turned on to write about the Fall of the Franc and mislead us over that.

It seems paradoxical that an article should impress us more if it is unsigned than if it is signed. But it does, owing to the weakness of our psychology. Anonymous statements have, as we have seen, a universal air about them. Absolute truth, the collected wisdom of the universe, seems to be speaking, not the feeble voice of a man. The modern newspaper has taken advantage of this. It is a pernicious caricature of literature. It has usurped that divine tendency towards anonymity. It has claimed for information what only belongs to creation. And it will claim it as long as we allow it to claim it, and to exploit the defects of our psychology. ' The High Mission of the Press.' Poor Press ! as if it were in a position to have a mission ! It is we who have a mission to it. To cure a man through the newspapers or through propaganda of any sort is impossible : you merely alter the symptoms of his disease. We shall only be cured by purging our minds of confusion. The papers trick us not so much by their lies as by their exploitation of our weakness. They are always confusing the two functions of words and insinuating that ' The Emperor of Guatemala is dead ' and ' A slumber did my spirit seal ' belong to the same category. They are always usurping the privileges that only uselessness may claim, and they will do this as long as we allow them to do it.

This ends our enquiry. The question ' Ought things to be signed ? ' seemed, if not an easy question, at all events an isolated one, but we could not answer it without considering what words are, and disentangling the two functions they perform. We decided pretty easily that information ought to be signed : common sense leads to this conclusion, and newspapers which are largely unsigned have gained by that device their undesirable influence over civilisation. Creation—that we found a more difficult matter. ' Literature wants not to be signed,' I suggested. Creation comes from the depths—the mystic will say from God. The signature, the name, belongs to the surface-personality, and pertains to the world of information, it is a ticket, not the spirit of life. While the author wrote he forgot his name ; while we read him we forget both his name and our own. When we have finished reading we begin to ask questions, and to study the book and the author, we drag them into the realm of information. Now we learn a thousand things, but we have lost the pearl of great price, and in the chatter of question and answer, in the torrents of gossip and examination papers we forget the purpose for which creation was performed. I am not asking for reverence. Reverence is fatal to literature. My plea is for something more vital : imagination. Imagination is as the immortal God which should assume flesh for the redemption of mortal passion (Shelley). Imagination is our only guide into the world created by words. Whether those words are signed or unsigned becomes, as soon as the imagination redeems us, a matter of no importance, because we have approximated to the state in which they were written, and there are no names down there, no personality as we understand personality, no marrying or giving in marriage. What there is down there—ah, that is another enquiry, and may the clergymen and the scientists pursue it more successfully in the future than they have in the past.

[1925]

Art for Art's Sake

An address delivered before the American Academy of
Arts and Letters in New York

I believe in art for art's sake. It is an unfashionable belief, and some of my statements must be of the nature of an apology. Sixty years ago I should have faced you with more confidence. A writer or a speaker who chose ' Art for Art's Sake ' for his theme sixty years ago could be sure of being in the swim, and could feel so confident of success that he sometimes dressed himself in aesthetic costumes suitable to the occasion—in an embroidered dressing-gown, perhaps, or a blue velvet suit with a Lord Fauntleroy collar ; or a toga, or a kimono, and carried a poppy or a lily or a long peacock's feather in his mediaeval hand. Times have changed. Not thus can I present either myself or my theme to-day. My aim rather is to ask you quietly to reconsider for a few minutes a phrase which has been much misused and much abused, but which has, I believe, great importance for us—has, indeed, eternal importance.

Now we can easily dismiss those peacock's feathers and other affectations—they are but trifles—but I want also to dismiss a more dangerous heresy, namely the silly idea that only art matters, an idea which has somehow got mixed up with the idea of art for art's sake, and has helped to discredit it. Many things, besides art, matter. It is merely one of the things that matter, and high though the claims are that I make for it, I want to keep them in proportion. No one can spend his or her life entirely in the creation or the appreciation of masterpieces. Man lives, and ought to live, in a complex world, full of conflicting claims, and if we simplified them down into the aesthetic he would be sterilised. Art for art's sake does not mean that only art matters, and I would also like to rule out such phrases as, ' The Life of Art,' ' Living for Art,' and ' Art's High Mission.' They confuse and mislead.

What does the phrase mean ? Instead of generalising, let us take a specific instance—Shakespeare's *Macbeth*, for example, and pronounce the words, ' *Macbeth* for *Macbeth's* sake.' What does that mean ? Well, the play has several aspects—it is educational, it teaches us something about legendary Scotland, something about Jacobean England, and a good deal about human nature and its perils. We can study its origins, and study and enjoy its dramatic technique and the music of its diction. All that is true. But *Macbeth* is furthermore a world of its own, created by Shakespeare and existing in virtue of its own poetry. It is in this aspect *Macbeth* for *Macbeth's* sake, and that is what I intend by the phrase ' art for art's sake.' A work of art— whatever else it may be—is a self-contained entity, with a life of its own imposed on it by its creator. It has internal order. It may have external form. That is how we recognise it.

Take for another example that picture of Seurat's which I saw two years ago in Chicago—' *La Grande Jatte.*' Here again there is much to study and to enjoy : the pointillism, the charming face of the seated girl, the nineteenth-century Parisian Sunday sunlight, the sense of motion in immobility. But here again there is something more ; ' *La Grande Jatte* ' forms a world of its own, created by Seurat and existing by virtue of its own poetry : ' *La Grande Jatte* ' *pour* ' *La Grande Jatte* ' : *l'art pour l'art.* Like *Macbeth* it has internal order and internal life.

It is to the conception of order that I would now turn. This is important to my argument, and I want to make a digression, and glance at order in daily life, before I come to order in art.

In the world of daily life, the world which we perforce inhabit, there is much talk about order, particularly from statesmen and politicians. They tend, however, to confuse order with orders, just as they confuse creation with regulations. Order, I suggest, is something evolved from within, not something imposed from without ; it is an internal stability, a vital harmony, and in the social and political category it has never existed except for the convenience of historians. Viewed realistically, the past is really a series of *dis*orders, succeeding one another by discoverable laws, no doubt, and certainly marked by an increasing growth of human interference, but disorders all the same. So that, speaking as a writer, what I hope for to-day is a disorder which will be more favourable to artists than is the present one, and which will provide them with fuller inspirations and better material conditions. It will not last—nothing lasts—but there have been some advantageous disorders in the past—for instance, in ancient

Athens, in Renaissance Italy, eighteenth-century France, periods in China and Persia—and we may do something to accelerate the next one. But let us not again fix our hearts where true joys are not to be found. We were promised a new order after the first world war through the League of Nations. It did not come, nor have I faith in present promises, by whomsoever endorsed. The implacable offensive of Science forbids. We cannot reach social and political stability for the reason that we continue to make scientific discoveries and to apply them, and thus to destroy the arrangements which were based on more elementary discoveries. If Science would discover rather than apply—if, in other words, men were more interested in knowledge than in power—mankind would be in a far safer position, the stability statesmen talk about would be a possibility, there could be a new order based on vital harmony, and the earthly millennium might approach. But Science shows no signs of doing this : she gave us the internal combustion engine, and before we had digested and assimilated it with terrible pains into our social system, she harnessed the atom, and destroyed any new order that seemed to be evolving. How can man get into harmony with his surroundings when he is constantly altering them ? The future of our race is, in this direction, more unpleasant than we care to admit, and it has sometimes seemed to me that its best chance lies through apathy, uninventiveness, and inertia. Universal exhaustion might promote that Change of Heart which is at present so briskly recommended from a thousand pulpits. Universal exhaustion would certainly be a new experience. The human race has never undergone it, and is still too perky to admit that it may be coming and might result in a sprouting of new growth through the decay.

I must not pursue these speculations any further—they lead me too far from my terms of reference and maybe from yours. But I do want to emphasise that order in daily life and in history, order in the social and political category, is unattainable under our present psychology.

Where is it attainable ? Not in the astronomical category, where it was for many years enthroned. The heavens and the earth have become terribly alike since Einstein. No longer can we find a reassuring contrast to chaos in the night sky and look up with George Meredith to the stars, the army of unalterable law, or listen for the music of the spheres. Order is not there.

In the entire universe there seem to be only two possibilities for it. The first of them—which again lies outside my terms of reference—is the divine order, the mystic harmony, which according to all religions is available for those who can contemplate it. We must admit its possibility, on the evidence of the adepts, and we must believe them when they say that it is attained, if attainable, by prayer. ' O thou who changest not, abide with me,' said one of its poets. ' *Ordina questo amor, o tu che m'ami,*' said another : ' Set love in order thou who lovest me.' The existence of a divine order, though it cannot be tested, has never been disproved.

The second possibility for order lies in the aesthetic category, which is my subject here : the order which an artist can create in his own work, and to that we must now return. A work of art, we are all agreed, is a unique product. But why ? It is unique not because it is clever or noble or beautiful or enlightened or original or sincere or idealistic or useful or educational —it may embody any of those qualities—but because it is the only material object in the universe which may possess internal harmony. All the others have been pressed into shape from outside, and when their mould is removed they collapse. The work of art stands up by itself, and nothing else does. It achieves something which has often been promised by society, but always delusively. Ancient Athens made a mess—but the *Antigone* stands up. Renaissance Rome made a mess—but the ceiling of the Sistine got painted. James I made a mess—but there was *Macbeth*. Louis XIV—but there was *Phèdre*. Art for art's sake ? I should just think so, and more so than ever at the present time. It is the one orderly product which our muddling race has produced. It is the cry of a thousand sentinels, the echo from a thousand labyrinths ; it is the lighthouse which cannot be hidden : *c'est le meilleur témoignage que nous puissions donner de notre dignité. Antigone* for *Antigone's* sake, *Macbeth* for *Macbeth's,* ' *La Grande Jatte* ' *pour* ' *La Grande Jatte.*'

If this line of argument is correct, it follows that the artist will tend to be an outsider in the society to which he has been born, and that the nineteenth century conception of him as a Bohemian was not inaccurate. The conception erred in three particulars : it postulated an economic system where art could be a full-time job, it introduced the fallacy that only art matters, and it overstressed idiosyncrasy and waywardness—the peacock-feather aspect—rather than order. But it is a truer conception than the one which prevails in official circles on my side of the Atlantic— I don't know about yours : the conception which treats the artist as if he were a particularly bright government advertiser and encourages him to be friendly and matey with his fellow citizens, and not to give himself airs.

Estimable is mateyness, and the man who achieves it gives many a pleasant little drink to himself and to others. But it has no traceable connection with the creative impulse, and probably acts as an inhibition on it. The artist who is seduced by mateyness may stop himself from doing the one thing which he, and he alone, can do—the making of something out of words or sounds or paint or clay or marble or steel or film which has internal harmony and presents order to a permanently disarranged planet. This seems worth doing, even at the risk of being called uppish by journalists. I have in mind an article which was published some years ago in the London *Times,* an article called ' The Eclipse of the Highbrow,' in which the ' Average Man ' was exalted, and all contemporary literature was censured if it did not toe the line, the precise position of the line being naturally known to the writer of the article. Sir Kenneth Clark, who was at that time director of our National Gallery, commented on this pernicious doctrine in a letter which cannot be too often quoted. ' The poet and the artist,' wrote Clark, ' are important precisely because they are not average men ; because in sensibility, intelligence, and power of invention they far exceed the average.' These memorable words, and particularly the words ' power of invention,' are the Bohemian's passport. Furnished with it, he slinks about society, saluted now by a brickbat and now by a penny, and accepting either of them with equanimity. He does not consider too anxiously what his relations with society may be, for he is aware of something more important than that —namely the invitation to invent, to create order, and he believes he will be better placed for doing this if he attempts detachment. So round and round he slouches, with his hat pulled over his eyes, and maybe with a louse in his beard, and—if he really wants one—with a peacock's feather in his hand.

If our present society should disintegrate—and who dare prophesy that it won't ?—this old-fashioned and démodé figure will become clearer : the Bohemian, the outsider, the parasite, the rat—one of those figures which have at present no function

either in a warring or a peaceful world.   It may not be dignified
to be a rat, but many of the ships are sinking, which is not
dignified either—the officials did not build them properly.   Myself, I would sooner be a swimming rat than a sinking ship—at
all events I can look around me for a little longer—and I remember
how one of us, a rat with particularly bright eyes called Shelley,
squeaked out, ' Poets are the unacknowledged legislators of the
world,' before he vanished into the waters of the Mediterranean.

What laws did Shelley propose to pass ?   None.   The legislation of the artist is never formulated at the time, though it
is sometimes discerned by future generations.   He legislates
through creating.   And he creates through his sensitiveness and
his power to impose form.   Without form the sensitiveness
vanishes.   And form is as important to-day, when the human
race is trying to ride the whirlwind, as it ever was in those less
agitating days of the past, when the earth seemed solid and the
stars fixed, and the discoveries of science were made slowly,
slowly.   Form is not tradition.   It alters from generation to
generation.   Artists always seek a new technique, and will continue to do so as long as their work excites them.   But form of
some kind is imperative.   It is the surface crust of the internal
harmony, it is the outward evidence of order.

My remarks about society may have seemed too pessimistic,
but I believe that society can only represent a fragment of the
human spirit, and that another fragment can only get expressed
through art.   And I wanted to take this opportunity, this vantage
ground, to assert not only the existence of art, but its pertinacity.
Looking back into the past, it seems to me that that is all there
has ever been : vantage grounds for discussion and creation, little
vantage grounds in the changing chaos, where bubbles have been
blown and webs spun, and the desire to create order has found
temporary gratification, and the sentinels have managed to utter
their challenges, and the huntsmen, though lost individually, have
heard each other's calls through the impenetrable wood, and the
lighthouses have never ceased sweeping the thankless seas.   In this
pertinacity there seems to me, as I grow older, something more
and more profound, something which does in fact concern people
who do not care about art at all.

In conclusion, let me summarise the various categories that
have laid claim to the possession of Order.

(1) The social and political category.   Claim disallowed on

the evidence of history and of our own experience. If man altered psychologically, order here might be attainable ; not otherwise.

(2) The astronomical category. Claim allowed up to the present century, but now disallowed on the evidence of the physicists.

(3) The religious category. Claim allowed on the evidence of the mystics.

(4) The aesthetic category. Claim allowed on the evidence of various works of art, and on the evidence of our own creative impulses, however weak these may be, or however imperfectly they may function. Works of art, in my opinion, are the only objects in the material universe to possess internal order, and that is why, though I don't believe that only art matters, I do believe in Art for Art's Sake.

[1949]

The Duty of Society to the Artist

A great deal has been said about the duty of the artist to society. It is argued that the poet, the novelist, the painter, the musician, has a duty to the community ; he is a citizen like everyone else ; he must pull his weight, he must not give himself airs, or ask for special terms, he must pay his taxes honourably, and keep the laws which have been made for the general good. That is the argument and it is a reasonable one. But there is another side : what is the duty of society to the artist ? Society certainly has a duty to its members ; it has a duty to the engineer who serves it loyally and competently : it must provide him with the necessary tools and not allow him to starve ; it has a duty to the stockbroker who is a competent dealer in stocks : since he is part of a financial system which it has accepted, it must support him and ensure him his due percentage. This is obvious enough. So what is its duty to the artist ? If he contributes loyally and competently, ought not society to reward him like any other professional man ?

Unfortunately the matter is not so simple. Art is a profession : that is quite true. The novelist or the musician has to learn his job just as the engineer or stockbroker has to learn his, and he too has to make both ends meet and needs to be paid or otherwise supported. But it's such a queer job. I will come back to it in a moment. I want first to consider society, the society we may expect to have after this war. We may expect a society that is highly centralised. It may be organised for peace : we hope it will. It may have to be organised against future wars, and if so, so much the worse. But in either case it will be very tightly knit ; it will be planned ; and it will be bureaucratic. Bureaucracy, in a technical age like ours, is inevitable. The advance of science means the growth of bureaucracy and the reign of the expert. And as a result, society and the state will be the same thing.

This has never happened in the past. Society used to be much more diffuse. The government was there, making laws and wars, but it could not interfere so much with the individual :

it had not the means. When I was a boy there was no wireless, no motor-cars : at an earlier date there were no telegrams, no railways : earlier still, no posts. You cannot interfere with people unless you can communicate with them easily. Society was diffuse, and in the midst of the diffusion the artist flourished. If he was a painter he painted for the king and the courtiers, who probably had some individual ideas about painting, or for the great aristocrats, or for the local squire, or for the church, which was not an individual but which knew what it wanted as regards subject matter. He lived in a society which was broken up into groups and he had the chance of picking the group which suited him. That society, after lasting for thousands of years, has suddenly hardened and become centralised, and in the future the only effective patron will be the state. The state is in a position to commission pictures, statues, symphonies, novels, epics, films, hot jazz—anything. It has the money, and it commands the available talent. It can and it will encourage the efficient engineer or stockbroker or butcher. What encouragement will it give to an artist ?

I am going to imagine an interview between an artist—a painter of genius I will suppose—and the appropriate state official whom I will call Mr. Bumble. The artist says, ' I want to paint the new police station : can I have the job ? ' Mr. Bumble is not interested in painting and he has no reason to suppose that the police care for it either ; still he does his duty, he looks up his instructions, and sees that though police stations are usually left plain there is no regulation against their being coloured. ' Yes, that would certainly be in order,' he says. ' I'm instructed to encourage art and I could give you the job, and I note you have suitable credentials. What sort of picture do you propose to paint ? '

' I shall see when I start,' replies the artist airily.

' See when you start ? Is not that a little vague ? I suppose that anyhow you will paint something which is edifying and inspiring ?—a figure of Justice, for instance.'

' I can't promise to do that. Indeed I don't feel inclined to edify or inspire. No doubt this state of ours is admirable, no doubt our police are a fine body of men—but no : I don't want to paint anything instructive.'

' Well, well,' says Mr. Bumble, and thinks how much easier it is to deal with a stockbroker. ' Well, you know about art and I don't, but I always assumed that art existed to make men into better citizens.'

' It does sometimes do that,' replies the artist, ' but not always, and I don't feel inclined to paint that type of picture just now. Sorry.'

Mr. Bumble, who is a thoroughly decent fellow, is sorry too, and then he has a good idea.

' Still there's light art, isn't there,' he says heavily, ' art which amuses and entertains. Provided the requirements of propriety are observed, there's no objection whatever to your painting something popular.'

' Yes, art does sometimes entertain,' replies the artist. ' But not always. And I don't feel inclined to paint that type of picture either.'

' May I ask what you do want to do ? '

' I want to experiment '.

' Experiment ? The walls of the new police station are no place for experiments '.

' I want to experiment. I want to extend human sensitiveness through paint. That's all that interests me. Perhaps when I've finished, the picture will instruct and inspire people. Perhaps it will amuse them. I don't know and I don't really care. I want to paint something which will be understood when this society of ours is forgotten and the police station a ruin.'

' The new police station a ruin when it has just cost thousands of pounds ? How preposterous ! '

' Yes, a ruin in the desert like Palmyra and Ankhor or Zimbabwe, a ruin like Borobudor or Ajanta ; which are remembered to-day not for their original purposes but because of the experiments, the discoveries made by artists upon their walls. A ruin like . . . '

But here Mr. Bumble holds up his hand. His patience is exhausted, he really cannot waste more time over this flibberty-gibbet.

' I can do nothing for you,' he says. ' You don't fit in. And if you won't fit into the state, how can you expect to be employed by the state ? '

The artist retorts, ' I know I don't fit in. And it's part of my duty not to fit in. It's part of my duty to humanity. I feel things, I express things, that haven't yet been felt and expressed, and that is my justification. And I ask the state to employ me on trust and pay me without understanding what I am up to.'

There my dialogue ends. Mr. Bumble refuses to give the commission, for it is a pretty tall order to be asked to pay for something which you do not understand ; he who pays the piper naturally hopes to call the tune.

I have made that conversation up in order to emphasise the fundamental difficulty which confronts the modern centralised state when it tries to encourage art. The state believes in education. But does art educate ? ' Sometimes, but not always ' is the answer ; an unsatisfactory one. The state believes in recreation. But does art amuse ? ' Sometimes, but not always ' is the answer again. The state does *not* believe in experiments, in the development of human sensitiveness in directions away from the average citizen. The artist *does*, and consequently he and the state—who will soon be his sole employer—must disagree.

So that is why there is a problem in the case of the artist which does not arise in the case of the butcher or the engineer. He never quite fits in. This did not matter in the loosely organised societies of the past, but it will matter in the future, where the community will be the only employer, and there is a danger and indeed a probability that art will disappear.

Perhaps I shall make this clearer if I quote from another dialogue, written by Plato. Plato, all through his life, was interested in the relation between the artist and the state, and was worried because the artist never quite fits in. He had himself the artistic temperament. In one of his earlier dialogues, the *Phaedrus*, he calls poetry

> a madness . . . the madness of those who are possessed of the Muses : which enters into a delicate mind, and there inspires frenzy . . . But he who having no touch of the Muses' madness in his soul, comes to the door and thinks he will get into the temple—he, I say, and his poems are not admitted : the sane man is nowhere at all when he enters into competition with a madman.

The sane man, whom Mr. Bumble represents, is certainly not inclined to subsidise madness : the state exists for the sane who have learned to fit in. Plato himself realised this, and in his later life he became enthusiastic about the state, and was obliged to change his attitude towards poetry and art. Personally he loved them as much as ever, but he saw they were disruptive, and he ended by banishing poets from the ideal community, on the ground that they upset people and that you never know what they will say next. He came round to Mr. Bumble's view.

Not sharing Plato's totalitarianism, I believe that Mr. Bumble ought to have given that commission. I see his difficulties. How, in the first place, was he to know that the applicant was not a fraud ? (He would have to rely on some advisory body here.) And in the second place even if he felt convinced that the artist was genuine as artists go, how should he feel justified in wasting public money on someone so useless ? (The answer here is that he must be educated, educated not so much to appreciate art as to respect it. Our officials, when they take up their posts, ought to be instructed in soothing words that there is something in this queer art business which they cannot understand and must try not to resent.)

By the way, I've assumed above that we shall have a stable future after the war. If the future were chaotic, the artist would become a Bohemian and an outsider, and the whole problem would alter.

[1942]

Does Culture Matter?

Culture is a forbidding word. I have to use it, knowing of none better, to describe the various beautiful and interesting objects which men have made in the past, and handed down to us, and which some of us are hoping to hand on. Many people despise them. They argue with force that cultural stuff takes up a great deal of room and time, and had better be scrapped, and they argue with less force that we live in a new world which has been wiped clean by science and cannot profit by tradition. Science will wipe us clean constantly, they hope, and at decreasing intervals. Broadcasting and the cinema have wiped out the drama, and quite soon we may hope for some new invention which will wipe out the cinema industry and Broadcasting House. In this constant scrubbing, what place can there be for the Brandenburg Concertos, or for solitary readings of Dante, or for the mosaics of Santa Sophia, or for photographs of them ? We shall all rush forward doing our work and amusing ourselves during the recreation hour with whatever gives least bother.

This prospect seems to me so awful that I want to do what I can against it, without too much attempt at fair-mindedness. It is impossible to be fair-minded when one has faith—religious creeds have shown this—and I have so much faith in cultural stuff that I believe it must mean something to other people, and anyhow want it left lying about. Faith makes one unkind : I am pleased when culture scores a neat hit. For instance, Sir Richard Terry, the organist of Westminster Cathedral, once made a remark which gave me unholy joy : speaking to some young musicians at Blackpool, he told them that they could be either men or crooners when they grew up, but not both. A storm in a cocktail resulted. The bands of Mr. Jack Payne and Mr. Henry Hall fizzed to their depths, and the less prudent members in them accorded interviews to the press. One crooner said that he and his friends could knock down Sir Richard and his friends any day, so they must be men. Another crooner said that he and his friends made more money than Sir Richard's friends, so they must be musicians. The pretentiousness and conceit of these amusement-mongers came out very strikingly. They appeared to be living in an eternal *thé dansant* which they mistook for the universe, and they couldn't bear being teased. For my own part, I don't mind an occasional croon or a blast in passing from a Wurlitzer organ, and Sir Richard Terry's speciality, madrigals, bore me ; nevertheless, the music represented by him and his peers is the real thing ; it ought to be defended and it has the right occasionally to attack. As a rule, it is in retreat, for there is a hostility to cultural stuff to-day which is disquieting.

Of course, most people never have cared for the classics, in music or elsewhere, but up to now they have been indifferent or ribald, and good-tempered, and have not bothered to denounce. ' Not my sort, bit tame,' or ' sounds like the cat being sick, miaou pussy,' or ' Coo, he must have felt bad to paint them apples blue ' —these were their typical reactions when confronted with Racine, Stravinsky, Cézanne. There was no to-do—just ' not my sort.' But now the good-humour is vanishing, the guffaw is organised into a sneer, and the typical reaction is ' How dare these so-called art-chaps do it ? *I'll* give them something to do.' This hostility has been well analysed by Mrs. Leavis, in her study of the English novel. She shows that though fiction of the best-seller type has been turned out for the last two hundred years, it has only lately realised its power, and that the popular novelist of to-day tends to be venomous and aggressive towards his more artistic brethren —an attitude in which he is supported by most of the press, and by the cheap libraries. Her attitude leads to priggishness ; but it is better to be superior than to kow-tow. There was once a curious incident, which occupied several inches on a prominent page of *The Times*. A popular comedian had been faded out on the air, and the B.B.C., generally so stiff-necked, were grovelling low in apology, and going into all kinds of detail in extenuation of their grave offence. When they had done, the comedian's comment was printed ; he professed himself appeased and consented to broadcast in the future. I wonder how much fuss a poet or a philosopher would have made if his talk had been cut short, and how many inches of regret he would have been given.

Incidents like this, so trivial in themselves, suggest that the past, and the creations that derive from the past, are losing their honour and on their way to being jettisoned. We have, in this age of unrest, to ferry much old stuff across the river, and the old stuff is not merely books, pictures and music, but the power to enjoy and understand them. If the power is lost the books, etc., will sink down into museums and die, or only survive in some fantastic caricature. The power was acquired through tradition. Sinclair Lewis, in *Babbitt*, describes a civilisation which had no tradition and could consequently only work, or amuse itself with rubbish; it had heard of the past, but lacked the power to enjoy it or understand. There is a grim moment at a mediumistic séance, when Dante is invoked. The company knew of Dante as the guy who got singed, so he duly appears in this capacity and returns to his gridiron after a little banter, with a pleased smirk. He has become a proper comic. And it would seem that he is having a similar if less extreme experience in Soviet Russia. He has been ferried across there, but he is condemned as a sadist; that is to say the power to understand him has been left behind. Certainly Dante wrote over the gates of Hell that they were made by the power, wisdom and love of God :

> Fecemi la divina Potestate,
> La somma Sapienza e il primo Amore,

and neither the Middle West nor the Soviets nor ourselves can be expected to agree with that. But there is no reason why we should not understand it, and stretch our minds against his, although they have a different shape. The past is often uncongenial as far as its statements are concerned, but the trained imagination can surmount them and reach the essential. Dante seems to me a test case. If people are giving him up it is a sign that they are throwing culture overboard, owing to the roughness of the water, and will reach the further bank sans Dante sans Shakespeare and sans everything.

Life on that further bank, as I conceive it, is by no means a nightmare. There will be work for all and play for all. But the work and the play will be split; the work will be mechanical and the play frivolous. If you drop tradition and culture you lose your chance of connecting work and play and creating a life which is all of a piece. The past did not succeed in doing that, but it can help us to do it, and that is why it is so useful.

Crooners, best-sellers, electrical-organists, funny-faces, dream-girls, and mickey-mice cannot do it—they throw the weight all to one side and increase the split. They are all right when they don't take themselves seriously. But when they begin to talk big and claim the front row of the dress-circle and even get to it, something is wrong. Life on that further bank might not be a nightmare, but some of us would prefer the sleep that has no dreams.

2

Cultivated people are a drop of ink in the ocean. They mix easily and even genially with other drops, for those exclusive days are over when cultivated people made only cultivated friends, and became tongue-tied or terror-struck in the presence of anyone whose make-up was different from their own. Culture, thank goodness, is no longer a social asset, it can no longer be employed either as a barrier against the mob or as a ladder into the aristocracy. This is one of the few improvements that have occurred in England since the last war. The change has been excellently shown in Mrs. Woolf's biography of Roger Fry ; here we can trace the decay of smartness and fashion as factors, and the growth of the idea of enjoyment.

All the same, we are a drop in the ocean. Few people share our enjoyment so far. Strictly between ourselves, and keeping our limited circulation in mind, let us put our heads together and consider for a moment our special problem, our special blessings, our special woes. No one need listen to us who does not want to. We whisper in the corner of a world which is full of other noises, and louder ones.

Come closer. Our problem, as I see it, is this : is what we have got worth passing on ? What we have got is (roughly speaking) a little knowledge about books, pictures, tunes, runes, and a little skill in their interpretation. Seated beside our gas-fires, and beneath our electric-bulbs, we inherit a tradition which has lasted for about three thousand years. The tradition was partly popular, but mainly dependent upon aristocratic patronage. In the past, culture has been paid for by the ruling classes ; they often did not know why they paid, but they paid, much as they went to church ; it was the proper thing to do, it was a form of social snobbery, and so the artists sneaked a meal, the author got a sinecure, and the work of creation went on. To-day, people are coming to the top who are, in some ways, more clear-sighted and honest than the ruling classes of the past, and they refuse to pay for what they don't want ; judging by the noises through the floor, our neighbour in the flat above doesn't want books, pictures, tunes, runes, anyhow doesn't want the sorts which we recommend. Ought we to bother him ? When he is hurrying to lead his own life, ought we to get in his way like a maiden-aunt, our arms, as it were, full of parcels, and say to him ' I was given these specially to hand on to you . . . Sophocles, Velasquez, Henry James . . . I'm afraid they're a little heavy, but you'll get to love them in time, and if you don't take them off my hands I don't know who will . . . please . . . please . . . they're really important, they're culture.'

His reply is unlikely to be favourable, but, snubbing or no snubbing, what ought we to do ? That's our problem, that's what we are whispering about, while he and his friends argue and argue and argue over the trade-price of batteries, or the quickest way to get from Balham to Ealing. He doesn't really want the stuff. That clamour for art and literature which Ruskin and Morris thought they detected has died down. He won't take the parcel unless we do some ingenious touting. He is an average modern. People to-day are either indifferent to the aesthetic products of the past (that is the position both of the industrial magnate and of the trade unionist) or else (the Communist position) they are suspicious of them, and decline to receive them until they have been disinfected in Moscow. In England, still the abode of private enterprise, indifference predominates. I know a few working-class people who enjoy culture, but as a rule I am afraid to bore them with it lest I lose the pleasure of their acquaintance. So what is to be done ?

It is tempting to do nothing. Don't recommend culture. Assume that the future will have none, or will work out some form of it which we cannot expect to understand. Auntie had better keep her parcels for herself, in fact, and stop fidgeting. This attitude is dignified, and it further commends itself to me because I can reconcile it with respect for the people arguing upstairs. Who am I that I should worry them ? Out of date myself, I like out of date things, and am willing to pass out of focus in that company, inheritor of a mode of life which is wanted no more. Do you agree ? Without bitterness, let us sit upon the ground and tell sad stories of the death of kings, ourselves the last of their hangers-on. Drink the wine—no one wants it, though it came from the vineyards of Greece, the gardens of Persia. Break the glass—no one admires it, no one cares any more about quality or form. Without bitterness and without conceit take your leave. Time happens to have tripped you up, and this is a matter neither for shame nor for pride.

The difficulty here is that the higher pleasures are not really wines or glasses at all. They rather resemble religion, and it is impossible to enjoy them without trying to hand them on. The appreciator of an aesthetic achievement becomes in his minor way an artist ; he cannot rest without communicating what has been communicated to him. This ' passing on ' impulse takes various forms, some of them merely educational, others merely critical ; but it is essentially a glow derived from the central fire, and to extinguish it is to forbid the spread of the Gospel. It is therefore impossible to sit alone with one's books and prints, or to sit only with friends like oneself, and never to testify outside. Dogmatism is of course a mistake, and even tolerance and tact have too much of the missionary spirit to work satisfactorily. What is needed in the cultural Gospel is to let one's light so shine that men's curiosity is aroused, and they ask why Sophocles, Velasquez, Henry James should cause such disproportionate pleasure. Bring out the enjoyment. If ' the Classics ' are advertised as something dolorous and astringent, no one will sample them. But if the cultured person, like the late Roger Fry, is obviously having a good time, those who come across him will be tempted to share it and to find out how.

That seems to be as far as we can get with our problem, as we whisper together in our unobtrusive flat, while our neighbours, who possess voices more powerful than our own, argue about Balham and Ealing over our heads. Remember, by the way, that we are not creative artists. The creative artist might take another line. He would certainly have more urgent duties. Our chief job is to enjoy ourselves and not to lose heart, and to spread culture not because we love our fellow men, but because certain things seem to us unique and priceless, and, as it were, push us out into the world on their service. It is a Gospel, and not altogether a benign one ; it is the zest to communicate what has been communicated. Works of art do have this peculiar pushful quality ; the excitement that attended their creation hangs about them, and makes minor artists out of those who have felt their power.

[1940]

The Raison d'Être of Criticism in the Arts

*An address delivered at a Symposium on Music
at Harvard University*

Believing as I do that music is the deepest of the arts and deep beneath the arts, I venture to emphasise music in this brief survey of the raison d'être of criticism in the arts. I have no authority here. I am an amateur whose inadequacy will become all too obvious as he proceeds. Perhaps, though, you will remember in your charity that the word amateur implies love. I love music. Just to love it, or just to love anything or anybody is not enough. Love has to be clarified and controlled to give full value, and here is where criticism may help. But one has to start with love ; one has, in the case of music, to want to hear the notes. If one has no initial desire to listen and no sympathy after listening, the notes will signify nothing, sound and fury, whatever their intellectual content.

The case *against* criticism is alarmingly strong, and much of my paper is bound to be a brief drawn up by the Devil's Advocate. I will postpone the evil day, and begin by indicating the case *for* criticism.

Most of us will agree that previous training is desirable before we approach the arts. We mistrust untrained appreciation, believing that it often defeats its own ends. Appreciation ought to be enough. But unless we learn by example and by failure and by comparison, appreciation will not bite. We shall tend to slip about on the surface of masterpieces, exclaiming with joy, but never penetrating. ' Oh, I do like Bach,' cries one appreciator, and the other cries, ' Do you ? I don't. I like Chopin.' Exit in opposite directions chanting Bach and Chopin respectively, and hearing less the composers than their own voices. They resemble investors who proclaim the soundness of their financial assets. The Bach shares must not fall, the Chopin not fall further, or one would have been proved a fool on the aesthetic stock exchange. The objection to untrained appreciation is not its naïveté but its tendency to lead to the appreciation of no one but oneself. Against such fatuity the critical spirit is a valuable corrective.

Except at the actual moment of contact—and I shall have much to say on the subject of that difficult moment—it is desirable to know why we like a work, and to be able to defend our preferences by argument. Our judgment has been strengthened and if all goes well the contacts will be intensified and increased and become more valuable.

I add the proviso ' if all goes well ' because success lies on the knees of an unknown God. There is always the contrary danger ; the danger that training may sterilise the sensitiveness that is being trained ; that education may lead to knowledge instead of wisdom, and criticism to nothing but criticism ; that spontaneous enjoyment, like the Progress of Poesy in Matthew Arnold's poem, may be checked because too much care has been taken to direct it into the right channel. Still it is a risk to be faced, and if no care had been taken the stream might have vanished even sooner. We hope criticism will help. We have faith in it as a respectable human activity, as an item in the larger heritage which differentiates us from the beasts.

How best can this activity be employed ? One must allow it to construct aesthetic theories, though to the irreverent eyes of some of us they appear as travelling laboratories, beds of Procrustes whereon Milton is too long and Keats too short. In an age which is respectful to theory—as for instance the seventeenth century was respectful to Aristotle's theory of the dramatic unities —a theory may be helpful and stimulating, particularly to the sense of form. French tragedy could culminate in Racine because certain leading strings had been so willingly accepted that they were scarcely felt. Corneille and Tasso were less happy. Corneille, having produced the *Cid*, wasted much time trying to justify its deviations from Aristotle's rules ; and Tasso wasted even more, for he published his theory of Christian Epic Poetry before he wrote the *Gerusalemme Liberata* which was to illustrate it. His epic was attacked by the critics because it deviated from what Aristotle said and also from what Tasso thought he might have said. Tasso was upset, became involved in three volumes of controversy, tried to write a second epic which should not deviate, failed, and went mad. Except perhaps in Russia, where the deviations of Shostakovitch invite a parallel, a theory in the modern world has little power over the fine arts, for good or evil. We have no atmosphere where it can flourish, and the attempts of certain governments to generate such an atmosphere in bureaus are unlikely to succeed. The construction of aesthetic theories and their comparison are desirable cultural exercises : the theories themselves are unlikely to spread far or to hinder or help.

A more practical activity for criticism is the sensitive dissection of particular works of art. What did the artist hope to do ? What means did he employ, subconscious or conscious ? Did he succeed, and if his success was partial where did he fail ? In such a dissection the tools should break as soon as they encounter any living tissue. The apparatus is nothing, the specimen all. Whether expert critics will agree with so extreme a statement is doubtful, but I do enjoy following particular examinations so far as an amateur can. It is delightful and profitable to enter into technicalities to the limit of one's poor ability, to continue as far as one can in the wake of an expert mind, to pursue an argument till it passes out of one's grasp. And to have, while this is going on, a particular work of art before one can be a great help. Besides learning about the work one increases one's powers. Criticism's central job seems to be education through precision.

A third activity, less important, remains to be listed, and since it lies more within my sphere than precision I will discuss it at greater length. Criticism can stimulate. Few of us are sufficiently awake to the beauty and wonder of the world, and when art intervenes to reveal them it sometimes acts in reverse, and lowers a veil instead of raising it. This deadening effect can often be dispersed by a well-chosen word. We can be awakened by a remark which need not be profound or even true, and can be sent scurrying after the beauties and wonders we were ignoring. Journalism and broadcasting have their big opportunity here. Unsuited for synthesis or analysis, they can send out the winged word that carries us off to examine the original.

There is in fact a type of criticism which has no interpretative value, yet it should not be condemned offhand. Much has been written about music, for instance, which has nothing to do with music and must make musicians smile. It usually describes the state into which the hearer was thrown as he sat on his chair at the concert and the visual images which occurred to him in that sedentary position. Here is an example, and a very lovely

one, from Walt Whitman. Whitman has heard ' one of Beethoven's master septets ' performed at Philadelphia (there is only
one Beethoven septet, but this the old boy did not know), and
the rendering of it on a ' small band of well-chosen and perfectly
combined instruments ' quite carried him away.

> Dainty abandon, sometimes as of Nature laughing on a
> hillside in the sunshine ; serious and firm monotonies, as of
> winds ; a horn sounding through the tangle of the forest, and
> the dying echoes ; soothing floating waves, but presently
> rising in surges, angrily lashing, muttering, heavy ; piercing
> peals of laughter for interstices ; now and then weird as Nature
> is herself in certain moods—but mainly spontaneous, easy,
> careless—often the sentiment of the postures of naked children
> playing or sleeping. It did me good even to see the violinists
> drawing their bows so masterly—every motion a study. I
> allowed myself, as I sometimes do, to wander out of myself.
> The conceit came to me of a copious grove of singing birds,
> and in their midst a simple harmonic duo, two human souls,
> steadily asserting their own pensiveness, joyousness.

Here is adorable literature, but what has it to do with Op. 20 ?
A poet's imagination has been kindled. He has allowed himself
to wander out of himself, but not into Beethoven's self, his
presumable goal. He has evoked the visual images congenial to
him, and though in the closing phrase there is a concert it is not
the one he attended, for it took place in his garden of Eden.

Another example of such criticism is to be found in Proust.
Proust is what Walt Whitman is not—sophisticated, soigné, rusé,
maladif. But he too listens to a septet and reacts to it visually,
he is carried off his seat into a region which has nothing to do
with the concert. It is the septet of Vinteuil, whom we have
hitherto known as the composer of a violin sonata. Vinteuil
himself, an obscure and unhappy provincial organist, has scarcely
appeared ; but his sonata, and particularly a phrase in it, *la petite
phrase*, has been an actor in the long-drawn inaction of the novel.
Character after character has listened to it, and has felt hope,
jealousy, despair, peace, according to the circumstances into which
la petite phrase has entered. We do not know what it sounds
like, but its arrival always means emotional heightening.

Towards the end of the novel, the hero goes to a musical
reception in Paris where a new work is to be performed. He

does not bother to look at the programme, being occupied by social trifles. It is a septet—the opening bars are sombre, glacial, as if dawn had not yet risen over the sea. He finds himself in an unknown world, where he understands nothing. Suddenly into this bewilderment there falls—*la petite phrase*, a reference to the sonata. He is listening to a posthumous work of Vinteuil, of whose existence he was unaware. Everything falls into shape. It is as if he has walked in an unknown region and come across the little gate which belongs to the garden of a friend. The septet expands its immensities, now comprehensible. The dawn rises crimson out of the sea, harsh midday rejoicings give way to more images, and the little phrase of the sonata, once virginal and shy, is august, quivering with colours, final, mature.

Now these visual wanderings are not entirely to my taste, nor perhaps to yours. Whitman's has its own naïve merit, but in the case of Proust, who is pretentious culturally, we feel uneasy. Shall we then say that they do not and cannot help us musically at all ? I think this is too severe. The septets of Beethoven and of Vinteuil have come no nearer to us, but we have been excited, we have been disposed to listen to sounds, we have been challenged to test the descriptions and to decide whether we agree with them. This general sharpening of interest is desirable. It can be effected in various ways : by a legitimate critic like Donald Tovey, by a grand old boy at Philadelphia, or by a snobby Frenchman in the Faubourg St. Germain. Not all ways are equally good. Those who hear music will always interpret it best. But those who don't hear it after the first few notes have also their use. Their wanderings, their visual images, their dreams, help to sharpen us. They recall us to the importance of sounds, and, their inferior in other ways, we may perhaps manage to listen to the sounds longer than they did.

Examples of higher musical value are to be found in the early journalism of Bernard Shaw. Though Shaw is a man of letters, like Whitman and Proust, and readily runs after his own thoughts and pictorial images, he does manage to remember the music. He can interpret as well as stimulate. He can say for instance of Haydn : ' Haydn would have been among the greatest had he been driven to that terrible eminence ; but we are fortunate enough in having had at least one man of genius who was happy enough in the Valley of Humiliation to feel no compulsion to struggle on through the Valley of the Shadow of Death.' What

a sensitive and just reflection ! How admirably it expresses that
turning away from the tragic so often displayed by Haydn—for
instance in the opening of the C Major Symphony, Op. 97 :
turning away not because he is afraid of tragedy, which would
discompose the listener, but because he prefers not to be tragic.
This is an essential in Haydn, and, apprehending it, Shaw con-
vinces us that he is inside music and could have criticised it more
deeply, had his career and his inclinations allowed.

I like, in this connection, jokes about music, the irresponsible
folly which sometimes kicks a door open as it flies. They too
may incline us to listen to sounds. When the English humorist,
Beachcomber, says ' Wagner is the Puccini of music,' he says
rather more than he says. Besides guying a well-worn formula,
he pierces Grand Opera itself, and reveals Brünnhilde and Butterfly transfixed on the same mischievous pin. I like, too, the
remark of an uncle of mine, a huntin', fishin', shootin', sportin'
sort of uncle, whose aversion to the arts was very genuine.
' They tell me,' he said one day thoughtfully, ' they tell me
music's like a gun ; it hurts less when you let it off yourself.'
Besides getting in a well-directed gibe, and discomposing my
aunt who adored Mendelssohn, he indicated very neatly the gulf
between artist on the one hand and critic on the other. Those
who are involved and those who appraise are never hurt in the
same way. This is, as a matter of fact, going to be our chief
problem here, and perhaps it will come the fresher because my
uncle hit at it in his slapdash fashion before striding back to his
dogs.

For now our trouble starts. We can readily agree that criticism has educational and cultural value ; the artist helps to
civilise the community, builds up standards, forms theories
stimulates, dissects, encourages the individual to enjoy the world
into which he has been born; and on its destructive side criticism
exposes fraud and pretentiousness and checks conceit. These
are substantial achievements. But I would like if I could to
establish its raison d'être on a higher basis than that of public
utility. I would like to discover some spiritual parity between
it and the objects it criticises, and this is going to be difficult.
The difficulty has been variously expressed. One writer—
Mr. F. L. Lucas—has called criticism a charming parasite ;
another—Chekhov—complains it is a gadfly which hinders

the oxen from ploughing ; a third—the eighteenth-century philosopher Lord Kames—compares it to an imp which distracts critics from their objective and incites them to criticise each other. My own trouble is not so much that it is a parasite, a gadfly, or an imp, but that there is a basic difference between the critical and creative states of mind, and to the consideration of that difference I would now invite your attention.

What about the creative state ? In it a man is taken out of himself. He lets down as it were a bucket into his subconscious, and draws up something which is normally beyond his reach. He mixes this thing with his normal experiences, and out of the mixture he makes a work of art. It may be a good work of art or a bad one—we are not here examining the question of quality—but whether it is good or bad it will have been compounded in this unusual way, and he will wonder afterwards how he did it. Such seems to be the creative process. It may employ much technical ingenuity and worldly knowledge, it may profit by critical standards, but mixed up with it is this stuff from the bucket, this subconscious stuff, which is not procurable on demand. And when the process is over, when the picture or symphony or lyric or novel (or whatever it is) is complete, the artist, looking back on it, will wonder how on earth he did it. And indeed he did not do it on earth.

A perfect example of the creative process is to be found in Kubla Khan. Assisted by opium, Coleridge had his famous dream, and dipped deep into the subconscious. Waking up, he started to transcribe it, and was proceeding successfully when that person from Porlock unfortunately called on business.

> Weave a circle round him thrice
> And close your eyes with holy dread,
> For he on honeydew hath fed
> And drunk the milk of Paradise—

and in came the person from Porlock. Coleridge could not resume. His connection with the subconscious had snapped. He had created and did not know how he had done it. As Professor John Livingston Lowes has shown, many fragments of Coleridge's day-to-day reading are embedded in Kubla Khan, but the poem itself belongs to another world, which he was seldom to record.

The creative state of mind is akin to a dream. In Coleridge's case it was a dream. In other cases—Jane Austen's for instance

—the dream is remote or sedate.   But even Jane Austen, looking back upon *Emma*, could have thought ' Dear me, how came I to write that ?   It is not ill-contrived.'   There is always, even with the most realistic artist, the sense of withdrawal from his own creation, the sense of surprise.

The French writer, Paul Claudel, gives the best description known to me of the creative state.   It occurs in *La Ville*.   A poet is speaking.   He has been asked whence his inspiration comes, and how is it that when he speaks everything becomes explicable although he explains nothing.   He replies :

> I do not speak what I wish, but I conceive in sleep,
> And I cannot explain whence I draw my breath, for it is my breath
>   which is drawn out of me.
> I expand the emptiness within me, I open my mouth, I breathe in
>   the air, I breathe it out.
> I restore it in the form of an intelligible word,
> And having spoken I know what I have said.

There is a further idea in the passage, which my brief English paraphrase has not attempted to convey : the idea that if the breathing in is *in*spiration the breathing out is *ex*piration, a pre-figuring of death, when the life of a man will be drawn out of him by the unknown force for the last time.   Creation and death are closely connected for Claudel.   I'm confining myself, though, to his description of the creative act, and ask you to observe how precisely it describes what happened in Kubla Khan.   There is conception in sleep, there is the connection between the sub-conscious and the conscious, which has to be effected before the work of art can be born, and there is the surprise of the creator at his own creation.

> Je restitue une parole intelligible,
> Et l'ayant dite, je sais ce que j'ai dit.

Which is exactly what happened to Coleridge.   He knew what he had said, but as soon as inspiration was interrupted he could not say any more.

After this glance at the creative state, let us glance at the critical.   The critical state has many merits, and employs some of the highest and subtlest faculties of man.   But it is grotesquely remote from the state responsible for the works it affects to expound.   It does not let down buckets into the subconscious. It does not conceive in sleep, or know what it has said after it has said it.   Think before you speak is criticism's motto ; speak before you think creation's. Nor is criticism disconcerted by people arriving from Porlock ; in fact it sometimes comes from Porlock itself. While not excluding imagination and sympathy, it keeps them and all the faculties under control, and only employs them when they promise to be helpful.

Thus equipped, it advances on its object. It has two aims. The first and the more important is aesthetic. It considers the object in itself, as an entity, and tells us what it can about its life. The second aim is subsidiary : the relation of the object to the rest of the world. Problems of less relevance are considered, such as the conditions under which the work of art was composed, the influences which formed it (criticism adores influences), the influence it has exercised on subsequent works, the artist's life, the lives of the artist's father and mother, prenatal possibilities and so on, straying this way into psychology and that way into history. Much of the above is valuable, but what meanwhile has become of Monteverdi's Vespers, or the Great Mosque at Delhi, or the Frogs of Aristophanes, or any other work which you happen to have in mind ? I throw these three objects at you because they happen to be in my own mind. I have been hearing the Vespers, seeing the Frogs, and thinking about the Delhi Mosque. If we wheel up an aesthetic theory —the best attainable, and there are some excellent ones—if we wheel it up and apply it with its measuring rods and pliers and forceps, its calipers and catheters, to Vespers, Mosque, and Frogs, we are visited at once by a sense of the grotesque. It doesn't work, two universes have not even collided, they have been juxtaposed. There is no spiritual parity. And if criticism strays from her central aesthetic quest to influences and psychological and historical considerations, something does happen then, contact is established. But no longer with a work of art.

A work of art is a curious object. Isn't it infectious ? Unlike machinery, hasn't it the power of transforming the person who encounters it towards the condition of the person who created it ? (I use the clumsy phrase 'towards the condition' on purpose.) We—we the beholders or listeners or whatever we are—undergo a change analogous to creation. We are rapt into a region near to that where the artist worked, and like him when we return to earth we feel surprised. To claim we actually entered his state and became co-creators with him there is presumptuous. However much excited I am by Brahms' Fourth

Symphony I cannot suppose I feel Brahms' excitement, and probably what he felt is not what I understand as excitement. But there has been an infection from Brahms through his music to myself. Something has passed. I have been transformed towards his condition, he has called me out of myself, he has thrown me into a subsidiary dream ; and when the passacaglia is trodden out, and the transformation closed, I too feel surprise.

Unfortunately this infection, this sense of co-operation with a creator, which is the supremely important step in our pilgrimage through the fine arts, is the one step over which criticism cannot help. She can prepare us for it generally, and educate us to keep our senses open, but she has to withdraw when reality approaches, like Virgil from Dante on the summit of Purgatory. With the coming of love, we have to rely on Beatrice, whom we have loved all along, and if we have never loved Beatrice we are lost. We shall remain pottering about with theories and influences and psychological and historical considerations—supports useful in their time, but they must be left behind at the entry of Heaven. I would not suggest that our comprehension of the fine arts is or should be of a nature of a mystic union. But, as in mysticism, we enter an unusual state, and we can only enter it through love. Putting it more prosaically, we cannot understand music unless we desire to hear it. And so we return to the earth.

Let us reconsider that troublesome object, the work of art, and observe another way in which it is recalcitrant to criticism. I am thinking of its freshness. So far as it is authentic, it presents itself as eternally virgin. It expects always to be heard or read or seen for the first time, always to cause surprise. It does not expect to be studied, still less does it present itself as a crossword puzzle, only to be solved after much re-examination. If it does that, if it parades a mystifying element, it is, to that extent, not a work of art, not an immortal Muse but a Sphinx who dies as soon as her riddles are answered. The work of art assumes the existence of the perfect spectator, and is indifferent to the fact that no such person exists. It does not allow for our ignorance and it does not cater for our knowledge.

This eternal freshness in creation presents a difficulty to the critic, who when he hears or reads or sees a work a second time rightly profits by what he has heard or read or seen of it the first time, and studies and compares, remembers and analyses, and often has to reject his original impressions as trivial. He may thus in the end gain a just and true opinion of the work, but he ought to remain startled, and this is usually beyond him. Take Beethoven's Ninth Symphony, the one in A. Isn't it in A ? The opening bars announce the key as explicitly as fifths can, leaving us only in doubt as to whether the movement will decide on the major or minor mode. In the fifteenth bar comes the terrifying surprise, the pounce into D minor, which tethers the music, however far it wanders, right down to the ineluctable close. Can one hope to feel that terror and surprise twice ? Can one avoid hearing the opening bars as a preparation for the pounce—and thus miss the life of the pounce ? Can we combine experience and innocence ? I think we can. The willing suspension of experience is possible, it is possible to become like a child who says ' Oh ! ' each time the ball bounces, although he has seen it bounce before and knows it must bounce.

It is possible but it is rare. The critic who is thoroughly versed in the score of the Ninth Symphony and can yet hear the opening bars as a trembling introduction in A to the unknown has reached the highest rank in his profession. Most of us are content to remain well-informed. It is so restful to be well-informed. We forget that Beethoven intended his Symphony to be heard always for the first time. We forget with still greater ease that Tchaikovsky intended the same for his Piano Concerto in B flat minor. Dubious for good reasons of that thumping affair, we sometimes scold it for being ' stale '—a ridiculous accusation, for it too was created as an eternal virgin, it too should startle each time it galumphs down the waltz. No doubt the Concerto, and much music, has been too often performed, just as some pictures have been too often looked at. Freshness of reception is exhausted more rapidly by a small or imperfect object than by a great one. Nevertheless the objects themselves are eternally new, it is the recipient who may wither. You remember how at the opening of Goethe's *Faust*, Mephistopheles, being stale himself, found the world stale, and reported it as such to the Almighty. The archangels took no notice of him and continued to sing of eternal freshness. The critic ought to combine Mephistopheles with the archangels, experience with innocence. He ought to know everything inside out, and yet be surprised. Virginia Woolf—who was both a creative artist and a critic— believed in reading a book twice. The first time she abandoned herself to the author unreservedly. The second time she treated him with severity and allowed him to get away with nothing he could not justify. After these two readings she felt qualified to discuss the book. Here is good rule of thumb advice. But it does not take us to the heart of our problem, which is super-rational. For we ought really to read the book in two ways at once. (And we ought to look at a picture in two ways at once, and to listen to music similarly.) We ought to perform a miracle the nature of which was hinted at by the Almighty when he said he was always glad to receive Mephistopheles in Heaven and hear him chat.

I would speak tentatively in the presence of an expert audience, but it seems to me that we are most likely to perform that miracle in the case of music. Music, more than the other arts, postulates a double existence. It exists in time, and also exists outside time, instantaneously. With no philosophic training, I cannot put my belief clearly, but I can conceive myself hearing a piece as it goes by and also when it has finished. In the latter case I should hear it as an entity, as a piece of sound-architecture, not as a sound-sequence, not as something divisible into bars. Yet it would be organically connected with the concert-hall performance. Architecture and sequence would, in my apprehension, be more closely fused than the two separate readings of a book in Virginia Woolf's.

The claim of criticism to take us to the heart of the Arts must therefore be disallowed. Another claim has been made for it, a more precise one. It has been suggested that criticism can help an artist to improve his work. If that be true, a raison d'être is established at once. Criticism becomes an important figure, a handmaid to beauty, holding out the sacred lamp in whose light creation proceeds, feeding the lamp with oil, trimming the wick when it flares or smokes. There must be many artists, musicians and others here, and it would be interesting to know whether criticism has helped them in their work, and if so how. Has she held up the lamp ? No doubt she illuminates past mistakes or merits, that certainly is within her power, but has the better knowledge of them any practical value ?

A remark of Mr. C. Day Lewis is interesting in this connection. It comes at the opening of *The Poetic Image*.

There is something formidable for the poet in the idea of criticism—something, dare I say it ? almost unreal. He writes a poem, then he moves on to a new experience, the next poem : and when a critic comes along and tells him what is right or wrong about the first poem, he has a feeling of irrelevance.

Something almost unreal. That is a just remark. The poet is always developing and moving on, and when his creative state is broken into by comments on something he has just put behind him, he feels bewildered. His reaction is ' What are you talking about ? Must you ? ' Once again, and in its purest form, the division between the critical and creative states, the absence of spiritual parity, becomes manifest. In its purest form because poetry is an extreme form of art, and is a convenient field for experiment. My own art, the mixed art of fiction, is less suitable, yet I can truly say with Mr. Day Lewis that I have nearly always found criticism irrelevant. When I am praised, I am pleased ; when I am blamed, I am displeased ; when I am told I am elusive, I am surprised—but neither the pleasure nor the sorrow nor the astonishment makes any difference when next I enter the creative state. One can eliminate a particular defect perhaps ; to sub- stitute merit is the difficulty. I remember that in one of my earlier novels I was blamed for the number of sudden deaths in it, which were said to amount to forty-four per cent of the fictional population. I took heed, and arranged that characters in sub- sequent novels should die less frequently and give previous notice where possible by means of illness or some other acceptable device. But I was not inspired to put anything vital in the place of the sudden deaths. The only remedy for a defect is inspiration, the subconscious stuff that comes up in the bucket. A piece of con- temporary music, to my ear, has a good many sudden deaths in it ; the phrases expire as rapidly as the characters in my novel, the chords cut each other's throats, the arpeggio has a heart attack, the fugue gets into a nose-dive. But these defects—if defects they be—are vital to the general conception. They are not to be remedied by substituting sweetness. And the musician would do well to ignore the critic even when he admits the justice of the particular criticism.

Only in two ways can criticism help the artist a little with his work. The first is general. He ought—if he keeps company at all—to keep good company. To be alone may be best—to be alone was that Fate reserved for Beethoven. But if he wishes to consort with ideas and standards and the works of his fellows —and he usually has to in the modern world—he must beware of the second-rate. It means a relaxation of fibre, a temptation to rest on his own superiority. I do not desire to use the words ' superior ' and ' inferior ' about human individuals ; in an individual so many factors are present that one cannot grade him. But one can legitimately apply them to cultural standards, and the artist should be critical here, and alive in particular to the risks of the clique. The clique is a valuable social device, which only a fanatic would condemn ; it can protect and encourage the artist. It is the artist's duty, if he wants to be in a clique, to choose a good one, and to take care it doesn't make him bumptious or sterile or silly. The lowering of critical standards in what one may call daily-studio life, their corruption by adulation or jealousy, may lead to inferior work. Good standards may lead to good work. That is all that there seems to be to say about this vague assistance, and maybe it was not worth saying.

The second way in which criticism can help the artist is more specific. It can help him over details, niggling details, minutiae of style. To refer to my own work again, I have certainly benefited by being advised not to use the word ' but ' so often. I have had a university education, you see, and it disposes one to overwork that particular conjunction. It is the strength of the academic mind to be fair and see both sides of a question. It is its weakness to be timid and to suffer from that fear-of-giving-oneself-away disease of which Samuel Butler speaks. Both its strength and its weakness incline it to the immoderate use of ' but.' A good many ' buts ' have occurred to-day, but not as many as if I had not been warned. The writer of the opposed type, the extrovert, the man who knows what he knows, and likes what he likes, and doesn't care who knows it—he should doubtless be subject to the opposite discipline ; he should be criticised because he never uses ' but ' ; he should be tempted to employ the qualifying clause. The man who has a legal mind should probably go easy on his ' if's.' Fiddling little matters. Yes, I know. The sort of trifling help which criticism can give the artist. She cannot help him in great matters.

With these random considerations my paper must close. The latter part of it has been overshadowed and perhaps obsessed by my consciousness of the gulf between the creative and critical states. Perhaps the gulf does not exist, perhaps it does not signify, perhaps I have been making a gulf out of a molehill. But in my view it does prevent the establishment of a first class raison d'être for criticism in the arts.   The only activity which can establish such a raison d'être is love.   However cautiously, with whatever reservations, after whatsoever purifications, we must come back to love.   That alone raises us to the co-operation with the artist which is the sole reason for our aesthetic pilgrimage. That alone promises spiritual parity.   My main conclusion on criticism has therefore to be unfavourable, nor have I succeeded in finding that it has given substantial help to the artists.

[1947]

The C Minor of that Life

Does 'Three Blind Mice' sound different when it is played in different keys? I ask for first aid on this problem. Of course if it is played high up it will sound different from when it is played low down ; the mice will squeak more shrilly. But that is not my problem. And, of course, if it is played first in one key and then in another, it will sound different the second time, owing to the relation between the keys ; the mice will seem increasingly insolent, or increasingly pathetic. But that again is not my problem. What I am muddling after is this : Is there any *absolute* difference between keys—a difference that is inherent, not relative ? Have they special qualities, and, if they have, can the qualities be named, and is there any key which is particularly suitable for 'Three Blind Mice' ?

I have battered my head against this for years—a head untrained musically, and unacquainted with any instrument beyond the piano. Perhaps, like many amateurs' problems, it is no problem, but one of those solemn mystifications which are erected by ignorance, and which would disappear under proper instruction. I continue to wonder whether keys have colours, or something analogous to colour (as the scales in Indian music have), whether they tint the tunes which are played in them, and which key would be most suitable for the Mice. C major ? And D major for Pop goes the Weasel ? Or is it the other way round ? Or does it not matter either way ?

The problem, if it is one, is connected with our sense of pitch. If we can't tell what note is being sounded, if we don't know what key the Mice are being played in, why then it can't matter to us in which key they are played. What the ear cannot hear, the heart cannot grieve. And I generally can't tell. My sense of pitch—though it does exist—is shaky and feeble and easily foiled by a few chromatics. I think I can tell when a tune is in C major, and I do frankly consider this key the most suitable for the Mice—it is straightforward, nurserified, unassuming. Mice in A flat would greatly overstate their

132

claims, for A flat is a delicate, suave gracious intimate refined key. And Mice in E would be presented far too brilliantly. I mention these three keys (C, A flat, and E) because I most readily detect them, and am therefore the more ready to ascribe them characteristics. Besides them, I sometimes spot F, which has the lyric quality of A flat, only less marked, and C sharp (D flat), which has the brilliancy of E, only more marked. Outside these five, it is usually guess-work for me.

The above are all major. More easily detected than any, and more interesting than any, because it moved so often through the mind and under the fingers of Beethoven, is the key of C minor. Perhaps because it evokes him, but perhaps because of something inherent in it, which attracted him, it appeals very readily to our sense of pitch, and if the Mice deserted their proper mode and put on its immensities, they would soon be run down. Beethoven, like myself, had feelings for certain keys, and he makes some quaint remarks about them. For instance, he calls B minor a 'black' key : rather odd—it never struck me as 'Black' ; brown is the utmost I would go to. Again he calls A flat 'barbaresco, not amoroso,' and here he is obviously wrong ! I have already defined the character of A flat ! Anyhow, if he did think it ' barbaresco,' why did he choose it for the slow movement of the Pathetic Sonata ? C sharp he calls 'maestoso.' Here he is quite right, and Wagner agrees with us, and has chosen this sparkling yet noble key for the closes both of Rheingold and of Götterdäm-merung ; the Gods go up to Walhalla and fall from it in C sharp.

But of C minor, the key he has made his own, Beethoven says nothing, so far as I know. He has invested in it deeply. If we lost everything he wrote except what is in this key, we should still have the essential Beethoven, the Beethoven tragic, the Beethoven so excited at the approach of something enormous that he can only just interpret and subdue it. It would be a pity to lose a Beethoven unbuttoned, a Beethoven yodelling, but this musician excited by immensities is unique in the annals of any art. No one has ever been so thrilled by things so huge, for the vast masses of doom crush the rest of us before we can hope to measure them. Fate knocks at our door ; but before the final tap can sound, the flimsy door flies into pieces, and we never learn the sublime rhythm of destruction.

The catalogue of the C minor items is a familiar one. Heading it is the Fifth Symphony. Then there is the great violin sonata—greater than the Kreutzer, many critics think. There is the third piano concerto. There is the Pathetic sonata, with its opening groan, and the last piano sonata (Op. III) with its opening dive into the abyss. There is the movement from the third Rasoumovsky Quartet, there are the thirty-two Variations. And there is probably a good deal more, some of it hidden away in works of other key-signatures. It would be absurd to press for similarities in items so different in intention and in date, but one has in all of them the conviction that Beethoven has found himself, that he is where he most wanted to be, that he is engaged in the pursuit of something outside sound—something which has fused the sinister and the triumphant.

There is a proof of this—at least it seems to me to be a proof—'indication' is the wiser word, no doubt—in the earliest of all the piano sonatas (Op. 2, No. 1). The key is F minor, and we go Mozarting ahead until we reach the last movement. This is a scrattling prestissimo, spitting triplets all over the place, and banging out not very amusing chords. After twenty bars, the triplets run down into the earth and re-emerge in the C minor key. Now the excitement begins. Beethoven, for the first time in his life, opens out. He plays with the new key for twelve bars, establishing it more firmly and heating himself up more at each note—and then out of it there soars a new tune, a tune in octaves, not loud, not elaborate, but tearing down the curtains and letting in the unknown light. As it sings itself out, the triplets get something to do which is worth doing, and when it ends and the banging chords re-enter, they talk sense. This knack of turning dullish stuff into great stuff is characteristic of Beethoven, and incidentally one of the reasons why one ought never to skip the repeats when playing him—for only at the repeat does one hear what the dullish stuff means. But it thrills me that he should have exercised the knack first in the key of C minor, and that from that attitude he should have prospected the wildest and most wonderful land of his empire.

Thus far have our Mice led us. Holding up their tails, let us count them. Firstly, there may be nothing in key. Secondly there can be nothing in key unless we have the sense of pitch. Thirdly, Beethoven thought, rightly or wrongly, that there was something in a key, and either chose C minor when he was in a particular mood, or was put into a particular mood after choosing it. Mozart's fondness for D major may also be noted, but in this respect, and indeed in others, Mozart did not go so far.

[1941]

Not Listening to Music

Listening to music is such a muddle that one scarcely knows how to start describing it. The first point to get clear in my own case is that during the greater part of every performance I do not attend. The nice sounds make me think of something else. I wool-gather most of the time, and am surprised that others don't. Professional critics can listen to a piece as consistently and as steadily as if they were reading a chapter in a novel. This seems to me an amazing feat, and probably they only achieve it through intellectual training; that is to say, they find in the music the equivalent of a plot; they are following the ground bass or expecting the theme to re-enter in the dominant, and so on, and this keeps them on the rails. But I fly off every minute: after a bar or two I think how musical I am, or of something smart I might have said in conversation; or I wonder what the composer—dead a couple of centuries— can be feeling as the flames on the altar still flicker up; or how soon an H.E. bomb would extinguish them. Not to mention more obvious distractions: the tilt of the soprano's chin or chins; the antics of the conductor, that impassioned beetle, especially when it is night time and he waves his shards; the affectation of the pianist when he takes a top note with difficulty, as if he too were a soprano; the backs of the chairs; the bumps on the ceiling; the extreme physical ugliness of the audience. A classical audience is surely the plainest collection of people anywhere assembled for any common purpose; contributing my quota, I have the right to point this out. Compare us with a gang of navvies or with an office staff, and you will be appalled. This, too, distracts me.

What do I hear during the intervals when I do attend? Two sorts of music. They melt into each other all the time, and are not easy to christen, but I will call one of them ' music that reminds me of something,' and the other ' music itself.' I used to be very fond of music that reminded me of something, and especially fond of Wagner. With Wagner I always knew where I was; he never let the fancy roam; he ordained that one phrase should recall the ring, another the sword, another the blameless fool and so on ; he was as precise in his indications as an oriental dancer. Since he is a great poet, that did not matter, but I accepted his leitmotiv system much too reverently and forced it on to other composers whom it did not suit, such as Beethoven and Franck. I thought that music must be the better for having a meaning. I think so still, but am less clear as to what ' a meaning ' is. In those days it was either a non-musical object, such as a sword or a blameless fool, or a non-musical emotion, such as fear, lust, or resignation. When music reminded me of something which was not music, I supposed it was getting me somewhere. ' How like Monet ! ' I thought when listening to Debussy, and ' how like Debussy ! ' when looking at Monet. I translated sounds into colours, saw the piccolo as apple-green, and the trumpets as scarlet. The arts were to be enriched by taking in one another's washing.

I still listen to some music this way. For instance, the slow start of Beethoven's Seventh Symphony invokes a grey-green tapestry of hunting scenes, and the slow movement of his Fourth Piano Concerto (the dialogue between piano and orchestra) reminds me of the dialogue between Orpheus and the Furies in Gluck. The climax of the first movement of the Appassionata (the ' più allegro ') seems to me sexual, although I can detect no sex in the Kreutzer, nor have I come across anyone who could, except Tolstoy. That disappointing work, Brahms' Violin Concerto, promises me clear skies at the opening, and only when the violin has squealed up in the air for page after page is the promise falsified. Wolf's ' Ganymed ' does give me sky—stratosphere beyond stratosphere. In these cases and in many others music reminds me of something non-musical, and I fancy that to do so is part of its job. Only a purist would condemn all visual parallels, all emotional labellings, all programmes.

Yet there is a danger. Music that reminds does open the door to that imp of the concert-hall, inattention. To think of a grey-green tapestry is not very different from thinking of the backs of the chairs. We gather a superior wool from it, still we do wool-gather, and the sounds slip by blurred. The sounds ! It is for them that we come, and the closer we can get up against them the better. So I do prefer ' music itself ' and listen to it and for it as far as possible. In this connection,

I will try to analyse a mishap that has recently overtaken the Coriolanus Overture. I used to listen to the Coriolanus for 'itself,' conscious when it passed of something important and agitating, but not defining further. Now I learn that Wagner, endorsed by Sir Donald Tovey, has provided it with a Programme : the opening bars indicate the hero's decision to destroy the Volscii, then a sweet tune for female influence, then the dotted-quaver-restlessness of indecision. This seems indisputable, and there is no doubt that this was, or was almost, Beethoven's intention. All the same, I have lost my Coriolanus. Its large-ness and freedom have gone. The exquisite sounds have been hardened like a road that has been tarred for traffic. One has to go somewhere down them, and to pass through the same domestic crisis to the same military impasse, each time the overture is played.

Music is so very queer that an amateur is bound to get muddled when writing about it. It seems to be more 'real' than anything, and to survive when the rest of civilisation decays. In these days I am always thinking of it with relief. It can never be ruined or nationalised. So that the music which is untrammelled and untainted by reference is obviously the best sort of music to listen to ; we get nearer the centre of reality. Yet though it is untainted, it is never abstract ; it is not like mathematics, even when it uses them. The Goldberg Variations, the last Beethoven Sonata, the Franck Quartet, the Schumann Piano Quintet and the Fourth Symphonies of Tchaikovsky and of Brahms certainly have a message. Though what on earth is it ? I shall get tied up trying to say. There's an insistence in music—expressed largely through rhythm ; there's a sense that it is trying to push across at us something which is neither an aesthetic pattern nor a sermon. That's what I listen for specially.

So music that is itself seems on the whole better than music that reminds. And now to end with an important point : my own performances upon the piano. These grow worse yearly, but never will I give them up. For one thing, they compel me to attend—no wool-gathering or thinking myself clever here—and they drain off all non-musical matter. For another thing, they teach me a little about construction. I see what becomes of a phrase, how it is transformed or returned, sometimes bottom upward, and get some notion of the relation of keys. Playing Beethoven, as I generally do, I grow familiar with his tricks, his

impatience, his sudden softnesses, his dropping of a tragic theme
one semitone, his love, when tragic, for the key of C minor,
and his aversion to the key of B major. This gives me a physical
approach to Beethoven which cannot be gained through the
slough of ' appreciation.' Even when people play as badly as
I do, they should continue : it will help them to listen.

[1939]

Not Looking at Pictures

Pictures are not easy to look at. They generate private fantasies, they furnish material for jokes, they recall scraps of historical knowledge, they show landscapes where one would like to wander and human beings whom one would like to resemble or adore, but looking at them is another matter, yet they must have been painted to be looked at. They were intended to appeal to the eye, but almost as if it were gazing at the sun itself the eye often reacts by closing as soon as it catches sight of them. The mind takes charge instead and goes off on some alien vision. The mind has such a congenial time that it forgets what set it going. Van Gogh and Corot and Michelangelo are three different painters, but if the mind is indisciplined and uncontrolled by the eye, they may all three induce the same mood, we may take just the same course through dreamland or funland from them, each time, and never experience anything new.

I am bad at looking at pictures myself, and the late Roger Fry enjoyed going to a gallery with me now and then, for this very reason. He found it an amusing change to be with someone who scarcely ever saw what the painter had painted. 'Tell me, why do you like this, why do you prefer it to that?' he would ask, and listen agape for the ridiculous answer. One day we looked at a fifteenth-century Italian predella, where a St. George was engaged in spearing a dragon of the plesiosaurus type. I laughed. 'Now, *what* is there funny in this?' pounced Fry. I readily explained. The fun was to be found in the expression upon the dragon's face. The spear had gone through its hooped-up neck once, and now startled it by arriving at a second thickness. 'Oh dear, here it comes again, I hoped that was all' it was thinking. Fry laughed too, but not at the misfortunes of the dragon. He was amazed that anyone could go so completely off the lines. There was no harm in it—but really, really! He was even more amazed when our enthusiasms coincided: 'I fancy we are talking about different things,' he would say, and we always were; I liked the mountain-back because it reminded me of a peacock, he because it had some structural significance, though not as much as the sack of potatoes in the foreground.

Long years of wandering down miles of galleries have convinced me that there must be something rare in those coloured slabs called ' pictures,' something which I am incapable of detecting for myself, though glimpses of it are to be had through the eyes of others. How much am I missing ? And what ? And are other modern sight-seers in the same fix ? Ours is an aural rather than a visual age, we do not get so lost in the concert hall, we seem able to hear music for ourselves, and to hear it as music, but in galleries so many of us go off at once into a laugh or a sigh or an amorous day-dream. In vain does the picture recall us. ' What have your obsessions got to do with me ? ' it complains. ' I am neither a theatre of varieties nor a spring-mattress, but paint. Look at my paint.' Back we go— the picture kindly standing still meanwhile, and being to that extent more obliging than music—and resume the looking business. But something is sure to intervene—a tress of hair, the half-open door of a summer-house, a Crivelli dessert, a Bosch fish-and-fiend salad—and to draw us away.

One of the things that helps us to keep looking is composition. For many years now I have associated composition with a diagonal line, and when I find such a line I imagine I have gutted the picture's secret. Giorgione's Castelfranco Madonna has such a line in the lance of the warrior-saint, and Titian's Entombment at Venice has a very good one indeed. Five figures contribute to make up the diagonal ; beginning high on the left with the statue of Moses, it passes through the heads of the Magdalene, Mary, and the dead Christ, and plunges through the body of Joseph of Arimathea into the ground. Making a right angle to it, flits the winged Genius of Burial. And to the right, apart from it, and perpendicular, balancing the Moses, towers the statue of Faith. Titian's Entombment is one of my easiest pictures. I look at photographs of it intelligently, and encourage the diagonal and the pathos to reinforce one another. I see, with more than usual vividness, the grim alcove at the back and the sinister tusked pedestals upon which the two statues stand. Stone shuts in flesh ; the whole picture is a tomb. I hear sounds of lamentation, though not to the extent of shattering the general scheme ; that is held together by the emphatic diagonal, which no emotion breaks. Titian was a very old man when he achieved this masterpiece ; that too I realise, but not immoderately. Composition here really has been a help, and it is a composition which no one can miss : the diagonal slopes as obviously as the band on a threshing-machine, and vibrates with power.

Unfortunately, having no natural aesthetic aptitude, I look for diagonals everywhere, and if I cannot find one think the composition must be at fault. It is a word which I have learnt —a solitary word in a foreign language. For instance, I was completely baffled by Velasquez's Las Meninas. Wherever was the diagonal ? Then the friend I was with—Charles Mauron, the friend who, after Roger Fry, has helped me with pictures most—set to work on my behalf, and cautiously underlined the themes. There is a wave. There is a half-wave. The wave starts up on the left, with the head of the painter, and curves down and up through the heads of the three girls. The half-wave starts with the head of Isabel de Velasco, and sinks out of the canvas through the dwarfs. Responding to these great curves, or inverting them, are smaller ones on the women's dresses or elsewhere. All these waves are not merely pattern ; they are doing other work too—e.g., helping to bring out the effect of depth in the room, and the effect of air. Important too is the pushing forward of objects in the extreme left and right foregrounds, the easel of the painter in the one case, the paws of a placid dog in the other. From these, the composition curves back to the central figure, the lovely child-princess. I put it more crudely than did Charles Mauron, nor do I sup-pose that his account would have been Velasquez's, or that Velasquez would have given any account at all. But it is an example of the way in which pictures should be tackled for the benefit of us outsiders : coolly and patiently, as if they were designs, so that we are helped at last to the appreciation of something non-mathematical. Here again, as in the case of the Entombment, the composition and the action reinforced one another. I viewed with increasing joy that adorable party, which had been surprised not only by myself but by the King and Queen of Spain. There they were in the looking-glass ! Las Meninas has a snap-shot quality. The party might have been taken by Philip IV, if Philip IV had had a Kodak. It is all so casual—and yet it is all so elaborate and sophisticated, and I suppose those curves and the rest of it help to bring this out, and to evoke a vanished civilisation.

Besides composition there is colour. I look for that, too, but with even less success. Colour is visible when thrown in my face—like the two cherries in the great grey Michael Sweertz group in the National Gallery. But as a rule it is only material for dream.

On the whole, I am improving, and after all these years I am learning to get myself out of the way a little, and to be more receptive, and my appreciation of pictures does increase. If I can make any progress at all, the average outsider should do better still. A combination of courage and modesty is what he wants. It is so unenterprising to annihilate everything that's made to a green thought, even when the thought is an exquisite one. Not-looking at art leads to one goal only. Looking at it leads to so many.

[1939]

THE ARTS IN ACTION

John Skelton

A Lecture given at the Aldeburgh Festival of 1950

John Skelton was an East Anglian ; he was a poet, also a clergyman, and he was extremely strange. Partly strange because the age in which he flourished—that of the early Tudors—is remote from us, and difficult to interpret. But he was also a strange creature personally, and whatever you think of him when we've finished—and you will possibly think badly of him —you will agree that we have been in contact with someone unusual.

Let us begin with solidity—with the church where he was rector. That still stands; that can be seen and touched, though its incumbent left it over four hundred years ago. He was rector of Diss, a market town which lies just in Norfolk, just across the river Waveney, here quite a small stream, and Diss church is somewhat of a landmark for it stands upon a hill. A winding High Street leads up to it, and the High Street, once very narrow, passed through an arch in its tower which still remains. The church is not grand, it is not a great architectural triumph like Blyborough or Framlingham. But it is adequate, it is dignified and commodious, and it successfully asserts its pre-eminence over its surroundings. Here our poet-clergyman functioned for a time, and, I may add, carried on.

Not much is known about him, though he was the leading literary figure of his age. He was born about 1460, probably in Norfolk, was educated at Cambridge, mastered the voluble inelegant Latin of his day, entered the church, got in touch with the court of Henry VII, and became tutor to the future Henry VIII. He was appointed ' Poet Laureate,' and this was confirmed by the universities of Cambridge, Oxford and Louvain. In the early years of Henry VIII he voiced official policy—for instance, in his poems against the Scots after Flodden. But, unfortunately for himself, he attacked another and a greater East Anglian,

T.C.D.   145   K

Cardinal Wolsey of Ipswich, and after that his influence declined. He was appointed rector of Diss in 1503, and held the post till his death in 1529. But he only seems to have been in residence during the earlier years. Life couldn't have been congenial for him there. He got across the Bishop of Norwich, perhaps about his marriage or semi-marriage, and he evidently liked London and the court, being a busy contentious fellow, and found plenty to occupy him there. A few bills and documents, a few references in the works of others, a little posthumous gossip, and his own poems, are all that we have when we try to reconstruct him. Beyond doubt he is an extraordinary character, but not one which it is easy to focus. Let us turn to his poems.

I will begin with the East Anglian poems, and with Philip Sparrow. This is an unusually charming piece of work. It was written while Skelton was at Diss, and revolves round a young lady called Jane, who was at school at a nunnery close to Norwich. Jane had a pet sparrow—a bird which is far from fashionable to-day, but which once possessed great social prestige. In ancient Rome, Catullus sang of the sparrow of Lesbia, the dingy little things were housed in gilt cages, and tempted with delicious scraps all through the middle ages, and they only went out when the canary came in. Jane had a sparrow, round which all her maidenly soul was wrapped. Tragedy followed. There was a cat in the nunnery by name Gib, who lay in wait for Philip Sparrow, pounced, killed him and ate him. The poor girl was in tears, and her tragedy was taken up and raised into poetry by her sympathetic admirer, the rector of Diss.

He produced a lengthy poem—it seemed difficult at that time to produce a poem that was not long. Philip Sparrow swings along easily enough, and can still be read with pleasure by those who will overlook its volubility, its desultoriness, and its joky Latin.

It begins, believe it or not, with a parody of the office for the dead ; Jane herself is supposed to be speaking, and she slings her Latin about well if quaintly. Soon tiring of the church service, she turns to English, and to classical allusions :

> When I remember again
> How my Philip was slain
> Never half the pain
> Was between you twain,
> Pyramus and Thisbe,

As then befell to me ;
I wept and I wailéd
The teares down hailéd,
But nothing it availéd
To call Philip again
Whom Gib our cat has slain.
Gib I say our cat
Worrowed him on that
Which I loved best. . . .
I fell down to the ground [1]

Then—in a jumble of Christian and antique allusions, most typical of that age—she thinks of Hell and Pluto and Cerberus —whom she calls Cerebus—and Medusa and the Furies, and alternately prays Jupiter and Jesus to save her sparrow from the infernal powers.

It was so pretty a fool
It would sit upon a stool
And learned after my school. . . .
It had a velvet cap
And would sit upon my lap
And would seek after small wormés
And sometimes white bread crumbés
And many times and oft
Between my breastés soft
It would lie and rest
It was proper and prest !
  Sometimes he would gasp
When he saw a wasp ;
A fly or a gnat
He would fly at that
And prettily he would pant
When he saw an ant
Lord how he would pry
After a butterfly
Lord how he would hop
After the grasshop
And when I said ' Phip Phip '
Then he would leap and skip
And take me by the lip.
Alas it will me slo
That Philip is gone me fro !

Jane proceeds to record his other merits, which include picking fleas off her person—this was a sixteenth century girls' school,

[1] The quotations are not verbally accurate. The text has been simplified for the purpose of reading aloud.

not a twentieth, vermin were no disgrace, not even a surprise, and Skelton always manages to introduce the coarseness and discomfort of his age. She turns upon the cat again, and hopes the greedy grypes will tear out his tripes.

> Those villainous false cats
> Were made for mice and rats
> And not for birdés small.
> Alas, my face waxeth pale . . .

She goes back to the sparrow and to the Church Service, and draws up an enormous catalogue of birds who shall celebrate his obsequies :

> Our chanters shall be the cuckoo,
> The culver, the stockdoo,
> The ' peewit,' the lapwing,
> The Versicles shall sing.

—together with other songsters, unknown in these marshes and even elsewhere. She now wants to write an epitaph, but is held up by her diffidence and ignorance ; she has read so few books, though the list of those she has read is formidable ; moreover, she has little enthusiasm for the English language—

> Our natural tongue is rude,
> And hard to be ennewed
> With polished termes lusty
> Our language is so rusty
> So cankered, and so full
> Of froward, and so dull,
> That if I would apply
> To write ornately
> I wot not where to find
> Terms to serve my mind.

Shall she try Latin ? Yes, but she will hand over the job to the Poet Laureate of Britain, Skelton, and, with this neat compliment to himself, Skelton ends the first part of Philip Sparrow.

He occupies the second part with praising Jane,

> This most goodly flower,
> This blossom of fresh colour
> So Jupiter me succour
> She flourishes new and new
> In beauty and virtue,

by-passes the sparrow, and enters upon a love poem :

> But wherefore should I note
> How often did I toot
> Upon her pretty foot
> It bruised mine heart-root
> To see her tread the ground
> With heeles short and round.

The rector is in fact losing his head over a schoolgirl, and has to pull himself up. No impropriety is intended, he assures us,

> There was no vice
> Nor yet no villainy,
> But only fantasy. . . .
> It were no gentle guise
> This treatise to despise
> Because I have written and said
> Honour of this fair maide,
> Wherefore shall I be blamed
> That I Jane have named
> And famously proclaimed?
> She is worthy to be enrolled
> In letters of gold.

Then he too slides into Latin and back into the office of the dead : *requiem aeternam dona eis Domine*, he chants.

This poem of Philip Sparrow—the pleasantest Skelton ever wrote—helps to emphasise the difference in taste and in style between the sixteenth century and our own. His world is infinitely remote ; not only is it coarse and rough, but there is an uncertainty of touch about it which we find hard to discount. Is he being humorous ? Undoubtedly, but where are we supposed to laugh ? Is he being serious ? If so, where and how much ? We don't find the same uncertainty when we read his predecessor Chaucer, or his successor Shakespeare. We know where they stand, even when we cannot reach them. Skelton belongs to an age of break-up, which had just been displayed politically in the Wars of the Roses. He belongs to a period when England was trying to find herself—as indeed do we to-day, though we have to make a different sort of discovery after a different type of war. He is very much the product of his times —a generalisation that can be made of all writers, but not always so aptly. The solidity of the middle ages was giving away beneath his feet, and he did not know that the Elizabethan age was coming—any more than we know what is coming. We have not the least idea, whatever the politicians prophesy. It is appropriate, at this point, to quote the wisest and most impressive lines he ever wrote—they are not well known, and probably they are only a fragment. They have a weight and a thoughtfulness which are unusual in him.

> Though ye suppose all jeopardies are passed
> And all is done that ye lookéd for before,
> Ware yet, I warn you, of Fortune's double cast,
> For one false point she is wont to keep in store,
> And under the skin oft festeréd is the sore ;
> That when ye think all danger for to pass
> Ware of the lizard lieth lurking in the grass.

It was a curious experience, with these ominous verses in my mind, to go to Diss and to find, carved on the buttress of the church, a lizard. The carving was there in Skelton's day ; that he noticed it, that it entered into his mind when he wrote, there is no reason to suppose. But its appearance, combined with the long grass in the churchyard, helped me to connect the present with the past, helped them to establish that common denominator without which neither has any validity.

> That when ye think all danger for to pass
> Ware of the lizard lieth lurking in the grass.

So true of the sixteenth century, so true of to-day ! There are two main answers to the eternal menace of the lizard. One of them is caution, the other courage. Skelton was a brave fellow —his opposition to Cardinal Wolsey proves that—but I don't know which answer he recommends.

But let us leave these serious considerations, and enter Diss church itself, where we shall be met by a fantastic scene and by the oddest poem even Skelton ever wrote ; the poem of 'Ware the Hawk.' Like Philip Sparrow, it is about a bird, but a bird of prey, and its owner is not the charming Jane, but an ill-behaved curate, who took his hawk into the church, locked all the doors, and proceeded to train it with the help of two live pigeons and a cushion stuffed with feathers to imitate another pigeon. The noise, the mess, the scandal, was terrific. In vain did the rector thump on the door and command the curate to open. The young man—one assumes he was young—took no notice, but continued his unseemly antics. Diss church is well suited to a sporting purpose, since its nave and choir are unusually lofty, and the rood-loft was convenient for the birds to perch on between the statues of the Virgin and St. John. Up and down he rushed, uttering the cries of his craft, and even clambering on to the communion table. Feathers flew in all directions and the hawk was sick. At last Skelton found ' a privy way ' in, and managed to stop him. But he remained impenitent, and threatened that another day he would go fox-hunting there, and bring in a whole pack of hounds.

Now is this an exaggeration, or a joke ? And why did Skelton delay making a poem out of it until many years had passed ? He does not—which is strange—even mention the name of the curate.

> He shall be as now nameless,
> But he shall not be blameless
> Nor he shall not be shameless.
> For sure he wrought amiss
> To hawk in my church at Diss.

That is moderately put. It was amiss. Winding himself up into a rage, he then calls him a peckish parson and a Domine Dawcock and a frantic falconer and a smeary smith, and scans history in vain for so insolent a parallel ; not even the Emperor Julian the Apostate or the Nestorian heretics flew hawks in a church. Nero himself would have hesitated. And the poem ends in a jumble and a splutter, heaps of silly Latin, a cryptogram and a curious impression of gaiety ; a good time, one can't help feeling, has been had by all.

How, though, did Skelton get into the church and stop the scandal ? Perhaps through the tower. You remember my mentioning that the tower of Diss church has a broad passage-way running through it, once part of the High Street. To-day the passage only contains a notice saying ' No bicycles to be left here,' together with a number of bicycles. Formerly, there was a little door leading up from it into the tower. That (conjectures an American scholar) may have been Skelton's privy entrance. He may have climbed up by it, climbed down the belfry into the nave, and spoiled, at long last, the curate's sport.

There is another poem which comes into this part of Skelton's life. It is entitled ' Two Knaves sometimes of Diss,' and attacks two of his parishioners who had displeased him and were now safely dead ; John Clerk and Adam Uddersall were their names. Clerk, according to the poet, had raged ' like a camel ' and now lies ' starke dead, Never a tooth in his head, Adieu, Jayberd, adieu,' while as for Uddersall, ' Belsabub his soule save, who lies

here like a knave.' The poem is not gentlemanly. Little that
Skelton wrote was. Not hit a man when he is down or dead ?
That's just the moment to wait for. He can't hit back.

The last East Anglian poem to be mentioned, is a touching
one : to his wife. As a priest, he was not and could not be
married, but he regarded his mistress as his legal consort, and
the poem deals with a moment when they were parting and
she was about to bear a child :

> 'Petually
> Constrained am I
> With weeping eye
>   To mourn and 'plain
> That we so nigh
> Of progeny
> So suddenly
>   Should part in twain.
>
> When ye are gone
> Comfort is none,
> But all alone
>   Endure must I
> With grievely groan
> Making my moan
> As it were one
>   That should needs die.

There is a story about the birth of this child which was written
down after Skelton's death, in a collection called *The Merry
Tales of Skelton*. According to it, there were complaints to
the bishop from the parish, which Skelton determined to quell.
So he preached in Diss church on the text *Vos estis*, you are,
and suddenly called out ' Wife ! bring my child.' Which the
lady did. And he held the naked baby out to the congregation
saying ' Is not this child as fair as any of yours ? It is not like
a pig or a calf, is it ? What have you got to complain about
to the bishop ? The fact is, as I said in my text, *Vos estis*, you
be, and have be and will and shall be knaves, to complayne of
me without reasonable cause.' Historians think that this jest-
book story enshrines a tradition. It certainly fits in with what
we know of the poet's fearless and abusive character.

Tenderness also entered into that character, though it did not
often show itself. Tenderness inspires that poem I have quoted,
and is to be found elsewhere in his gentle references to women ;

for instance, in the charming ' Merry Margaret,' which often appears in anthologies.

> Merry Margaret
>   As midsummer flower,
> Gentle as falcon
>   Or hawk of the tower :
> With solace and gladness
> Much mirth and no madness
> All good and no badness.

And in the less known but still more charming poem ' To Mistress Isabel Pennell ' which I will quote in full. Isabel was a little girl of eight—even younger than Jane of the sparrow. (' Reflaring,' near the beginning of the poem, is ' redolent.' ' Nept ' means catmint.)

> By Saint Mary, my Lady,
> Your mammy and your daddy
> Brought forth a goodly baby.
>   My maiden Isabel,
>   Reflaring rosabel,
>   The fragrant camomel :
>   The ruddy rosary,
>   The sovereign rosemary
>   The pretty strawberry
>   The columbine, the nept,
>   The jelofer well set,
>   The proper violet :
>   Ennewed your colour
>   Is like the daisy flower
>   After the April shower ;
>   Star of the morrow gray,
>   The blossom on the spray
>   The freshest flower of May :
>   Maidenly demure,
>   Of womanhood the lure ;
>   Wherefore I make you sure
>   It were an heavenly health,
>   It were an endless wealth,
>   A life for God himself
>   To hear this nightingale
>   Among the birdés small
>   Warbelling in the vale :
>   Dug dug,
>   Jug jug,
>   Good year and good luck,
>   With chuck, chuck, chuck, chuck !

Women could touch his violent and rugged heart and make it gentle and smooth for a little time.   It is not the dying tradition of chivalry, it is something personal.

But we must leave these personal and local matters, and turn to London and to the political satires.   The main group is directed against Cardinal Wolsey.   The allusions are often obscure, for though Skelton sometimes attacks his great adversary openly, at other times he is covering his tracks, and at other times complimentary and even fulsome.   The ups and downs of which have furnished many problems for scholars.   Two points should be remembered.   Firstly, Skelton is not a precursor of the Reformation ;   he has sometimes been claimed as one by Protestant historians.   He attacked the abuses of his church—as exemplified in Wolsey's luxury, immorality and business.   He has nothing to say against its doctrines or organisation and was active in the suppression of heresy.   He was its loyal if scandalous son.

Secondly, Wolsey appears to have behaved well.   When he triumphed, he exacted no vengeance.   Perhaps he had too much to think about.   The story that Skelton died in sanctuary in St. Margaret's, Westminster, fleeing from the Cardinal's wrath, is not true.   He did live for the last years of his life in London, but freely and comfortably ;   bills for his supper parties have been unearthed.   And though he was buried in St. Margaret's it was honourably, under an alabaster inscription.   Bells were pealed, candles were burned.   Here again we have the bills.

The chief anti-Wolsey poems are ' Speke Parrot,' ' Colin Clout,' ' Why come ye not to Court ? ' and the cumbrous Morality play ' Magnificence.'

Speke Parrot—yet another bird ;   had Skelton a bird complex ? ornithologists must decide—Speke Parrot is one of those convenient devices where Polly is made to say what Polly's master hesitates to say openly.   Poor Polly !   Still master is fond of Polly, and introduces him prettily enough.

> Parrot is no churlish chough nor no fleckéd pie,
>   Parrot is no penguin that men call a carling,
> Parrot is no woodcock, nor no butterfly,
>   Parrot is no stammering stare that men call a starling,
>   But Parrot is my own dear heart and my dear darling,
> Melpomene, that fair maid, she burnished his beak :
> I pray you, let Parrot have liberty to speak.

Skelton's genuine if intermittent charm continues into the next stanza :

> Parrot is a fair bird for a lady
>   God of his goodness him faméd and wrought ;
> When parrot is dead, he doth not putrify.
>   Yet all things mortal shall turn unto nought,
>   Except man's soul, that Christ so dearly bought ;
> That never may die, nor never die shall—
> Make much of Parrot, the popinjay royal.

The ' popinjay royal '—that is to say the bird of King Henry VIII, whose goodness and generosity Wolsey abuses. And parrot, given his beak, says many sharp things against the Cardinal, who ' carrieth a king in his sleeve ' and plays the Pope's game rather than his liege's. Subtly and obscurely, with detailed attention to his comings and goings, the great man is attacked. It is a London poem, which could not have been written in a Norfolk rectory.

Much more violent is 'Why come ye not to Court ? ' where the son of the Ipswich butcher gets brutally put in his place.

> Why come ye not to court ?
> To which court ?
> To the king's court
> Or to Hampton Court ?
> The king's court should have the excellence
> But Hampton Court hath the pre-eminence.

And at Hampton Court Wolsey rules, with

> his base progeny
> And his greasy genealogy,
> He came of the sang royall
> That was cast out from a butcher's stall. . . .
> With lewd conditions coated
> As hereafter be noted—
> Presumption and vainglory,
> Envy, wrath and lechery,
> Covertise and gluttony,
> Slothful to do good,
> Now frantic, now stark mad.

As for ' Colin Clout.' The title is the equivalent of Hodge or the Man in the Street, from whose point of view the poem is supposed to be written. It is a long rambling attack on bishops, friars, monks, and the clergy generally, and Wolsey comes in for his share of criticism. I will quote from it not the abusive passages, of which you are getting plenty, but the dignified and devout passage with which it closes. Skelton was after all inside the church he criticised, and held its faith, and now and then he reminds us of this.

> Now to withdraw my pen
> And now a while to rest
> Meseemeth it for the best.
>   The forecastle of my ship
> Shall glide and smoothly slip
> Out of the waves wild
> Of the stormy flood
> Shoot anchor and lie at road
> And sail not far abroad
> Till the coast be clear
> And the lode-star appear
> My ship now will I steer
> Towards the port salu
> Of our Saviour Jesu
> Such grace that He us send
> To rectify and amend
> Things that are amiss
> Where that his pleasure is.   Amen.

It is a conventional ending, but a sincere one, and reminds us that he had a serious side ; his ' Prayer to the Father of Heaven ' was sung in the church here, to the setting of Vaughan Williams. He can show genuine emotion at moments, both about this world and the next. Here are two verses from ' The Manner of the World Nowadays,' in which he laments the decay of society.

> Sometimes we sang of mirth and play
> But now our joy is gone away
> For so many fall in decay
>   Saw I never :
> Whither is the wealth of England gone ?
> The spiritual saith they have none,
> And so many wrongfully undone
>   Saw I never.

' Magnificence,' the last of the anti-Wolsey group, is a symbol for Henry VIII, who is seduced by wicked flatterers from his old counsellor (i.e. from Skelton himself). Largess, Counter-feit-Countenance, Crafty-Conveyance, Cloaked-Collusion and Courtly-Abusion are some of the names, and all are aspects of Wolsey. At enormous length and with little dramatic skill they ensnare Magnificence and bring him low. By the time

Stage 5, Scene 35 is reached he repents, and recalls his former adviser, and all is well.

Well, so much for the quarrel between Skelton and Wolsey—between the parson from Norfolk and the Cardinal from Suffolk, and Suffolk got the best of it. Skelton may have had right on his side and he had courage and sincerity, but there is no doubt that jealousy came in too. At the beginning of Henry VIII's reign he was a very important person. He had been the King's tutor, he went on a semi-diplomatic mission, and as Poet Laureate he was a mouthpiece for official lampoons. With the advent of Wolsey, who tempted the king with pleasure, his importance declined, and he did not live to see the days when Henry preferred power to pleasure, and Wolsey fell.

The satires against the Scots, next to be mentioned, belong to the more influential period of Skelton's life. They centre round the Battle of Flodden (1513). King Henry's brother-in-law, James IV of Scotland, had challenged him, had invaded England, and been killed at Flodden, with most of his nobility. Skelton celebrates the English victory with caddish joy. In quoting a few lines, I do not desire to ruffle any sensitive friends from over the Border. I can anyhow assure them that our Poet Laureate appears to have got as good as he gave :

> King Jamie, Jemsy, Jocky my jo,
> Ye summoned our king—why did ye so
> To you nothing it did accord
> To summon our king your sovereign lord ? . . .
> Thus for your guerdon quit are ye,
> Thanked be God in Trinitie
> And sweet Saint George, our Lady's knight
> Your eye is out : adew, good-night.

And still more abusively does he attack an enemy poet called Dundas who wrote Latin verses against him.

> Gup, Scot,
> Ye blot
> Set in better
> Thy pentameter
> This Dundas
> This Scottish ass,
> He rhymes and rails
> That Englishmen have tails. . . .
> Shake thy tail, Scot, like a cur
> For thou beggest at every man's door

> Tut, Scot, I say
> Go shake thee dog, hey. . . .
> Dundas,
> That drunk ass. . . .
> Dundee, Dunbar
> Walk Scot,
> Walk sot
> Rail not so far.

The accusation that Englishmen have tails is still sometimes made, and is no doubt as true as it ever was. I have not been able to find out how Dundas made it, since his poem has vanished. We can assume he was forcible. Nor have I quoted Skelton in full, out of deference to the twentieth century. He is said to have written it in his Diss rectory. That is unlikely—not because of its tone, but because it implies a close contact with affairs which he could only have maintained at Court.

Our short Skeltonic scamper is nearing its end, but I must refer to the ' Tunning of Elinor Rumming,' one of the most famous of Skelton's poems. Elinor Rumming kept a pub—not in East Anglia, but down in Surrey, near Leatherhead. The poem is about her and her clients, who likewise belonged to the fair sex.

> Tell you I will
> If that you will
> A while be still
> Of a comely Jill
> That dwelt on a hill:
> She is somewhat sage
> And well worn in age
> For her visage
> It would assuage
> A man's courage . . .
> Comely crinkled
> Wondrously wrinkled
> Like a roast pig's ear
> Bristled with hair.

You catch the tone. You taste the quality of the brew. It is strong and rumbustious and not too clean. Skelton is going to enjoy himself thoroughly. Under the guise of a satirist and a corrector of morals, he is out for a booze. Now the ladies come tumbling in :

> Early and late
> Thither cometh Kate

Cisly and Sare
With their legs bare
And also their feet
Fully unsweet
Their kirtles all to-jagged
Their smocks all to-ragged,
With titters and tatters
Bring dishes and platters
With all their might running
To Elinor Rumming
To have of her tunning.

They get drunk, they tumble down in inelegant attitudes, they trip over the doorstep, they fight—Margery Milkduck, halting Joan, Maud Ruggy, drunken Alice, Bely and Sybil, in they come. Many of them are penniless and are obliged to pay in kind and they bring with them gifts often as unsavoury as the drink they hope to swallow—a rancid side of bacon for example—and they pawn anything they can lay their hands on, from their husband's clothes to the baby's cradle, from a frying pan to a side saddle. Elinor accepts all. It is a most lively and all-embracing poem, which gets wilder and lewder as it proceeds. Then Skelton pulls himself up in characteristic fashion.

My fingers itch
I have written too mich
Of this mad mumming
Of Elinor Rumming.

And remembering that he is a clergyman and a Poet Laureate he appends some Latin verses saying that he has denounced drunken, dirty and loquacious women, and trusts they will take his warning to heart. I wonder. To my mind he has been thoroughly happy, as he was in the church at Diss when the naughty curate hawked. I often suspect satirists of happiness— and I oftener suspect them of envy. Satire is not a straight trade. Skelton's satires on Wolsey are of the envious type. In Elinor Rumming and Ware the Hawk I detect a coarse merry character enjoying itself under the guise of censoriousness.

Thought is frank and free :
To think a merry thought
It cost me little nor nought.

One question that may have occurred to you is this : was Skelton typical of the educated parish priest of his age ? My own impression is that he was, and that the men of Henry VIII's reign, parsons and others, were much more unlike ourselves than we suppose, or if you prefer it, much odder. We cannot unlock their hearts. In the reign of his daughter Elizabeth a key begins to be forged. Shakespeare puts it into our hands, and we recover, on a deeper level, the intimacy promised by Chaucer. Skelton belongs to an age of transition : the silly Wars of the Roses were behind him ; he appears even to regret them, and he could not see the profounder struggles ahead. This makes him ' difficult,' though he did not seem so to himself. His coarseness and irreverence will pain some people and must puzzle everyone. It may help us if we remember that religion is older than decorum.

Of his poetry I have given some typical samples, and you will agree that he is entertaining and not quite like anyone else, that he has a feeling for rhythm, and a copious vocabulary. Some-times—but not often—he is tender and charming, occasionally he is devout and very occasionally he is wise. On the whole he's a comic—a proper comic, with a love for improper fun, and a talent for abuse. He says of himself in one of his Latin verses, that he sings the material of laughter in a harsh voice, and the description is apt ; the harshness is often more obvious than the laughter, and leaves us with a buzzing in the ears rather than with a smile on the face. Such a row ! Such a lot of complaints ! He has indeed our national fondness for grumb-ling—the government, the country, agriculture, the world, the beer, they are none of them what they ought to be or have been. And although we must not affix our dry little political labels to the fluidity of the past (there is nothing to tie them on to), it is nevertheless safe to say that temperamentally the Rector of Diss was a conservative.

On what note shall we leave him ? A musical note commends itself. Let me quote three stanzas from a satire called ' Against a comely Coistroun '—that is to say, against a good-looking kitchen-boy. The boy has been conjectured to be Lambert Simnel, the pretender to the crown of England. He was silly as well as seditious, and he fancied himself as a musician and ' curiously chanted and currishly countered and madly in his musicks mockishly made against the Nine Muses of politic poems and poets matriculate '—the matriculate being Skelton, the Poet Laureate. Listen how he gets basted for his incompe-tence : you may not follow all the words, but you can hear the blows fall, and that's what matters :

> He cannot find it in rule nor in space,
> He solfas too haute, his treble is too high
> He braggeth of his birth, that born was full base,
> His music without measure, too sharp is his *Mi*,
> He trimmeth in his tenor to counter pirdewy,
> His descant is busy, it is without a mean
> Too fat is his fancy, his wit is too lean.
>
> He rumbleth on a lewd lute ' Roty bully joys '
> Rumble down, tumble down, hey go now now !
> He fumbleth in his fingering an ugly good noise,
> It seemeth the sobbing of an old sow !
> He would be made much of, an he wist how ;
> Well sped in spindles and turning of tavells ;
> A bungler, a brawler, a picker of quarrels.
>
> Comely he clappeth a pair of clavichords
> He whistleth so sweetly, he maketh me to sweat ;
> His descant is dashed full of dischords
> A red angry man, but easy to entreat :
> An usher of the hall fain would I get
> To point this proud page a place and a room
> For Jack would be a gentleman, that late was a groom.

Kitchen-boy Simnel, if it be he, was evidently no more a performer than he was a prince.   Yet I would have liked to have him here now, red, angry, good looking, and making a hideous noise, and to have heard Skelton cursing him as he screeched. The pair of them might have revived for us that past which is always too dim, always too muffled, always too refined.   With their raucous cries in your ears, with the cries of the falconer in Diss Church, with the squawkings of Speke Parrot, and the belchings of Elinor Rumming, I leave you.

[1950]

Julius Caesar

While I was considering what to say about *Julius Caesar*, I happened to go to a school entertainment. It was a large primary school, and the boys mostly came from working class homes ; little boys—the eldest couldn't have been fourteen. They acted some scenes out of this very play. They did not act them well—how should they ? They had not had the time to rehearse, they forgot their words and said them too fast, also there was not the money to buy properties with : the Roman Senators wore towels and curtains and anything they could scrounge and a solitary garland of green cardboard was handed from Caesar to Brutus and from Brutus to Antony as the occasion required. The audience were more interested in identifying their offspring than in following the plot. Remarks could be heard such as, ' There he is, that one's Tom,' and there were squeals from babies who were lifted up in their mothers' arms to see better, and seemed critical of what they saw. I was critical myself—yet I had an odd feeling of pleasure and of awe, and certain words of Cassius after the murder came into my mind.

> How many ages hence
> Shall this our lofty scene be acted o'er,
> In states unborn and accents yet unknown !

If Shakespeare had been present with us in that school, he might not have been flattered but he would not have been surprised, for what he expected to occur has occurred : the play lives.

> O Julius Caesar ! thou art mighty yet :
> Thy spirit walks abroad.

It was walking with us as well as circumstances permitted : it was part of the civilisation of England and of all who read English.

The general immortality of Shakespeare is too vast a subject. Let us keep to this particular play. Why has it caught on ? It is about some old Romans who murdered one of their number and were finally defeated by his friends. The incident was chronicled by a Greek historian, Plutarch, and Shakespeare read a translation of it and turned out a play somewhere about 1600. It seems to have been a success from the first. And we to-day, though we may not rank it with the Great Four—*Hamlet, Othello, Lear, Macbeth*—always hail it as a typical example of his genius, and are excited when the curtain rises.

It is exciting—that is one reason for its popularity. Although it is not carefully constructed like a Greek play or a classical French play, although it is not as cunning in its advance as *Othello* or *Macbeth*, yet it does succeed in startling us and holding us. It effects this by three well-timed explosions. The first of these explosions is of course the murder itself. The preparation for this is masterly—the growth of the conspiracy, omens, storms, apparitions, Portia's forebodings, Calpurnia's dream, the tempting of Caesar to the Senate House, the failure of Artemidorus to save him, the luring away of Antony : and then the deed. And the murder is followed by a second explosion ; Antony's funeral speech. The excitement is revived and increased instead of dropping. After that indeed there is a lull and a failure to interest, until we come to the plains of Philippi and the third explosion : the quarrel in the tent between Brutus and Cassius. This is so unexpected, so natural psychologically and so touching that it produces a tremendous effect, and after it, his nerves all exhausted, Brutus beholds Caesar's ghost. I do not mean that these three explosions, these three famous scenes, are the only reason for the play's popularity. But they do provide the excitement, and if a drama does not excite the ordinary man it may satisfy its contemporaries, but it has no chance of being acted ' in states unborn and accents yet unknown.'

The second reason for popularity is the character drawing, and particularly the character of Brutus. Before I come to it, I am going to risk a generalisation about Shakespeare. He was an Elizabethan dramatist, and I do not think the Elizabethans were conscientious over their characters ; they would often alter them in the middle in order to get on with the play. Beaumont and Fletcher contain glaring examples of this. Good men become bad and then good again : traitors turn into heroes and vice versa without any internal justification. And Shakespeare sometimes does it too. There is an example—not a glaring one—in this play, in the character of Casca. Casca first appears as extremely polite and indeed servile to Caesar. ' Peace ho ! Caesar speaks,' he cries. Then he shows himself to Brutus and Cassius as a sour blunt contradictious fellow, who snaps them up when they speak and is grumpy when they invite him to supper. You may say this is subtlety on Shakespeare's part, and that he is indicating that Casca is a dark horse. I don't think so. I don't think Shakespeare was bothering about Casca —he is merely concerned to make the action interesting and he alters the character at need. Later on, during the thunderstorm, Casca becomes different again ; he walks about with a drawn sword, is deeply moved by the apparitions, and utters exalted poetry. At the murder-scene he wounds Caesar in the neck, and then we hear of him no more. His usefulness is over. Contrast Shakespeare here with a modern writer, like Tolstoy. Tolstoy is conscientious over his characters, he has a personal responsibility to each of them, he has a vital conception of them, and though they are full of contradictions, those contradictions are true to life. Contrast Casca with Dolohov in *War and Peace.* Shakespeare often doesn't mind about his people. And when I am reading him one of my difficulties is to detect when he does mind and when he doesn't. This may be heresy on my part, but it seems to me that a great deal of Shakespearean criticism is invalid because it assumes that his characters are real people, and are never put in just to make the play go. The play's the thing, I suggest.

It is delightful when the characters are real, when Shakespeare does bother about them. Brutus is real, so is Cassius, so is Antony, so perhaps is Caesar himself. Brutus is an intellectual who can do things, who is not (like Hamlet) hampered by doubts. He can do things—but he always does them wrong : his advice is invariably fatal, from the moment of the murder down to the battle of Philippi. He cannot realise that men seek their own interests, for he has never sought his own, he has lived nobly among noble thoughts, wedded to a noble wife. He is kind to his servant. Everything he does is touched with fineness. Yet Brutus is not frigid. He just avoids being a prig. We are able to take him to our hearts. And with him is associated the worldly but far from contemptible Cassius. Those two speak the same language though they sometimes use different words. And against them is opposed Mark Antony —brilliant, sensuous, devoted to Caesar, but heartless otherwise, and treacherous. These three support the play. The character of Caesar is—difficult : Shakespeare does not present him sympathetically. He makes a few fine remarks like

> It seems to me most strange that men should fear :
> Seeing that death, a necessary end,
> Will come when it will come.

But goes on to talk bombast and to assert that he and Danger

> . . . are two lions litter'd in one day
> And I the elder and more terrible.

Do you detect a contemporary voice here ? I do. It is Mussolini's. His infirmities are insisted on : his epilepsy, his deafness. He is pompous, conceited, showing-off, dictatorial. Indeed, some modern producers have stressed this and have presented *Julius Caesar* as a study in Fascism. But when Caesar is dead, his spirit is mighty, and haunts Brutus and wins. I don't know what to make of this. If Shakespeare were a modern writer I should be more clear about his conception. I should be certain that he has planned Caesar to be little in life and great in death. But, being an Elizabethan, is it possible that he may be altering Caesar as he alters Casca, for the sake of the play ?

Excitement—and enough real people. Here are two of the reasons why *Julius Caesar* lives, and why, after more than three hundred years, it is acted by primary school boys. At the end of the performance to which I have referred, after Brutus, aged twelve, had suicided himself, and fallen with rather a thump, another of the children came forward, in his little brown suit, to speak the epilogue. The epilogue was not by Shakespeare. It ran as follows :

> I come to say our play is done
> We hope you have enjoyed the fun.

The child then retired. He had spoken briefly but justly. Shakespeare is fun. There are murders and ghosts, jealousy, remorse, despair, there is *Othello*, there is *Lear*, there is even *Timon of Athens*—but—how shall I put it ? Shakespeare never grumbles. He denounces life but he never complains of it ; he presents even its tragedies for our enjoyment.

[1942]

The Stratford Jubilee of 1769

Half-way through the eighteenth century the world of culture was convulsed by the fall of a mulberry tree. A clergyman had cut it down, since it overhung his house, and he could not have supposed that anyone would have objected to such a natural proceeding. But he had reckoned without the *Zeit-geist*. The mulberry tree had been planted by Shakespeare, and the worship of Shakespeare was just ready to begin. A storm of indignation arose, which the clergyman increased by refusing to pay his rates ; he was hounded out of Stratford, and it was decreed that no one of his name (which was fortunately Gastrell) should ever be allowed to reside there again. The fallen tree became a sacred object. Relics were made from its wood, and one of these—a casket—was sent up by the Corporation to Garrick, the leading actor of the day. Inside the casket was a flattering address, and the freedom of the town. Now Garrick was already a Shakespeare expert : he had improved the last act of *Hamlet* almost out of recognition, besides transfiguring *Romeo and Juliet*, and he was delighted with the attention. In a letter, still preserved, he thanks the Corporation warmly for the ' elegant and inestimable box,' and he decided to organise a celebration at Stratford which should place the bard's fame and his own upon a permanent and mutual basis.

It is not the first Shakespeare celebration. The first may have resulted in the death of Shakespeare. Drayton and Jonson, it is said, paid a visit to their friend in 1616, and drank him into his grave. But this only rests on the testimony of another clergyman ; nor do we know much about a celebration for which there is historical evidence—the festivities of 1746. These were held in a meadow near the church for the purpose of restoring Shakespeare's monument, and brought in £12 10s., not a large sum, but sufficient to do considerable damage. So Garrick had his precedents. But he worked on a larger scale and in accordance with his own vivid personality. From the stage of Drury Lane he announced that :

On Avon's Banks, where flowers eternal blow,
Like its full stream our gratitude shall flow,

and he planned a three days' Jubilee for the autumn of 1769 which should include almost everything except the performance of a Shakespeare play—turtles and fireworks, processions, masked balls and transparencies, all centering round a rotunda on the model of Ranelagh to be erected on the Bancroft. 'Why bring in Shakespeare?' the purist will murmur. But why not? There is no reason to suppose that Shakespeare would have minded being brought in, or that he would have found a rotunda less congenial than the formidable precipices of red brick which await him to-day a few yards down stream.

The graver and grander minds of the epoch held aloof from 'Garrick's Vagary.' They suspected frivolity and self-advertisement. Gray was dubious. Doctor Johnson went to Brighton. Horace Walpole, over in Paris, announced with concern that the French were laughing at us. The French were welcome to laugh at us. Quaffing our mulberry tree goblets, wearing our mulberry tree medals, waving our 'Shakespeare Ribbands in imitation of the Rainbow which unites the colours of all parties,' and singing :

The pride of all nations was the Sweet Willey O
The first of the Swains
He gladdened the plains
None ever was like to the Sweet Willey O—

—what did we care for the French? And here were the cannons and guitars to usher in the dawn, and there was 'Judith', an oratorio by Isaac Bickerstaffe, being performed in the church to the music of Dr. Arne, and there was Boswell dressed as a Corsican chief with 'Corsica Boswell' in his hat, and duchesses as witches, and Garrick wearing Shakespeare's own gloves, and the Birthplace in Henley Street illuminated, and the Jubilee Stakes won by a jockey who admitted that he had no great taste for reading. All—all was English ; so what more did we want ?

Well, one thing more : less English weather.

Ye gods, how it rained ! It poured and poured for the whole three days ; the procession had to be given up, the fireworks would not go off, the Jubilee Stakes were run knee-deep, and as a final irony the Avon rose during the midnight masquerade and isolated the rotunda. With great difficulty were the ladies got out of it in time ; screaming and splashing and dressed as witches, Cordelias and what not, they were led over slippery planks to their coaches through darkness and storm.   The horses tugged, the wheels sank two feet in water and mud, the Bancroft became a raging sea, and no one in these circumstances paid any attention to Boswell, who tried to recite a poem of his own composition about Corsica, with a mulberry wood staff in his hand.

Nor was the weather the only disappointment.   The citizens of Stratford failed to give satisfaction too.   They seem to have been in the grip of two passions—fear and avarice—and the oddest tales about them occur in the contemporary newspapers. Many of them thought that Garrick was the Devil, and barred themselves up in their houses ; they were terrified by the decorations, particularly by a transparency of Caliban and Trinculo, and their belief that God's Judgment impended was confirmed by the abnormal floods.   Others, more courageous, sallied forth through the sheets of rain to fleece the visitors.   Ninepence was charged for washing out a pocket-handkerchief, one-and-sixpence for the Temple of the Graces, and two shillings for telling the time.   One of the victims gives details of his expenses.   It cost him £49 from London and back for the three days, and he was trying to do things as cheaply as he could.   Certainly the cult of Shakespeare starts off with rather a jerk.

However, Garrick managed to recite his Dedication Ode, which was to him and to his patrons the chief item in the Jubilee. He said it with gusto, in spite of a cut chin, caused through the drunkenness of his barber, and he stood in the middle of a line of female singers, who led the choruses.   The Ode is an empty piece of writing, but its tone is significant ; it blends the exalted and the intimate.   The same note is struck in Gainsborough's portrait.   There Garrick is depicted with his arm round Shakespeare's waist—if a bust can be said to have a waist.   His expression is at once loyal and independent. ' Stick to me and I will stick to you,' he seems to be saying. It is pleasant to reflect that Shakespeare did not betray him. Although he lost heavily over the fiasco, he got his money back, and more than back, on the stage of Drury Lane, where he presented his ' Stratford Jubilee' with enormous success during the following winter.

[1932]

Gibbon and his Autobiography

It was at Rome on the 15th of October 1764, as I was musing amidst the ruins of the Capitol while the bare-footed friars were singing vespers in the Temple of Jupiter, that the idea of writing the decline and fall of the city first started to my mind.

The sentence is a very famous one, and anyhow the words 'decline and fall' give the clue to it. It is written by Edward Gibbon the historian, and is telling us in his *Autobiography* how he came to write the great history which has made his name immortal. Gibbon has been in my thoughts lately. I often have occasion to go to Putney, now a suburb of London, where he was born. I see the church at the end of Putney Bridge, close to which he resided as a little boy, and the river which he must have contemplated. Resided, contemplated ; I use those pompous words on purpose, for even as a little boy Gibbon was not playful or frisky. I cannot imagine him bowling his hoop down Putney High Street, or fishing for sticklebacks in the Thames. But I can imagine him 'residing' there, and thus he comes into my thoughts.

I also think of him because I have been re-reading the *Decline and Fall* and have been trying to find parallels between the collapse of the Mediterranean civilisation which he there describes and the apparent collapse of world-civilisation to-day. I have not found many parallels, but I do think it strengthens our outlook occasionally to glance into the past, and to lift our eyes from the wave that threatens to drown us to the great horizons of the sea of history, where personal safety no longer signifies. Gibbon is a great navigator of the sea of history— the greatest whom this country, or perhaps any, has produced— and his work has the majesty, the precision and the reliability of a well-built ship ; I had almost added ' the poetry and the beauty of a ship,' though it is not, strictly speaking, beautiful. Because of my visits to Putney and because of this graver reason I am chatting about him now.

After a sickly childhood at Putney, and an unsatisfactory

term at Oxford, Gibbon led a very happy life as well as a diligent one.   His health improved, he made good friends—particularly Lord Sheffield who edited the *Autobiography*—he worked unceasingly, and after the moment at Rome which he has just described, he worked according to a plan.   Study and amusement were to him the same thing : he did not split his life into ' work ' and ' recreation,' which is what most people do and have to do to-day ; he belonged to the eighteenth century, and he has all the stateliness and the sanity of that limited but admirable age. He died just as the industrial era was starting.   I don't think he would have understood it, and it certainly could not have produced him.   Later historians, such as Macaulay or Carlyle, are always fussing about something or other—worrying about the underdog or preaching the gospel of work.   Gibbon never fusses.   He is an aristocrat.   The underdog never unduly distresses him, and he never preaches the gospel of work because work to him was the same as amusement : he often interchanges those two words, which we regard as opposites.   In the house of his friend, Lord Sheffield, or in his own house in Switzerland, unremitting, unperturbed, he pursued his congenial task, and as the great history went on, and was published volume after volume, he began to realise that to this delightful labour another delight might be added, namely posthumous fame ; which has indeed been granted to him.   Although the *Decline and Fall* came out nearly two hundred years ago, it is still the leading authority on its period.   Macaulay and Carlyle need correcting and supplementing, but the history of Gibbon stands firm. This is an amazing achievement.   He is read because of his accuracy to fact and his sound historical judgment : not merely because he is a master of style.

Now this success—this command over his material and over the circumstances of daily life—had to be paid for.   Everything has to be paid for, and Gibbon paid by curtailing his passions. He was not an ardent character, he disapproved of enthusiasm, he disliked religion, and the raptures of lovers moved him either to ribaldry or to contempt.   Once he, too, had been in love, with a Swiss girl, but his father had disapproved, and sensible young Edward, seeing storms ahead, had given her up without difficulty.   ' I sighed as a lover.   I obeyed as a son ' is the famous phrase in which he records this.   He could be affectionate and grateful—to Lord Sheffield, to the rather tiresome old aunt who had been good to him when he was a boy at Putney, but he never developed his emotions. For this he has been blamed. But if you develop your emotions, for that also you have to pay—everything has to be paid for, and he would have impaired the particular qualities that made him great. To me he remains an attractive character, despite his formalism and worldliness. I like to think of him not only writing and reading at his desk, but in society, fashionably dressed, for he was quite the beau, and shaped like a balloon, for he was extremely fond of good food and became plump. The balloon was supported on little legs which twinkled and turned with immense rapidity as Gibbon bowed right and left to the company, and it supported in its turn a face of quite unusual ugliness. Yes ! poor Edward was excessively plain. Once he was taken to see an old French lady who was blind and was accustomed to pass her hands over the faces of visitors, to realise their appearance. When she touched Gibbon's face, the old lady was so startled by what she felt that she exclaimed : ' Mais c'est une mauvaise plaisanterie.' She could not believe it was a face at all. No doubt Gibbon was sensitive over this—people the shape of balloons often are. But he had many recompenses. He had wisdom, learning, good taste, tolerance, and he lived in an age when those qualities were appreciated as they are not to-day. We could not have a Gibbon to-day. Our conditions forbid it. The war says no. Totalitarianism says no. The social conscience also says no. For good and for evil our faces are turned away from the eighteenth century which he adorned and exemplified. Our historians are either fanatics or scientists, and he was neither. He was a man of letters, equipped for evoking and interpreting the past. The great ship of his genius ploughs seas which, according to theorists, should lie beyond his range, and we can only thank the human star that this is so, that he lived, and lived just when he did.

His *Autobiography* is one of the minor masterpieces of its century. It is a formal, self-conscious work, written to be read, it is intelligent, entertaining, dignified, and often amusing : there is, for instance, a devastating account of contemporary Oxford, which Cambridge at all events has never forgotten. Here's a passage from it where Cambridge also gets involved. He is discussing which is the senior foundation—a question which still agitates their dons. And he calmly remarks :

Perhaps in a separate annotation I may coolly examine the fabulous and real antiquities of our sister universities, a question which has kindled such fierce and foolish disputes among their fanatic sons. In the meanwhile it will be acknowledged that these venerable bodies are sufficiently old to partake of all the prejudices and infirmities of age. The schools of Oxford and Cambridge were founded in a dark age of false and barbarous science [Gibbon was blind to the achievements of mediaevalism] : and they are still tainted by the vices of their origin. Their primitive discipline was adapted to the education of priests and monks : and the government still remains in the hands of the clergy, an order of men whose manners are remote from the present world and whose eyes were dazzled by the light of philosophy.

He spent but fourteen months at Oxford, 'the most idle and unprofitable of my whole life,' and the *Autobiography* goes on to describe his expulsion because he had lapsed into Romanism, his salutary travels on the Continent, the growth of his mental powers, his service in the militia (an invaluable practical training for the future historian), his residences in Switzerland, and the slowly maturing achievement of the *Decline and Fall*. Don't look for gaiety here or for spontaneity, but you will find wit, shrewdness, and the pardonable weightiness of a man who knows that he has genius and has used it properly. The book, by the way, is not Gibbon's own arrangement, but a compilation made by Lord Sheffield out of several separate memoirs which he had left behind him. Sheffield did his work well, so we are quite right, though not quite accurate, in referring to the book as Gibbon's *Autobiography*.

I will conclude with another quotation from it, where he describes how, twenty-seven years after its conception in Rome, the colossal enterprise of the *Decline and Fall* is concluded at Lausanne in Switzerland.

I have presumed to mark the moment of conception : I shall now commemorate the hour of my final deliverance. It was on the day, or rather on the night of the 27th of June, 1787, between the hours of eleven and twelve, that I wrote the last lines of the last page in a summer house in my garden. After laying down my pen, I took several turns in a berceau or covered walk of acacias, which commands a prospect of

the country, the lake and the mountains.   The air was temper-
ate, the sky was serene, the silver orb of the moon was reflected
from the waters and all Nature was silent.   I will not dis-
semble the first emotions of joy on the recovery of my freedom
and perhaps the establishment of my fame.   But my pride
was soon humbled, and a sober melancholy was spread over
my mind by the idea that I had taken my everlasting leave
of an old and agreeable companion, and that whatever might
be the future fate of my history, the life of the historian must
be short and precarious.

There is great English, and a great rounded life !   It is not our
English or our life, and it would be useless for us in our twentieth-
century circumstances to imitate either the style or the conduct
of Gibbon.   We have to carry on differently.   But he is a
landmark and a signpost—a landmark of human achievement :
and a signpost because the social convulsions of the Roman
Empire as described by him sometimes pre-figure and indicate
these convulsions which shake the whole world to-day.

[1942]

Voltaire and Frederick the Great

Two hundred years ago a Frenchman paid a visit to a German. It is a famous visit. The Frenchman was delighted to come to Germany, his German host delighted to welcome him. They were more than polite to one another, they were enthusiastic, and each thought, ' I am sure we are going to be friends for ever.' Yet the visit was a disaster. They still talk about it in Germany to-day, and they say it was the Frenchman's fault. And they still talk about it in France. And I'm going to talk about it now, partly because it makes such a good story, and partly because it contains a lesson for us all, even though it did happen two hundred years back.

The Frenchman was Voltaire. People to-day sometimes think of Voltaire as a person who sneered at everything, and made improper jokes. He was much more than that, he was the greatest man of his age, indeed he was one of the greatest men whom European civilisation has produced. If I had to name two people to speak for Europe at the Last Judgment I should choose Shakespeare and Voltaire—Shakespeare for his creative genius, Voltaire for his critical genius and humanity. Voltaire cared for the truth, he believed in tolerance, he pitied the oppressed, and since he was a forceful character he was able to drive his ideas home. They happen to be my own ideas, and like many other small people I am thankful when a great person comes along and says for me what I can't say properly for myself. Voltaire speaks for the thousands and thousands of us who hate injustice and work for a better world.

What did he do ? He wrote enormously : plays (now forgotten) ; short stories, and some of them are still read—especially that masterpiece, *Candide*. He was a journalist, and a pamphleteer, he dabbled in science and philosophy, he was a good popular historian, he compiled a dictionary, and he wrote hundreds of letters to people all over Europe. He had correspondents everywhere, and he was so witty, so up-to-date, so on the spot that kings and emperors were proud to get a letter from Voltaire and hurried to answer it with their own hand.

He is not a great creative artist. But he is a great man with a powerful intellect and a warm heart, enlisted in the service of humanity. That is why I rank him with Shakespeare as a spiritual spokesman for Europe. Two hundred years before the Nazis came, he was the complete anti-Nazi.

I am so fond of him that I should like to add he had a perfect character. Alas, he hadn't ! He was a bundle of contradictions and nerves. Although he loved truth he often lied. Although he loved humanity he was often malicious. Though generous he was a money-maker. He was a born tease. He had no dignity. And he was no beauty to look at either—a gibbering monkey of a man, very small, very thin, with a long sharp nose, a bad complexion and beady black eyes. He overdressed, as little people sometimes do, and his wig was so large that it seemed to extinguish him.

That is the Frenchman who sets out for Berlin on June 13, 1751 ; the German whom he is about to visit is Frederick the Great, King of Prussia.

Frederick is one of the founders of modern Germany, and Hitler has made a careful study of him. He plunged Europe into wars to advance his ambitions. He believed in force and fraud and cruelty, and in doing everything himself. He had a genius for organising, he preferred to employ inferior men, and he despised the human race. That is the dividing line between him and Voltaire. Voltaire believed in humanity. Frederick did not. ' You don't know this damned race of men,' he once exclaimed. ' You don't know them. I do.' He was a cynic, and having had a very unhappy childhood he felt till the end of his life that he had not been properly appreciated ; and we know how dangerous such men can be, and what miseries they can bring upon themselves and others.

But there was another side to Frederick. He was a cultivated, sensitive gentleman. He was a good musician, he had read widely, and he had made a careful study of French. He even composed a number of French poems—they are not good, still they serve to show that to him German wasn't everything. He was, in this way, more civilised than Hitler. There was no Nordic purity nonsense about him. He did not think that Germany was destined to rule the world : he knew that the world is a very complicated place, and that we have to live and let live in it ; he even believed in freedom of speech.

'People can say what they like as long as I do what I like' was the way he put it. One day, as he went through Berlin he saw a caricature of himself on a wall, and all he said was : 'Oh— hang it down lower so that it can be seen better.'

The visit began in a whirl of compliments. Voltaire called Frederick 'The Solomon of the North,' Frederick declared that of all his victorious titles the most precious was Possessor of Voltaire. He made his guest a court official, housed him royally, gave him a handsome salary, and promised an extra salary to his niece, Madame Denis, if she would come to keep house for him. (We shall hear more of poor Madame Denis in a minute.) Witty conversation, philosophic discussion, delicious food—Frederick liked good food, though he was careful to get it cheap. Everything seemed perfect—but ! Not long after his arrival, Voltaire wrote a letter to a friend in France in which the ominous little word 'But' keeps occurring.

'The supper parties are delicious. The King is the life of the company. But. I have operas and comedies, reviews and concerts, my studies and books. But, but. Berlin is fine, the princesses charming, the maids of honour handsome. But.' We can interpret this But. It is the instinctive protest of the free man who finds himself in the power of a tyrant. Voltaire, for all his faults, was a free man. Frederick had charm and intelligence. But—he was a tyrant.

The visit went very slowly. Voltaire did several tiresome things. He got mixed up in a shady financial transaction, he quarrelled with another Frenchman who was in the king's service, he drank too much chocolate, and when the king rationed him he revenged himself by taking the wax candles out of the candle- sticks and selling them. All very undignified. And—worst of all—he laughed at the king's French poems. Frederick, like Hitler, fancied himself as an artist, and he had often employed his guest to polish his verses up. Now he was told that the tiresome little monkey was poking fun at him and quoting him all over the place—a serious matter this, for some of the poems were imprudent, and intended for private circulation only. The Solomon of the North was vexed. He thought : 'No doubt my visitor is a genius, but he is making more trouble than he's worth, and he's disloyal.' And Voltaire thought : 'No doubt my host is a mighty monarch, but I would rather worship him from a distance.' He left Berlin, after a stay of two years, which had gradually become more and more uncomfortable for both parties.

But that is not the end.   The real bust-up was yet to come. It occurred at Frankfurt, where Voltaire was waiting for Madame Denis to join him.   Frankfurt did not belong to the King of Prussia.   He had no legal authority there at all, but he had his 'Gestapo' and he worked through them to interfere with personal liberty.   He discovered that Voltaire had taken away from Berlin (it seems by accident) a copy of the wretched French poems, flew into a passion and ordered Voltaire's luggage to be searched.   As always, he employed second-rate people and they went too far.   They not only searched Voltaire's luggage but they imprisoned him and bullied him night and day in the hope of extracting information which would please their royal master.   It is an incredible affair, a real foretaste of Nazi methods.   Voltaire tried to escape ; he was stopped at the gates of Frankfurt and dragged back, and Madame Denis, who now arrived to join her uncle, was also arrested and ill-treated. Madame Denis was a stout, emotional lady, with some pretensions as an actress.   She was not one to suffer in silence and she soon made Europe ring with her protests.   Voltaire's health broke down and he feigned to be more ill than he really was : he ran from his tormentors into an inner room and gasped 'Will you not even allow me to be sick ?'   His secretary rushed up to assist him, and Voltaire, while making all the motions of vomiting, whispered in his ear, 'I am pretending ! I am pretending !'   He loved fooling people ; he could be mischievous even in his misery, and this is to me an endearing trait.

Frederick saw things had gone too far.   Voltaire and his niece were released, and in later years the two great men corresponded almost as enthusiastically as before.   But they were careful not to meet and Voltaire at all events had learnt a lesson.   Berlin had taught him that if a man believes in liberty and variety and tolerance and sympathy he cannot breathe the air of the totalitarian state.   It all may seem nice upon the surface—But ! The tyrant may be charming and intelligent—but ! The machinery may work perfectly—but ! Something is missing : the human spirit is missing.   Voltaire kept faith with the human spirit.   He fought its battle against German dictatorship two hundred years before our time.

[1941]

George Crabbe and Peter Grimes

A Lecture given at the Aldeburgh Festival of 1948

Before I come to George Crabbe or to Peter Grimes the poem, or to Peter Grimes the opera, I must speak of Aldeburgh.

The situation of this place is curious. A slight rise of the ground—I'll call it a hill, though the word is too emphatic—projects from the fenlands of Suffolk towards the North Sea. On this hill stands the church, a spacious Gothic building with very broad aisles, so that it has inside rather the effect of a hall. At the foot of the hill lies the town—a couple of long streets against which the sea is making an implacable advance. There used to be as many as five streets—three of them have disappeared beneath the shallow but violent waters, the house where Crabbe was born is gone, the street that has been named after him is menaced, the Elizabethan moot hall, which used to be in the centre of the place, now stands on a desolate beach. During the past twelve months the attack has been frightening. I can remember a little shelter erected for visitors on the shingle. Last autumn it was at the edge of a cliff, so that fishermen at the high tide actually sat in it to fish. This spring it has vanished, and the waters actually broke into the High Street—huge glassy waves coming in regularly and quietly, and each exploding when it hit the shore with the sound of a gun. This sort of attack went on a hundred and fifty years ago, when Crabbe was alive, but the zone of operation lay further out. To-day, only the hill is safe. Only at the church, where he preached, and where his parents lie buried, is there security and peace.

North and south of the hill lie marshes. The marshland to the north requires no comment, but that to the south is peculiar, and I had it in mind when I called the situation of Aldeburgh ' curious.' It is intersected by the river Alde which flows due east,—but when it is within fifty yards of the sea it turns due south, and does not reach the sea for twelve miles, being divided from it by a narrow ridge of shingle. Here again the waves are attacking, and are trying to break through the barrier that keeps them from the river. If they succeed—and they have had some success—Aldeburgh will be menaced on its flank and the valuable town grazing lands will disappear into the slime of the estuary.

It is with this estuary of the Alde that we are mainly concerned to-day. It is here, and not on the open sea or the sea front, that the action of the poem of Peter Grimes takes place. There used to be a little port on the estuary, Slaughden Quay. It was important in Crabbe's day, and was well defined even in my own earlier visits to the district. It is now battered and derelict and the sea may wash across into it at the next great storm. Here Crabbe worked as a boy, rolling casks of butter about, and much he hated it. Hence Peter Grimes set out to fish. The prospect from Slaughden, despite desolation and menace, is romantic. At low tide the great mud flats stretch. At high tide the whole area is a swirl of many-coloured waters. At all times there are birds and low woodlands on the further bank, and, to the north, Aldeburgh sheltering among a few trees, and still just managing to dominate her fate.

I wanted to evoke these sombre and touching scenes as best I could, in order to give a local habitation and a name to what follows. Crabbe without Aldeburgh, Peter Grimes without the estuary of the Alde, would lose their savour and tang. Now for my story, and the first point I have to make is that Crabbe disliked his native town. Born here in 1754, he grew to manhood in straitened circumstances. He was afraid of his odd rough father who made him roll the casks about; then he was apprenticed to an apothecary; he hated that too, he couldn't even handle a boat properly, he was no use at all. One grim day in the winter of 1779, he walked to the bleak and cheerless Marsh Hill, gazed at a muddy stretch of water called the Leech Pond, and decided to clear out. Leaving these shores ' where guilt and famine reign,' he set out to seek his fortune in London as a poet. He nearly died of starvation first, and he was rescued not by his fellow townsmen, but by the generosity and insight of Edmund Burke. Burke recognised his genius and had faith in his integrity. From that moment his fortunes were assured; he abandoned medicine and turned to the church for his profession, took orders, and returned to Aldeburgh three years later in the unexpected rôle of a triumphant curate.

Again he was unhappy, and no wonder. For he had not concealed his opinions on his home-town, and had indeed described it to Lord Shelburne as a venal little borough in Suffolk. He knew what he thought of his parishioners and they, for their part, regarded him as an ill-tempered intellectual who, having failed to heal men's bodies, proposed to interfere with their souls. The emotions are recorded with which he mounted the pulpit of Aldeburgh church for the first time. 'I had been unkindly received in the place—I saw unfriendly countenances about me, and, I am sorry to say, I had too much indignation—though mingled I hope with better feelings—to care what they thought of me or my sermon.' The tension only lasted a few months. He got transferred. He was appointed domestic chaplain to the Duke of Rutland, moved away inland into Leicestershire, where he was happy or anyhow cosy. But his distaste for his native town had been confirmed. Everything seemed to incommode him there. Even his hopes of discovering a new species of trefoil on the beach were dashed. 'If I can once more shake off my complaints,' he writes, 'and gain a little life and spirit, I verily believe I shall publish an account of my plant.' But Sir Joseph Banks reported that the trefoil had been catalogued already. And when towards the end of his life, he indulged in a visit of sentimentality, what were the results?

> Beccles is the home of past years and I could not walk through the streets as a stranger. It is not so at Aldeburgh. There a sadness mingles with all I see or hear; not a man is living whom I knew in my early portion of life; my contemporaries are gone, and their successors are unknown to me and I to them.

Beccles, Leicestershire, Wiltshire—anywhere else. It is rare to discover in his writings a reference to his native town that is neither melancholy nor satirical.

Crabbe's antipathy to his birthplace was to play an essential part in the creation of Peter Grimes. It was not a straightforward antipathy. It was connected with a profound attraction. He might leave Aldeburgh with his body, but he never emigrated spiritually; here on the plane of creation was his home and he could not have found a better one. This Borough made him a poet, through it he understood Suffolk, and through East Anglia he approached England. He remains here, however far he seems to travel, whatever he says to the contrary. His best work describes the place directly—the Village, the Parish Register, the

Borough—and its atmosphere follows him when he attempts other themes.

> The few dull flowers that o'er the place are spread
> Partake the nature of their fenny bed ;
> Here on its wiry stem with rigid bloom
> Grows the salt lavender that lacks perfume ;
> Here the dwarf sallows creep, the septfoil harsh
> And the soft slimy mallow of the marsh.
> Low on the ear the distant billows sound
> And just in view appears their stony bound
> No hedge nor tree conceals the glowing sun. . . .

Dull, harsh, stony, wiry, soft, slimy—what disobliging epithets, and yet he is in love with the scene. And the love becomes explicit in a prose footnote which he appends to the passage.

> Such is the vegetation of the fen when it is at a small distance from the ocean ; and in this case, there arise from it effluvia strong and peculiar, half saline, half putrid, which would be considered by most people as offensive and by some as danger- ous ; but there are others to whom singularity of taste or association of ideas has rendered it agreeable and pleasant.

The sights and the sounds are not beautiful, the smells are putrid, yet through the singularity of his taste and the associations they bring to him he loves them and cannot help loving them. For he had the great good luck to belong to a particular part of England and to belong to it all his life.

This attraction for the Aldeburgh district, combined with that strong repulsion from it, is characteristic of Crabbe's uncomfort- able mind. Outwardly he did well for himself, married money and ended up as a west country pluralist. Inwardly he remained uneasy, and out of that uneasiness came his most powerful poems. It is natural to remember Wordsworth in connection with him. They were contemporaries, and they had this in common, that they were regional and that their earliest impressions were the most durable. But there the resemblance between them ends. Wordsworth—his superior genius apart—had a power of harmon- ising his experiences which was denied to Crabbe. He could encircle them with the sky, he could overawe them with tremen- dous mountains. Crabbe remains down amongst them on the flat, amongst pebbles and weeds and mud and driftwood, and within earshot of a sea which is no divine ocean. Thus based, he is capable of considerable achievements, and the contradictory impulses possessing him generated Peter Grimes.

We know how this sombre masterpiece originated. When Crabbe was trying to be a doctor he came across an old fisherman who had had a succession of apprentices from London and a sum of money with each. The apprentices tended to disappear and the fisherman was warned he would be charged with murder next time. That is the meagre material upon which a poet's imagination worked. According to Edward Fitzgerald—who was a persistent student of Crabbe—the fisherman's name was Tom Brown. Anyhow, he is transformed into Peter Grimes.

The poem occurs in the series of ' The Borough,' which was written for the most part away from Aldeburgh, and finished there in 1809. As a narrative, it is one of the best of the series, and it is prefaced by quotations from *Macbeth* and *Richard III* which fix the emotional atmosphere and warn us that the murdered apprentices will live again. It opens with a father-motive ; like Crabbe himself, Peter Grimes hates his own father —a pious old fisherman who makes him go to church—and breaks away from him abusively, on one occasion striking him on the head and felling him. Murder is not done, but the wish to murder has been born.

> The father groan'd ' If thou art old ' said he,
> ' And hast a son, thou wilt remember me.'

Peter was indeed to beget sons, though not in the flesh. For the present he gets drunk, and when his father passes away, indulges in maudlin grief. It is a prelude to the main tragedy.

Freed from control, the young fisherman proposes to enjoy life—' the life itself ' he has called it exultantly—and gambles and drinks. But money is required for such joys, so he develops into a poacher and trespasser, a rustic Ishmael. Then come the sadistic lines :

> But no success could please his cruel soul
> He wish'd for one to trouble and control ;
> He wanted some obedient boy to stand
> And bear the blow of his outrageous hand ;
> And hoped to find in some propitious hour
> A feeling creature subject to his power,

and the first of the apprentices arrives, a product of the eighteenth-century workhouse system. Everyone knows he is being mis-handled and starved, no one protects him,

> and some on hearing cries
> Said calmly 'Grimes is at his exercise'—

a phrase which is effectively introduced into Peter Grimes the opera.

> Thus lived the lad in hunger, peril, pain,
> His tears despised, his supplications vain :
> Compelled by fear to lie, by need to steal,
> His bed uneasy and unblessed his meal,
> For three sad years the boy his torture bore,
> And then his pains and trials were no more.

The second apprentice follows, also with premium, and he too dies. Peter's explanation is that he was playing on the main mast at night, fell into the well where the catch was kept and hit his head. The jury exonerate him. The third apprentice is a delicate well-mannered child, who rouses the townsfolk to pity and charity and whom Peter dares not beat too hard. He disappears during a voyage at sea. Peter had his fish and wanted to sell it in the London market. They encountered a storm, the boat leaked, the boy fell ill and before Peter could make harbour both the fish and the boy had died. Such anyhow was Peter's account. But

> The pitying women raised a clamour round
> And weeping said 'Thou hast thy prentice drown'd.'

The mayor forbade him to hire any more apprentices (as in the opening of the opera) and none of his neighbours would help him, so henceforward he carried on his trade alone, and melancholy invades him.

Now begin the depths, and I would add the flats of the poem —using 'flat' in no derogatory sense, but to indicate the glassy or muddy surface upon which the action now proceeds and through which at any moment something unexpected may emerge. Nothing is more remarkable, in the best work of Crabbe, than the absence of elevation. As a preacher, he may lift up his eyes to the hills. As a poet he was fascinated by

> The bounding marsh-bank and the blighted tree ;
> The water only, when the tides were high,
> When low, the mud half-cover'd and half dry ;
> The sun-burnt tar that blisters on the planks,
> And bank-side stakes in their uneven ranks ;
> Heaps of entangled weeds that slowly float,
> As the tide rolls by the impeded boat.

That is what attracts him—flatness—and upon it the most tragic of his poems deploys. The idea of regeneration, so congenial to Wordsworth and the Lake District, does not appeal to this son of the estuary. Those who sin on the lines of Peter Grimes must sink and sink—incapable ever of remorse, though not of fear, incapable of realising the sun except as a blistering heat, and incapable of observing the stars.

> When tides were neap, and, in the sultry day,
> Through the tall bounding mud banks made their way,
> There anchoring, Peter chose from man to hide,
> There hang his head . . .
> Here dull and hopeless he'd lie down and trace
> How sidelong crabs had scrawl'd their crooked race
> Or sadly listen to the tuneless cry
> Of fishing gull or clanging golden-eye . . .
> He nursed the feelings these dull scenes produce,
> And loved to stop beside the opening sluice . . .

The hanging of the head, the dullness, the nursing of dullness, the lying down motionless in a motionless boat, the dreary contemplation of nature in her trickling exhaustion, the slow downward bending paralysis of the once active man—they present what the poet too had experienced and the clergyman had combated or ignored. They spring from the attraction and from the repulsion exercised on Crabbe by the surrounding scenery, from the dual feeling which I analysed earlier.

We must consider Crabbe's sensitiveness to dreams in a moment—we are not quite in the world of dreams yet. Peter is still sane and awake. The only sign of abnormality is that he avoids three particular places in the estuary of the Alde ; when near them he rows away whistling until they are out of sight. It would seem that here and there the surface of the water is thinner than elsewhere, more liable to be broken from below. He becomes a solitary, seeks men and curses them, and they curse him and he retires to his boat. For a whole winter no one sees him. Next summer, he is afloat as before, but no longer fishing. He is gazing, hypnotised by the three places in the stream. ' Dost thou repent ? ' he is asked. The words have a crystallising effect and shatter him. Quitting his boat, he goes raving mad, rushes over the countryside and is caught and carried to the parish infirmary. Here, half nightmare, half vision, the story culminates. Grimes himself takes up the tale in the sedate eighteenth century couplets and the formal diction which Crabbe could not and perhaps did not desire to forgo.

'I'll tell you all,' he said, 'the very day
When the old man first placed them in my way:
My father's spirit—he who always tried
To give me trouble, when he lived and died—
When he was gone he could not be content
To see my days in painful labour spent,
But would appoint his meetings, and he made
Me watch at these, and so neglect my trade.

' 'T was one hot noon, all silent, still, serene,
No living being had I lately seen;
I paddled up and down and dipp'd my net,
But (such his pleasure) I could nothing get,—
And so I sat and look'd upon the stream,
How it ran on, and felt as in a dream:
But dream it was not: No!—I fix'd my eyes
On the mid stream and saw the spirits rise:
I saw my father on the water stand,
And hold a thin pale boy in either hand;
And there they glided ghastly on the top
Of the salt flood, and never touch'd a drop:
I would have struck them, but they knew th' intent,
And smiled upon the oar, and down they went.

'Now, from that day, whenever I began
To dip my net, there stood the hard old man—
He and those boys: I humbled me and pray'd
They would be gone;—they heeded not, but stay'd:
Nor could I turn, nor would the boat go by,
But, gazing on the spirits, there was I:
They bade me leap to death, but I was loth to die:
And every day, as sure as day arose,
Would these three spirits meet me ere the close;
To hear and mark them daily was my doom,
And "Come," they said, with weak, sad voices, "come."
To row away, with all my strength I tried,
But there were they, hard by me in the tide,
The three unbodied forms—and "Come," still "come," they cried.

'There were three places, where they ever rose,—
The whole long river has not such as those—
Places accursed, where, if a man remain,
He'll see the things which strike him to the brain;
And there they made me on my paddle lean,
And look at them for hours;—accursed scene!
When they would glide to that smooth eddy-space,

Then bid me leap and join them in the place ;
And at my groans each little villain sprite
Enjoy'd my pains and vanish'd in delight.

'In one fierce summer-day, when my poor brain
Was burning hot, and cruel was my pain,
Then came this father-foe, and there he stood
With his two boys again upon the flood :
There was more mischief in their eyes, more glee,
In their pale faces when they glared at me :
Still did they force me on the oar to rest,
And when they saw me fainting and oppress'd,
He, with his hand, the old man, scoop'd the flood,
And there came flame about him mix'd with blood ;
He bade me stoop and look upon the place,
Then flung the hot-red liquor in my face ;
Burning it blazed, and then I roar'd for pain,
I thought the demons would have turn'd my brain.

'Still there they stood, and forced me to behold
A place of horrors—they can not be told—
Where the flood open'd, there I heard the shriek
Of tortured guilt—no earthly tongue can speak :
"All days alike ! for ever ! " did they say,
"And unremitted torments every day "—
Yes, so they said '—But here he ceased, and gazed
On all around, affrighten'd and amazed ;
Then dropp'd exhausted, and appear'd at rest,
Till the strong foe the vital powers possess'd ;
Then with an inward, broken voice he cried,
'Again they come,' and mutter'd as he died.

Crabbe is explicit on the character of Peter Grimes, and
appends an interesting note. 'The mind here exhibited is one
untouched by pity, unstung by remorse and uncorrected by
shame.' And he shrewdly observed that 'no feeble vision, no
half-visible ghost, not the momentary glance of an unbodied
being nor the half audible voice of an invisible one would be
created by the continual workings of distress on a mind so
depraved and flinty.' Grimes is tough, hard and dull, and the
poet must be tough with him, tougher than Shakespeare had to
be with Macbeth, who possessed imagination. He must smash
him up physically with penury, disease and solitude, and then
place indubitable spectres in his path. Physical sufferings have
their effect on any nature :

and the harder that nature is, and the longer time required
upon it, so much the more strong and indelible is the impres-

sion. This is all the reason I am able to give why a man of feeling so dull should yet become insane, and why the visions of his distempered brain should be of so horrible a nature.

The poet sees his literary problem very clearly. A sensitive Grimes would mean a different poem. He must make him a lout, normally impervious to suffering, though once suffering starts it is likely to take a strange form.

Grimes in a normal state would be inarticulate. He can only address us effectively through nightmares, and skilful use is made, at the close, of that dream state with which Crabbe was himself too familiar for his own happiness. He recognised its value for his work. He once told Lady Scott, Sir Walter's wife, ' I should have lost many a good bit, had I not set down at once things that occurred in my dreams,' and he kept a lamp and writing material by his bedside in order to record them before they were forgotten. Many of them were unpleasant. He suffered himself from a recurrent one, induced perhaps by opium. He would dream that he was teased by boys who were made of leather so that when he beat them they felt nothing. ' The leather lads have been at me again,' he would remark in fatigued tones at the rectory breakfast table. Dreams of all types occur in his work. ' The World of Dreams ' and ' Sir Eustace Grey ' are terrifying. There is a poignant one at the close of ' The Parting Hour ' where a desolate man dreams that his wife and children are with him in an enchanting tropical land. And there is a nightmare, rivalling Grimes' in terror and exceeding it in subtlety, where an imprisoned highwayman, condemned to death for murder, dreams that he is innocent and is walking in exquisite weather down to the sea with the girl he loves, and with his sister. The three young people pass through the lanes and over the sheep walk, ' Where the lamb browses by the linnet's bed,' cross the brook and behold

> The ocean smiling to the fervid sun—
> The waves that faintly fall and slowly run—
> The ship at distance and the boats at hand :
> And now they walk upon the sea-side sand,
> Counting the number and what kind they be,
> Ships softly sinking in the sleepy sea.

On it flows, with a gentleness and sensuousness unusual with Crabbe, in order that the awakening may be the more terrible. They admire

those bright red pebbles that the sun
Through the small waves so softly shines upon :
And those live lucid jellies which the eye
Delights to trace as they swim glittering by ;
Pearl-shells and rubied starfish they admire,
And will arrange above the parlour-fire—
Tokens of bliss—

Then the nightmare asserts itself, the surface is broken :

Oh ! horrible ! a wave
Roars as it rises—save me Edward ! save !
She cries :—Alas ! the watchman on his way
Calls, and lets in—truth, terror, and the day !

This famous passage is more dramatic and more sensitive than anything in Grimes. More human values are involved, so there is more to lose, the sudden reversal in fortune is only too typical of sleep, and the wave joins the horrors of imagination to those of fact. We are back in the prison which we had forgotten. Truth re-establishes itself, the more relentless for its withdrawal when the criminal walked with those he had loved and lost.

As for Peter Grimes. He has gone to hell and there is no doubt about it. No possibility of mercy intervenes. A simple rough fisherman over whom some would have sentimentalised, he is none the less damned, the treacherous flatness of the estuary has opened at last. He will sink into the fire and the blood, the only torments he can appreciate. His father has brought him to disaster—that is his explanation, and the father-motive which preluded the tragedy has re-emerged. To push the motive too hard is to rupture the fabric of the poem and to turn it into a pathological tract, but stressed gently it helps our understanding. The interpretations of Freud miss the values of art as infallibly as do those of Marx. They cannot explain values to us, they cannot show us why a work of art is good or how it became good. But they have their subsidiary use : they can indicate the condition of the artist's mind while he was creating, and it is clear that while he was writing Peter Grimes Crabbe was obsessed by the notion of two generations of males being unkind to one another and vicariously punishing unkindness. It is the grandsire-grandson alliance against the tortured adult.

The other motive—also to be stressed cautiously—is the attraction-repulsion one. Peter tries to escape from certain places on the stream, but he cannot, he is always drifting back to them.

Crabbe is always drifting back in the spirit to Aldeburgh. The poet and his creation share the same inner tension, the same desire for what repels them. Such parallels can often be found between the experiences of a writer, and the experiences of a character in his books, but the parallels must be drawn lightly by the critic, for the experiences have usually been transformed out of recognition and the moral climate changed. To say that Crabbe is Peter Grimes would make that prosperous clergyman indignant and would be false. To say that Crabbe and Grimes share certain psychological tensions might also make him indignant, but it would be true.

And now let us consider Peter Grimes the opera ; or rather the libretto, for we shall not be much concerned with its music. The circumstances of its creation are remarkable. The composer, Benjamin Britten, a Suffolk man, was away in the United States, and read there with feelings of nostalgia the poems of Crabbe. They recalled his own country to him, they inspired him, and commissioned by the American conductor, Koussewitzky, he wrote the opera. It has been accepted as a great work ; it has become a national possession and been performed all over the world, and it is a work for which I myself have deep affection.

Now since it bears the same title as the poem people often assume that it is Crabbe set to music. This is not the case. The opera diverges widely from its original, and it is interesting to examine the changes which the composer and his librettist, Mr. Montagu Slater, have thought fit to make. They had every right to make them. A composer is under no obligation to stick to his original : his duty is to be original himself. Sometimes he chooses to stick. Verdi's Otello, for instance, follows Shakespeare closely—the only addition being the credo introduced for Iago. Bizet's Carmen, on the other hand, diverges from Prosper Mérimée's story of the same name, and Donizetti's Lucia di Lammermoor owns only the wildest obligations to Sir Walter Scott.

The plot of Peter Grimes and the character of its hero are closely interwoven. The curtain rises on the trial of Peter for murdering an apprentice. The scene is the Moot Hall, and the date is 1830—about fifty years later than the presumable date for the action of the poem. Peter is let off with a warning and we gather that he was innocent. Ellen Orford, the schoolmistress —who is introduced, with much alteration, from another poem— believes in him, and he hopes to make good and marry her ; he hates being an outcast. Then the scene changes to the beach and to that music of the work-a-day sea which always brings tears into my eyes, it is so lovely, the townsfolk gather, the pleasant time-serving rector (borrowed from another poem) passes, Auntie and her dubious if desirable nieces appear out of another poem at the entrance of the Boar. Peter cannot get help with his boat, people shun him, but he hears of a possible apprentice in the Ipswich workhouse, and Ellen goes off to fetch the boy. The weather turns to storm and the scene to the interior of the Boar. There, in a terrific moment, Peter bursts in on the riotous company. There is silence and he meditates aloud on the Great Bear, the Pleiades, the impossibility of deciphering fate upon the revolving sky. He is revealed as the exception, the poet. The uproar resumes, Ellen enters with the new apprentice, and Peter takes him ' home ' amongst cries of derision.

' Home ' is an upturned boat on the edge of a cliff. Much has happened by the time we reach it—much gossip about Peter's brutality and some evidence of it. The ill-assorted pair enter—the boy terrified, Peter now irritable, now gentle, trying to make friends, dreaming of marriage with Ellen. The neighbours are heard approaching to look into the rumours of cruelty. Peter, enraged, hurries the boy off to their fishing, pushes him out through the cliff door, he slips, falls, and is killed. The next act is a manhunt; there is evidence of murder, voices shout through the fog. Peter realises that all is up. He launches his boat, sails out into the darkness in it, and sinks it. The new day begins and with it the music of the work-a-day sea. Someone sights a sinking boat, but it is too far off to be rescued or identified, and no one is interested, and all is as if nothing had ever been. The chorus gathers, the curtain falls slowly, the opera is over.

It amuses me to think what an opera on Peter Grimes would have been like if I had written it. I should certainly have starred the murdered apprentices. I should have introduced their ghosts in the last scene, rising out of the estuary, on either side of the vengeful greybeard, blood and fire would have been thrown in the tenor's face, hell would have opened, and on a mixture of Don Juan and the Freischütz I should have lowered my final curtain. The applause that follows is for my inward ear only. For what in the actual opera have we ? No ghosts, no father, no murders, no crime on Peter's part except what is caused by the far greater crimes committed against him by society. He is the misunderstood Byronic hero. In a properly constituted community, he would be happy, but he is too far ahead of his surroundings, and his fate is to drift out in his boat, a private Viking, and to perish unnoticed while work-a-day life is resumed. He is an interesting person, he is a bundle of musical possibilities, but he is not the Peter Grimes of Crabbe.

You remember the words in which Crabbe describes his hero. He is hard and dull, flinty, impervious to sensations, and it was a problem to Crabbe to make such a character suffer. 'The mind here exhibited is one untouched by pity, unstung by remorse, and uncorrected by shame.' And he gazes downward. Whereas Grimes in the opera is sensitive, touched by pity, stung by remorse, and corrected by shame, he needs no apparitions to remind him of his errors and he lifts up his eyes to the stars. We leave him with the knowledge that it is society who sinned, and with compassion.

The community is to blame. That is one implication of the opera, and Mr. Montagu Slater in his introduction suggests that the implication is to be found in Crabbe himself and that the poet-clergyman was ahead of his times. And the date of the action is put forward into 1830, the year of revolution, and extracted from the placid eighteenth century where it was originally embedded. There is benefit in this operatically, but it cannot be justified from Crabbe. Crabbe satirised society. He did not criticise it. Doctrinally he was a Tory parson, equally averse to idleness and to enthusiasm, and he ascribed human miseries to human frailties and to fate. As his biographer Huchon remarks, 'He had nothing of the radical or rebel in him. To make him a sort of early Cobbett is to take a strangely mistaken idea of his character and his ideas . . . He remained essentially bourgeois.' The implication of a social problem combines with the changes in the action and the transformation of Grimes' character to make the opera very different from the poem. The first time I heard it, this worried me rather. I knew the poem well, and I missed its horizontality, its mud. I was puzzled at being asked by Grimes to lift up my eyes to the stars. At the second hearing my difficulty disappeared, and I accepted the opera as an independent masterpiece, with a life of its own.

It is time to leave both the opera and the poem behind. I would like in conclusion to go beyond them and revert to the obscure person, who lived at Aldeburgh about two hundred years ago, and whose name was perhaps Tom Brown. He got apprentices from London, they kept disappearing, and he was warned. That is all we know. But he caught the attention of a young surgeon who afterwards specialised in poetry and turned him into Peter Grimes. Two centuries pass. A young musician out in America reads Peter Grimes. It catches his attention, and inspires him to create an opera. Is that how works of art are born? Do they all depend on a Tom Brown? No, they depend on the creative imagination which will find a Tom Brown somewhere or other, and will accrete round him until he is transformed. So I do not suggest that Aldeburgh need raise a statue to this obscure and unattractive citizen. Still the fact remains that he happens to be genesis in the whole affair. He is the first step in a series of creative events which has produced your Festival, and if he could ever see anything and if he can see anything now he is feeling surprised.

[1948]

Bishop Jebb's Book

One hundred and thirty-six years ago, John Jebb, who was afterwards Bishop of Limerick, Ardfert, and Aghadoe, bought a folio-size note-book. He paid nine and ninepence for it to William Watson and Son, Booksellers, 7 Capel Street, Dublin, which was not dear, for it contains six quires of paper. And what paper ! paper manly yet seductive, paper which persuades the lagging and corrects the errant pen, sustains the heavy ink, retains the light, tempts even the twentieth century into calligraphy. In its depths there are two watermarks : one of Britannia, seated in a shield beneath a crown, the other of the date 1799 beneath intertwined initials. The reference must be to the union of England and Ireland, and when the Bishop bought the book he must have felt that that little problem at all events was solved. The book is bound in boards, and strong quarter-calf, but the leather recently cracked, like much else in my time, and one of the covers is now loose. This would distress me, if there was anyone to whom I could hand on the book, as it has been handed down to me. But there is no one, and even if I were a clergyman with grandchildren there would be no one. Bequests are coming to their natural end, traditions are retiring to that insecure fortress, the museum. There is not time for the personal memory-sogged past, and there is not room for it either. If after my death—which interests me less than his interested the Bishop— the book should survive, the important thing in it will be the blank pages. Still delightful to write on, they may profit posterity.

The name of the Bishop of Limerick has resounded greatly in my family, but rather megaphonically, like the name of a station shouted out by too energetic a porter. One was so near it that one could not hear it. The bishop, the bishop, the blessed bishop, the bishop's concern, the bishop's regret, his just displeasure, his condescension, his escape from drowning at Rostrevor, his paralysis alleviated at Leamington, all boomed against each other and echoed internally. And when one got outside the family vault there was an even greater obstacle : universal silence. No one had heard of the Blessed Bishop.

Scholars would verify him, ecclesiastics recall him after anxious thought, but he seemed quite lost to general fame. Like a train which has been despatched in a particular direction, he could be located in that direction and that only. That direction now seems to be me. I have inherited his book. Opening it I read the initial entry. 'Begun this common-place book at Cashel Wednesday Novem^{er} 11, 1804'—in red ink. Signed 'John Jebb' in black ink. And pencilled 'Afterwards Bishop of Limerick' by my grandfather.

That was just about the time those two got to know one another. They were both young, strange as it seems—Jebb not thirty. Never averse to the great, he was hanging around the Archbishop of Cashel, and, never idle, he was composing a sermon for the Dublin Magdalen Asylum. But he put all aside when my grandfather, who was a student at Trinity, Dublin, called, and he spoke to him of the superiority of Euripides over Sophocles, of Spenser, Shakespeare, Milton, Dryden, Pope, all through the night. A friendship began, which only ended with his death, thirty years later. When he became bishop my grandfather became his chaplain, courier and trumpeter. When my grandfather wanted to marry, it was the bishop who conducted negotiations for him, just as it was the bride's sisters who conducted them for her. Notes flew between the ponderous parties and have been preserved : the milieu by this time is Clapham and the Clapham Sect. After enormous fuss and copious admonition, the marriage was approved. It was a happy one, and the bride had the additional joy of living under the bishop's roof and nursing him when he ailed. In his will he left them his silver shoe-buckles. So it is alleged. As a matter of fact, they got a little more, this book and others, for instance, but not much more. That made no difference to their devotion. My grandmother, who was the daughter of a banker, may have had her private thoughts, but she did not voice them, and my grandfather, who was absolutely unworldly and who became increasingly provincial, went on from height to height. He wrote his hero's life, he edited his sermons, he published his letters, he called his own first-born after him, and so strong was the force of his will that when he died in his turn, the echoing name persisted for a while, and the bishop, the bishop, the blessed bishop could be heard even in the present century by those who held their ear to the ground.

The first two pages of the commonplace book are ruled for
an index : a beautiful piece of work.   Each letter of the alphabet
has a section, and each section is subdivided into five, one for
each vowel.   When the bishop entered a thought, he underlined
the first word in it, and referred appropriately in the index to
its page.   Thus Pa in the index has reference to pages 6 and 12,
where ' Pastoral Care ' and ' Parnel's beautiful Hymn to Content-
ment ' are discussed.   Po 14 directs us to the Poor in Spirit.
The index is beautiful rather than effective, and in continuing
the book I have disdained it.   He did not write in the book
much, and has only filled up eighteen of its pages.   His unworthy
successor (as I must tediously term myself) has filled over a
hundred pages, so perhaps it is my book.   But two hundred
pages remain virgin, so it is still nobody's.   I know what my
grandfather would think of my sacrilegious temerity.   The
sacred volume has passed unsullied from Cashel to Limerick, to
Clapham, to quiet rectories in Kent and Essex, and here I am
scribbling notes about Marx in it, or copying extracts from
Madame de Sévigné.   I don't know what the bishop himself
would think : he is too far away ; indeed I cannot imagine him
taking any notice.   The spiders' threads one throws backwards
into the past seldom stick.   As a rule, they encounter complete
non-recognition, and return to one.

What do I think of him ?   Well, he had a beautiful hand-
writing, anyhow, when he took trouble, small and crystalline ;
some of his notes at the time of his chaplain's marriage are
marvellous—one can scarcely see the piety for the penmanship.
And when he hurt his right hand he learnt to write almost as
beautifully with his left.   Also there is a portrait of him which
I find sympathetic.   It is a sketch by George Richmond, and
shows his head sagging forward over a desk upon some papers :
the forehead is large, the mouth and chin are planed away by
foreshortening.   But this is not much to go on, and eulogies add
nothing.   He was of good family and clever, a scholar and a
gentleman, he was efficient at church business, he kept in touch
with influential patrons in Dublin and London.   If there is
anything Irish in him, or of Ireland, it does not appear.   Attended
by his faithful satellite, he moves complacently through tragic
skies.

But it is amusing to see how the book progresses.   While not
keeping up the index, I have followed the bishop in underlining

the first word of every entry, and in ruling a line, clumsily of course, to the left of every page. His spirit also saves me from scandal : we both tend to be non-intimate on the subjects of letters and life, and to saddle Seneca or Ibsen with anything which we do not quite want to say. It would do his reputation no harm if the whole collection was published, and mine no good. His last five entries are : Human Life, Platonists and Stoicks, Miracles, Philosophy, Miracles. My first five entries are : Commonplaces, Isolation, Resentment, Change of Plan, Moll Flanders. I will conclude by transcribing his entry, ' Journal or Diary ' :

> The utility of keeping one has been dwelt on by many persons remarkable for great attainments and piety. Dr. Johnson said that a full and unreserved one would be a very good exercise, and would yield great satisfaction when the particulars were faded from remembrance. He began one himself twelve or fourteen times, but never could persevere. The great thing to be recorded, he said, is the state of one's own mind ; and you should write down everything you remember ; for you cannot judge at first what is bad or good ; and write immediately while the impression is fresh, for it will not be the same a week afterwards. Pleasant for a man to review his own mind.
>
> I should wish at no very distant date to begin a Journal. The great danger will be that I may be tempted to deal disingenuously with myself in it. If I could write an *honest* report of my own mind it would under God's blessing do me good. I date this, that if I feel indisposed to put my present resolution in hand I may be shamed into it.

Janry 25, 1806. J. J.

A Journal was duly started, but it has perished.

[1940]

Henry Thornton

On March the 31st and April the 1st an exhibition will be held at Clapham, where lived my great-grandfather, and in the school that has been named after him : the Henry Thornton School. The exhibition will be partly commercial and technical, but it will have an historical side, including a collection of prints of Old Clapham ; Battersea Rise, my ancestor's home, will be included, and he and the life he stood for will be offered again to the public, it may be for the last time.

What sort of life was it ? Let his friend and executor, Sir Robert Inglis, testify : ' His piety was fervent, and yet sober ; his liberality was magnificent and yet discriminating ; his charity was large and yet not latitudinarian ; his self-denial was rigorous yet unobtrusive.' This is a very fair estimate. Like the man himself, it does not go too far. There is also extant a charming portrait of him by Hoppner, but this does not go too far either ; calmness, moderation and restraint dominate in its well-ordered scheme. Mr. Thornton's chin is firm without ferocity, his mouth ascetic without fanaticism, his forehead intelligent without fire, in his right hand is a parliamentary bill. The restless modern mind, skimming over all these solidities, finds nothing to laugh at, nothing to condemn, and nothing to die for, and becomes unsympathetic, partly through envy. Here is neither a sinner, a mystic, nor an artist—types which the modern mind can comprehend, and in whose presence it does not feel rebuked. Here is only a successful banker, an extensive philanthropist, a devout Christian, and affectionate husband and a judicious father, a loyal friend, an upright citizen, an incorruptible M.P. :

> Nor place or pension e'er got he
> For self or for connection ;
> We shall not tax the Treasury
> By Thornton's re-election.

Sound : but not exciting ; not even inspiring.

He has two claims on the notice of posterity : a volume of *Family Prayers*, and an *Essay on Paper Credit*.

The prayers were composed from time to time, to be read

aloud to his own household at Battersea Rise. In the end, there
were over sixty of them, one for each morning and evening in
the month. With characteristic modesty, he never thought of
publishing them, but they were copied by friends and circulated
among other members of the Clapham Sect, and twenty years
after his death Sir Robert Inglis gathered them into a volume.
This had an enormous success. Between 1834 and 1854 it ran
into thirty-one editions, and within living memory our family
were still receiving royalties from its sales. The prayers are of
the usual evangelical type. They consist of vague contrition,
vague thankfulness, and somewhat precise instructions to God on
the subject of His own attributes. They borrow their cadences
from the Book of Common Prayer and from unimaginative
recollections of the Bible, all the splendours and the strangenesses
of sacred literature are absent, and it is difficult to understand why
their smooth rhetoric was preferred when so much better was
to hand, and why the use of them became in the mid-nineteenth
century the distinctive sign of true Evangelism :

> O God, who hast commanded us in Thy word to call upon
> Thy name, and hast declared that Thou hearest and answerest
> the prayers of those who make their supplications unto Thee,
> we desire now to offer up our petitions, under a deep sense
> of our unworthiness, and of Thy manifold and great mercies.

This level is consistently maintained through all sixty prayers ;
the prose never rises, never falls. ' Manifold and great mercies,'
indeed ! What can the words have conveyed to the reader or
to the family and the servants who listened to them from opposite
ends of the great library at Battersea Rise ? To us they mean
nothing at all. We get something quite different out of them :
no meaning, but an aroma, the aroma of a vanished society, the
sense of well-to-do people on their knees, the solid chairs into
which the elbows dig, the antimacassared backs against which
the foreheads rest, the voice of the master of the house, confront-
ing his Maker in a monotone, and, if the hour be morning, the
great virgin breakfast table, clothed all in white like a bride.
For three generations it was a problem to religious Englishmen
whether the breakfast dishes should come in before prayers and
so get cold, or should come in after, which meant a wait, and
an unpleasant sense of hanging in a void between two worlds.
I do not know which decision my great-grandfather took, but

there is a story that in later years his daughter Marianne read the same passage out of the Bible again and again, because she was paralysed by the sight of the cat eating the ham, and felt unable to stop either the cat or herself.

Family Prayers went out with the family. When the children were limited and the servants went into factories and the death-duties cut property to pieces, these daily gatherings of piety and plenty came to a natural end. Little houses have been built to-day upon the noble lawns of Battersea Rise, and upon the site of its great library which William Pitt designed, and those little houses listen to the religious service on the wireless, if they listen at all. Distracted by earthly chores, they hear from Broadcasting House the voice of an enlightened clergyman who tries to make religion realistic and definite and to give spiritual tips ; he vibrates like a weathercock to international troubles, he grapples with daily trivialities, he enhaloes the ticket collectors, bus conductors, waitresses, and L.C.C. ambulances whom we encounter during the drab suburban day ; he even glances at pet animals. A modern St. Francis, he believes in detail. The Henry Thornton prayers avoid detail, they generalise, they are a discipline and an institution, their well-worn phrases, ' manifold mercies ' and the rest of it, would interfere with the general effect if they bore too clear-cut a meaning. The Clapham Sect listened, rose from its knees, ate, and then made money—made as much as ever it could, and then gave as much as it could away. The activity in either direction was immense. Thanks to the economic conditions of the times, wealth rushed down these worthy people's throats from morn to eve, and not being psychologists they thought it would have no effect upon their souls if they purged themselves promptly. The devil is subtler than that. He, like Christ, understands the deceitfulness of riches : the deceitfulness which many a bitter example now brings to the light. Wealth always fattens the person who swallows it, no matter how promptly he purges, and it is significant that in spite of his fabulous charities Henry Thornton left all his nine children extremely well off, and that some of his money has even descended to myself. Very little ; the last trickle of the golden stream before it expires in the sands of taxation. Still, enough to remind me that there was an age when to get rich and to be good were harmonious.

A similar hope is held by the Quakers, to whom the Clapham

Sect has sometimes been compared. They hold it with better
reason, because they have what the Claphamites lacked : a
touch of mysticism, a sense of the unseen, and a capacity for
martyrdom. These impulses, whatever their objective value,
do purge the soul, in a way which alms-giving and self-examina-
tion cannot ; they do lift the participant into a region outside
money, whereas charity only keeps man running to and fro,
from his business to his deserving cause, and then back to his
business. He relieves distress, which the miser doesn't, but he,
too, is bound on the wheel. This indifference to the unseen
seems to me the great defect in my great-grandfather's set, and
the reason why they have not made a bigger name in history.
It came out in everything—in the books they collected, in the
letters my great-aunts wrote to one another, and in the comments which they made upon life, which are surprisingly dry
for people so pious. Poetry, mystery, passion, ecstasy, music,
don't count.

Henry Thornton's second claim on the notice of posterity is
his treatise on Paper Money. It has lately been re-edited, with
an introduction by an eminent economist, Professor Hayek.
Both his father and his brother were directors of the Bank of
England, and he married the daughter of a wealthy Yorkshire
merchant. Thanks to his training and to his ability, he became
one of the leading bankers of his age, in close touch with the
provincial banking system which was then springing up, and
also in touch with developments in London and with questions
of foreign exchange and foreign trade. His treatise which he
published in 1802 had a great effect at the time, and was to be
praised by John Stuart Mill, but it was eclipsed by the work of
Ricardo, and was almost forgotten by the end of the century.
At the time of the War it was rediscovered by economists in
America, and according to Professor Hayek, it is important for
students of the present situation ; he speaks of Thornton's
acumen, great intellectual power, and width of outlook, and
states that the treatise extends far beyond the occasion which
evoked it, and is a major contribution to the science of banking.

To the general public the theory of Paper Credit is as remote
as Family Prayers, and I wonder with what emotion, if with
any, they will see the name of my ancestor when they visit the
Clapham exhibition. They will remember him, perhaps, as the
man who helped Wilberforce to free the slaves—a great work,

to be sure, and a work which now needs all doing over again. For the world has not progressed as Henry Thornton hoped. The evils in human nature, which he realised, and the evils in commercialism, which he could not realise, have combined to pull it down, and the religious remedies he proposed seem to-day formal and trifling. But they worked well enough in his own circle and on himself. His manuscript diary is in my possession, and I will transcribe from it the final sentence, which was written only a few months before his death in 1815, at the age of fifty-five :

I think if it should please God to gild the evening of the life of my most beloved wife with a few more rays of comfort, sustaining her delicate body and making our children more and more evidently pious, which would be one great joy to her soul, if He should also afford to me that measure of success in business which shall enable me to prepare a good and safe station for my successor in the Banking house in which I am concerned, and if He shall also keep me from falling into any new temptations and dangers, I may consider myself as highly favoured by Providence, for how few can I discover round me who have half my prosperity, or who can look with so little reason for apprehension on a numerous family of children.

[1939]

William Arnold

Oakfield, or Fellowship in the East is not a masterpiece, yet I read it with intense interest, for the reason that its author was Matthew Arnold's brother. Matthew Arnold is of all the Victorians most to my taste : a great poet, a civilised citizen, and a prophet who has managed to project himself into our present troubles, so that when we read him now he seems to be in the room. I took up this novel by his brother with a curiosity that has not been disappointed. It is a strange, quixotic, disillusioned work and it hands out no bouquets, either to Indians or to Englishmen working in India.

Their father, the famous headmaster, helped to start the present public-school system, and laid stress on character and on individual morality. He represented the middle-class conscience, and his children grew up convinced that life meant duty, and hopeful that Christianity meant truth. William Arnold was born in 1828 ; he was educated at Rugby and Oxford, spending his holidays in the Lakes where the Arnolds had a much-loved house, and he decided to serve humanity in India. Desire for adventure may have contributed, for he went to India as a soldier, as an ensign in the 58th native infantry. Then he changed over to the civil service. He became assistant commissioner to the Punjab, and finally director of education there in 1853. While still assistant commissioner, he published *Oakfield* under the pseudonym of ' Punjabi.' The novel was criticised as an anonymous attack on an honourable body of men (how well one knows the phrase !), so he issued a second edition under his own name. His hero is, like himself, educated at Oxford, has also a home in the Lakes, also joins the Indian army in his twenties, and also switches over to the administration. William Arnold and Oakfield are indeed the same person.

The story makes depressing reading. Oakfield lands at Calcutta full of enthusiasm and the desire to serve, but he gets no pleasure out of India, except from the initial thrill of tropical scenery. He works hard at languages and ' passes ' in Hindustani and Persian, but gains no understanding of native life, which he regards with a sort of respectful despair. ' All the talk as to the magnificent work of civilising Asia through British influence in India is humbug,' he concludes, 'and it has grieved many generous hearts before now to find it so.' Until the point of divergence between Eastern and Western mentality has been discovered, co-operation is impossible. And though Christianity may be true, to preach it to India is to begin at the wrong end : ' physical improvement first, then intellectual, then spiritual ; that seems the natural order of things.' Oakfield is honourable, intelligent, and critical—a typical Arnold combination—and he does not shrink from remarking ' the Manchester folks want cotton and when cotton is wanted England is ready to begin and consider its duty to India.'

His immediate problem, however, is military life and social intercourse with his fellow officers. He is first stationed up the river at Hajeepoor in a bad regiment. The drinking and gambling, the rudeness to the natives, the general lack of propriety and decency keep him in his bungalow as much as possible, and when he does dine in the mess a brother officer sings an improper song and he walks out as a protest. This episode moved me to irreverent laughter, and I am not surprised that the young man was unpopular in his regiment. Nor is he surprised. He is perfectly willing to suffer for his priggishness, since it is part of the high and consistent standard maintained by him in con- sequence of his education and home life. He is then transferred to Meerut, to a regiment with better traditions, and he gives us a long description of his voyage with congenial companions up the river. The description ignores the river, Allahabad at the moment of the Magh Mela being dismissed with the briefest reference. What interests Oakfield and his fellow passengers is the state of the English Church, the Tractarian Movement at Oxford, the possibilities and the dangers of reform, the positions of Roman Catholicism and of Dissent. India is passed with a puzzled sigh, with a sense of ignorance and impotence. The new regiment is reached, and the most exciting part of the novel begins. For though the officers are gentlemanly and smart, they too are affected by the general laxity of European morals in the East ; they are shallow and wordly, they get into debt, and, for all their talk of honour, they are unchivalrous to women. Oakfield makes the acquaintance of a civil servant, Middleton, and of his sister, and the moment comes when Miss Middleton's name is mentioned too familiarly in the mess. He protests to the senior officer present, and obtains no satisfaction. He is then insulted by Miss Middleton's traducer, and he ought by the unwritten code of honour to challenge him to a duel. He refuses to do so, and when he is challenged he refuses to fight. He is brave enough to endure the charge of cowardice. All this part of the novel is elevated and fine : the writing remains flat, for William Arnold was not an artist. Finally Oakfield loses his temper, turns on his tormentors in an unconventional way and castigates one of them with a horse-whip. There is an appalling row, followed by a ponderous court-martial. Oakfield is acquitted, in view of the provocation he has received and of the illegality of duelling, but his position is no pleasanter in his new regiment than it had been in his old one after the improper song. He carries on with a high hand.

Then comes the second Sikh war, and at the battle of Chillian-walla he rescues the regimental standard, which has been captured, and rehabilitates himself. He carries on as before. The approval of people whom he does not approve means nothing to this stiff-necked young man. He resigns his commission and becomes a magistrate, and he works on and on, longing to get home. We are occasionally given glimpses of his home, and the English lakes gleam in the pages of the book with a radiance denied to the Ganges. Finally he is invalided to England and there is a poignant passage where as he leaves Calcutta he passes a boatful of young men arriving, enthusiastic about their careers as he had once been about his. He returns to his family, dying —although he does not know it—and with long-drawn Victorian pathos the story closes. One day he inveighs against his official drudgery and cries, ' Must I go on patiently, taking a bushel of falsehood for a grain of truth, casting my bread upon the waters, resume my work in India ? Oh ! ' he exclaimed suddenly, ' I cannot do it.' He is told that he will not have to do it. His upright arid career is at an end. He will never have to see India again.

Even to-day, when conditions both in India and in England are so different, *Oakfield* is a disquieting book. It is so sincere, and it states so fearlessly truths which are unwelcome to the governors and to the governed. If it is priggish, it sticks to its guns ; and if it is ineffective it is well aware of its limitations. The characters are long-winded and the action cumbrous. But it has the Arnold integrity. It is the work of a man whose brother was a genius, and who was akin to that brother morally. By a final touch of irony, the novel is even more autobiographical than its author supposed. It is prophetic as well as retrospective, for William Arnold was destined to fizzle out in much the same way as his hero. He wearied of his work in India ; his wife died there ; and, like Oakfield, he was invalided home ; he too longed to see Westmorland and the Lakes, but, less fortunate here, he died as he was being carried off the boat at Gibraltar. He was only thirty-one. He passes out of history. But at the moment of his disappearance he is transfigured. Matthew Arnold takes him up and glorifies him. Two of his poems, the ' Stanzas from Carnac ' and ' A Southern Night,' are an elegy on his dead young brother, and should be read as an epilogue to *Oakfield*. ' A Southern Night ' is more than an elegy, for it faces up to the tragedy of the inhibited career. There had been no splendour for poor William Arnold. He and his wife—they are ' spent ones of a work-day age,' they are all too typical of our time, and it is strange, thinks the poet, that they should have been buried so romantically—she by the Himalayan heights, he by these Mediterranean waters.

> Strange irony of fate, alas,
>   Which, for two jaded English, saves,
> When from their dusty life they pass,
>   Such peaceful graves !
>
> In cities should we English lie,
>   Where cries are rising ever new,
> And men's incessant stream goes by—
>   We who pursue
>
> Our business with unslackening stride,
>   Traverse in troops, with care-fill'd breast,
> The soft Mediterranean side,
>   The Nile, the East,
>
> And see all sights from pole to pole,
>   And glance, and nod, and bustle by,
> And never once possess our soul
>   Before we die.
>
> Not by those hoary Indian hills,
>   Not by this gracious Midland sea
> Whose floor to-night sweet moonshine fills,
>   Should our graves be.

Thus is William Arnold glorified—he and Oakfield, whom he had made in his image—and the eternal freshness of poetry descends upon his punkah-swept life. There is certainly some beauty in the world—the poet knows it and connects the dead brother with that beauty :

> And what but gentleness untired,
>   And what but noble feelings warm,
> Wherever shown, howe'er inspired,
>   Is grace, is charm ?
>
> What else is all these waters are,
>   What else is steep'd in lucid sheen,
> What else is bright, what else is fair,
>   What else serene ?
>
> Mild o'er her grave, ye mountains, shine !
>   Gently by his, ye waters, glide !
> To that in you which is divine
>   They were allied.

[1944]

'Snow' Wedgwood

The interesting correspondence between Robert Browning
and Julia Wedgwood features a broken friendship and provides
yet another example of the leisurely misunderstandings in which
the nineteenth century indulged. Our ancestors were well
equipped for the game of epistolary cross-purposes. They had
plenty of time, plenty of servants, and they nourished grievances,
cherished remarks and entertained regrets with a lavishness which
is impossible for their hustled descendants. They had ample
opportunities for refining, expanding, correcting, and impairing
personal relationships. We may feel, in our slap-dash way,
that they might have been happier if they had written less, but
we must admit that they gave full marks to an important subject.
'Love, to most of us, is quite as much the discipline as the
refreshment of life,' writes Miss Wedgwood, and Browning,
though proner to paganism, is obliged to agree.

He and she got to know one another in 1864, shortly after
Elizabeth Barrett's death. Browning was already famous ;
Julia (' Snow ') Wedgwood was still young. She had an assured
position as a member of a respectable, cautious, high-minded
middle-class family which managed, somehow or other, to
include unconventionality in its make-up ; the unconventionality
of the Wedgwood clan is notable and very English, and saved
it from being stuffy. As the great-granddaughter of Josiah
Wedgwood the potter, as the granddaughter of Sir James
Mackintosh and the niece of Charles Darwin, she represented a
sound intellectual tradition. Though diffuse, earnest and exacting, she was not a prig, and she and the great poet could correspond comfortably. Some of his letters to her are very good ;
in one of them he re-writes ' Enoch Arden,' in another he
re-creates the sufferings of Keats. There was mutual sympathy,
they were happy, they were becoming intimate. Too intimate ?
Anyhow, she suddenly broke off the connection, and declined
to see Mr. Browning any more. She gives her reasons, with
circumspection and delicacy, in a letter of which three versions
exist, and she takes all the blame (if blame there is to be) upon

herself.　Browning is frightfully nice, as men often are immedi-
ately after a snub, but he feels a fool and their correspondence
dies.

Two years later (they thought it was three years, but it was
actually two) they began to write to one another again, chiefly
on the high topic of 'The Ring and the Book.' Julia has
hardened in the interval, she is no longer ecstatic, and, as a critic
who will presently produce a work called *The Moral Ideal*,
she deplores Mr. Browning's preoccupation with Evil and chides
him for it carefully. 'You know,' she writes, 'you owe us an
adequate translation of what your wife was to you.' He replies
rather irritably that he owes no such translation to anyone ; she
insists that he does, and that ends it.　Mixed up with their
literary and philosophic bout is their personal muddle—they
rake up the past and try to understand it better.　Just why had
they broken ?　Had Miss Wedgwood heard a report of something which Browning had said or had not said about her, and
what in either case was it ?　Why did Browning suppose she
had written to him as she did write ?　They reached no conclusion except a respectful peevishness.

Mr. Richard Curle, who edits this correspondence, provides
an introduction which makes ' Snow ' much too portentous and
bleak a female.　She was not like that—at least she was not like
that when I knew her in her later days.　Her deafness made her
formidable for strangers, but she was polite and cordial, extremely
modest about her work, and decidedly gay.　Her support of the
Woman's Movement, like her contributions to the *Spectator*
under Hutton, has of course been forgotten : the world hasn't
the time.　But she had fine qualities, of the heart as well as of
the head, and they ought to be recorded ; she could, for instance,
make a close friendship outside her own class, and though it is
easy enough to do this to-day, owing to the social break-up, it
was not easy to do it in the nineteenth century, when the Victorian
fabric was still intact, and drawing-rooms seemed drawing-rooms
and housemaids housemaids for ever.

[1937]

William Barnes

It is surprising that William Barnes has not been more widely worshipped. Perhaps there was a touch of pride in his gentleness, which led him to conceal himself from notoriety beneath the veil of the Dorset dialect. The veil is slight : anyone can lift it after half an hour's reading. Yet it seems to have served his purpose, and to have confined him to the audience whom he loved. He should have been a popular poet, for he writes of matters which move everyone and in a way which everyone can understand. There is no mysticism in him beyond the trust that we shall, through the goodness of God, be reunited to the dead whom we have loved. There is no difficult or disturbing view of society, no crankiness, no harshness of diction or thought. He is truly, sweetly, affectionately, a Yes-man, and considering how many worthless Yes-men are being boosted to-day as national assets, it is surprising that he should have been left alone, he a clergyman, he a schoolmaster, he of the soil. Propaganda has passed him by. He has been left where he wished, to his own people, and to the few outsiders who have cared to lift the veil and win an easy and a rich reward. To read him is to enter a friendly cottage where a family party is in full swing. One misses many of the allusions, one is not connected with the party by blood, yet one has no sense of intrusion. The party, like all unsophisticated gatherings, welcomes the entire human race. And when, to the jokes and the chatter, there is added the scent of the roses at the casement, and the sighing of the wind down the lane, and the memory of the past loveliness and kindness that are gone—and faith in the future loveliness and kindness that will return with the next generation—the effect is overwhelming. It is impossible to read a poem like ' Woak Hill ' without tears in one's eyes. Or rather, if one has not tears in one's eyes at the end of ' Woak Hill ' one has not read it. It is impossible to praise the author of ' Uncle and Aunt ' in the balanced language of the study. ' I shake hands with you in my heart,' wrote an old Dorsetshire servant from her London basement-kitchen. Those are the words in which he has to be praised.

If, suspicious of so much amiability, we start pulling him to pieces, we discover that contrary to expectation he is a scholar. Like A. E. Housman, he knew exactly what he was doing in verse, and he knew what others had done. He sang Dorset because he had to, but not without premeditation ; he was not the gifted rustic who smudged some of the effects in Burns. ' Woak Hill ' itself is composed in an elaborate Persian metre, the Pearl, and even those who discount its pathos are obliged to admire its dexterity. Other poems are written as Ghazels, others imitate or adapt recondite Bardic metres, and all of them have their words in the right places. Light words—rose-petals of words, withered leaves, red dowst o' the ridges ; but they fall into their places with the assurance of marble.

> Sweet Be'mi'ster, that bist a-bound
> By green an' woody hills all round,
> Wi' hedges, reache'n up between
> A thousan' vields o'zummer green,
> Where elems' lofty heads do drow
> Their sheädes vor haÿ-meäkers below,
> An' wild hedge-flow'r's do charm the souls
> O' maïdens in their evenèn strolls.

The technical skill of ' wild hedge-flow'r's ' is notable ; the verse is heavily pulled up by the lightest element in its subject-matter. We pause, we put on the brake for flowers, and the scenes through which we have been sliding coalesce and are saved from too much smoothness. In the last line the natural speed of the verse is released. Forward we go again, after having been clamped by beauty. It is amazing that a writer who always puts the heart first can so keep his head. His genius worked not by a series of happy hits but by using the poetic intelligence, and it is the more amazing since his prose-intelligence was provincial. He believed, for instance, that only Anglo-Saxon words should be employed in English, and he wrote a philological grammar in which vowels become ' breath-sounds,' and consonants ' clippings.' To believe this and yet to create touching poetry in which Anglo-Saxon words are mainly employed is a unique achievement.

His life—except for the loss of his beloved wife and for an occasional trouble over his school—was a very happy one. His temperament, though profound, was equable. He was rooted where he could grow, and was never assailed by lusts or nervestorms. He could live through the Labourers' Revolt of 1830 without its shadows falling across his verse, and he could help his neighbour, Colonel Shrapnel, with some mathematical formulae. Good Colonel Shrapnel was working out a new type of explosive. When the railway was extended to Dorchester it vexed some people, but he and his pupils found some fine geological specimens in the chalk cuttings. Even the new stove so unwisely installed at St. Peter's did not function fatally.

> The carbonic acid gas [writes his daughter] which rose from beneath the floor of the aisles had first the effect of making the little children drop down insensible, and one by one they were carried out. Next the more delicate young people succumbed, among whom were two or three of William Barnes's household. At length even the strong ones began to suffer and went out in groups, leaving the rector preaching to empty benches, very much bewildered to know what was happening, for the heavy fumes had not yet reached him in the pulpit. The streets were full of groups of suffering people, helping to support others more suffering than themselves. One young woman fell into a swoon which lasted three hours.'

All this he survived. The little trials of life, like its deeper sorrows, were accepted by him bravely, and with the belief that joy must prevail. For the joy beyond death he had the authority of his Church ; for joy upon earth he could point to the recurring generations of village life :

> Vor daughters ha' mornen when mothers ha' night,
> An' there's beauty alive when the feäirest is dead ;
> As when woone sparklèn weäve do sink down from the light,
> Another do come up an' catch it instead.

Yet the heart retains its preferences and joy is compatible with personal loss :

> Smile on, happy maïdens ! but I shall noo mwore
> Zee the maïd I do miss under evenèn's dim sky,
> An' my heart is a-touch'd to see you avore
> The doors, vor to chatty an' zee vo'k goo by.

Out of the goodness of his heart, his muse commends sweetness, modesty, innocent mirth, piety, domesticated manliness. He never destroys and seldom criticises, and those who believe that no poetry can be great unless it is rebellious will condemn him as too Sunday-schoolish. But a muse can attend a Sunday school. She disobeys all rules. ' There can be no art without love,' he wrote. That too is a rule, and therefore not universally true, but it is true of his own art. He gathered up all the happiness and beauty he could see around him, he invented more, he poured it out as a continuous offering upon the countryside, and when he was told that the offering would from its nature perish he replied : ' To write in what some may deem a fast outwearing speech-form may seem as idle as the writing of one's name in snow on a spring day. I cannot help it. It is my mother tongue, and it is to my mind the only true speech of the life that I draw.'

In his old age, as he sat by the fire in the comfortable rectory at Came, he heard the garden gate clanging behind some friends who had just left him, perhaps for ever. The sound moved him to poetry, and he called his daughter and began to dictate ' The Geäte a-vallèn to.'

> In the zunsheen of our summers
>   Wi' the hay time now a-come
> How busy wer we out a'vield
>   Wi' vew a-left at hwome,
> When waggons rumbled out ov yard,
>   Red-wheeled wi' body blue,
> And back behind 'em loudly slamm'd
>   The geäte a-vallèn to.

When he had finished dictating he paused, and listened to the sounds clanging back through the centuries. ' Observe that word " geäte ",' he said. ' That is how King Alfred would have pronounced it, and how it was called in the Saxon Chronicle, which tells us of King Edward, who was slain at Corfe's geäte.' He paused again and continued : ' Ah ! if the Court had not been moved to London, then the speech of King Alfred, of which our Dorset is the remnant, would have been the Court language of to-day.'

William Barnes had not many regrets, but this was one of them.

[1939]

Three Stories by Tolstoy

Three short-stories by Tolstoy—namely *The Cossacks*, *The Death of Ivan Ilyitch*, and *The Three Hermits*—may help us towards an understanding of him.

They are very different, these stories. *The Cossacks* is an early work, full of adventure, it swings ahead, it's about war and love and mountains and ambushes, and it takes place at the foot of the Caucasus. *The Death of Ivan Ilyitch*, written later, is a story of illness and suffering indoors, where we never breathe the fresh air. *The Three Hermits* (also a late work) is a folk-tale about some Holy Men who were so stupid that they could not even learn the Lord's Prayer.

The three stories, although so different, have one thing in common. They all teach that simple people are best. That was Tolstoy's faith. It took various forms at various times of his life and led him into all sorts of contradictions—sometimes he believed in fighting, sometimes in non-violence and passive resistance, sometimes he was a Christian, sometimes he wasn't, was sometimes an ascetic, sometimes a voluptuary, but the idea that simple people are best underlies all his opinions from start to finish. He was himself far from simple—one of the most complex and difficult characters with whom the historian of literature has to deal, he was an aristocrat, an intellectual, a landowner who thought property wrong, he was ravaged with introspection and remorse. But that's his faith, simplicity.

In one of his earlier revolts against society he had retired to the Caucasus and joined the Russian Army there. At that time conditions were primitive, and savage tribes would descend from the mountains to raid the lowlands to the north. To check them the Russian Government subsidised the Cossacks, who were almost equally wild. The Cossacks lived in their own villages, but were a military organisation who manned outposts and co-operated with the regular army. They were independent and charming, they loved violence and pleasure, and the women as well as the men went free. The life warmed Tolstoy's imagination, and is responsible for his first masterpiece. *The*

Cossacks is loosely written and the plot is simple. A young Russian officer is stationed in a village and falls in love with a Cossack girl, Marianka. She is betrothed to a wild local youngster, who has made good by killing a tribesman. There are complications, and just as the Russian thinks he has won the girl over, the young Cossack is desperately wounded by the tribesman's brother; Marianka turns away from the officer in fury and returns to her own people, whom she had been tempted to desert. Thus epitomised, the plot sounds thin and stagey, but it is alive by the character-drawing, by the wealth of incident, and by the splendid descriptions of scenery. It's a story of youth, written by a young man.

> Yes, this is the kind of man I am [says one of the Cossacks]. I am a hunter and there isn't another hunter in the regiment like me. I can find and show you every kind of animal and bird—what they are and where they are, I know all about them. And I have got dogs and two guns and nets and a mare and a falcon; got everything I want, thank God! You perhaps may become a real hunter but don't boast of it. I will show you everything. That's the kind of man I am! I will find the scent for you. I know the beast. I know where his lair is and where he goes to drink or lie down. I will make a shooting hut and I will sit there all night and keep watch for you. What is the use of sitting at home? One only gets warm and gets drunk. And then the women come and make a row, and one's angry. Whereas there— you go out and you smooth down the reeds and you sit and watch as a brave young fellow should. You look up at the sky and see the stars : you look at them and guess the time. The wood stirs and you hear a little noise, and a boar comes out to roll in the mud. You hear how the young eagles cry and how the cocks or the geese in the village answer them— geese only till midnight of course. All this I know.

The Cossacks was published in 1863. It made a great sensation in Russia. He followed it with *War and Peace* and *Anna Karenina*, and by the time he wrote *The Death of Ivan Ilyitch* he was famous.

Ivan Ilyitch is a successful public servant who rises to become a judge. He is a decent fellow—he has had to pull strings to get on, of course, but everyone has to do that—if you're in the civil service yourself you realise that, don't you ? He married, and for love. Romance doesn't last, of course, and by the time he and his wife are middle-aged they quarrel a good deal. That's not unusual—if you yourself are middle-aged you've experienced it perhaps. When he becomes a judge he takes a charming house at St. Petersburg. He is interested in the house, and supervises its decorating, climbs on a ladder to show a workman how to hang a curtain ; he slips and in saving himself knocks his side against the corner of a picture frame. The bruised place aches a little, but the discomfort soon passes off, and that's nothing, is it ? He went on with his worldly and respectable life, attended the courts, got in with the best people, gave parties. He had a terrible row with his wife over some cakes. She called him a fool because he had ordered too many and he threatened her with divorce. You know the sort of thing. Still it passed. The only trouble was—he didn't feel quite well. There was a nasty taste in his mouth at times, his temper got worse, and there was an uncomfortable feeling—not exactly a pain—in his side, where he had banged it against the picture frame. He is persuaded to consult the doctor who diagnoses—either a loose kidney or appendix trouble. He resumes his daily life—but the pain gets worse.

I won't inflict on you further details of this gruesome story— the most powerful Tolstoy ever wrote. The end is—agonising death, death embittered by Ivan Ilyitch's knowledge that he is in everyone's way, and that they will be thankful when he is gone, and by the polite pretence around him that he is going to recover. In this bitterness there is one compensation. Among his servants is a young peasant called Gerasim, whose job it is to do the rough work in the house. Gerasim is strong, good-tempered and unsophisticated, and spends his time in doing things for other people without making any fuss. ' Death will come to all of us, so what's a little trouble, your honour ? ' says Gerasim. And Ivan Ilyitch discovers before the end that something is wrong with his life ; unlike Gerasim he has lived only for himself —even when he was in love with his wife it was for the sake of his own pleasure, and that's what has been wrong. The illumination comes, and at the supreme moment he understands. ' In the place of death there was light.'

In *The Death of Ivan Ilyitch* Tolstoy criticises modern civilisation. In *The Three Hermits* he shows what civilisation needs.

A bishop, an excellent man, is on a voyage, and hears of an island where three hermits live, saving their souls. He determines to visit them, and finds them indeed holy and sincere, but so ignorant that they do not even know the Lord's Prayer. He teaches them, but they are so stupid that they have the greatest difficulty in learning it; they try again and again, one gets it right, another gets it wrong; however, the Bishop is patient, and does not re-embark until the lesson is learnt. He has the satisfaction of leaving the hermits in a row on the shore, saying the Lord's Prayer fairly accurately. By now it is night and the full moon has risen. The ship continues her course, and in the middle of the night something is seen following her rapidly over the sea. It is the Three Hermits. They have forgotten the Lord's Prayer, and they are running over the surface of the waves to ask the Bishop to teach them again.

You will see now what I mean by saying Tolstoy believes in simple people. And he believed in a different sort of simplicity at various times in his life. When he was young, and himself a bit of a rip, he believed in the Cossacks, because they were spontaneous and loved animal violence and pleasure. In *The Death of Ivan Ilyitch* he has shifted his affection to the Russian peasant, Gerasim, who is placid and imperturbable and unselfish. And in *The Three Hermits* he recommends a third type—the saint who is an imbecile in the world's judgment, but walks on the water through the powers of the spirit. Tolstoy was inconsistent. Here are some of his inconsistencies, and they laid him open to attack. But he never wavered in his central faith: simplicity.

Do you yourself believe in simplicity as a cure for our present troubles? And if so, how do you think simplicity can be worked in a world that has become industrialised? Tolstoy's outlook was agricultural: he never realised the implications of the machine.

[1942]

Edward Carpenter

Edward Carpenter was born at Brighton one hundred years ago. Few people recall him to-day, and those who do probably dismiss him as a crank. But he was a remarkable fellow, lovable, charming, energetic, courageous, possibly great, and he was once an inspiration in the world of Labour. He deserves commemoration.

He came of respectable upper-middle-class parentage. He grew up in stodgy comfort, with no conception of the lives of the poor, and he set forth on what promised to be a typically Victorian career. He went to Cambridge, choosing Trinity Hall as his college because it was ' so gentlemanly,' read mathematics, rowed, became a Fellow and took orders. Here a little hitch occurred. He had had the religious doubts appropriate to his period, and after he was a clergyman they increased and he was physically ill, and felt that something deeper than his consciousness was pushing him out of the Church : ' You've got to go, you've got to go,' something said, and he went.

His experience, so far, was not unusual. Other thoughtful and decent young men would become curates in the hope of doing good and then have to be unfrocked, to the dismay of their families. Leslie Stephen is another example. What was unusual with Carpenter was that his difficulties were only partly theological. With him it was really a case of social maladjustment. He was not happy in the class into which he had been born. He wanted to live and work with the manual labourers. As soon as he got clear of the Church he realised this, settled in Sheffield, and that district, then far from gentility, became his home. Here were the people who suited him : artisans, unemployed, toughs, it is to them that his heart went out and his heart was stronger than his head, although he had a good head. His action does not seem revolutionary to-day, for he retained his private income of five hundred a year throughout. But it was very revolutionary at the time ; it astonished people, and he did not revolt from a sense of duty or in order to make

217

a splash, but because he wanted to. He lived with working-class people, adopted many of their ways, worked hard physically, market-gardened, made and wore sandals, made (but did not wear) a Saxon tunic. He may not have got into another class, but he certainly discarded his own and gained happiness by doing so, and at the end of his life, when I came to know him, he rather mistrusted me because, like himself, I had had the disadvantage of a university education.

His heart made him a socialist. Would he be recognised as one to-day ? It was the socialism of Shelley and Blake. He strove to destroy existing abuses such as landlordism and capitalism, and all he offered in their place was love. He was not interested in efficiency or organisation, or party discipline, nor in industrialism, though he tried to be. He believed in Liberty, Fraternity and Equality—words now confined to platforms and perorations. He saw the New Jerusalem from afar, from the ignoble slough of his century, and there is no doubt that it does look more beautiful from a distance. When the armies of the down-trodden enter its gate, as thanks in part to his efforts they are doing to-day, the New Jerusalem becomes a more ordinary city, where the party leaders book the best rooms. Moreover, he was a mystic, and when he was asked how he combined his socialism with his mysticism, he answered, in his gay, quaint way : ' I like to hang out my red flag from the ground floor, and then go up above to see how it looks '—a striking answer, but not sound trade unionism. Except by people now elderly, Carpenter must be forgotten to-day in the labour movements he helped to found. He would not in the least mind. He was absolutely selfless.

This early ardour poured over into a famous volume of poems, *Towards Democracy* (1883). They are in the style and in the spirit of Walt Whitman and have been called Whitman and water—a gibe which amused their author. They expressed his faith, and his love for the individual and for the beauty of nature. These were the only two things he cared about, and he says so repeatedly, sometimes in an economic utterance, like *Civilisation, Its Cause and Cure*, sometimes in philosophic speculation, as in *The Art of Creation*, sometimes in aesthetic criticism (*Angels' Wings*), sometimes in works on sex (*Love's Coming of Age* and *The Intermediate Sex*), and best of all is his autobiography, *My Days and Dreams*, written at the end of his life. He demands from society the furtherance of these two things : all else is nonsense. His prose is good, and reveals his sensible and affectionate character. He may have worn sandals, refused to eat meat, supported women's rights before they were fashionable, and disbelieved in vivisection, but he was far, far from being a fool, and the reader who opens him patronisingly will encounter something challenging and tough.

Needless to say, Carpenter had no racial prejudice, and a visit to Ceylon, which he made at the invitation of a Tamil friend, completed his development, and gave him a metaphysical background to the personal emotions and the socialist hopes which he had developed in England. He sat at the feet of an Adept, and he described the elusive experience in *A Visit to a Gnani*. As he had looked outside his own class for companionship, so he was obliged to look outside his own race for wisdom. This done, he reached equilibrium. He always gave me the feeling that he had dominated his material and knew where he was in the world and what he wanted. Whether one agreed with him, whether one thought him practical, became a minor question.

He died at Guildford, in 1929. He had worked for a socialism which should be non-industrial, unorganised and rooted in the soil. Society was far from such a socialism when he wrote, and it is further than ever from it to-day. But that is not the whole of his work.

[1944]

Webb and Webb

Beatrice Webb, who has just died, was one of the great English women of our age. But any homage to her must begin with a summary of her work, for that is what she herself would have wished. Personal gossip, personal relationships, successes, failures —all these she held to be irrelevant : what mattered in her view was work ; have you worked ? What is your work ?

Her work was the investigation of society. She began in the eighties and nineties of the last century, by contributing to an ' inquest ' into the social conditions of London. This inquest was conducted by her cousin Charles Booth, took seventeen years to publish and ran into many volumes of letterpress and maps ; its main aim was the analysis of poverty, particularly in the East End. She followed it by an independent study of the Co-operative Movement in Great Britain, from the seventeenth century until her own day. Then—after her marriage with Sidney Webb—she collaborated with him, and the first outcome of this was their *Minority Report* on the Poor Law. Both of them had sat on a Royal Commission to examine the problem of poverty : it had issued a report from which they dissented, and in their Minority Report they set in motion the Socialist and Labour campaign for the break-up of the existing Poor Law system. They then produced, amongst other books, the *History of Trade Unionism* ; its sequel *Industrial Democracy*, a treatise in seven volumes on *English Local Government*, and finally, turning from England to Russia, they investigated conditions there and produced yet another monumental survey : *Soviet Communism*.

Such was her work. Who was she ?

She was the daughter of a successful railway director, Richard Potter, and she grew up in the heart of Victorianism, amongst the amenities which the nineteenth century lavished upon a happy few. There were nine Miss Potters, and between the country houses and the town houses of their parents they had a very pleasant time. Not a frivolous time, for there was in this wealthy family a strong vein of Puritanism and of intellectual seriousness. Herbert Spencer was a close friend, and through him the girl got to know George Eliot, Professor Huxley, G. H. Lewes, etc. It was a full interesting life, based economically upon capitalism, politically on liberalism, and philosophically upon individualism, and for the nine Miss Potters it was all very well. But what was going on outside this comfortable existence, these lofty and satisfactory thoughts ? Beatrice began to wonder. She knew that ' the poor ' existed, and she read in the reports of company directors such phrases as ' water plentiful and labour docile.' But she wanted to know more.

Although her family was prosperous, it had the advantage of humble connections, who had not risen in the world and were still cotton-operators in Lancashire. She got into touch with them, through her old nurse, and made their acquaintance, at first under an assumed name. She liked them, they her, and it is worth noting that she, who was by temperament institutional and bureaucratic, first contacted her subject matter on the human side. Critics have complained that she was unsympathetic to the individual, and she herself avows that a million sick have always seemed to her more worthy of self-sacrificing devotion than a solitary sick child. She did not believe in a local and sentimental pity. Nor did she believe that poverty could be cured by charity. It could only be cured by altering the conditions in which the poor lived, conditions can't be altered until they are ascertained, and hence her belief in Commissions of Enquiry and note-taking, and questionnaires, and her ultimate conversion to socialism and state-control, and all that her parents detested. Later on when I met her—she was an elderly lady then and a very grand one—I was equally struck by the rigidity of her opinions and by the human charm with which those opinions were expressed. And, reading her early experiences in *My Apprenticeship*, I have come to understand how such a combination occurred.

Her conversion to socialism and to marriage occurred at the same time. About 1890 the firm of Webb and Webb, as they called it, was founded, and few unions have been so productive of private happiness and of public good. They worked as one person : to both of them, the great object in life was work, and the same type of work. When either of them voiced an opinion, they invariably used the word ' we.' ' We think that . . .', ' We cannot support the present tendency towards . . .' and so on. It was not a royal ' we,' or a

conceited one.   It was rather the well-considered pronouncement
of the firm of Webb and Webb.   I remember thinking when
I visited them in their country home that if I could have con-
futed the pronouncement, it would have been instantly withdrawn.   All I could do was to babble, 'Well I don't somehow
feel like that myself.'   My remark was listened to, was dismissed,
and the next pronouncement followed.   I leant back in my
deep arm-chair without any feeling that I had been snubbed.
The atmosphere was authentic and noble.   They were too
serious to score.   She sat on one side of the great hygienic fireplace, he on the other—she tall and graceful, he short and compact, and in front of the fire lay a third personage, the dog.
The dog formed no part of any social survey and consequently
had the Webbs in his power ;   whatever they instructed him to
do he did the reverse.   But the human problem lay completely
under their control.   Alternately they would rise, stand in front
of the fire, and begin a sentence beginning 'we.'   William
Nicholson's portrait of them shows them thus ;   a splendid
conversation-piece ;   there are the Webbs, and the fireplace and
the dog, and strewn papers, and augustness radiating, and singleness of purpose and unity of faith.[1]

For lunch we had mutton, greens, potatoes, rice pudding—
simplest of menus, but supreme in quality and superbly cooked ;
never have I eaten such mutton, greens, potatoes, rice.   Then
Sidney Webb took me for a walk.   The dog decided to come
too, and instantly vanished into a wood.   'I cannot think why
he always does this,' said his master thoughtfully.   We continued
alone to the open country, through a tract appropriately devoid
of birds, and here in the silence he uttered a sentence about himself and his wife :   'Our age this year is a hundred and fifty-
seven,' he said, adding: 'our combined ages.'   When I recall
that charming sentence to-day I think too of the closing words
of her autobiography, *My Apprenticeship*.   There she speaks of
'Our Partnership : a working comradeship founded in a common faith and made perfect by marriage ;   perhaps the most
exquisite, certainly the most enduring, of all the varieties of
happiness.'   Soon after we returned from the walk the hired car
came round to remove me.   They escorted me to it, attentive
and courteous to the last, and as soon as it started they started to
go back to their work.   That was the only time I saw the Webbs,

[1] This picture is now in the London School of Economics.

and I could never have been intimate with them : only those who worked with them could be that, and my own schemes for improving society run upon different lines. But it is a great honour to have met them, and a great enlargement of experience, and I want in particular to pay homage to her who passed away this month in her sleep at the individual age of eighty-five.

[1943]

[224]

A Book that Influenced Me

It was rather a little book, and that introduces my first point. One's impulse, on tackling the question of influence, is to search for a great book, and to assume that here is the force which has moulded one's outlook and character. Looking back upon my own half-century of reading, I have no doubt which my three great books have been : Dante's *Divine Comedy*, Gibbon's *Decline and Fall*, and Tolstoy's *War and Peace*. All three are great both in quality and in bulk. Bulk is not to be despised. Combined with quality, it gives a long book a pull over a short one, and permits us to call it monumental. Here are three monuments. But they have not influenced me in the least, though I came across them all at an impressionable age. They impressed me by their massiveness and design, and made me feel small in the right way, and to make us feel small in the right way is a function of art ; men can only make us feel small in the wrong way. But to realise the vastness of the universe, the limits of human knowledge, the even narrower limits of human power, to catch a passing glimpse of the mediaeval universe, or of the Roman Empire on its millennial way, or of Napoleon collapsing against the panorama of Russian daily life—that is not to be influenced. It is to be extended. Perhaps those three books were too monumental, and human beings are not much influenced by monuments. They gaze, say ' Oh ! ' and pass on unchanged. They are more likely to be influenced by objects nearer their own size ? Anyhow, that has been my own case.

The book in question is Samuel Butler's *Erewhon*, a work of genius, but with Dante, Gibbon and Tolstoy setting our standards not to be called great. It has been better described as ' a serious book not written too seriously.'

Published as far back as 1872, it is difficult to classify—partly a yarn, partly an account of Utopia, partly a satire on Victorian civilisation. It opens with some superb descriptions of mountain scenery : this part is taken from Butler's New Zealand experiences. The hero is a bit of a scamp, and not so much a living character as a vehicle for the author's likes and dislikes, and for his mischievousness. He has left England under a cloud for a distant colony, with the intention of converting some lost tribe to Christianity at a handsome profit. He hears that beyond the mountain range there are terrible figures, and still more terrible sounds. He sets out, and presently discovers enormous and frightful statues, through whose hollow heads the wind moans. They are the guardians of Erewhon. Struggling past them, he enters the unknown country, and the fantasy proper begins. The descent on the further side beyond the statues is exquisitely related, and the scenery now suggests the Italian slopes of the Alps. He is politely imprisoned by the mountaineers until instructions as to his disposal can come up from the capital. But there are two hitches. One of them occurs when his watch is discovered on him. The other is with his jailer's daughter, Yram (Erewhonian for Mary). He and she get on well, and when he catches a cold he makes the most of it, in the hope of being cosseted by her. She flies into a fury.

By now he has learnt the language, and is summoned to the capital. He is to be the guest of a Mr. Nosnibor and the account of Mr. Nosnibor puzzles him. ' He is,' says his informant, ' a most delightful man, who has but lately recovered from embezzling a large sum of money under singularly distressing circumstances ; you are sure to like him.' What can this all mean ? It's wrong to have a watch, wrong to catch a cold, but embezzlement is only a subject for sympathy. The reader is equally puzzled, and skilfully does Butler lead us into the heart of this topsy-turvy country, without explaining its fantasies too soon. Take the Musical Banks. Erewhon, it seems, has two banking systems, one of them like ours, the other is Musical Banking. Mr. Nosnibor, as befits a dubious financier, goes constantly to the first sort of bank, but never attends the offices of the second, though he is ostensibly its ardent supporter. Mrs. Nosnibor and her daughters go once a week. Each bank has its own coinage, the coins of the musical banks being highly esteemed, but of no commercial value, as the hero soon discovers when he tries to tip one of its officials with them. Just as in Swift we read for a bit about the Yahoos without realising that he intends them for ourselves, so we read about the Musical Banks, and only gradually realise that they caricature the Church of England and its connections with Capitalism. There was a great row over this chapter as soon as it was understood ; the 'enfant terrible,' as he called himself, had indeed heaved a brick. He also shocked people by reversing the positions of crime and illness. In Erewhon it is wicked to be ill—that is why Yram was angry when the hero had a cold. Embezzlement, on the other hand, is a disease. Mr. Nosnibor is treated for it professionally and very severely. 'Poor papa,' says his charming daughter, 'I really do not think he will steal any more.' And as for possessing a watch—all machinery invented after a certain date has been destroyed by the Erewhonians, lest it breeds new machines, who may enslave men. And there are further brilliant inventions—for instance, the College of Unreason, who teach a Hypothetical Language, never used outside their walls, and in whom we must reluctantly recognise the ancient universities of Oxford and Cambridge, and their schools of Latin and Greek. And there is the worship of the Goddess Ydgrun (Mrs. Grundy) ; the worship is mostly bad, yet it produces a few fine people, the High Ydgrunites. These people were conventional in the right way : they hadn't too many ideals, and they were always willing to drop a couple to oblige a friend. In the High Ydgrunites we come to what Butler thought desirable. Although a rebel, he was not a reformer. He believed in the conventions, provided they are observed humanely. Grace and graciousness, good temper, good looks, good health and good sense ; tolerance, intelligence, and willingness to abandon any moral standard at a pinch. That is what he admired.

The book ends, as it began, in the atmosphere of adventure. The hero elopes with Miss Nosnibor in a balloon. The splendid descriptions of natural scenery are resumed, they fall into the sea and are rescued, and we leave him as secretary of the Erewhon Evangelisation Company in London, asking for subscriptions for the purpose of converting the country to Christianity with the aid of a small expeditionary force. 'An uncalled-for joke ?' If you think so, you have fallen into one of Butler's little traps. He wanted to make uncalled-for jokes. He wanted to write a serious book not too seriously.

Why did this book influence me ? For one thing, I have the sort of mind which likes to be taken unawares. The frontal full-dress presentation of an opinion often repels me, but if it be insidiously slipped in sidewise I may receive it, and Butler

is a master of the oblique.   Then, what he had to say was congenial, and I lapped it up.   It was the food for which I was
waiting.   And this brings me to my next point.   I suggest that
the only books that influence us are those for which we are ready,
and which have gone a little farther down our particular path
than we have yet got ourselves.   I suggest, furthermore, that
when you feel that you could almost have written the book
yourself—that's the moment when it's influencing you.   You
are not influenced when you say, ' How marvellous !   What a
revelation !   How monumental.   Oh ! '   You are being extended.   You are being influenced when you say ' I might
have written that myself if I hadn't been so busy.'   I don't
suppose that I could have written the *Divine Comedy* or the
Decline and Fall.   I don't even think I could have written the
Antigone of Sophocles, though of all the great tragic utterances
that comes closest to my heart, that is my central faith.   But I
do think (quite erroneously) that I could have turned out this
little skit of Erewhon if the idea of it had occurred to me.   Which
is strong evidence that it has influenced me.

Erewhon also influenced me in its technique.   I like that idea
of fantasy, of muddling up the actual and the impossible until
the reader isn't sure which is which, and I have sometimes tried
to do it when writing myself.   However, I mustn't start on
technique.   Let me rather get in an observation which was put
to me the other day by a friend.   What about the books which
influence us negatively, which give us the food we don't want,
or, maybe, are unfit for, and so help us to realise what we do
want ?   I have amused myself by putting down four books
which have influenced me negatively.   They are books by great
writers, and I have appreciated them.   But they are not my
sort of book.   They are : the *Confessions* of St. Augustine,
Macchiavelli's *Prince*, Swift's *Gulliver*, and Carlyle on *Heroes
and Hero Worship*.   All these books have influenced me negatively,
and impelled me away from them towards my natural food.
I know that St. Augustine's *Confessions* is a ' good ' book, and
I want to be good.   But not in St. Augustine's way.   I don't
want the goodness which entails an asceticism close to cruelty.
I prefer the goodness of William Blake.   And Macchiavelli—
he is clever—and unlike some of my compatriots I want to be
clever.   But not with Macchiavelli's cold, inhuman cleverness.
I prefer the cleverness of Voltaire.   And indignation—Swift's

indignation in *Gulliver* is too savage for me; I prefer Butler's in *Erewhon*. And strength—yes, I want to be strong, but not with the strength of Carlyle's dictator heroes, who foreshadow Hitler. I prefer the strength of Antigone.

[1944]

Our Second Greatest Novel?

Most people agree that Tolstoy's *War and Peace* is the greatest novel that western civilisation has produced. Which novel is the second greatest? I suggest Marcel Proust's *A la Recherche du Temps Perdu*.

Proust was the son of a doctor. He had some Jewish blood in him, and provides another example of the gifts which that wonderful race has given to the world. He was born in 1871, in a French country town which he has immortalised and imparadised as Combray. He went to Paris and entered literary society and smart society, and Paris also has he immortalised—as Dante immortalised the Inferno. He had bad health, and he has immortalised illness. Retiring more and more from the world, sleeping by day, shutting himself up in a room which was lined with cork, he worked and worked, and strove with the aid of memory to throw his sensations and experiences into a work of art. He succeeded. The enormous novel which resulted is not as warm-hearted or as heroic or as great as *War and Peace*. But it is superior as an artistic achievement ; it is full of echoes, exquisite reminders, intelligent parallels, which delight the attentive reader, and at the end, and not until the end, he realises that those echoes and parallels occur as it were inside a gigantic cathedral ; that the book, which seemed as we read it so rambling, has an architectural unity and pre-ordained form.

The first volume came out in 1913. There are seven volumes in all—seven sub-novels, with the same characters occurring in them, and endless cross references between them. Proust died before the entire work had been published. To the last moment he was dictating, struggling against a high fever, and refusing to take any nourishment except iced beer. What mattered to him was not life, which he had found unsatisfactory, but art, which alone makes any meaning out of life. On his last day, in November 1922, at three in the morning, he summoned his secretary and dictated a noble passage about the duty of a novelist to do his work as it ought to be done, basing it on laws of goodness, scrupulousness and sacrifice which seem to be derived from

229

some other world.   As a result of the effort of dictation, an
abscess burst in his lung and he died.   Proust was not a very
attractive man, or a healthy one.   But he possibly produced the
second greatest European novel, and he raised that rather tiresome word ' art ' to an importance and a sublimity which we
cannot neglect.

The story is told through a narrator or hero who more or less
resembles Proust himself ; who grows up with his mother and
grandmother—the only characters displaying human integrity ;
who moves from Combray to the meretricious charm of Paris ;
who goes into aristocratic society and is disillusioned by it ;
who goes in for love and is still more disillusioned ; who falls
ill, and, prematurely aged, finds that his world has aged too yet
is none the less fascinating as an object for observation.   That is
my first point.   The second is this : what really matters in the
book is not events but the remembering of events.   Many tragic
events occur and many funny ones, but they take their final shape
in the meditations of the narrator.   The novel is called not
' Things Past ', but the ' Remembrance of Things Past '.   For all
its realism, it has about it something of a day dream.   It plays
about with time.   It reconsiders the same episode, the same
characters, and reaches new results.   It keeps turning the stuff
of life about and looking through it from this direction and
that.

The famous ' little phrase ' (*la petite phrase*) in the music of
Vinteuil serves as an example.   This ' little phrase ' becomes
almost an actor, and an actor constantly appearing in a new
part.   We first hear the name of Vinteuil in hideous circumstances.   The composer is dead—an obscure little country organist
unknown to fame—and his daughter is defiling his memory.
The horrible scene is to radiate in several directions—everything
radiates in Proust.   Much later, a violin sonata is being performed in Paris and a little phrase from its slow movement
catches the ear of Swann, and steals into his life.   Swann is in
love with a worthless creature, Odette, and it attends his love.
The love affair goes wrong, like most affairs in Proust, the phrase
is forgotten.   Then it breaks out again when he is ravaged with
jealousy, and now it attends his misery and past happiness at
once, without losing its own divine character.   Who wrote the
violin sonata ?   On hearing it is by Vinteuil, Swann says : ' H'm,
I once knew a wretched little organist of that name.   It couldn't

be by him.' But it is, and Vinteuil's daughter, who seemed so infamous, has piously transcribed her father's work and published it. Her nature is many-sided, like most natures in Proust.

That seems all. The 'little phrase' crosses the book again, but as an echo. Then hundreds, indeed thousands of pages on, when Vinteuil has become a national glory and there is talk of raising a statue to him in the town where he has been so wretched and so obscure, another work of his is performed—a posthumous string sextet. The hero listens—he is in an unknown rather terrible universe while a sinister dawn reddens the sea. Suddenly for him and for the reader too, the 'little phrase' of the sonata recurs—half-heard, changed, but giving complete orientation, so that he is back in the country of his childhood with the knowledge that it belongs to the unknown. It gives memory a shock, and these shocks and their emotional consequences are Proust's main concern.

So my first point was that the narrator or hero is more or less Proust himself, and my second point—a difficult one, for it takes us into his central problem—is that he is concerned not with events and people as Tolstoy is, but with memories of events and people, and that consequently his novel often has the quality of a day dream, in which the ordinary sequence of time gets interrupted and mixed up. My third point—a straightforward one—is the social scene. He gives a brilliant and malicious picture of the French aristocracy forty or fifty years ago. It was an aristocracy which had wealth and style, but no sense of responsibility, no connection with the land, and no faith in anything except its own superiority to the rest of mankind. Proust saw through it and bowed down to it. He was both a satirist and a snob. He gives, too, a picture and a disagreeable one of the bourgeoisie, who force themselves up through the social fabric as the story proceeds, and who are typified by the detestable Monsieur and Madame Verdurin. The working classes come in, as servants and parasites, and are not handled amiably either. The only people who are treated with respect are the hero's mother and grandmother, women incapable of worldliness and meanness, and the artists who, like Proust himself, strive to *understand* the disappointing scene and to give it afterwards a coherence and a beauty it never possesses at the time.

Point number four : Proust as a drawer of character. He is masterly. We live with his people, we see them develop, they behave incredibly, and later on we see why. When they contradict themselves they only become more real. It is an immense gallery of portraits, in which predominate the superb Duchess of Guermantes, and the sinister yet touching Baron de Charlus. Even if people only appear for a few minutes, we know them, and hundreds of pages on we shall recognise them if they reappear. The characters are often falling in love with one another, and—here is point number five perhaps—I must allude to Proust's theory of love. It is a gloomy theory and I do not agree with it. He thought, to be brief, that the more deeply people fall in love, the more they distorted one another, so that passion is a certain prelude to misunderstanding. He thought, too, that jealousy is inevitable, and that its arrival means the renewal of a love which might otherwise have mercifully died. Long tracts in the latter part of the work are devoted to the ' hero's ' affair with Albertine. They make depressing reading, and most people skip them.

It is important when tackling Proust to be patient and to be intelligent. He makes no concessions to stupidity. Some writers —and they are great writers—do make concessions. Dickens does, and even Tolstoy does. Proust does not. He expects a constant awareness, both from the mind and from the senses. He was an individualist, he was an invalid, he was a bit of a snob, he belonged to a society which was decadent, and he had no interest in social reform. How dare I suggest that such a creature produced the second best European novel ? I dare, because I do not believe that this art business can be swept aside. No violence can destroy it, no sneering can belittle it. Based on an integrity in man's nature which lies deeper than moral integrity, it rises to heights of triumph which give us cause to hope. Proust was an artist and a tremendous one ; he found in memory the means of interpreting and humanising this chaotic world, and he has given the results in *Remembrance of Things Past*.

[1943]

Gide and George

Two modern writers of European reputation, the Frenchman André Gide and the German Stefan George, offer contrasted reaction to the present chaos. I will begin with Gide.

Gide is an old man now.[1] He has written a number of novels including *The Immoralist*, his most disquieting work, *The Caves of the Vatican*, expressing his pagan side, and *The Narrow Gate*, which expresses his Protestant pietistic side. He has also written criticisms and plays, and a fascinating and frank autobiography of his early life, he has kept journals, been active at conferences, helped to run the chief French literary magazine. And now he is an old man. And when his country collapsed three years ago he might naturally have done what some French writers actually did—that is to say, collaborated with Hitler or at all events with Vichy. He refused. Retiring to unoccupied France, he continued to express truths which he alone, owing to his prestige, was able to get into print. Instead of playing for safety, he used his high position to uphold still higher the torch of freedom. Then Hitler advanced again and occupied the south. Gide got away to Tunis, and when the Allied Armies captured it this spring they found him there. He has honoured us as well as his own country by his conduct, and he has advanced the republic of letters.

Yet I do not want to present Gide as a hero. He would not wish it and he isn't the type. He is not a hero. He is a humanist. The humanist has four leading characteristics—curiosity, a free mind, belief in good taste, and belief in the human race—and all four are present in Gide. His curiosity—he is always enquiring, he's interested in society and its break up, in his own character and other people's, in virtues and in vices too : in forgery as much as in the ecstasies of the saints : in self-denial and in self-indulgence. And secondly, he has a free mind. He is indifferent to authority, and he is willing to pay the penalty for independence. For example, he once went to the Congo, and he was so disgusted by economic imperialism and its exploitation of the

[1] He died in February, 1951.

African Negro, that he became a communist, at some personal inconvenience. Later on he went to Russia, and what he saw of communism there compelled him at even greater inconvenience to renounce it. I'm not saying either of these decisions is correct. I only want to point out that here's a man with a free mind, indifferent to authority, indifferent sometimes to logic, indifferent to everything except what he believes to be true. He has remained an individualist in an age which imposes discipline. His third characteristic is that he believes in good taste. Gide is a literary man, not a scientist, not a prophet, and his judgments tend to be aesthetic. He's subtle and elusive—sometimes annoyingly so—he sets great store by charm, he's more interested in harmony than in doctrine.

Fourth, he believes in humanity. He is not cynical about the human race. And consequently—for it is a consequence—he has no class prejudice and no colour prejudice. I remember so well the last time I met him : it was in an international congress of writers at Paris in the 'thirties, and he had to make a speech. A tall, willowy figure, he undulated on the platform above the vast audience, rather full of airs and graces and inclined to watch his own effects. Then he forgot himself and remembered the human race and made a magnificent oration. His thesis was that the individual will never develop his individuality until he forms part of a world society. As his thought soared, his style became fluid, and sentimentality passed into affection. He denied that humanity would cease to be interesting if it ceased to be miserable, and imagined a social state where happiness will be accessible to all, and where men, because they are happy, will be great. At that time the menace of Fascism was already darkening our doorways, and it seemed to us, as we listened to Gide, that here was a light which the darkness could not put out. It is not easy, in a few words, to give a picture of a very complicated individual ; let me anyhow make it clear that he reacts to the European tragedy as a humanist, that the four characteristics of humanism are curiosity, a free mind, belief in good taste, and belief in the human race, and that he has been prepared to suffer for his beliefs : they have not been just for the study and the cloister ; and consequently men honour him.

Now there are other reactions to the European tragedy besides humanism. Let us turn to Stefan George and see what he did in the face of the approaching darkness—George, a fine lyric poet, a sincere man of high ideals and of an iron will. He died exactly ten years ago, in 1933, after the establishment of Hitler's power. He was born in a very different Germany, in 1868. Well educated, and versed in European culture, he thought of his country as one among many, and owed a special debt, in his early poems, to France. By nature he was a recluse. He wrote for a small circle of friends and was accepted by them as their chief. Then he had an intense personal experience which exalted his poetry but did not improve his judgment, and as a result of that experience the circle of friends hardened into a cult, and George almost assumed the airs of a priest. Domineering and humourless, he trained his young disciples and began to send them out into the world. He taught them to despise the common man and to despise women, to prefer instinct to brains, and to believe in good birth, and in state organisation. A friend of mine who attended the University of Heidelberg used to see these disciples of George in the streets, ' almost dancing, tall, graceful and athletic, with their heads thrown back, as if they were trying to avoid the sight of common humanity.' It seemed like the coming of a new aristocracy, and George himself was a natural aristocrat, just as Gide is a natural democrat. He was an exceptional person, highly gifted as a poet, a lofty idealist with something of a prophet's grandeur. He knew it, and he made the mistake of thinking that when a person is exceptional he ought to be a leader The idea of leadership, so seductive and so pernicious both for the leaders and the led, invaded this fine artist. The swastika was stamped on the covers of his latest books, his poems spoke of a Fuehrer and a New Reich, and he found a cure for the evils of his age not in humanism, like Gide, but in authority. That was his reaction to the approaching European tragedy : authoritarianism.

The Nazis were not slow to take him up. From their point of view he was one of them. The National Socialists, it has been well said, have a peculiar gift for adopting and defiling ideas that have been of real value in their time, and they did not spare Stefan George. They patronised him and he had the misery of seeing his work exploited by cads—the greatest misery which a fastidious writer can undergo. He saw his ideals put into practice by Hitler, and it was more than he could stand. Doctor Goebbels wrote to him—no doubt with Hitler's approval—and offered him high honours as a poet in the gangster state. To his glory, he never answered the letter. Germany had become intolerable, and in 1933 he went away to Switzerland to die. That is his end—a sad end but a dignified one. The poet whom the Nazis claim as their own could not stand their foulness and preferred to die in exile.

Creative writers are always greater than the causes that they represent, and I have not interpreted either Gide or George to you in this brief summary of their respective attitudes. I have, for instance, conveyed nothing of the quality of their emotion or their style, nor is it possible to do so except by quotations. But they neatly illustrate two contrasted reactions in this age of misery : the humanist's reaction, and the authoritarian's.

[1943]

Gide's Death

I never knew Gide well, but we exchanged letters now and then, and I saw something of him in Paris at an international writers' conference in 1935. Like many others at that date, he was then hopeful of the Russian experiment, he was not scared by its economic and social heresies, and he had not foreseen its contempt for individual freedom or its regimentation of the intellect and of taste. He made a moving speech at the conference about the greatness of Man, who will become greater still when no men suffer from misery or want. He was the humanist unafraid.

He was also as slippery as a trout. He entertained myself and a friend at a restaurant, stood us a delightful dinner with promise of a still more delightful talk after it, and then—*il se sauva* when the coffee arrived, he saved himself, he was gone. André Malraux went with him. I still remember the disappearance of those two distinguished backs, and our mild disappointment. In what diverse directions were they finally to vanish ! That, too, none of us then foresaw.

I saw Gide once more, after Paris. He did not see me. It was in a remote valley in the Crau, in Provence. He was leaning over a bridge with a friend, looking at a rushing turbid stream, silent, and looking upstream. It is thus that I most clearly see him. Distinguished as ever, he was also content. I realised more clearly how much he had got out of life, and had managed to transmit through his writings. Not life's greatness—greatness is a nineteenth century perquisite, a Goethean job. But life's complexity, and the delight, the difficulty, the duty of registering that complexity and of conveying it. Unlike some others who have apprehended complexity, he was a hard worker. He wrote and wrote and travelled and wrote, and oh how he has helped us in consequence ! He has taught thousands of people to mistrust façades, to call the bluff, to be brave without bounce and inconsistent without frivolity. He is the humanist of our age —not of other ages, but of this one.

His equipment contained much that was unusual and bewildering. He was what *The Times* obituary notice of him sagely termed ' heterodox ' (*i.e.* homosexual), he had in many ways a pagan outlook, yet he had also a puritanical and religious outlook, which was inherent in his upbringing and sometimes dominated him. He had also, and above all, a belief in discovering the truth and following it. This comes out in the fascinating exchange of letters between him and Paul Claudel. Claudel, an authoritative authoritarian, had much that Gide believed himself to lack —more genius, more influence, more money, more will-power, more everything—and he tried to impose his formidable personality upon his correspondent, and to convert him to his own strongly-held views. He was a fisher of men. He cast his net. But the fish escaped. Wavering, yielding, tempted, flustered, Gide nevertheless slipped through the meshes and continued his undulating course upstream. *Il se sauva.* He saved himself instead of being saved, and left Paul Claudel planted on the bank.

Gide had not a great mind. But he had a free mind, and free minds are as rare as great, and even more valuable at the present moment. He has died at the age of eighty-one. No one could wish old people to live on in days like these, yet I wish he had found time to write me a promised letter on the subject of *Howards End.* Year after year I have heard through mutual friends that he was contemplating one. It would have been a precious and a provocative possession.

[1951]

Romain Rolland and the Hero

There died a couple of months ago a French writer who is of international importance. Whether he was a great writer is debatable, but he did address all humanity, not merely his own nation. Romain Rolland is not as celebrated to-day as he was a quarter of a century back, when he seemed to be of the first rank, and to have almost the stature of Tolstoy. There are two reasons for this decline in reputation. He did not fulfil his early promise as a novelist, the world did not fulfil his hopes; and he started out with passionate hopes. He became isolated, he was partly forgotten.

He was born in 1866. Although he came from the heart of France, and became a professor at Paris, he had strong Teutonic sympathies, which we must bear in mind if we are to understand him. He had an enormous admiration for German music, and for much German literature, and he cherished a rather Teutonic cult for the great man. With him, the cult was beneficent, for greatness, in his vision, meant not power over others, not dictator-ship, but creation, exploration. All the same, his life-long insist-ence on the Hero is not very French, and it has its distant parallel in the sinister cult which has produced Hitler. He combined hero worship with belief in the people, and by ' the people,' he meant not the stodgy ' common man ' who is being so boosted by our administrators to-day, but the people as a fiery instinc-tive emotional force, the people who made the French Revolu-tion. The ' hero ' and the ' people ' were his twin stars, and whenever they shine he sees his way through the uncongenial tangle of his century.

His most important work is the enormous novel, *John Chris-topher*. The theme of it is the hero as musician. There are ten volumes, and I can remember our excitement at the beginning of the century when they were coming out. We were full of hopes then, easily-held hopes, we did not know the severity of the problems which Fate was reserving for us, and the volumes were both civilised and inspiring, and how few books are both ! They were intensely human, they had integrity, they possessed the culture of the past, yet they proclaimed that culture is not time-bound or class-bound, it is a living spirit to be carried on. ' Have you read the latest *John Christopher*?' we were saying. ' Has he got to Paris yet?' As the series proceeded, our excitement slackened. However, the author pushed his great achievement through, and was awarded the Nobel Prize for literature in 1916. Romain Rolland had entered the first world-war. He was shattered by it to an extent which we can scarcely comprehend. To-day we are all of us tougher, and though we still cherish hopes they are protected by a very necessary crust of cynicism. We are no longer surprised. He—who had known what was best in Germany, and there was much good in that Germany—he, who was an inheritor of France, saw the two precious civilisations destroying each other, and the imperialism of Russia slinking up behind. While loyal to France, he became an internationalist, and a precursor of the League of Nations, and addressed to the youth of his country a pamphlet entitled *Above the Battle*.

> For the finer spirits of Europe there are two dwelling places : our earthly fatherland, and the City of God. Of the one we are the guests, of the other the builders. To the one let us give our lives and our faithful hearts ; but neither family, friend nor fatherland nor aught that we love has power over the spirit. The spirit is the light. It is our duty to lift it above tempests, and thrust aside the clouds that threaten to obscure it : to build higher and stronger, dominating the injustice and hatred of nations, the walls of that city wherein the souls of the whole world may assemble.

The title *Above the Battle* was unfortunate. It suggested that the writer felt himself superior to his fellows, and it annoyed people who were brave or vulgar-minded or both—and it is possible to be both. He became unpopular in his own country, and stayed for the rest of the war in Switzerland working on prisoners' relief. When peace came he had some further success as a dramatist. He had always been interested in a People's Theatre, where the people could be given what they understood and could participate in, and not what the upper classes thought nice for them. He had longed for the popular stage of ancient Greece to be reborn in the modern world. And he had himself written plays, dealing with mass-revolution and freedom (a play

on Danton, for instance), and some of these were performed,
under the direction of Reinhardt. But it is as the author of
John Christopher and *Above the Battle* that he is best remembered.

Romain Rolland knew and understood a great deal about
music, and whatever he says is worth reading. He wrote a long
and important work on Beethoven, also on Handel ; he could
appreciate composers as diverse from one another as Berlioz and
Hugo Wolf. He did not like Brahms—most Frenchmen and
many Germans do not—and he had only a contemptuous tolerance for Debussy. What he demanded was vitality, robustness
from which alone the mysterious filaments of the spirit can
sprout. He felt music as a breath from the vanished centuries,
to be transformed by our lungs into the song of the moment and
the prophecy of the future ; music is the god which each generation must make into flesh. It was the deepest thing for him,
and anyone who has felt its depth is bound to join in homage
to him. I am not qualified to say whether he is a sound musical
interpreter. He is certainly a thrilling one, and here is the
heart of him, without doubt. There is a scene in the opening
volume of *John Christopher* where the hero, still a baby, touches
the piano for the first time, and experiments in the marriage of
sounds. I have never come across a scene like it in literature,
for it is not merely poetic, not merely good child psychology :
it seems to take us inside a special chamber of the human spirit,
and make us co-creators.

The opening volumes of *John Christopher* are the best. They
take place in a little princely city of the old Germany, on the
banks of the Rhine. The child's forbears have been musicians
here for generations in a quiet way, but he himself is anything
but submissive and he does not fit in. The young Beethoven
is in the writer's mind, and he has supplied other details from
his own youth. Explosive, moody, inconsiderate, uncouth,
John Christopher is all the same good, affectionate, generous,
trustful. He suffers atrociously from poverty, and the cruelty
of his drunken father, and from fear of death which is only
tempered by his disgust at life. Violent longings, powers outside him shake him. His genius is recognised, but not fully
recognised : he is too large for the little town, and when he is
actually rude to its Grand Duke he is expelled and escapes to
France. In these early volumes we get, besides the impression
of genius and character, a brilliant and sympathetic account of

the old Germany which will never return ; we sit in little shops
and go for Sunday walks or to a performance at the local opera ;
we make love, with discretion, to this girl or that ; we are
narrow-minded and serious, and past us all the time flows the
Rhine. *Dawn* and *Morning* (volumes one and two) are delightful.
In volume five we get to Paris and the interest rather flags.
John Christopher's comments and escapades are less exciting and
his surroundings have lost their vividness. He discovers, after
a good deal of grumpiness, that Paris is not France, gets into touch
with the people, and makes close friends with a fine-natured
Frenchman, Olivier. By now he is famous, and there is a touching episode when he visits a provincial admirer—a humble and
sincere old man whom he has never seen. The visit is a success
—just a success ; we are on tenterhooks all the time lest it be
a failure, for the great musician is extremely irritable and the
humble old man is an admirer of Brahms, and a bit of a bore.

The final volume, *The New Day*, passes into mysticism. The
hero, mortally sick, finds himself fording a river which is partly
the Rhine of his youth, partly the river of death. The crossing
is hard, and on his shoulder is seated a child. Heavier grows
the burden, and from the bank he has left come cries of ' You'll
never succeed.' He stumbles, he is drowning—and then the
water becomes shallow. The sun rises. Bells burst into music,
and he reaches the further shore. John Christopher is saved.
And he has not merely saved himself. He is not just the artist.
He is Christopher the saint. He has carried on his shoulders,
through the troubles of our century, the divine spirit of man,
so that it may live and grow. ' Child, who are you ? ' he asks.
And the child answers, ' I am the day which is going to be born.'

I don't think the work will live like another French panorama-
novel of the period—the novel of Proust. It is too episodic and
diffuse, the conception sags, the satire is often journalistic and
the style flat. But Romain Rolland was a far bigger person than
Proust from the social and moral point of view ; he cared about
other people and tried to help them, he fought for a better world
constantly and passionately, and he moved across frontiers towards internationalism as surely as the Rhine moves through
Germany to the universal sea. He may be forgotten to-day,
but insight and sincerity such as his will return to a world which
needs them badly, and through other lips he will inspire youth
once more and clarify its hopes.   [1945]

A Whiff of D'Annunzio

Poet, hero, and cad, D'Annunzio presents a test problem to the Englishman. Byron, to whom he has been compared, was difficult enough, and was sent by us on a continental pilgrimage from which he has never returned. D'Annunzio is even more troublesome, since his poetry is more poetical than Byron's, his heroism more histrionic and his caddishness not an aristocratic freak but innate in his bones and bowels. And he has no sense of humour—the 'saving grace' as we are pleased to call it. Faced by such a problem, the Englishman becomes uncritical and unjust, thinks himself profound when he castigates and acute when he is merely being nasty, refuses to admit that an ill-bred egoist can be a genius and a leader of men, and suspects shoddiness because there is no underlying moral worth. D'Annunzio, a very great southerner, is not thus to be judged. His standards are not ours, and if we ask him to sign a suburban gentlemen's agreement he will impale us contemptuously upon the point of his pen as he did President Wilson. How are we to approach him ? His secretary and sometime publisher, Signor Tom Antongini, has written a book which may help us. It is not much of a book, but it breathes his atmosphere and accepts his ideals.

His leading passion was the Renaissance passion for earthly immortality. And he knew that immortality cannot be won by talking. Effort must accompany advertisement, and as a writer, a patriot, and a lover, he worked very hard. By the time he died he had a number of books to his credit, a still larger number of mistresses, and the city of Fiume. It is no small haul. It is a substantial hostage against oblivion. So long as Italy is Italy, he will not be forgotten. He, Paderewski, and T. E. Lawrence stand out as the three artists who achieved fame as men of action during the 1914–1918 war, and of the three he is the most spectacular. He will win the prize which he wanted and which he certainly deserves.

There is another prize—the silence that does not even say it is silent ; D'Annunzio knew nothing about that. In some words which were engraved in his retreat, the Vittoriale—words which his biographer accepts as mysterious but which we find muddled—he claims to approach the gods *Princeps et Praeco*, as a Prince and a Herald. He was always heralding, always heading some sumptuous embassy of his own creation, always clothing his actions in a gorgeous rhetoric which concealed them. Here again, he belongs to the garrulous, restless, processional Italian Renaissance. 'I go to awake the Dead,' cried the fifteenth-century scholar Cyriac of Ancona, meaning that he was getting on with his Greek studies. 'I go towards the Light,' cries D'Annunzio, meaning that he has ratted in the Chamber of Deputies from the Conservatives to the Socialists. The actions are not unimportant, the phrases are striking. But the Light, the Dead, remain as they were, in silence.

Signor Antongini, who was with him while he was writing *The Martyrdom of St. Sebastian*, is interesting in this connection. He suggests that that particular play was inspired not by religious mysticism but by a pair of female legs. D'Annunzio was full of spiritual ideas, but he could not use them until he had had the good fortune to see Ida Rubinstein dancing in a ballet. Then he exclaimed, ' Here are the legs of St. Sebastian for which I have been searching in vain all these years,' and poetry poured from his pen. No doubt the anecdote exaggerates, still it emphasises the point that his contacts with life were sensuous and local in their character ; certain gestures, certain limbs, certain spots of soil in the Abruzzi and elsewhere, served as jumping-off grounds for his art, and impelled him into orations about human destiny. Nothing he writes is profound. Yet he is never superficial, because he is excited by what he touches and sees, or hopes to touch. ' We ate oranges as if they were bread.' Why has this phrase, in its half-remembered Italian, lingered in my mind for nearly thirty years ? It is a phrase from his drama *The Dead City*, and, placed where he placed it, it brought out the taste of the newly picked fruit and the feeling of it between the lips and the teeth ; not pulp, not juice, but a unity, bread-like, divine. The characters—poor mortals, they had fallen in love as they should not—discussed such an orange amidst the aridities of Greece, and it passed as a tangible presence behind the veil of their prose, it lent importance to their fate, like the peaches and pears surrounding

a Crivelli Madonna.   There are several lists in Signor Antongini's tribute, which will repel the reader by their triviality
and expensiveness, yet he had better study them, because they
indicate D'Annunzio's aesthetic sources—lists of fruits, mottoes,
scents, horses, villas, women, dogs.   Most of these, including the
women, had to be renamed after the poet handled them, so that
he might have an additional sense of power.   They are defiled
by his possessiveness, but they are evidently necessary to his
art.

The women deserve particular attention, from Duse the Divine
down to poor Madame de B——, whose confessions fill an entire
chapter.   She describes her first and last visit to the poet's villa
at Florence.   ' On the pillar on the left I read " Beware of the
dog " and on that on the right " Beware of the master." ' Her
knees trembled, she rang the bell.   ' The first shock in store was
for my nostrils, the air was heavy with incense,' and before many
minutes she had been seduced.   A few minutes more, and she
was bowling away in a carriage lined like a coffin with roses.
She told Signor Antongini of her fall many years later.   It had
become her great, her tender memory.   He mentioned her name
with due discretion to his employer, who only said : ' Madame
de B——? I think I remember her vaguely.   She was at the
time of *La Figlia di Jorio*.'

By now we are well into the waters of the Mediterranean.
Our trouble is that, to the northerner, such an inscription as
' Beware of the dog—Beware of the master ' is essentially comic.
Yet neither Signor Antongini nor D'Annunzio nor Madame
de B—— finds anything funny in it or anything vulgar : it is
to them a cynical proclamation of virility, which she who ignores
ignores at her peril.   This makes them antipathetic, so we must
remind ourselves in conclusion that the Mediterranean is also the
sea of courage and of splendour.   D'Annunzio's courage is un-
questionable.   He possessed both grit and dash ; he could urge
Italy into the War, fight in the trenches, fly over Vienna, occupy
and administer Fiume against the approval of the Allies and of
his own Government, and he could watch his own appendix be
cut out under a local anaesthetic.   And his splendour—that too
is incontestable, although by our standards it is often encumbered
by *bric-à-brac*.   He could write like music, like scents, like religion,
like blood, like anything, he could sweep into the folds of his
magnificent prose whatever took his fancy, and then assert it was

sacred. There has been nobody like him. Fascism wisely accepted him after a little demur, and we had better do the same. We can anyhow hail him by two of the titles which he claims : poet and hero.

[1938]

The Complete Poems of C. P. Cavafy

The first English translation of Cavafy was made by Cavafy.
The occasion is over thirty years ago now, in his flat, 10 Rue
Lepsius, Alexandria ; his dusky family-furnished flat. He is back
from his work in a government office ; the Third Circle of
the Irrigation employs him as it might have employed many of
his heroes. I am back from my work, costumed in khaki ; the
British Red Cross employs me. We have been introduced by
an English friend, our meetings are rather dim, and Cavafy is
now saying with his usual gentleness, ' You could never understand my poetry, my dear Forster, never.' A poem is produced
—' The God Abandons Antony '—and I detect some coincidences
between its Greek and public school Greek. Cavafy is amazed.
' Oh, but this is good, my dear Forster, this is very good indeed,'
and he raises his hand, takes over, and leads me through. It
was not my knowledge that touched him but my desire to know
and to receive. He had no idea then that he could be widely
desired, even in the stumbling North. To be understood in
Alexandria and tolerated in Athens was the extent of his ambition.

Since that distant day, many other translators have had a
shot. The shooter most to my taste is George Valassopoulo.
He had the advantage of working with the poet and he has
brought much magic across ; Cavafy is largely magic. But
Valassopoulo only translated, and only wished to translate, some
of the poems. What was needed, and has been happily found,
is a translator for them all, for all the hundred and fifty-four of
them : Professor John Mavrogordato. This eminent scholar
has done a most valuable piece of work, lucid, faithful, intelligent ;
he has enabled us to read what Cavafy wanted to say, and to
read it in its proper perspective. For Cavafy as a historical poet,
or as an erotic poet, or an introspective one, would fail to convey
that Mediterranean complexity. We need all of him if we are
to understand anything.

All the poems are short. They are learned, sensuous, ironic,
civilised, sensitive, witty. Where's their centre ? Courage enters,
though not in an ordinary nor a reputable form. Cavafy

appreciates cowardice also, and likes the little men who can't be consistent or maintain their ideals, and can't know what is happening and have to dodge.

> Be afraid of grandeurs, O my soul;
> And if you cannot conquer your ambitions
> With hesitations always and precautions
> Follow them up.

Be afraid, if you are Caesar, of that obscure person in the crowd; he may be Artemidorus trying to warn you against death. Be afraid lest, into your comfortable flat, Pompey's head is carried on a trencher. Be afraid if, like Nero, you lie asleep, of the obscure tumblings in the cupboard; your little household gods are falling over each other in terror, because they, not you, can hear the approaching footsteps of the Erinyes. And if you are brave your courage is only genuine when, like those who fought at Thermopylae, you know you are certain to perish.

Courage and cowardice are equally interesting to his amoral mind, because he sees in both of them opportunities for sensation. What he envies is the power to snatch sensation, to triumph over the moment even if remorse ensues. Perhaps that physical snatching is courage; it is certainly the seed of exquisite memories and it is possibly the foundations of art. The amours of youth, even when disreputable, are delightful, thinks Cavafy, but the point of them is not that: the point is that they create the future, and may give to an ageing man in a Rue Lepsius perceptions he would never have known.

> The years of my youth, my life of pleasure—
> How clearly I see the meaning of them now.
> What unnecessary, what vain repentances . . .
> But I did not see the meaning then.

> Under the dissolute living of my youth
> Were being formed the intentions of my poetry,
> The province of my art was being planned.
> And that is why my repentances were never lasting.
> My resolutions to control myself, to change,
> Used to endure for two weeks at most.

The attitude recalls Proust's, but the temperament differs. Cavafy is never embittered, never the invalid. He is thankful to have lived, and 'Young men even now are repeating his verses. His visions pass before their lively eyes, and even now they are moved by his revelation of beauty.' He has something of the antique faith in fame. He is not a super-sensitive Frenchman. He is not English. He is not even British. Alexandria's his home.

> Environment, of house, of city centres, city quarters
> Which I look upon and where I walk ; years and years.
> I have created you in the midst of joy and in the midst of sorrows ;
> With so many circumstances, with so many things.
> And you have been made sensation, the whole of you, for me.

Alexandria is the city which he creates and over which he leans, meditative, when sorrows and triumphs recur ; the city over which Antony, nearly two thousand years before him, may have leant when the music sounded and the God abandoned him. It is in Alexandria that he died in 1933 at the age of seventy ; the Greek Hospital lay close by to receive him.

His material as a poet, then, begins with his own experiences and sensations : his interest in courage and cowardice and bodily pleasure, and so on. He begins from within. But he never makes a cult of himself or of what he feels. All the time he is being beckoned to and being called to by history, particularly by the history of his own race. History, too, is full of courage, cowardice, lust, and is to that extent domestic. But it is something more. It is an external inspiration. And he found in the expanses and recesses of the past, in the clash of great names and the tinkle of small ones, in the certified victories and slurred defeats, in the jewels and the wounds and the vast movements beginning out of nothing and sometimes ending nowhere : he found in them something that transcended his local life and freshened and strengthened his art. Demurely, ironically he looks into the past, for he knew the answers. Cleopatra did not win Actium. Julian did not reinstate paganism. Anna Comnena took the wrong side. The senate sit in state to receive the barbarians ; news comes that there are no more barbarians, so the senate have nothing to do. Sometimes there is a double irony ; the Prince from western Libya impresses the Alexandrians by his reticence and dignity ; he is actually a most ordinary youth, who dare not speak because of his awful Greek accent,

> and he suffered no little discomfort,
> Having whole conversations stacked inside him.

'Exactly what I feel in England,' a Greek friend remarked to me. The irony became triple as he spoke, and Cavafy would have appreciated this further turn of the screw.

There is however nothing patronising in his attitude to the past, nor have his cameos the aloofness of Hérédia. The warmth of the past enthralls him even more than its blunders, and he can give the sense of human flesh and blood continuing through centuries that are supposed to be unsatisfactory. A tomb here, an inscription there ; coloured glass worn by an Emperor and Empress at their coronation because they have no jewels. Sometimes the supernatural appears, and not always ominously : as in ' One of their Gods ', it may enrich voluptuousness :

> When one of them was passing through the market
> Of Seleukeia, about the hour of evenfall,
> Like a tall, a beautiful, a perfect youth,
> With the joy of incorruptibility in his eyes,
> With his black and perfumed hair,
> The passers-by would look at him,
> And one would ask another if he knew him,
> And if he was a Greek of Syria, or a stranger. But a few
> Who observed with greater attention
> Would understand and draw aside ;
> And while he disappeared under the arcades,
> In the shadows and in the lights of evening,
> Going towards the quarter which at night only
> Lives, with orgies and debauchery,
> And every kind of drunkenness and lust,
> They would wonder which it could be of Them,
> And for what disreputable sensuality
> He had come down to the streets of Seleukeia
> From those Majestical All-holy Mansions.

The idea that the Divine should descend to misbehave, so shocking to the Christian, comes naturally enough to a paganising Greek, and the poem (which I first knew in a Valassopoulo translation) sums up for me much that is characteristic. And how admirable is its construction ! Only two sentences, and the second one descending and descending until the final abrupt ascent.

His attitude to the past did not commend him to some of his contemporaries, nor is it popular to-day. He was a loyal Greek, but Greece for him was not territorial. It was rather the influence that has flowed from his race this way and that through the ages, and that (since Alexander the Great) has never disdained to mix with barbarism, has indeed desired to mix ;

the influence that made Byzantium a secular achievement. Racial purity bored him, so did political idealism. And he could be caustic about the claims of the tight-lipped little peninsula overseas. ' Aristocracy in modern Greece ? ' he once exclaimed. ' To be an aristocrat there is to have made a corner in coffee in the Peiraeus in 1849.' The civilisation he respected was a bastardy in which the Greek strain prevailed, and into which, age after age, outsiders would push, to modify and be modified. If the strain died out—never mind : it had done its work, and it would have left, far away upon some Asian upland, a coin of silver, stamped with the exquisite head of a Hellenising king. Pericles, Aristides, Themistocles, schoolroom tyrants : what did they know of this extension which is still extending, and which sometimes seemed (while he spoke) to connote the human race ?

Half humorously, half seriously, he once compared the Greeks and the English. The two peoples are almost exactly alike, he argued ; quick-witted, resourceful, adventurous. ' But there is one unfortunate difference between us, one little difference. We Greeks have lost our capital—and the results are what you see. Pray, my dear Forster, oh pray, that you never lose your capital.'

That was in 1918. British insolvency seemed impossible then. In 1951, when all things are possible, his words make one think —words of a very wise, very civilised man, words of a poet who has caught hold of something that cannot be taken away from him by bankruptcy, or even by death.

[1951]

Virginia Woolf

The Rede Lecture, delivered in the Senate House, Cambridge

When I was appointed to this lectureship the work of Virginia Woolf was much in my mind, and I asked to be allowed to speak on it. To speak on it, rather than to sum it up. There are two obstacles to a summing up. The first is the work's richness and complexity. As soon as we dismiss the legend of the Invalid Lady of Bloomsbury, so guilelessly accepted by Arnold Bennett, we find ourselves in a bewildering world where there are few headlines. We think of *The Waves* and say ' Yes —that is Virginia Woolf ': then we think of *The Common Reader*, where she is different, of *A Room of One's Own* or of the preface to *Life as we have known it* : different again. She is like a plant which is supposed to grow in a well-prepared garden bed—the bed of esoteric literature—and then pushes up suckers all over the place, through the gravel of the front drive, and even through the flagstones of the kitchen yard. She was full of interests, and their number increased as she grew older, she was curious about life, and she was tough, sensitive but tough. How can her achievement be summed up in an hour ? A headline sometimes serves a lecturer as a life-line on these occasions, and brings him safely into the haven where he would be. Shall I find one to-day ?

The second obstacle is that 1941 is not a good year in which to sum up anything. Our judgments, to put it mildly, are not at their prime. We are all of us upon the Leaning Tower, as she called it, even those of us who date from the nineteenth century, when the earth was still horizontal and the buildings perpendicular. We cannot judge the landscape properly as we look down, for everything is tilted. Isolated objects are not so puzzling ; a tree, a wave, a hat, a jewel, an old gentleman's bald head look much as they always did. But the relation between objects—that we cannot estimate, and that is why the verdict must be left to another generation. I have not the least faith that anything which we now value will survive historically (something which we should have valued may evolve, but that is a different proposition) ; and maybe another generation will dismiss Virginia Woolf as worthless and tiresome. However, this is not my opinion, nor I think yours ; we still have the word, and I wonder whether I cannot transmit some honour to her from the university she so admired, and from the central building of that university. She would receive the homage a little mockingly, for she was somewhat astringent over the academic position of women. ' What ? I in the Senate House ? ' she might say. ' Are you sure that is quite proper ? And why, if you want to discuss my books, need you first disguise yourselves in caps and gowns ? ' But I think she would be pleased. She loved Cambridge. Indeed, I cherish a private fancy that she once took her degree here. She, who could disguise herself as a member of the suite of the Sultan of Zanzibar, or black her face to go aboard a Dreadnought as an Ethiopian [1]—she could surely have hoaxed our innocent praelectors, and, kneeling in this very spot, have presented to the Vice-Chancellor the exquisite but dubious head of Orlando.

There is, after all, one little life-line to catch hold of : she liked writing.

These words, which usually mean so little, must be applied to her with all possible intensity. She liked receiving sensations —sights, sounds, tastes—passing them through her mind, where they encountered theories and memories, and then bringing them out again, through a pen, on to a bit of paper. Now began the higher delights of authorship. For these pen-marks on paper were only the prelude to writing, little more than marks on a wall. They had to be combined, arranged, emphasised here, eliminated there, new relationships had to be generated, new pen-marks born, until out of the interactions, something, one thing, one, arose. This one thing, whether it was a novel or an essay or a short story or a biography or a private paper to be read to her friends, was, if it was successful, itself analogous to a sensation. Although it was so complex and intellectual, although it might be large and heavy with facts, it was akin to the very simple things which had started it off, to the sights, sounds, tastes. It could be best described as we describe them. For it was not about something. It was something. This

---

[1] See Adrian Stephen, *The Dreadnought Hoax*. See, still more, an unpublished paper which she herself once wrote for a Women's Institute, leaving it helpless with laughter.

is obvious in ' aesthetic ' works, like *Kew Gardens* and *Mrs. Dalloway* ; it is less obvious in a work of learning, like the *Roger Fry*, yet here too the analogy holds. We know, from an article by R. C. Trevelyan, that she had, when writing it, a notion corresponding to the notion of a musical composition. In the first chapter she stated the themes, in the subsequent chapters she developed them separately, and she tried to bring them all in again at the end. The biography is duly about Fry. But it is something else too ; it is one thing, one.

She liked writing with an intensity which few writers have attained, or even desired. Most of them write with half an eye on their royalties, half an eye on their critics, and a third half eye on improving the world, which leaves them with only half an eye for the task on which she concentrated her entire vision. She would not look elsewhere, and her circumstances combined with her temperament to focus her. Money she had not to consider, because she possessed a private income, and though financial independence is not always a safeguard against commercialism, it was in her case. Critics she never considered while she was writing, although she could be attentive to them and even humble afterwards. Improving the world she would not consider, on the ground that the world is man-made, and that she, a woman, had no responsibility for the mess. This last opinion is a curious one, and I shall be returning to it ; still, she held it, it completed the circle of her defences, and neither the desire for money nor the desire for reputation nor philanthropy could influence her. She had a singleness of purpose which will not recur in this country for many years, and writers who have liked writing as she liked it have not indeed been common in any age.

Now the pitfall for such an author is obvious. It is the Palace of Art, it is that bottomless chasm of dullness which pretends to be a palace, all glorious with corridors and domes, but which is really a dreadful hole into which the unwary aesthete may tumble, to be seen no more. She has all the aesthete's characteristics : selects and manipulates her impressions ; is not a great creator of character ; enforces patterns on her books ; has no great cause at heart. So how did she avoid her appropriate pitfall and remain up in the fresh air, where we can hear the sound of the stable boy's boots, or boats bumping, or Big Ben ; where we can taste really new bread, and touch real dahlias ?

She had a sense of humour, no doubt, but our answer must go a little deeper than that hoary nostrum. She escaped, I think, because she liked writing for fun. Her pen amused her, and in the midst of writing seriously this other delight would spurt through. A little essay, called *On being Ill*, exemplifies this. It starts with the thesis that illness in literature is seldom handled properly (de Quincey and Proust were exceptional), that the body is treated by novelists as if it were a sheet of glass through which the soul gazes, and that this is contrary to experience. There are possibilities in the thesis, but she soon wearies of exploring them. Off she goes amusing herself, and after half a dozen pages she is writing entirely for fun, caricaturing the type of people who visit sick-rooms, insisting that Augustus Hare's *Two Noble Lives* is the book an invalid most demands, and so on. She could describe illness if she chose—for instance, in *The Voyage Out*—but she gaily forgets it in *On being Ill*. The essay is slight, still it does neatly illustrate the habit of her mind. Literature was her merry-go-round as well as her study. This makes her amusing to read, and it also saves her from the Palace of Art. For you cannot enter the Palace of Art, therein to dwell, if you are tempted from time to time to play the fool. Lord Tennyson did not consider that. His remedy, you remember, was that the Palace would be purified when it was inhabited by all mankind, all behaving seriously at once. Virginia Woolf found a simpler and a sounder solution.

No doubt there is a danger here—there is danger everywhere. She might have become a glorified diseuse, who frittered away her broader effects by mischievousness, and she did give that impression to some who met her in the flesh ; there were moments when she could scarcely see the busts for the moustaches she pencilled on them, and when the bust was a modern one, whether of a gentleman in a top hat or of a youth on a pylon, it had no chance of remaining sublime. But in her writing, even in her light writing, central control entered. She was master of her complicated equipment, and though most of us like to write sometimes seriously and sometimes in fun, few of us can so manage the two impulses that they speed each other up, as hers did.

The above remarks are more or less introductory. It seems convenient now to recall what she did write, and to say a little about her development. She began back in 1915 with *The*

Voyage Out—a strange, tragic, inspired novel about English tourists in an impossible South American hotel ; her passion for truth is here already, mainly in the form of atheism, and her passion for wisdom is here in the form of music. The book made a deep impression upon the few people who read it. Its successor, *Night and Day*, disappointed them. This is an exercise in classical realism, and contains all that has characterised English fiction, for good and evil, during the last two hundred years : faith in personal relations, recourse to humorous side-shows, geographical exactitude, insistence on petty social differences : indeed most of the devices she so gaily derides in *Mr. Bennett and Mrs. Brown*. The style has been normalised and dulled. But at the same time she published two short stories, *Kew Gardens*, and *The Mark on the Wall*. These are neither dull nor normal ; lovely little things ; her style trails after her as she walks and talks, catching up dust and grass in its folds, and instead of the precision of the earlier writing we have something more elusive than had yet been achieved in English. Lovely little things, but they seemed to lead nowhere, they were all tiny dots and coloured blobs, they were an inspired breathlessness, they were a beautiful droning or gasping which trusted to luck. They were perfect as far as they went, but that was not far, and none of us guessed that out of the pollen of those flowers would come the trees of the future. Consequently when *Jacob's Room* appeared in 1922 we were tremendously surprised. The style and sensitiveness of *Kew Gardens* remained, but they were applied to human relation- ships, and to the structure of society. The blobs of colour continue to drift past, but in their midst, interrupting their course like a closely sealed jar, stands the solid figure of a young man. The improbable has occurred ; a method essentially poetic and apparently trifling has been applied to fiction. She was still uncertain of the possibilities of the new technique, and *Jacob's Room* is an uneven little book, but it represents her great departure, and her abandonment of the false start of *Night and Day*. It leads on to her genius in its fullness ; to *Mrs. Dalloway* (1925), *To the Lighthouse* (1927), and *The Waves* (1931). These successful works are all suffused with poetry and enclosed in it. *Mrs. Dalloway* has the framework of a London summer's day, down which go spiralling two fates : the fate of the sensitive worldly hostess, and the fate of the sensitive obscure maniac ; though they never touch they are closely connected, and at the same moment we lose sight of them both. It is a civilised book, and it was written from personal experience. In her work, as in her private problems, she was always civilised and sane on the subject of madness. She pared the edges off this particular malady, she tied it down to being a malady, and robbed it of the evil magic it has acquired through timid or careless thinking ; here is one of the gifts we have to thank her for. *To the Lighthouse* is, however, a much greater achievement, partly because the chief characters in it, Mr. and Mrs. Ramsay, are so interesting. They hold us, we think of them away from their surroundings, and yet they are in accord with those surroundings, with the poetic scheme. *To the Lighthouse* is in three movements. It has been called a novel in sonata form, and certainly the slow central section, conveying the passing of time, does demand a musical analogy. We have, when reading it, the rare pleasure of inhabiting two worlds at once, a pleasure only art can give : the world where a little boy wants to go to a lighthouse but never manages it until, with changed emotions, he goes there as a young man ; and the world where there is pattern, and this world is emphasised by passing much of the observation through the mind of Lily Briscoe, who is a painter. Then comes *The Waves*. Pattern here is supreme—indeed it is italicised. And between the motions of the sun and the waters, which preface each section, stretch, without interruption, conversation, words in inverted commas. It is a strange conversation, for the six characters, Bernard, Nevill, Louis, Susan, Jinny, Rhoda, seldom address one another, and it is even possible to regard them (like Mrs. Dalloway and Septimus) as different facets of one single person. Yet they do not conduct internal monologues, they are in touch amongst themselves, and they all touch the character who never speaks, Percival. At the end, most perfectly balancing their scheme, Bernard, the would-be novelist, sums up, and the pattern fades out. *The Waves* is an extraordinary achievement, an immense extension of the possibilities of *Kew Gardens* and *Jacob's Room*. It is trembling on the edge. A little less—and it would lose its poetry. A little more—and it would be over into the abyss, and be dull and arty. It is her greatest book, though *To the Lighthouse* is my favourite.

It was followed by *The Years*. This is another experiment in the realistic tradition. It chronicles the fortunes of a family through a documented period. As in *Night and Day*, she deserts poetry, and again she fails. But in her posthumous novel *Between the Acts* she returns to the method she understood. Its theme is a village pageant, which presents the entire history of England, and into which, at the close, the audience is itself drawn, to continue that history ; ' The curtain rose ' is its concluding phrase. The conception is poetic, and the text of the pageant is mostly written in verse. She loved her country —the country that is the countryside, and emerges from the unfathomable past. She takes us back in this exquisite final tribute, and she points us on, and she shows us through her poetic vagueness something more solid than patriotic history, and something better worth dying for.

Amongst all this fiction, nourishing it and nourished by it, grow other works. Two volumes of *The Common Reader* show the breadth of her knowledge and the depth of her literary sympathy ; let anyone who thinks her an exquisite recluse read what she says on Jack Mytton the foxhunter. As a critic she could enter into anything—anything lodged in the past, that is to say ; with her contemporaries she sometimes had difficulties. Then there are the biographies, fanciful and actual. *Orlando* is, I need hardly say, an original book, and the first part of it is splendidly written : the description of the Great Frost is already received as a ' passage ' in English literature, whatever a passage may be. After the transformation of sex things do not go so well ; the authoress seems unconvinced by her own magic and somewhat fatigued by it, and the biography finishes competently rather than brilliantly ; it has been a fancy on too large a scale, and we can see her getting bored. But *Flush* is a complete success, and exactly what it sets out to be ; the material, the method, the length, accord perfectly, it is doggie without being silly, and it does give us, from the altitude of the carpet or the sofa-foot, a peep at high poetic personages, and a new angle on their ways. The biography of Roger Fry—one should not proceed direct from a spaniel to a Slade Professor, but Fry would not have minded and spaniels mind nothing—reveals a new aspect of her powers, the power to suppress herself. She indulges in a pattern, but she never intrudes her personality or overhandles her English ; respect for her subject dominates her, and only occasionally—as in her description of the divinely ordered chaos of Fry's studio with its still-life of apples and eggs labelled ' please do not touch '—does she allow her fancy to play.

Biographies are too often described as 'labours of love,' but the *Roger Fry* really is in this class ; one artist is writing with affection of another, so that he may be remembered and may be justified.

Finally, there are the feminist books—*A Room of One's Own* and *Three Guineas*—and several short essays, etc., some of them significant. It is as a novelist that she will be judged. But the rest of her work must be remembered, partly on its merits, partly because (as William Plomer has pointed out) she is sometimes more of a novelist in it than in her novels.

After this survey, we can state her problem. Like most novelists worth reading, she strays from the fictional norm. She dreams, designs, jokes, invokes, observes details, but she does not tell a story or weave a plot, and—can she create character ? That is her problem's centre. That is the point where she felt herself open to criticism—to the criticisms, for instance, of her friend Hugh Walpole. Plot and story could be set aside in favour of some other unity, but if one is writing about human beings, one does want them to seem alive. Did she get her people to live ?

Now there seem to be two sorts of life in fiction, life on the page, and life eternal. Life on the page she could give ; her characters never seem unreal, however slight or fantastic their lineaments, and they can be trusted to behave appropriately. Life eternal she could seldom give ; she could seldom so portray a character that it was remembered afterwards on its own account, as Emma is remembered, for instance, or Dorothea Casaubon, or Sophia and Constance in *The Old Wives' Tale*. What wraiths, apart from their context, are the wind-sextet from *The Waves*, or Jacob away from *Jacob's Room* ! They speak no more to us or to one another as soon as the page is turned. And this is her great difficulty. Holding on with one hand to poetry, she stretches and stretches to grasp things which are best gained by letting go of poetry. She would not let go, and I think she was quite right, though critics who like a novel to be a novel will disagree. She was quite right to cling to her specific gift, even if this entailed sacrificing something else vital to her art. And she did not always have to sacrifice ; Mr. and Mrs. Ramsay do remain with the reader afterwards, and so perhaps do Rachel from *The Voyage Out*, and Clarissa Dalloway. For the rest—it is impossible to maintain that here is an immortal portrait gallery. Socially she is limited to the upper-middle professional classes, and she does not even employ many types. There is the bleakly honest intellectual (St. John Hirst, Charles Tansley, Louis, William Dodge), the monumental majestic hero (Jacob, Percival), the pompous amorous pillar of society (Richard Dalloway as he appears in *The Voyage Out*, Hugh Whitbread), the scholar who cares only for young men (Bonamy, Neville), the pernickety independent (Mr. Pepper, Mr. Banks) ; even the Ramsays are tried out first as the Ambroses. As soon as we understand the nature of her equipment, we shall see that as regards human beings she did as well as she could. Belonging to the world of poetry, but fascinated by another world, she is always stretching out from her enchanted tree and snatching bits from the flux of daily life as they float past, and out of these bits she builds novels. She would not plunge. And she should not have plunged. She might have stayed folded up in her tree singing little songs like *Blue-Green* in the *Monday or Tuesday* volume, but fortunately for English literature she did not do this either.

So that is her problem. She is a poet, who wants to write something as near to a novel as possible.

I must pass on to say a little—it ought to be much—about her interests. I have emphasised her fondness for writing both seriously and in fun, and have tried to indicate how she wrote : how she gathered up her material and digested it without damaging its freshness, how she rearranged it to form unities, how she was a poet who wanted to write novels, how these novels bear upon them the marks of their strange gestation— some might say the scars. What concerns me now is the material itself, her interests, her opinions. And not to be too vague I will begin with food.

It is always helpful, when reading her, to look out for the passages which describe eating. They are invariably good. They are a sharp reminder that here is a woman who is alert sensuously. She had an enlightened greediness which gentlemen themselves might envy, and which few masculine writers have expressed. There is a little too much lamp oil in George Meredith's wine, a little too much paper crackling on Charles Lamb's pork, and no savour whatever in any dish of Henry James', but when Virginia Woolf mentions nice things they get right into our mouths, so far as the edibility of print permits. We taste their deliciousness. And when they are not nice, we taste them equally, our mouths awry now with laughter. I will

not torture this great university of Oxbridge by reminding it of
the exquisite lunch which she ate in a don's room here in the
year 1929 ; such memories are now too painful. Nor will I
insult the noble college of women in this same university—
Fernham is its name—by reminding it of the deplorable dinner
which she ate that same evening in its Hall—a dinner so lowering
that she had to go to a cupboard afterwards and drink something
out of a bottle ; such memories may still be all too true to fact.
But I may without offence refer to the great dish of Bœuf en
Daube which forms the centre of the dinner of union in *To the
Lighthouse*, the dinner round which all that section of the book
coheres, the dinner which exhales affection and poetry and
loveliness, so that all the characters see the best in one another
at last and for a moment, and one of them, Lily Briscoe, carries
away a recollection of reality. Such a dinner cannot be built
on a statement beneath a dish-cover which the novelist is too
indifferent or incompetent to remove. Real food is necessary,
and this, in fiction as in her home, she knew how to provide.
The Bœuf en Daube, which had taken the cook three days to
make and had worried Mrs. Ramsay as she did her hair, stands
before us ' with its confusion of savoury brown and yellow
meats and its bay leaves and its wine ' ; we peer down the shiny
walls of the great casserole and get one of the best bits, and like
William Banks, generally so hard to please, we are satisfied.
Food with her was not a literary device put in to make the book
seem real. She put it in because she tasted it, because she saw
pictures, because she smelt flowers, because she heard Bach,
because her senses were both exquisite and catholic, and were
always bringing her first-hand news of the outside world. Our
debt to her is in part this : she reminds us of the importance of
sensation in an age which practises brutality and recommends
ideals. I could have illustrated sensation more reputably by
quoting the charming passage about the florists' shop in *Mrs.
Dalloway*, or the passage where Rachel plays upon the cabin
piano. Flowers and music are conventional literary adjuncts.
A good feed isn't, and that is why I preferred it and chose it to
represent her reactions. Let me add that she smokes, and now
let the Bœuf en Daube be carried away. It will never come
back in our lifetime. It is not for us. But the power to
appreciate it remains, and the power to appreciate all distinction.
    After the senses, the intellect. She respected knowledge, she

believed in wisdom. Though she could not be called an optimist, she had, very profoundly, the conviction that mind is in action against matter, and is winning new footholds in the void. That anything would be accomplished by her or in her generation, she did not suppose, but the noble blood from which she sprang encouraged her to hope. Mr. Ramsay, standing by the geraniums and trying to think, is not a figure of fun. Nor is this university, despite its customs and costumes : she speaks of ' the light shining there—the light of Cambridge.'

No light shines now from Cambridge visibly, and this prompts the comment that her books were conditioned by her period. She could not assimilate this latest threat to our civilisation. The submarine perhaps. But not the flying fortress or the land mine. The idea that all stone is like grass, and like all flesh may vanish in a twinkling, did not enter into her consciousness, and indeed it will be some time before it can be assimilated by literature. She belonged to an age which distinguished sharply between the impermanency of man and the durability of his monuments, and for whom the dome of the British Museum Reading Room was almost eternal. Decay she admitted : the delicate grey churches in the Strand would not stand for ever ; but she supposed, as we all did, that decay would be gradual. The younger generation—the Auden-Isherwood generation as it is convenient to call it—saw more clearly here than could she, and she did not quite do justice to its vision, any more than she did justice to its experiments in technique—she who had been in her time such an experimenter. Still, to belong to one's period is a common failing, and she made the most of hers. She respected and acquired knowledge, she believed in wisdom. Intellectually, no one can do more ; and since she was a poet, not a philosopher or a historian or a prophetess, she had not to consider whether wisdom will prevail and whether the square upon the oblong, which Rhoda built out of the music of Mozart, will ever stand firm upon this distracted earth. The square upon the oblong. Order. Justice. Truth. She cared for these abstractions, and tried to express them through symbols, as an artist must, though she realised the inadequacy of symbols.

They come with their violins, said Rhoda ; they wait ; count ; nod ; down come their bows. And there is ripples and laughter like the dance of olive trees. . . .

' Like ' and ' like ' and ' like '—but what is the thing that
lies beneath the semblance of the thing ?   Now that lightning
has gashed the tree and the flowering branch has fallen . . .
let me see the thing.   There is a square.   There is an oblong.
The players take the square and place it upon the oblong.
They place it very accurately ; they make a perfect dwelling-
place.   Very little is left outside.   The structure is now visible ;
what is inchoate is here stated ; we are not so various or so
mean ; we have made oblongs and stood them upon squares.
This is our triumph ; this is our consolation.

The consolation, that is to say, of catching sight of abstractions.
They have to be symbolised, and ' the square upon the oblong '
is as much a symbol as the dancing olive trees, but because of
its starkness it comes nearer to conveying what she seeks.
Seeking it, ' we are not so various or so mean ' ; we have added
to the human heritage and reaffirmed wisdom.
The next of her interests which has to be considered is society.
She was not confined to sensations and intellectualism.   She
was a social creature, with an outlook both warm and shrewd.
But it was a peculiar outlook, and we can best get at it by looking at a very peculiar side of her : her feminism.
Feminism inspired one of the most brilliant of her books—
the charming and persuasive *A Room of One's Own* ; it contains
the Oxbridge lunch and the Fernham dinner, also the immortal
encounter with the beadle when she tried to walk on the college
grass, and the touching reconstruction of Shakespeare's sister—
Shakespeare's equal in genius, but she perished because she had
no position or money, and that has been the fate of women
through the ages.   But feminism is also responsible for the
worst of her books—the cantankerous *Three Guineas*—and for
the less successful streaks in *Orlando*.   There are spots of it all
over her work, and it was constantly in her mind.   She was
convinced that society is man-made, that the chief occupations
of men are the shedding of blood, the making of money, the
giving of orders, and the wearing of uniforms, and that none
of these occupations is admirable.   Women dress up for fun or
prettiness, men for pomposity, and she had no mercy on the
judge in his wig, the general in his bits and bobs of ribbon, the
bishop in his robes, or even on the harmless don in his gown.
She felt that all these mummers were putting something across

over which women had never been consulted, and which she at any rate disliked. She declined to co-operate, in theory, and sometimes in fact. She refused to sit on committees or to sign appeals, on the ground that women must not condone this tragic male-made mess, or accept the crumbs of power which men throw them occasionally from their hideous feast. Like Lysistrata, she withdrew.

In my judgment there is something old-fashioned about this extreme feminism ; it dates back to her suffragette youth of the 1910's, when men kissed girls to distract them from wanting the vote, and very properly provoked her wrath. By the 1930's she had much less to complain of, and seems to keep on grumbling from habit. She complained, and rightly, that though women to-day have won admission into the professions and trades they usually encounter a male conspiracy when they try to get to the top. But she did not appreciate that the conspiracy is weakening yearly, and that before long women will be quite as powerful for good or evil as men. She was sensible about the past ; about the present she was sometimes unreasonable. However, I speak as a man here, and as an elderly one. The best judges of her feminism are neither elderly men nor even elderly women, but young women. If they, if the students of Fernham, think that it expresses an existent grievance, they are right.

She felt herself to be not only a woman but a lady, and this gives a further twist to her social outlook. She made no bones about it. She was a lady, by birth and upbringing, and it was no use being cowardly about it, and pretending that her mother had turned a mangle, or that her father Sir Leslie had been a plasterer's mate. Working-class writers often mentioned their origins, and were respected for doing so. Very well ; she would mention hers. And her snobbery—for she was a snob—has more courage in it than arrogance. It is connected with her insatiable honesty, and is not, like the snobbery of Clarissa Dalloway, bland and frilled and unconsciously sinking into the best arm-chair. It is more like the snobbery of Kitty when she goes to tea with the Robsons ; it stands up like a target for anyone to aim at who wants to. In her introduction to *Life as we have known it* (a collection of biographies of working-class women edited by Margaret Llewellyn Davies) she faces the fire. ' One could not be Mrs. Giles of Durham, because one's body had never stood at the wash-tub ; one's hands had never wrung and scrubbed and chopped up whatever the meat is that makes a miner's supper.' This is not disarming, and it is not intended to disarm. And if one said to her that she could after all find out what meat a miner does have for his supper if she took a little trouble, she would retort that this wouldn't help her to chop it up, and that it is not by knowing things but by doing things that one enters into the lives of people who do things. And she was not going to chop up meat. She would chop it badly, and waste her time. She was not going to wring and scrub when what she liked doing and could do was write. To murmurs of ' Lucky lady you ! ' she replied, ' I am a lady,' and went on writing. ' There aren't going to be no more ladies. 'Ear that ? ' She heard. Without rancour or surprise or alarm, she heard, and drove her pen the faster. For if, as seems probable, these particular creatures are to be extinguished, how important that the last of them should get down her impressions of the world and unify them into a book ! If she didn't, no one else would. Mrs. Giles of Durham wouldn't. Mrs. Giles would write differently, and might write better, but she could not produce The Waves, or a life of Roger Fry.

There is an admirable hardness here, so far as hardness can be admirable. There is not much sympathy, and I do not think she was sympathetic. She could be charming to individuals, working-class and otherwise, but it was her curiosity and her honesty that motivated her. And we must remember that sympathy, for her, entailed a tremendous and exhausting process, not lightly to be entered on. It was not a half-crown or a kind word or a good deed or a philanthropic sermon or a godlike gesture ; it was adding the sorrows of another to one's own. Half fancifully, but wholly seriously, she writes :

> But sympathy we cannot have. Wisest Fate says no. If her children, weighted as they already are with sorrow, were to take on them that burden too, adding in imagination other pains to their own, buildings would cease to rise ; roads would peter out into grassy tracks ; there would be an end of music and of painting ; one great sigh alone would rise to Heaven, and the only attitudes for men and women would be those of horror and despair.

Here perhaps is the reason why she cannot be warmer and more human about Mrs. Giles of Durham.

This detachment from the working-classes and Labour re-inforces the detachment caused by her feminism, and her attitude to society was in consequence aloof and angular. She was fascinated, she was unafraid, but she detested mateyness, and she would make no concessions to popular journalism, and the ' let's all be friendly together' stunt. To the crowd—so far as such an entity exists—she was very jolly, but she handed out no bouquets to the middlemen who have arrogated to themselves the right of interpreting the crowd, and get paid for doing so in the daily press and on the wireless. These middlemen form after all a very small clique—larger than the Bloomsbury they so tirelessly denounce, but a mere drop in the ocean of humanity. And since it was a drop whose distinction was proportionate to its size, she saw no reason to conciliate it.

' And now to sum up,' says Bernard in the last section of *The Waves*. That I cannot do, for reasons already given ; the material is so rich and contradictory, and ours is not a good vintage year for judgments. I have gone from point to point as best I could, from her method of writing to her books, from her problems as a poet-novelist to her problems as a woman and as a lady. And I have tried to speak of her with the directness which she would wish, and which could alone honour her. But how are all the points to be combined ? What is the pattern resultant ? The best I can do is to quote Bernard again. ' The illusion is upon me,' he says, ' that something adheres for a moment, has roundness, weight, depth, is completed. This, for the moment, seems to be her life.' Bernard puts it well. But, as Rhoda indicated in that earlier quotation, these words are only similes, comparisons with physical substances, and what one wants is the thing that lies beneath the semblance of the thing ; that alone satisfies, that alone makes the full statement.

Whatever the final pattern, I am sure it will not be a depressing one. Like all her friends, I miss her greatly—I knew her ever since she started writing. But this is a personal matter, and I am sure that there is no case for lamentation here, or for the obituary note. Virginia Woolf got through an immense amount of work, she gave acute pleasure in new ways, she pushed the light of the English language a little further against darkness. Those are facts. The epitaph of such an artist cannot be written by the vulgar-minded or by the lugubrious. They will try, indeed they have already tried, but their words make no sense.

It is wiser, it is safer, to regard her career as a triumphant one. She triumphed over what are primly called ' difficulties,' and she also triumphed in the positive sense : she brought in the spoils. And sometimes it is as a row of little silver cups that I see her work gleaming. ' These trophies,' the inscription runs, ' were won by the mind from matter, its enemy and its friend.'

[1941]

Two Books by T. S. Eliot

I

NOTES TOWARDS THE DEFINITION OF CULTURE

There is T. S. Eliot who is a poet, and there are also two Mr. Eliots who write criticism. The poet does not enter into this particular volume ; his great achievement lies elsewhere, and it has been awarded the highest possible honours, both in this country and abroad.

The two critics do enter. They dominate the scene, and although they never contradict one another there is a difference between them which must be noted. They differ according to the audiences they address. Most of the book is addressed to sophisticated and highly educated people, and it is, on the whole, not satisfactory. At the end of it, three broadcasts are printed ; these were intended for popular audiences and they are a success. It would seem that when Mr. Eliot is wishing to instruct his prose remains lucid, considerate and assured ; his excellent hand-book on Dante is an example of this. When on the other hand he is writing for people who may answer him back, he becomes wary and loads his sentences with qualifications and precautions which make them heavy. The very title of the book is ominous. It is not about culture nor about a definition of culture, nor does it even offer notes on a definition. It offers ' notes towards the definition.' By its caution and astuteness the title forestalls many possible objections. But what cumbersome English !

The broadcasts were intended for a German-speaking audience, and were translated into German for that purpose. In the first of them, Mr. Eliot speaks of the unity of European culture, and ascribes the richness of English to our continental connection. In the second, he describes the break-up of European culture during the last twenty years, and refers to the *Criterion*, the admirable review which he once edited. The third broadcast is the least satisfactory, because he advances in it towards a definition of culture, and then retires without making it clear how far he has been. Culture is connected with the family, if we interpret the family rightly.   It is also connected—in certain circumstances—with much else.   It is assuredly connected with Christianity.   Here we reach firmer ground.   We feel—and he would wish us to feel—that his religious faith is more important to him than anything else, and that art and literature are only valid in their relation to it.   The relation may be negative : 'only a Christian culture could have produced Voltaire and Nietzsche.'   But as far as Europe is concerned the relation must exist.   Where there is not Christianity there is nothing.   And it has to be Christianity of an approved type : Mr. Eliot grows increasingly theological.   Smartly over the knuckles does he rap a certain book called *The Churches Survey Their Task.*   They surveyed it wrongly.   The rap occurs in the main body of the work.   Here we may pursue, in greater detail and with superior caution, the ideas exposed in the broadcasts.   There is much that is subtle and profound, much that is provocative, and we are bound to admit at the end that culture is even more important than we guessed.   Unfortunately she has not become more accessible.   Through the criss-cross of reservations and postulates we can scarcely catch sight of her outline, or see where she is going.

The book is prefaced by a quotation from Lord Acton : 'I think our studies ought to be all but purposeless.'   The quotation does not seem appropriate in view of Mr. Eliot's purposeful interest in polemical Christianity.   Acton, too, was a deeply religious man.   But he was also a convinced liberal, and Mr. Eliot, for all his many-sidedness, cannot be described as that.

[1949]

2

THE COCKTAIL PARTY. A COMEDY

A comedy where one of the characters is crucified on an ant-hill is not comic in the usual sense of the word, and readers of *The Cocktail Party* will do well to arm themselves against difficulties.   On the stage, those difficulties may diminish : the play was well received when it was produced at the Edinburgh Festival last year, and it is having a tremendous success in New York.   The faces and voices and clothes of the characters may help to establish a perspective which is unobtainable through words.

Where does the mere reader find himself?

In an operating-theatre—a spiritual one. He has realised in the first act that something is wrong with some of the characters, perhaps with all of them ; they chatter miserably and endlessly, and drink unprofitably, and Lavinia, the wife who should be helping Edward her husband to throw the party, has just deserted him. In the second act the reader gets a dramatic surprise —his big laugh, if the phrase be permissible. He discovers that three of the worthless guests were really doctors, who were mingling with their unsuspecting patients in order to gather information about them. Surgeon-in-chief is Sir Henry Harcourt-Reilly, previously an anonymous buffoon and now enthroned in his consulting room. With him work Julia, previously mistaken for an ill-natured feckless old woman, and Alex, mistaken for a globe-trotter with pseudo-connections which turn out to be genuine. The patients arrive. Edward and Lavinia are confronted with one another, to their mutual indignation, and the similarity of their cases emphasised. They are refused any spectacular cure. They are followed by Celia, the girl with whom Edward has intrigued. Celia's position is different, is unique. She has a sense of sin—not for anything specific, but a general sense, and she desires to ' atone.' A way is pointed out to her, and accepted by her, no fee is charged her, and she is assigned to a ' sanatorium ' the outcome of which no one can foresee, not even the experts. A fourth patient is expected, but he is too much immersed in worldliness, and does not come. The act ends in a solemn and touching libation to the safety of Celia. It has become clear to the reader that he is actually in the presence of the Church, which is directing its children, through its priesthood, on their appropriate paths.

In the third act he learns what has happened. Edward and Lavinia are reconciled, are living together happily and civilly in their old flat, and are about to throw yet another cocktail party. It is the best they can achieve. Their quarrel was not important, nor is their reconciliation. The worldly young man has become still more worldly. As for Celia, we hear that she has chosen the path of Devotion and Dedication, has become a nurse and a nun, and has perished agonisingly amongst savages. Her sufferings are dwelt on, are indeed gloated over, and no doubt this is consonant with the author's religious outlook and with his ' comedy.' But aesthetically, the sufferings disturb the reader and distract him. The Christian ethic of atonement, which has been impending over his head since the end of the second act, comes down with too sudden a bump. He hears the doctor-priests analysing the successful martyrdom as they sip their drinks, and he wonders.

The difficulties of *The Cocktail Party* do not extend to its diction. It is most beautifully and lucidly written. T. S. Eliot can do whatever he likes with the English language. This time he has selected a demure chatty verse-form which seems to be like prose, but it is full of turns and subtle echoes, and always open for the emotional intensity he occasionally needs. On the stage, such diction may well carry all before it, and, reinforced by sound stage-craft, may place affairs in a less puzzling perspective.

[1950]

The Ascent of F.6

This play is not easy to focus. It is short and straightforward, yet at least four pairs of spectacles are necessary before we can examine it properly. Let us start by looking at it through a heroic pair.

Behold Michael Ransom, known to his friends as M. F. ! He is a gifted, sensitive, ascetic, altruistic mountaineer, who crowns a noble life with a glorious death. Aeroplanes locate his body on the summit of the virgin peak known as F.6, which he alone has scaled. His body perishes, his name liveth for evermore. A national hero, akin to Colonel Lawrence in temperament aud to Captain Scott in fate—that is what we see through this pair of spectacles, but the play is by Messrs. Auden and Isherwood, and the spectacles soon slip off the nose and smash into nasty splinters. Try another pair.

Try the politico-economic outlook. F.6 now appears to be situated on the boundary of two colonies, British Sudoland and Ostnian Sudoland, and the expedition to scale it is really a political ramp. The British and the Ostnians are racing one another to the top, for reasons of prestige, and if the British lose they will have trouble with the natives down in the coffee plantations, and no dividends. Thus viewed, the play becomes a satire of familiar type, the type instituted over thirty years ago by Hilaire Belloc in his brilliant novel *Mr. Burden*. The situation is old, the machinery up to date, for Auden and Isherwood can show us the working up of public opinion through broadcasting. Little Mr. and Mrs. Everyman in their poky flat—they are caught by the F.6 propaganda, they listen spellbound to the important personages who come to the microphone ; as they hear about the terrible mountain and the glorious young man, their own lives become less drab and boring, and they actually dash off and have a week-end at Hove, though they can ill afford it, as they realise on their return. ' He belongs to *us* now,' they cry, as they gaze at the obelisk erected to Ransom, after his death, by Big Business. Sudoland is safe. The natives work. The coffee comes. The curtain falls.

But focus again; this time upon Ransom himself. F.6 now appears as a test for his character, which he fails to surmount. He suffers from the last infirmity of noble minds: thinking he pursues virtue and knowledge, he really pursues power. And at the crisis, in the nightmare-cloud on the summit, he sees that his motive has been impure, and, as evidence of this, the ghosts of the friends whom he has killed. He has sacrificed them in devoting himself. He had tried to turn back, but as soon as he set foot on the mountain all were doomed.

Why is F.6 so fatal? Chormopuloda the natives call it, and it is haunted by a demon, they say. There is a monastery by the upper glacier, and the monks there spend their time less idly than might be supposed, restraining the demon by their meditations from irrupting on to the plains. The abbot explains to Ransom that the demon takes different forms for its temptations; he does not reveal that to Ransom himself it will take the form of his own mother. Mrs. Ransom has appeared earlier in the play. It is she who made her son go, when he shrank from the temptation of power. She wants him to be brave, for her sake, and to be happy, provided she supervises his happiness. Cornelia, the mother of the Gracchi! For her other son, James, is the politician who organises the ramp. Cornelia-Jocasta! For our final pair of spectacles is provided by Freud. When the cloud lifts from the summit of the mountain, Ransom finds his mother waiting for him, reabsorbing that which she has sent forth, frustrating that which she has created. He has never escaped her. He re-enters the womb. The lyric final suggests 'Peer Gynt,' but there is a bitterness in it which neither Ase nor Solveig conveys. She sings to her little boy:

> Reindeer are coming to drive you away
> Over the snow on an ebony sleigh,
> Over the mountains and over the sea
> You shall go happy and handsome and free.

But the chorus retorts:

> True, Love finally is great,
> Greater than all; but large the hate,
> Far larger than Man can ever estimate.

Mother-love, usually sacrosanct, becomes a nasty customer in this exciting play.

The Ascent of F.6 is a tragedy in a modern mode, full of funniness and wisecracks. It is not an entertainment, for all its light-heartedness, because its details fit in to its grave general plan. Unlike its predecessor, *The Dog beneath the Skin*, it moves onward instead of after its own tail ; the changes from poetry to prose, from monastery to mike, advance the action, the amusing subordinate characters never blur the genius and the pathos of Ransom.

[1936]

The Enchafèd Flood

T. E. Lawrence, that desert hero, once told me that he did not think highly of the sea. He considered it overrated. He enjoyed teasing sailormen and found them easy game, and when on board would make such remarks to them as, ' I've been sitting upstairs on the verandah. I think I'll go now and rest in my room.' Their infuriated reactions amused him. He never crossed the line, I think, but he would have regarded that ordeal as an opportunity for experiencing vulgarity. He was the aggressive landlubber—a refreshing type and a modern one. The landlubber gets covered with tar and chucked overboard, he turns green and is sick, but he has had his laugh and his say. He has made fun of the sea.

Sacrilege !

Yet the sea to-day certainly is in retreat. Occasionally it reasserts itself, as in the Kontiki expedition, and occasionally, through the fringe of oil and dead birds and the chonking and bobbing of metal objects, we catch a glimpse of it from the shore. But it is in retreat poetically. A poet is needed to arrest it, to restore Neptune his majesty, to wet Canute his feet, to float the Old Man in the Boat. Auden is such a poet. He has the necessary power, and a contemporary vision that can include the past. He takes us back to the romantics, including Lear, he lends us their ears and their fears, and with their help revivifies the mass of water from whose shallows we came, and contrasts that mass with the desert, into which we try to retreat, and with the City, which we are trying to build and have never built. The nineteenth century helps him—Wordsworth, Shelley, Blake, Tennyson, Melville, Baudelaire, Rimbaud, Ibsen, Kierkegaard. They understand the expedition, the setting out, the heroic leap, and sometimes they understand how expeditions end. The age of reason cannot help. Voltaire, Rousseau, understand nothing. They cannot with their common sense interpret this trinity of Sea, Desert, City. They mock on, mock on. And, their salutary mirth in my ears, I turn me to *The Enchafèd Flood*.

It reprints lectures. Critics who have decided that lectures

274

must not be reprinted will doubtless complain of it on this account ; anyhow it is a good old game, complaining of Auden, and a safe one. The admonitory note, the professional quote, are certainly present in him, but underlying them is imaginative passion, and the words ' We must love one another or die.' The effort to grasp the universe, and where it threatens us, persists here as in his poems. The threat alters because we alter, and neither seas nor deserts now menace directly. They are symbols. And he plunges us into that world of symbols which is so chancy in its effects, and from which we emerge illuminated, or dazed. For myself, I am not too dazed. That is what happens to me when reading this writer. He elicits a response which I cannot always explain. Because he once wrote ' We must love one another or die,' he can command me to follow him.

The first section, ' The Sea and the Desert,' contrasts and compares these protagonists. They are alike in that they are wildernesses, which beckon to the outlaw and the hero, and they both contain earthly paradises—the Happy Island and the Oasis respectively. They differ in that the sea breeds life. The blessed creatures and the slimy things seen by the Ancient Mariner dwell there, so does Moby Dick ; it is wild and lonely but vital. To the city of to-day—the squalid unbuilt or ruined city—the sea still calls, though its waters choke and destroy us as soon as they are tasted. Its romance is more powerful than the desert's —and T. E. Lawrence knew this really.

The second section, ' The Stone and the Shell,' interprets a dream of Wordsworth's with which the book started. Wordsworth dreamt that he encountered a knight, half Ishmael and half Don Quixote, who held in the one hand a stone, which belongs to the desert and symbolises precise knowledge, and in the other hand a shell, symbolic of poetry and prophecy, and murmurous of the sea. Both the stone and the shell are needed for the perfect city, but the knight must know how to control their opposing magics. He cannot, the waters gain on him, and Wordsworth awakes. Auden has at this point much symbolism on his hands—an extensive bag of tricks. He too fails to control it, I think ; anyhow this is the section of the book where I found myself getting dazed. I felt I had strayed into a conjuror's parlour, and that the objects hurtling around me were not real. It is a feeling one often experiences when reading the romantics, and it comes and it goes.

It has gone in the final section. This is called 'Ishmael—Don Quixote.' The two types of heroes are analysed, Ishmael more particularly, and there is a discussion of Moby Dick. Melville is very profoundly explored to-day, especially in the United States, and like all ploughed-up authors his surface has got rather bumpy. Fortunately Auden is a poet, who understands what poems feel like as well as what they mean, and who does not rely too much upon incest and castration. The sea guides him : perhaps through his Icelandic blood. Real and symbolic voyages coincide and by the end of the discussion we have a clearer vision of Ahab's tragedy.

The Enchafèd Flood, it should now appear, is itself a poem. Though its tone is critical, it is not constructed like a lecture course or a thesis. Brooding in it is the ruined or unbuilt city, and we must either build it or die. We cannot escape any more to the sands or the waves and pretend they are our destiny. We have annihilated time and space, we have furrowed the desert and spanned the sea, only to find at the end of every vista our own unattractive features. What remains for us, whither shall we turn ? To the city which we have not yet built, to the unborn polity, to the new heroism.

The heroic image to-day is not the nomad wanderer through the desert or over the ocean, but the less exciting figure of the builder, who renews the ruined walls of the city. Our temptations are not theirs. We are less likely to be tempted by solitude into Promethean pride : we are far more likely to become cowards in the face of the tyrant who would compel us to lie in the service of the False City. It is not madness we need to flee but prostitution. Let us, reading the logs of their fatal but heroic voyages, remember their courage.

Auden's hope—reinforced in his case by Christian dogma—is the world's hope and its only hope. For some of us who are non-Christian there still remains the comfort of the non-human, the relief, when we look up at the stars, of realising that they are uninhabitable. But not there for any of us lies our work or our home.

[1951]

Forrest Reid

When one has been friends with a writer for thirty-five years, and he dies, and one is asked to write about him—well one wishes to write about him, but the books recede, and little details, of doubtful interest to the public, take their place. No doubt Forrest Reid's trilogy of *Young Tom*, *The Retreat* and *Uncle Stephen* is a unique chronicle of boyhood. No doubt, again, *Apostate* is a memorable spiritual biography. Nor will *Illustrators of the Sixties* be superseded. But smaller things intrude. Moreover, to those who knew and loved him, he was more than a creator of books. He existed in his own right, and by the right of being unlike anyone else. His integrity, his affection, his patience and humorous irritability, his prejudices and occasional ruefulness about them—how can it all be conveyed without overdoing the tang or missing it out? Good temper, bad temper —which was it? One didn't know, didn't care, only knew that there was a great deal of it and that its charm was irresistible. He was the most important person in Belfast, and, though it would be too much to say that Belfast knew him not, I have sometimes smiled to think how little that great city, engaged in its own ponderous purposes, dreamed of him or indeed of anything. He who dreamed and was partly a dream. A dream compounded not only of visions, Mediterranean and Celtic, but of the ' moral fragrance ' which he prized and pursued and diffused.

Into which falls his voice. ' Och, it'll do you no harm '—of whisky. Or ' Tea or coffee ? Tea, I think. It's apt to be the more successful.' Or ' What did he want to use that foul language for ? Remus only gave him a wee nip.' For Remus and all dogs he had unbounded love. For cats he entertained a proportionate regard, and his visits to Bloomsbury were rendered tolerable by a cemetery, where cats confabulated upon some railed-in tombs. Except for its animals, which included moles, he did not appreciate England. He came over to the place mainly to play croquet, in which he was expert, and, whirled from one championship ground to another in a car, acquired a special view of its geography. Each time it was nicer to him than he expected, which showed what he had been thinking in the intervals.

For his own country, for Northern Ireland, his feeling was passionate—a regional feeling, not political, and not hardening into theories. Happy the man who has such feelings, happy the district for which they are felt ! He has given to the Lagan, and Newcastle Co. Down, and Ballycastle something which they can keep for ever, if they are worthy.

He entered no cultural swim, and for this his independence of character was responsible. He could not fit into any clique, he was never the right shape, and, though not truculent or aggressive, he never softened his opinions. For a long time he maintained that all women novelists, with the exception of Jane Austen, are bad, which did not commend him to the sisterhood. When his loyalty was once given it was irremovable. Year in, year out, whatever the metropolitan fashions, he reverenced Henry James. He had indeed hoped for closer literary contact with James, but the Master was scared of *The Garden God*, a Platonic but Hellenic romance, and somewhat withdrew. Reid was hurt and surprised, but not affronted. His high estimate of James's character and art did not waver. Another loyalty went out to Walter de la Mare, to whom he has devoted a detailed and affectionate study.

His critical attitude, especially about poetry, was childish and firm. Poems are people. They either evoke a sympathetic response from us or they do not, and if they do not we had better move away. In his last book, *Milk of Paradise*, he writes : ' After all, the personal appeal in poetry is everything, because without it, for the particular reader concerned, there *is* no poetry.' What a contrast to the highly equipped modern critic who, until he has applied his tests and noted how the poem reacts to them, cannot know whether the poem is good, and if good, good in what way and how good in that way ! Reid kept to what he liked. This might have made his outlook arbitrary and whimsical, but he was saved here by the inner gravity of his spirit, and his natural good taste. In *Milk of Paradise* he quotes, and discusses on an even note, hackneyed poems like ' Lucy Gray,' recondite poems like Dobell's ' Orphan's Song,' and controversial excerpts from Poe. There was his heart, thus it happened to respond. He left others to their own responses, nor was he curious to discover what these were.

Believing as he did (and asI do) in the past, he would approve a reference to our first meeting. It was in 1911, the year *The Bracknels* was published. I had written to thank him for that delicate and disturbing novel, without knowing who he was or where he lived. I received an answer from round the corner. We were both of us in Belfast, and from this happy coincidence much depended. He and his friends invited me to lunch, the first of their endless hospitalities. There was pheasant—a delicious meal and an attentive dog. In the afternoon we rowed through sunlight and shadow up the Lagan, then a lovely stream haunted by his sort of ghosts. In the next year when *Following Darkness* appeared, it was dedicated to me. Perhaps that is why I have a special feeling for it. Some critics sensed Satanism in its title, and became excited. Idiots, they had forgotten Puck's ' Following darkness like a dream.' Towards the end of his life, he rewrote *Following Darkness* as *Peter Waring*, but I have never cared to read this later version. The earlier is so connected with happy visits to Ireland, with the Mourne Mountains, with cats and dogs muddling round a fire, with the glint from his spectacles and the turns in his voice.

[1947]

English Prose between 1918 and 1939

The W. P. Ker Lecture delivered in the University of Glasgow

This is a period between two wars—the Long Week-End it has been called—and some of the books published in it look backward—like Siegfried Sassoon's *Memoirs of an Infantry Officer* —and try to record the tragedy of the past ; others look forward and try to avert or explain the disaster which overtook Europe in the thirties.   And even when they are not directly about a war—like the works of Lytton Strachey or Joyce or Virginia Woolf—they still display unrest or disillusionment or anxiety, they are still the products of a civilisation which feels itself insecure.   The French lady, Madame de Sévigné, writing letters during the wars of the late seventeenth century, can feel tranquil. The English lady, Jane Austen, writing novels in the Napoleonic wars, can feel tranquil.   Those wars were not total.   But no one can write during or between our wars and escape their influence. There, then, is one obvious characteristic of our prose.   It is the product of people who have war on their mind.   They need not be gloomy or hysterical—often they are gay and sane and brave—but if they have any sensitiveness they must realise what a mess the world is in, and if they have no sensitiveness they will not be worth reading.

We can conveniently divide the long week-end into two periods—the 1920's and the 1930's.   The division is not hard and fast, still it is helpful.   The twenties react after a war and recede from it, the thirties are apprehensive of a war and are carried towards it.   The twenties want to enjoy life and to understand it : the thirties also want to understand but for a special purpose : to preserve civilisation.   They are less detached.   In *Life among the English* Rose Macaulay contrasts the two periods neatly :

> The twenties were, as decades go, a good decade : gay, decorative, intelligent, extravagant, cultured.   There were booms in photography, Sunday films and theatre clubs, surrealism, steel furniture, faintly obscure poetry, Proust, James Joyce, dancing, rink-skating, large paintings on walls of rooms.

The next decade was more serious, less cultured, less aesthetic, more political. The slump blew like a cold draught at its birth, war stormed like forest fire at its close : between these two catastrophes Communists and Fascists battled and preached, and eyes turned apprehensively across the north sea towards the alarming menace which had leaped up like a strident jack-in-the-box from a beer-cellar to more than a throne.

Rose Macaulay is a wise guide, tolerant, generous-minded, liberal, courageous, cheerful, and her judgments of society and social values are always sound. She sums up the two decades very well.

But of course there is more to say. There are influences in this world more powerful than either peace or war. And we cannot get a true idea of our period and the books it produces until we look deeper than fashions or politics or the achievements and failures of generals. For one thing, there is a huge economic movement which has been taking the whole world, Great Britain included, from agriculture towards industrialism. That began about a hundred and fifty years ago, but since 1918 it has accelerated to an enormous speed, bringing all sorts of changes into national and personal life. It has meant organisation and plans and the boosting of the community. It has meant the destruction of feudalism and relationship based on the land, it has meant the transference of power from the aristocrat to the bureaucrat and the manager and the technician. Perhaps it will mean democracy, but it has not meant it yet, and personally I hate it. So I imagine do most writers, however loyally they try to sing its praises and to hymn the machine. But however much we detest this economic shift we have to recognise it as an important influence, more important than any local peace or war, which is going on all the time and transforming our outlooks. It rests on applied science, and as long as science is applied it will continue. Even when a writer seems to escape it, like T. E. Lawrence, he is conditioned by it. T. E. Lawrence hated the progress of industrialism, he hated what your city of Glasgow and my city of London stand for. He fled from it into the deserts of Arabia and the last of the romantic wars, in the search of old-time adventure, and later on into the deserts of his own heart. I think he was right to fly, because I believe that a writer's duty often exceeds any duty he owes to society, and that he often ought to lead a forlorn retreat. But of course the flight failed. Industrialism did T. E. Lawrence in in the long run, and it was not by the spear of an Arab but by a high-power motor-bike that he came to his death.[1] We must face the unpleasant truths that normal life to-day is a life in factories and offices, that even war has evolved from an adventure into a business, that even farming has become scientific, that insurance has taken the place of charity, that status has given way to contract. You will see how disquieting all this is to writers, who love, and ought to love, beauty and charm and the passage of the seasons, and generous impulses, and the tradition of their craft. And you will appreciate how lost some of them have been feeling during the last quarter of a century, and how they have been tempted to nostalgia like Siegfried Sassoon, or to disgust like Evelyn Waugh and Graham Greene.

But this economic movement, from the land to the factory, is not the only great movement which has gathered strength during our period. There has been a psychological movement, about which I am more enthusiastic. Man is beginning to understand himself better and to explore his own contradictions. This exploration is conveniently connected with the awful name of Freud, but it is not so much in Freud as in the air. It has brought a great enrichment to the art of fiction. It has given subtleties and depths to the portrayal of human nature. The presence in all of us of the subconscious, the occasional existence of the split personality, the persistence of the irrational especially in people who pride themselves on their reasonableness, the importance of dreams and the prevalence of day-dreaming—here are some of the points which novelists have seized on and which have not been ignored by historians. This psychology is not new, but it has newly risen to the surface. Shakespeare was subconsciously aware of the subconscious, so were Emily Brontë, Herman Melville and others. But conscious knowledge of it only comes at the beginning of the century, with Samuel Butler's *The Way of All Flesh*, and only becomes general after 1918—partly owing to Freud. It gathers strength now, like the economic movement, and, like it, is independent of war or peace. Of course, writers can be stupid about it, as about anything else, they can apply it as a formula instead of feeling it as a possibility ; the stupid psychologist who applies his (or her) formula in season or out

[1] See Christopher Caudwell, *Studies in a Dying Culture* ; a brilliant criticism of the period from a communist standpoint.

and is always saying ' you think you don't but you do ' or ' you think you do but you don't ' can be absolutely maddening. But the better minds of our age—what a rich harvest they have reaped ! Proust in France to begin with ; Gertrude Stein and her experiments in uninhibited talk—not too successful in her own case but influential : Dorothy Richardson's novels, another pioneer in this country : the later work of D. H. Lawrence, the novels of Virginia Woolf, Joyce, de la Mare, Elizabeth Bowen. History too has profited. This new method of examining the human individual has helped to reinterpret the past. Aldous Huxley's *Grey Eminence* is one example—it gives a fresh view of Cardinal Richelieu and his adviser Father Joseph—a fresh view of their insides. Livingston Lowes' *The Road to Xanadu* is another example : a fresh view of the genius and make-up of Coleridge. And then there is the great work of a Christian historian, Arnold Toynbee, *A Study of History*, which regards history as a record of what men think and feel as well as of what they assert and achieve, and tries, with this extra material to account for the rise and fall of civilisations. Professor Toynbee comes to the conclusion that they rise and fall in accord with a religious law, and that except the Lord build the house their labour is but lost that build it ; or, if you prefer the language of Freud to that of the Old Testament, that the conscious must be satisfactorily based on the subconscious.

So though we are justified in thinking of our period as an interval between two wars we must remember that it forms part of larger movements where wars become insignificant : part of an economic movement from agriculture to industrialism, and of a psychological movement which is reinterpreting human nature. Both these movements have been speeded up, and writers have in my judgment been worried by the economic shift but stimulated by the psychological. Remember too, in passing, another factor, and that is the shift in physics exemplified by the work of Einstein. Can literary men understand Einstein ? Of course they cannot—even less than they can understand Freud. But the idea of relativity has got into the air and has favoured certain tendencies in novels. Absolute good and evil, as in Dickens, are seldom presented. A character becomes good or evil in relation to some other character or to a situation which may itself change. You can't measure people up, because the yard-measure itself keeps altering its length. The best exponent

of relativity in literature known to me is Proust, though there
are instances in English too. Most of Proust's people are odious,
yet you cannot have the comfort of writing any of them off as
bad. Given the circumstances, even the most odious of them all,
Madame Verdurin, can behave nobly. Proust and others have
this attitude—not because they know anything about science,
but because the idea of relativity, like the idea of the subconscious
self, has got about and tinged their outlook.

A word must now be said on the special character of prose.
Prose, unlike poetry, does two things. It serves us in daily
life and it creates works of art. For instance, I travelled from
Euston to Glasgow on prose, I am talking prose now, and, like
M. Jourdain, I am astonished at finding myself doing so. For
prose, besides serving our practical ends, also makes great
literature.

Now, one of the problems which a critic has to tackle is that
these two uses of prose are not water-tight, and one of these is
as it were constantly slopping over into the other. The practical
popular prose is always getting into the deliberate artistic prose
which makes books. Indeed, if it didn't, the artistic prose
couldn't live very long as it would get stale and stuffy. It has
to be replenished by contemporary speech. And in this period
of ours there has been a great deal of this replenishment. New
words and phrases—and, what is more important, the new habits
of thought expressed by them—are rapidly absorbed by authors
and put into books. That is one tendency of our period, and it
may be called, for want of a better word, the popular tendency.
The writer feels himself part of his people. He enters or wants
to enter into their ways. And he wants to be understood by
them, and so he tries to be informal and clear. I'll give several
examples of it. Here is a little example, taken from letter-
writing. In 1918, if I had had a letter from a stranger it would
certainly have begun ' Dear Sir.' To-day, if I have a letter from
a stranger, it will probably begin ' Dear Mr. Forster.' One form
of address doesn't mean more than another, but the convention
is a more friendly one. I expect it came in, like other speak-
easies, from America. It shows which way the wind of words
is blowing. Another sign is the speeches of public men. Public
men are becoming less formal—some of them because of the
influences of the radio, for they know if they broadcast too

pompously listeners will switch off. Others are informal by instinct, like Winston Churchill, whose speeches sound and read more democratic than those of the Prime Ministers of the last war. Novelists too—they practise the friendly unpatronising tone ; Christopher Isherwood's *Mr. Norris changes Trains* is an example of this. Isherwood—who is extremely intelligent— always writes as if the reader were equally intelligent. He is an example of democratic good manners. He trusts his public. Another novelist—Ernest Hemingway—introduces a new technique of conversation. Another straw which shows which way this wind is blowing is the tendency of official notices and proclamations to become more intelligible. They do so reluctantly, for the bureaucrat who gives his meaning clearly is afraid he may be giving something else away too. Still they do it. They tend to issue orders which we understand. And since we live under orders, this is a good thing.

I could continue this list of the popular tendencies in prose. We have had an example in the demand from high quarters for Basic English—and I expect it is a useful commercial idea though I cannot see what it has to do with literature, or what it can do to literature, except impoverish it. I'll conclude with an example of another kind, a reference to the English of the Authorised Version of the Bible. This, the great monument of our seventeenth-century speech, has constantly influenced our talk and writing for the last three hundred years. Its rhythm, its atmosphere, its turns of phrase, belonged to our people and overflowed into our books. Bunyan, Johnson, Blake, George Eliot, all echo it. About ten years ago an edition of the Bible came out called *The Bible designed to be read as Literature.* Its publication gave some of us a shock and caused us to realise that the English of the Authorised Version had at last become remote from popular English. This was well put in a review by Somerset Maugham. The English of the Bible, he agreed, is part of our national heritage, but it is so alien to our present idiom that no writer can study it profitably. I shall soon be quoting from a writer who has studied it, still Somerset Maugham is right on the whole, and there is now an unbridgeable gulf between ourselves and the Authorised Version as regards style, and the gulf widened about 1920, when those other influences we have discussed became strong. Quotations from the Bible still occur, but they support my contention : they are usually conventional and insensitive, introduced because the author or speaker wants to be impressive without taking trouble. Listen to the following advertisement of 'Cable and Wireless' in *The Times* of July 28th, 1943. The advertisement is reporting a speech made by a cabinet minister, Colonel Oliver Stanley, at a Cable and Wireless staff lunch :

> When the end comes, when victory is won, then history will begin to assess merit. We shall all of us be searching our conscience. . . . We shall be discussing who succeeded and who failed . . . I have no doubt at all, when we come to discuss the part that Cable and Wireless has played, what the verdict of the nation will be—' Well done thou good and faithful servant.'

No doubt Cable and Wireless has done and deserved well, but I do not feel it can be suitably congratulated in the words of St. Matthew's Gospel, and if the English of the Bible had been in Colonel Stanley's blood instead of in his cliché-box I do not think he would have used such words. It is an example of insensitiveness to the Authorised Version and of the complete divorce between Biblical and popular English. (A similar example, this time of insensitiveness to Milton, was the slogan 'They also serve' on a war-workers' poster.)

So much for this popular tendency in prose. I have suggested that it takes various forms, bringing freshness and informality and new usages and democratic good manners into literature, but also bringing vulgarity and flatness. Now for the other tendency to which I will attach the name esoteric ; the desire on the part of writers—generally the more distinguished writers— to create something better than the bloodshed and dullness which have been creeping together over the world. Such writers are often censured. You may complain that Lytton Strachey, Virginia Woolf, James Joyce, D. H. Lawrence and T. E. Lawrence have done little to hearten us up. But you must admit they were the leading writers of our age. It is an age that could not produce a Shakespeare or even a Madame de Sévigné or a Jane Austen : an age in which sensitive people could not feel comfortable, and were driven to seek inner compensation : an age similar in some ways to that which caused St. Augustine to write *The City of God*. St. Augustine, though he looked outside him, worked within. He too was esoteric. These writers look outside them and find their material lying about in the world. But they arrange it and re-create it within, temporarily sheltered from the pitiless blasts and the fog.

A further word on T. E. Lawrence. *The Seven Pillars of Wisdom* is a most enigmatic book. Lawrence made good in the world of action and was what most of us regard as a hero—brave, selfless, modest, and kind by nature yet ruthless at need, loyal and the inspirer of loyalty, magnetic, a born leader of men, and victorious at Damascus in the last of the picturesque wars. Such a man, even if not happy, will surely be true to type. He will remain the man of action, the extrovert. But when we read the *Seven Pillars* we find beneath the gallant fighting and the brilliant description of scenery—sensitiveness, introspection, doubt, disgust at the material world. It is the book of a man who cannot fit in with twentieth-century civilisation, and loves the half-savage Arabs because they challenge it. This comes out in the following quotation : note in the final sentence the hit at ' vested things ' ; at the innate commercialism of the west which ruined the peace of Versailles.

Their mind [the Arabs'] was strange and dark, full of depressions and exaltations, lacking in rule, but with more of ardour and more fertile in belief than any other in the world. They were a people of starts, for whom the abstract was the strongest motive, the process of infinite courage and variety, and the end nothing. They were as unstable as water, and like water would perhaps finally prevail. Since the dawn of life, in successive waves, they had been dashing themselves against the coasts of flesh. Each wave was broken, but, like the sea, wore away ever so little of the granite on which it failed, and some day, ages yet, might roll unchecked over the place where the material world had been, and God would move over the face of those waters. One such wave (and not the least) I raised and rolled before the breath of an idea till it reached its crest, and toppled over and fell at Damascus. The wash of this wave, thrown back by the resistance of vested things, will provide the matter of the following wave, when in fullness of time the sea shall be raised once more.

The *Seven Pillars* for all its greatness is too strange a book to be typical of a period, and the same applies to another curious masterpiece, James Joyce's *Ulysses*. For a typical example I'd take Lytton Strachey's *Queen Victoria*. This is important for several reasons. It came out at the beginning of our period, it is an achievement of genius, and it has revolutionised the art of biography. Strachey did debunk of course ; he hated pomposity, hypocrisy and muddle-headedness, he mistrusted inflated reputations, and was clever at puncturing them, and he found in the Victorian age, which had taken itself very, very seriously, a tempting target for his barbed arrows. But he was much more than a debunker. He did what no biographer had done before : he managed to get inside his subject. Earlier biographers, like Macaulay and Carlyle, had produced fine and convincing pictures of people ; Lytton Strachey makes his people move ; they are alive, like characters in a novel : he constructs or rather reconstructs them from within. Sometimes he got them wrong ; his presentation of General Gordon has been questioned, so has his brilliant later work on Elizabeth and Essex. But even when they are wrong they seem alive, and in the *Queen Victoria* his facts have not been seriously challenged ; and, based on dry documents, a whole society and its inhabitants rise from the grave, and walk about. That was his great contribution. He was a historian who worked from within, and constructed out of the bones of the past something more real and more satisfactory than the chaos surrounding him. He is typical of our period, and particularly of the twenties—throughout them his influence is enormous ; to-day it has declined, partly because people are again taking themselves very very seriously, and don't like the human race to be laughed at, partly because Strachey had some tiresome imitators, who have brought his method into discredit. However that doesn't matter. Reputations always will go up and down. What matters is good work, and *Queen Victoria* is a masterpiece. It is a pageant of the historical type, but as the grand procession passes we—you and I, we little readers, are somehow inside the procession, we mingle unobserved with royalty and statesmen and courtiers and underlings, and hear their unspoken thoughts.

Even a frivolous passage, like the one about the Boy Jones, has its historical function. Lytton Strachey was a gay person who loved fun and nonsense, and he knew how to make use of them in his work. Through the episode of the enigmatic Boy Jones, an undersized youth who repeatedly entered Buckingham Palace and hid there in the year 1840, was discovered under sofas, and confessed that he had ' helped himself to soup and other eatables,

sat upon the throne, seen the Queen, and heard the Princess Royal
squall,' Strachey recreates the domestic confusion existing there,
and makes the period come alive. Then he passes on to more
serious topics.

What was he serious about ? Not about political ideals or
social reform. Like T. E. Lawrence, he was disillusioned though
in another way. He believed, however, in wit and aristocratic
good manners, and he was implacable in his pursuit of truth.
He believed, furthermore, in fidelity between human beings.
There, and there only, the warmth of his heart comes out. He
is always moved by constant affection, and the Queen's love for
the Prince Consort, and for his memory, makes the book glow
and preserves it from frigidity. Strachey's belief in affection,
like his fondness for fun, is too often forgotten. Here is the
famous passage describing the Queen's death, with which the
book closes. He begins by being the dignified historian ; then
he dismisses his subject tenderly, and launches the Queen as it
were on an ebbing tide, carrying her backwards through the
manifold joys of life till she vanishes in the mists of her birth.

By the end of the year the last remains of her ebbing strength
had almost deserted her ; and through the early days of the
opening century it was clear that her dwindling forces were
kept together only by an effort of will. On January 14, she had
at Osborne an hour's interview with Lord Roberts, who had
returned victorious from South Africa a few days before.
She inquired with acute anxiety into all the details of the war ;
she appeared to sustain the exertion successfully ; but, when
the audience was over, there was a collapse. On the following
day her medical attendants recognised that her state was hopeless ; and yet, for two days more, the indomitable spirit fought
on ; for two days more she discharged the duties of a Queen
of England. But after that there was an end of working ;
and then, and not till then, did the last optimism of those about
her break down. The brain was failing, and life was gently
slipping away. Her family gathered round her ; for a little
more she lingered, speechless and apparently insensible ; and,
on January 22, 1901, she died.

When, two days previously, the news of the approaching
end had been made public, astonished grief had swept over
the country. It appeared as if some monstrous reversal of the

course of nature was about to take place. The vast majority
of her subjects had never known a time when Queen Victoria
had not been reigning over them. She had become an indis-
soluble part of their whole scheme of things, and that they
were about to lose her appeared a scarcely possible thought.
She herself, as she lay blind and silent, seemed to those who
watched her to be divested of all thinking—to have glided
already, unawares, into oblivion. Yet, perhaps, in the secret
chambers of consciousness, she had her thoughts, too. Perhaps
her fading mind called up once more the shadows of the past
to float before it, and retraced, for the last time, the vanished
visions of that long history—passing back and back, through
the cloud of years, to older and ever older memories—to
the spring woods at Osborne, so full of primroses for Lord
Beaconsfield—to Lord Palmerston's queer clothes and high
demeanour, and Albert's face under the green lamp, and
Albert's first stag at Balmoral, and Albert in his blue and
silver uniform, and the Baron coming in through a doorway,
and Lord M. dreaming at Windsor with the rooks cawing in
the elm-trees, and the Archbishop of Canterbury on his knees
in the dawn, and the old King's turkey-cock ejaculations, and
Uncle Leopold's soft voice at Claremont, and Lehzen with the
globes, and her mother's feathers sweeping down towards her,
and a great old repeater-watch of her father's in its tortoise-
shell case, and a yellow rug, and some friendly flounces of
sprigged muslin, and the trees and the grass at Kensington.

You'll remember what I said before about the new psychology
being in the air, and this last long lovely drifting sentence,
with its imaginings of the subconscious, could not have been
created at an earlier date.

A word on the authors whom I have mentioned. I have kept
to those who may be said to belong to our period, who were
formed by it, and received its peculiar stamp. Authors like
Arnold Bennett, Galsworthy, Wells, Belloc, Chesterton, Frank
Swinnerton, Norman Douglas, Bertrand Russell, Lowes Dickinson, George Moore, Max Beerbohm, did good work after 1920,
and some of them are still active. But they got their impressions
and formed their attitudes in an earlier period, before the first
of the two world-wars. D. H. Lawrence presents a special difficulty. Does he come in or not? His finest novels, *The White*

Peacock and *Sons and Lovers* were published round about 1912 and he displays all his life a blend of vision and vituperation which seem to date him further back still—right back to Carlyle.   On the other hand, he was alive to the new economics and the new psychology, and well aware, when he died in 1930, that the war to end war had ended nothing but the Victorian peace.   My own feeling is that he does come into our survey.

To sum up my remarks.   Our period : a long week-end between two wars.   Economic and psychological changes already in existence intensify.   Writers are intimidated by the economic changes but stimulated by the psychological.   Prose, because it is a medium for daily life as well as for literature, is particularly sensitive to what is going on, and two tendencies can be noted : the popular, which absorbs what is passing, and the esoteric, which rejects it, and tries to create through art something more valuable than monotony and bloodshed.   The best work of the period has this esoteric tendency.   T. E. Lawrence, though heroic in action, retreats into the desert to act.   Lytton Strachey is disillusioned, except about truth and human affection.

As for assessing the value of our period, I am disposed to place it high, and I do not agree with those numerous critics who condemn it as a failure, and scold mankind for enjoying itself too much in the twenties and for theorising too much in the thirties.   We are plunged in a terrific war, and our literary judgments are not at their best.   All our criticism is or ought to be tentative.   And tentatively I suggest that the long week-end did valuable work, and I ask you to pause before you yield to the prevalent tendency to censure it.

[1944]

An Outsider on Poetry

I have written very little poetry in my life, and only two lines of modern poetry. Here they are:

> I will pull down Hastings, you shall see
> Companion to India as a boat gnawed.

I wrote them last year in a dream, and managed on waking to transcribe them before the censor stopped me—that censor who from Porlock or elsewhere always attends on our sleep and prevents us from communicating what we have learnt in it. On their merits I need not pronounce. They seem to me poetry because they scan and modern because they are obscure and minatory. Most feebly credentialled by them, I approach the thirty-six poets of *Poetry of the Present*, Mr. Geoffrey Grigson's Anthology of the thirties and forties.

One has need of some sort of credential. The outsider, the proser, even if he is modest and sensitive, goes wrong in the poetry-world very quickly. He can hear music, he can recognise ideas, but the marriage between music and ideas, out of which the poem is born, often eludes him, with the result that his judgment is unreliable, he praises where he ought to blame, and vice versa. He is constantly entering a world for which he is not prepared. He is prepared for the poetry of the past. Critics have laid down the lines within which he may wander. But the present demands an unaided opinion, which he hesitates to give. The safer course is not to read the stuff, and to hold the comfortable hope that what is worthy in it will survive. Meanwhile the poets are far from comfortable, for if they are not read they will not get published. Their fate is symbolic: the present indifference to contemporary poetry—contrasting so lamentably with the curiosity of the twenties and thirties—is part of the general menace to literature.

I read it from time to time myself. I cannot pretend to be as curious about it as I am about contemporary music, but now and then, perhaps through some personal experience, perhaps through my profound belief that poets know best, I venture, I venture into the present's whirlpool, and find something hitting my hand. It is uncommonly like a stone, and since it may not be a precious stone practical people ignore it. There however the stone is. Through some slight affinity in myself, I hold it, I remove it from the waters with respect, I listen and look. There's been discomfort here. That is my first impression. The person who has created this little object does not find the universe a soft or sunny spot. Through his imagination, he has heard danger coming, he has seen war-clouds, he has felt the social-tremble underfoot, and maybe he has detected disunion in his own heart. He is minatory like my own doggerel. How should he not be? It began with Auden and the various people who have complained of Auden have never managed to avoid his note,

> never will be perfect like the fountains;
> We live in freedom by necessity,
> A mountain people dwelling among mountains.

The threat may be lifted to the heroic, it may be subdued into an anxiety, it may be masked by compassion or sharpened by satire, but in some form or other it is the heritage of most of the contributors to this volume.

> The blackbirds sing and I see no end of agony,
>   The pink and the white blossom
> Spangles the chestnuts, the theatres pour into the streets
> The unimaginative. And the earth renews
> In Europe its solar gaiety, and the earth moves on
>   To no destination.
>   (*Kenneth Allott*)

> What's to become of the world if Money should suddenly die?
> Should suddenly take a toss and go down crash on his head?
> If the dance suddenly finished, if they stopped the runaway bus,
> If the trees stopped racing away?
> If our hope come true and he dies, what's to become of us? . . .
>   (*Bernard Spencer*)

> When I was born on Amman hill
> A dark bird crossed the sun,
> Sharp on the floor the shadow fell;
> I was the youngest son.

> And when I went to the County School
> I worked in a shaft of light.
> In the wood of the desk I cut my name:
> Dai for Dynamite.

The tall black hills my brothers stood ;
Their lessons all were done.
From the door of the school when I ran out
They frowned to watch me run . . .

(Vernon Watkins)

The seven-branched cactus
Will never sweat wine :
My own bleeding feet
Shall furnish the sign.

The rock says ' Endure.'
The wind says ' Pursue '
The sun says ' I will suck your bones
And afterwards bury you.'

(Sidney Keyes)

That seems the generalisation to which the outsider can cling
as the little objects dash against his hand ; minatory : the anxiety
of those who, through their temperament, apprehend more than
the rest of us, and have special powers for communicating their
dreams. It is only a generalisation, and the poem I most admired
stands right beyond it on the calm lake of oriental philosophy :

But now beyond question, the swans sail on together,
Wing answering wing, as parting of a breath
Is close to its indrawing,
And the god in one sees himself in the other,
For his self-knowledge is the sailing of two swans.
But the swans do not know themselves possessed,
They go on their own way in their distant world.

(E. J. Scovell)

And there are other poems which express no view but rest
content with the immediate sensation, the present image :

The scent of the conifers, sound of the bath,
The view from my bedroom of moss-dappled path,
As I struggle with double-end evening tie,
For we dance at the Golf Club, my victor and I.

(John Betjeman)

Wild Wilbur paces by the caves
His limbs are long his smile is wide
His hands are dangling side by side
His eyes are fixed upon the waves.

The birds sing in his healthy ears
The waves spill round his anklesocks
Sometimes he spits upon the rocks
Sometimes he picks his nose with tears. . . .

(James Kirkup)

That contemporary poetry should often be obscure and odd never surprises me ; the poet, however traditional his equipment, is always an innovator and likely to puzzle his elders. He has seen something old in a new way, and he may even have seen something new. When reading him it is desirable to be good tempered ; so many readers get cross out of a sense of duty ; they are proud of being irritated by modern verse, and of detecting any affectations in it. They enjoy sneering at it, and one small thing that we can do for it and for literature generally is to call their bluff and ask them to explain why they are sneering.

[1949]

Mohammed Iqbal

I met Iqbal once, thirty years ago, and only in passing. He is dead now and lies in honour outside the great mosque in Lahore, his own city. I visited his grave last winter. He is constantly mentioned in India—quite as often as Tagore, with whom he is contrasted. Over here he is little known ; so I shall venture to allude to him, although I can only read him in translation.

Iqbal was an orthodox Moslem, though not a conventional one. He was highly educated, and partly in Europe ; he was not cosmopolitan, and the basis of his culture remained Oriental. By profession he was a lawyer. He wrote both prose and poetry. The poems are mostly in Urdu, some are in Persian, and a few in Punjabi. As for his politics, he was once in sympathy with a united India, but in later life he changed, and adherents of Pakistan now claim him as a prophet. Whatever his opinions, he was no fanatic, and he refers to Hindus and to Christians with courtesy and respect.

All the same he was a fighter. He believed in the Self—the Self as a fighting unit—and his philosophy is not an enquiry into truth but a recommendation as to how the fight should be carried on. Fight we must, for man is the vice-regent of God upon earth. We must fortify our personalities. We must be hard. We must always be in a state of tension and try to be supermen. In one poem, Satan complains to God that men are not worth tempting because they are weak and have never discovered their Selves :

> O master of all . . .
> Association with mankind has debased me.
> Take back from me this doll of water and clay.[1]

So might the button-moulder in Ibsen's play complain of Peer Gynt. Iqbal reminds us of Nietzsche too. Renunciation of the Self is a form of cowardice, and therefore a crime. We cannot bear one another's burdens, and we must not expect to be redeemed.

[1] The translations are from an interesting monograph by Mr. S. A. Vahid, published in Lahore.

Now he combines this doctrine of hardness and of the Self with a capacity for mysticism. The combination makes him remarkable as a poet. Even in a translation, one can see the sudden opening-up of vistas between the precepts. It is not the mysticism that seeks union with God. On this point the poet is emphatic. We shall see God perhaps. We shall never be God. For God, like ourselves, has a Self, and he created us not out of himself but out of nothing. Iqbal dislikes the pantheism which he saw all around him in India—for instance, in Tagore— and he castigates those Moslem teachers who have infected Islam with it. It is weakening and wrong to seek unity with the divine. Vision—perhaps. Union—no.

Such—if an outsider may summarise—is his philosophy. It is not a philosophy I like, but that is another matter. There is anyhow nothing vague about it, nothing muzzy. It gives us a shock and helps us to see where we are. It is non-Christian. It is, in a sense, anti-humanitarian. It inspires him to write poems. They follow the orthodox forms, but they contain matter which is excitingly modern. Take, for instance, this poem in which Man defiantly addresses God on the ground that Man has proved the better artist of the two :

> Thou didst create night but I made the lamp.
> Thou didst create clay but I made the cup.
> Thou didst create the deserts, mountains, and forests,
> I produced the orchards, gardens and the groves :
> It is I who make the glass out of stone
> And it is I who turn a poison into an antidote.

Or consider this strange poem on the subject of Lenin. Lenin has died, and finds himself in the presence of the deity whom he had supposed to be an invention of the priests. He is not intimidated, but speaks his mind. God exists, to be sure. But whose God is he? The starving peasant's? The God of the East, who worships the white men? Or of the West, who worships the Almighty Dollar?

> Thou art All-Powerful, O Lord, but in thy world
> The lot of the hapless labourer is very hard !
> When will this boat of Capitalism be wrecked?
> Thy world is waiting for the Day of Reckoning.

The angels are moved by the dead Bolshevik's bluntness, and

they sing to their Lord like the angels at the opening of Goethe's *Faust*, but not in the same strain :

> Intellect is still unbridled. Love is not localised.
> O painter divine, Thy painting is still imperfect.
> Lying in ambush for mankind are the vagabond, the exploiter and
>   the monk.
> In thy universe the old order still continueth.

The Almighty is moved in his turn. He bows to the criticism of Lenin, and he orders the angels to burn every cornstalk in the field which does not nourish the cultivator, to give the sparrow strength to fight the falcon, and to smash up the glasshouse of modern civilisation. Iqbal never identifies hardness with oppression, or the Self with selfishness. The superman he seeks may come from any class of society.

Here is an uncontroversial lyric, ' Loneliness.' The poet is speaking, and his words gain pathos when we remember his creed of hardness :

> To the sea-shore I went and said to a restless wave,
> ' Thou art always in quest of something. What ails thee ?
> There are a thousand bright pearls in thy bosom,
> But hast thou a heart like mine in thy breast ? '
> It merely trembled, sped away from the shore, and said nothing.
>
> I betook myself to the presence of God, passing beyond the sun and
>   the moon, and said :
> ' In thy world not a single particle knows me,
> The world has no heart, and this earthly being of mine is all heart.
> The garden is charming, but is not worthy of my song.'
> A smile came to his lips, but he said nothing.

Mohammed Iqbal is a genius and a commanding one, and though I often disagree with him and usually agree with Tagore, it is Iqbal I would rather read. I know where I am with him. He is one of the two great cultural figures of modern India, and our ignorance about him is extraordinary.

[1946]

Syed Ross Masood

Contributed to the Memorial Number of an Urdu Journal

Masood had many English friends, but I may claim to be the oldest and most intimate of them. I have known him since 1907, and we kept in touch the whole time. I have been with him in England and in Switzerland and have twice visited him in India [1] and have also been his guest in France and in Germany. I cannot speak of our affection here—it is not the time or the place—but I am thankful to pay this tribute to it and to his memory. There never was anyone like him and there never will be anyone like him. He cannot be judged as ordinary men are judged. My own debt to him is incalculable. He woke me up out of my suburban and academic life, showed me new horizons and a new civilisation and helped me towards the understanding of a continent. Until I met him, India was a vague jumble of rajahs, sahibs, babus, and elephants, and I was not interested in such a jumble : who could be ? He made everything real and exciting as soon as he began to talk, and seventeen years later when I wrote *A Passage to India* I dedicated it to him out of gratitude as well as out of love, for it would never have been written without him.

Masood was essentially an artist. Those who knew him as an official may be surprised at this statement, but though his career was of a practical character his temperament was aesthetic. He lived by his emotions and instincts, and his standards were those of good taste. ' Don't be so damned inartistic ' he would say if he wanted to criticise my conduct. For logic, and for ethical consistency, he had very little use. He had an artist's recklessness over money ; he was fantastically generous, incredibly hospitable, and always happiest when he was giving something away. He was a patron of the arts and a connoisseur ; he loved good books, coins and engravings : when he went to Japan, he made a collection of coloured prints there, and gave them to me afterwards. His aesthetic judgments were not always sound, but they

[1] First at his home in Aligarh, and then in Hyderabad, Deccan, where he was Director of Education.

were always vehement and came from the very depths of his being. As a young man he had an unbounded admiration for the poetry of Alfred de Musset, and in later life when a play of Tolstoy's was put on in London and took his fancy he went to see it eight times. A professional critic may smile at his enthusiasms, but men of wider outlook will understand them, and recognise their sincerity and their stimulating effect on others. One might disagree with him but he never left one cold. With his temperament, he naturally felt most at home in the country that has honoured art most, and that country is neither India nor England but France. He loved Paris, and he spoke French well.

What did he think of the English? He handled them splendidly. If they patronised him, he let them have it back, very politely, and I have often been amused at the way in which Englishmen and Englishwomen who had begun by giving themselves airs were obliged to drop them, and to yield to his masterful personality and his charm. There is a story that he was once involved in a ' railway-carriage ' incident. He was stretched full-length in an empty compartment when a British officer bounced in and said ' Come on ! get out of this.' Masood looked up quietly and said, ' D'you want your head knocked off? ', whereupon the officer exclaimed, ' I say, I'm awfully sorry, I didn't know you were that sort of person,' and they became excellent friends. Whether this story be true or not, it is certainly true that on another occasion when returning on a P. & O. he contracted to shave an Australian miner all the way from Bombay to Marseilles for the sum of one guinea, and that he kept the contract. That was how he handled the Anglo-Saxons. He overwhelmed them by his energy and his unconventionality of address.

That was how he handled them, but what did he think of them? Leaving aside his English friends, whom he placed in a class apart, what did he feel about the Ruling Race as a whole? Perhaps his private thoughts are best expressed in a remark which has always amused me : ' As for your damned countrymen, I pity the poor fellows from the bottom of my heart, and give them all the help I can.' He was irritated by the English, he was sometimes bitter about them, but he realised that they were awkwardly placed in India, and he extended, half humorously, his sympathy towards them in their plight. He did not really dislike them, and I attribute his tolerance to his early upbringing ;

when he was a little boy at Aligarh, he lived with Sir Theodore and Lady Morison, and his life-long friendship with both of them coloured his outlook and made him less exacting.

Masood's real work, of course, lay with his own community in his own country, and those who shared it will write about him best. But I knew him very well, from a particular angle, and I have tried to keep to that angle in this inadequate contribution to his memory. When his official career is described, it must not be forgotten that he was essentially an artist, and I have tried to emphasise this. And when his services to Islam, to India, and to the Urdu language are commemorated, it must not be forgotten that he was loved and indeed adored by men and women who differed from him in creed, race, and speech, but were able nevertheless to recognise his genius and the greatness of his heart.

[1937]

A Duke Remembers

Men, Women and Things, the Duke of Portland's reminiscences, is more of a bag than a book. The reader who opens it will assist at a tremendously aristocratic shoot, where many birds fall dead but none are wantonly wounded. In the foreground move the guns, always titled and often royal, then come the highly-paid keepers, and further off, also doing their duty and drawing their screw, slink the beaters. It is a very good-tempered book. Great names hurtle through the air, to fall at our feet with scarcely a feather disarranged. It is also a self-assured book, hence its strength. If the writer stopped to think what he was aiming at, he would be lost, the pen would drop from his hand. But he never stops, he just writes, just as he just shoots, dresses or rides. He has worn the best clothes all his life, killed the best animals, and had the best friends, and with the same flair he uses the best words. Hit or miss ! There's no getting away from that truth, is there ? and it's a hit all the time with the Duke of Portland. Duke, Duke, you're cute, as those lively if backward people the Americans would say. Oh Duke, give us more ! And this is indeed the third volume of his reminiscences. They make the pleasantest reading, that is to say he is so loyal to his peers, so considerate to his dependants and so resourceful and jolly when confronted with the plebs that we do not notice the triviality of their subject-matter or their narrowness of outlook.

> In her younger days, ' Skittles ' often hunted with the Quorn hounds, riding horses which were lent her by an admirer of Hebrew origin, who hunted from Melton. One day he and his horse fell into a brook. ' Skittles ' jumped over them both, turned round, kissed her hand and said, ' Moses in the bulrushes, I see.' This is only one of the many good stories I have heard about ' Skittles.'

There is something faintly wrong in this good story about Skittles, but we dash past it, the racy anecdote carries us. We join too in the baiting of various provincial Mayors. Mayors are absurd, they show the wrong sort of awe at the approach of royalty, with the result that a drop of sweat falls from the nose of one of them on to Queen Alexandra's glove. 'Fortunately the Lady in Waiting had a handkerchief at hand,' so no real harm was done. (The mentality of the Duke here is precisely that of the Mayor, but he doesn't notice that, nor do we.) We relish, too, the wit of Sir Frederick Milner. Interrupted at a political meeting by a radical grocer, Sir Frederick dubbed him 'Treacle Tommy.' The grocer was furious and retorted with 'Frothy Fred,' but this was not nearly as clever, and when the election results came out it was the 'froth' that rose to the top, while the 'treacle' sank to the bottom, its natural home.

Yes, the general effect of the book is pleasant. The writer is a man of energy, good humour and natural sense, who has inherited and enhanced a great name, held a high post in the royal household, and found the world agreeable. He does not like the present day. Women are plainer, driving deteriorates, of the thirteen great London houses of his youth only four remain as private residences, and as for the country, the estates around Welbeck are let, or empty, and their staffs of servants are seeking employment elsewhere. Such are the results of Treacle Tommy and time. But the Duke is too good a sportsman to grumble : 'For all this, I believe human nature is and always will be the same ; it may therefore be only the outward and visible form of things which has so much altered. I hope the new world, though I do not always agree with its ways, holds just as many possibilities of happiness, good fellowship, and enjoyment of life as that which I knew, and shall try to some extent to describe.'

In a sentence such as this the landed aristocrat seems the only democrat, and our hearts go out to him. But he is far away from us really. His touches of arrogance and patronage, his childish interest in uniforms, and the clouds of retainers behind which he can retire combine to make him a very queer bird. No doubt the arrogance is unconscious, but the aristocrat does practise, more than most men, the art of switching off when a person or a situation incommodes him. Graciousness and bleakness alternate. Hence the mixed impression he makes upon the general public, and the reprisals he occasionally provokes. A regrettable incident once happened at Nottingham. Lord Roberts, attended by the Duke himself, was decorating veterans there, and one of the men, just as the ribbon was going to be pinned on him, opened his coat and out popped the head of a kitten. A kitten was the last thing which the Commander-in-Chief had expected, and he so hated cats that he stepped back and trod on the Duke's toe. All must deplore the veteran's conduct, yet the public is bound to pop out a kitten occasionally, or it would burst. It has, every now and then, to remind the governing classes that they must not take themselves and their awards too seriously, and if it is ever afraid to do this England will cease to be England.

[1937]

A working-class man I know—he grew up in a Gloucester-shire village—has told me of the reactions of the villagers there to the parson thirty years back. The parson was not disliked, he was a kindly, friendly fellow, who had the right word for every occasion. But when the right word was spoken and he passed out of earshot, swinging his stick and looking right and left at the sky, the villagers came into their own for a moment, and used foul language about him. They had to, to clear their chests and to get rid of their feeling of incompetence. To preserve their manhood and their self-respect, they had to splutter a little smut.

Mrs. Miniver, the gifted heroine of Miss Jan Struther's sketches, invites a similar reaction. She, too, has the right word for every occasion. What answer can the villagers make to a lady who is so amusing, clever, observant, broad-minded, shrewd, demure, Bohemian, happily-married, triply-childrened, public-spirited and at all times such a lady? No answer, no answer at all. They listen to her saying the right things, and are dumb. They watch her doing the right things in the right way, and are paralysed. Even if they disgrace themselves by spluttering smut in her hearing, she is not put out, for the class to which she and the parson belong has grown an extra thickness of skin in the last thirty years. 'Touchée!' she would exclaim, with her little ringing laugh, and pass on untouched. She is too wonderful with the villagers, she has them completely taped. Taximen, too. One day she overhears two ridiculous fat bottled-nosed taximen talking about the subconscious self. She takes the absurdity back to her husband, whose sense of humour coincides with her own, and if the taximen had turned the tables and ridiculed *her* she would have taken that back, too. She has learnt the defensive value of honesty, which was unknown to her immediate forebears, and consequently nothing short of physical violence can ever do her in. Even when the High-landers take off their trousers at the Games she is not discon-

[1] The book, not the film.

certed ; it is the governess who looks the other way. And she writes so well, knowing just where to place each word. And she has delighted thousands upon thousands of readers of *The Times* and been the subject of two *Times* leaders and of innumerable letters to *The Times* calling her charming, and she has been a clue in *Times* crossword puzzles. Why do a few of us stand glum by the roadside as the gallant little pageant passes ? Is it not just our own silly jealousy that prevents us from following in her train ?

Perhaps. But there is another possibility, which is more interesting to examine. It concerns the odd social fabric of these islands. Mrs. Miniver is beyond doubt a lady. But she is equally certainly not an aristocrat. Although her name is vaguely heraldic and her son at Eton and her brother-in-law the McQuern of Quern, she comes out of the top-drawer but one. She thinks she is in the top drawer of all, and that her good behaviour is the best kind of behaviour. It may be morally the best. But socially—no, and her quiet assurance that she is socially 'it' becomes rather trying. There is something the little lady has not got—some grace or grandeur, some fierce eccentricity, some sense of ancient lineage or broad acres lost through dissipation, something which makes patronage acceptable, even if it hurries the patron to the guillotine. She may be able to give chapter and verse for a distinguished ancestry, but distinction does not course in her blood. She has her own style, but she has not Style. Look at her treatment of poverty. She and her husband are poorish and not ashamed of it, which is very nice of them, but a fatal error for those who wish to seem always in the right. Her shabby old car, her unsnobbishness in living only in Kent, are deftly exploited, and serve to snub another lady who has smarter cars and lives in Gloucestershire. But dinginess is a dangerous weapon. It may break in the hand if used carelessly. She assumes that it will work in the social sphere as effectively as it does in the humorous and the moral, and that she can create the atmosphere of Madame de Sévigné by behaving like Mrs. Carlyle.

That—so far as one can put one's finger upon an elusive spot —is the trouble with Mrs. Miniver and with the class to which she and most of us belong, the class which strangled the aristocracy in the nineteenth century, and has been haunted ever since by the ghost of its victim. It is a class of tradesmen and professional men and little Government officials, and it has come into power consequent on the Industrial Revolution and Reform Bills and the Death Duties. But it has never been able to build itself an appropriate home, and when it asserts that an Englishman's home is his castle, it reveals the precise nature of its failure. We who belong to it still copy the past. The castles and the great mansions are gone, we have to live in semi-detached villas instead, they are all we can afford, but let us at all events retain a Tradesman's Entrance. The Servants' Hall has gone ; let the area-basement take its place. The servants themselves are going ; Mrs. Miniver had four, to be sure, but many a suburban mistress batters the registry offices in vain. The servants are unobtainable, yet we still say, ' How like a servant ! ' when we want to feel superior and safe. Our minds still hanker after the feudal stronghold which we condemned as uninhabitable.

This is not a great tragedy, according to present standards of sadness. Something much worse than middle-class complacency and facetiousness has got loose in the world to-day. But it is worth noting, and the working classes sometimes note it for themselves, and let out a hoot. They have something which the middle classes have not and the aristocracy once had ; spontaneity, natural gaiety, recklessness. They are losing it, for their betters have insisted upon their being insured, and insurance always has a soddening effect upon the spirits. But they retain enough of it to miss the point of the jokes in *Punch*, and to make rude noises when moral worth dons a plumed hat and masquerades as social distinction. There is a natural sympathy between the top drawer and the bottom. The ' castle ' and the ' hovel ' have understood one another, and have even approximated in type. Those who had everything have felt easy in the presence of those who had nothing ; and vice versa. A society constituted thus was not just and could not be permanent, but in the intervals of persecution and rebellion there was a harmony in the fabric of England which has been lost. The top drawer has now gone. The bottom drawer is being reorganised and dusted out. The top drawer but one makes its little jokes and imposes its whimsies and ideals as if nothing else was obtainable. And certainly there are worse things. But there are other things.

People still go on studying the English National Character. And Mrs. Miniver furnishes useful material. But the world moves so fast under the relentless lash of science that national characteristics are not likely to be of much importance in the future. They have a factitious value, especially in wartime, because they are exploited by rival governmental gangs, but the forces that form human nature have moved elsewhere. Just as Gloucestershire and Kent have become alike, so will England, Germany, Russia, and Japan become alike. Internationalism, unavowed or avowed, is a cert. Bloodstained or peaceful, it is coming. As it looms on the eastern horizon, the little differences of the past lose their colour, and the carefully explored English temperament seems in particular scarcely worth the bother that has been taken over interpreting it.

[1939]

In My Library

You are soon in my library and soon out of it, for most of the books are contained in a single room. I keep some more of them in a bedroom and in a little sitting-room and in a bathroom cupboard, but most of them are in what we will politely term the library. This is a commodious apartment—twenty-four feet by eighteen—and a very pleasant one. The ceiling is high, the paint white, the wallpaper ribboned-white, and the sun, when it shines, does so through lofty windows of early Victorian Gothic. Even when it does not shine, the apartment remains warm and bright, for it faces south. Round the walls are a dozen wooden bookcases of various heights and shapes, a couple of them well designed, the others cheap. In the middle of the room stands a curious object; a bookcase which once belonged to my grandfather. It has in its front a little projecting shelf supported on two turned pillars of wood, and it has a highly polished back. Some say it is a converted bedstead. It stood in a similar position in the middle of his study over a hundred years ago—he was a country clergyman. Bedstead or not, it is agreeable and original and I have tried to fill it with volumes of gravity, appropriate to its past. Here are the theological works of Isaac Barrow, thirteen volumes, full morocco, stamped with college arms. Here are the works of John Milton, five volumes, similarly garbed. Here is Evelyn's Diary in full calf, and Arnold's *Thucydides* and Tacitus and Homer. Here are my grandfather's own works bearing titles such as *One Primeval Language*, *The Apocalypse its own Interpreter* and *Mohammedanism Unveiled*. Have you read my grandfather's works? No? Have I read them? No.

My grandfather then is one of the influences that I can trace in my little collection. I never knew him in the flesh. He must have been rather alarming. His character was dogmatic and severe and he would not approve of some of the company which I oblige him to keep to-day. For close by, in a bookcase between the two windows, lurk works of another sort—Anatole France, Marcel Proust, Hérédia, André Gide—the type of Frenchman whose forerunners he denounced in a sermon preached to his village in 1871 on the occasion of the Fall of Paris. It is ironical that the book belonging to him which I most cherish should be a French book. This is a great encyclopaedia in fifty-two volumes—the *Biographie Universelle* of 1825. Each volume bears his dignified bookplate with our family arms and also the bookplate of Sir James Mackintosh, its previous owner. It is in bad condition—all the backs off—but it is a useful work of reference of the leisurely type, and makes excellent reading. There is nothing slick about it. It dates from the days before the world broke up, and it is a good thing occasionally to go back to these days. They steady us.

The next influence I have to note is that of his daughter, my aunt. I inherited her possessions and had to sell or give away most of her books before I could fit into my present quarters. But I kept what I liked best, and enough to remind me of her cultivated and attractive personality. She was a maiden lady of strong character, and a great reader, particularly of good prose. Trollope, Jane Austen, Charlotte Yonge, Malory, sound biographies of sound Victorians—these have come down from her. Books on birds also—Bewick and Morris. The birds remind me of her bookplate. She had a charming personal one of a foliated arabesque round a shield, and from the arabesque peep out birds, dogs and a squirrel—some of the living creatures who surrounded her country home where she led a quiet, happy and extremely useful life. She was interested in crafts—she started classes for leather-work in the village. She was herself a designer and worker, she designed and executed book-covers which were made up at the binder's, and my shelves (to which we now return) are enriched by several examples of her skill. Here are the Letters of Charles Darwin (whom she had known), and Ruskin's *Praeterita*, and Ruskin's *Giotto*—a fine example in pigskin, introducing the legendary O of Giotto and her own initials. The most ambitious of all her bindings—the *Rubaiyat of Omar Khayyam*—I gave away after her death to an oriental friend. I still miss that lovely book and wish I possessed it. I still see the charming design with which she decorated its cover —polo players adapted from an ancient Persian miniature—a design for which the contemporary dust jacket is a poor substitute.

However I am contemporary myself and I must get on to myself and not linger amongst ancestral influences any longer.

What did I bring to my library? Not much deliberately. I have never been a collector, and as for the first edition craze, I place it next door to stamp collecting—I can say no less. It is non-adult and exposes the book-lover to all sorts of nonsense at the hands of the book-dealer. One should never tempt book-dealers. I am myself a lover of the interiors of books, of the words in them—an uncut book is about as inspiriting as a corked up bottle of wine—and much as I enjoy good print and good binding and old volumes they remain subsidiary to the words : words, the wine of life. This view of mine is, I am convinced, the correct one. But even correctness has had its disadvantages and I am bound to admit that my library, so far as I have created it, is rather a muddle. Here's one sort of book, there's another, and there is not enough of any sort of book to strike a dominant note. Books about India and by Indians, modern poetry, ancient history, American novels, travel books, books on the state of the world, and on the world-state, books on individual liberty, art-albums, Dante and books about him—they tend to swamp each other, not to mention the usual pond of pamphlets which has to be drained off periodically. The absence of the collector's instinct in me, the absence of deliberate choice, have combined with a commendable variety of interests to evolve a library which will not make any definite impression upon visitors.

I have not a bookplate—too diffident or too much bother. I cannot arrange books well either ; shall it be by subjects or by heights ? Shall a tall old Froissart stand beside *The Times Atlas*, or beside a tiny Philippe de Commines ? I do not bang or blow them as much as I should, or oil their leather backs, or align those backs properly. They are unregimented. Only at night, when the curtains are drawn and the fire flickers, and the lights are turned off, do they come into their own, and attain a collective dignity. It is very pleasant to sit with them in the firelight for a couple of minutes, not reading, not even thinking, but aware that they, with their accumulated wisdom and charm, are waiting to be used, and that my library, in its tiny imperfect way, is a successor to the great private libraries of the past. 'Do you ever lend books ? ' someone may say in a public-spirited tone of voice at this point. Yes, I do, and they are not returned, and still I lend books. Do I ever borrow books ? I do, and I can see some of them unreturned around me. I favour reciprocal dishonesty. But the ownership of the things does give me peculiar pleasure, which increases as I get older. It is of the same kind, though not so strong, as the desire to possess land. And, like all possessiveness, it does not go down to the roots of our humanity. Those roots are spiritual. The deepest desire in us is the desire to understand, and that is what I meant just now when I said that the really important thing in books is the words in them—words, the wine of life—not their binding or their print, not their edition value or their bibliomaniac value, or their uncuttability.

One's favourite book is as elusive as one's favourite pudding, but there certainly are three writers whom I would like to have in every room, so that I can stretch out my hand for them at any moment. They are Shakespeare, Gibbon and Jane Austen. There are two Shakespeares in this library of mine, and also two outside it, one Gibbon, and one outside it, one Jane Austen and two outside it. So I am happily furnished. And, of course, I have some Tolstoy, but one scarcely wants Tolstoy in every room. Shakespeare, Gibbon and Jane Austen are my choice, and in a library one thinks of Gibbon most. Gibbon loved books but was not dominated by them. He knew how to use them. His bust might well stand on my grandfather's bookcase, to my grandfather's indignation.

[1949]

The London Library

In May 1841 the London Library was launched on the swelling tides of Victorian prosperity. It celebrates its centenary among the rocks. It is unharmed at the moment of writing—not a volume out of action—but the area in which it stands is cloven by the impacts of the imbecile storm. All around it are the signs of the progress of science and the retrogression of man. Buildings are in heaps, the earth is in holes. Safe still among the reefs of rubbish, it seems to be something more than a collection of books. It is a symbol of civilisation. It is a reminder of sanity and a promise of sanity to come. Perhaps the Nazis will hit it, and it is an obvious target, for it represents the tolerance and the disinterested erudition which they so detest. But they have missed it so far.[1]

Why should a private subscription library, which appeals to only a small section of the community, arouse exalted thoughts?

The answer to this question is to be found in the Library's history, and in its present policy. Speakers at its annual meetings are fond of saying that it is unique, which is more or less true, and that it is typically English, which greatly understates its claims. It is not typically English. It is typically civilised. It pays a homage to seriousness and to good sense which is rare in these islands and anywhere. It has cherished the things of the mind, it has insisted on including all points of view, and yet it has been selective. Ephemeral books, popular successes, most novels, many travelogues and biographies have been excluded from its shelves. And technical treatises, such as have helped to make the mess outside, have not been encouraged either. Of course it has had its lapses; one can find trash in it, and specialisation-lumber also. But its policy has always been to send those who want trash to the chain-libraries, and those who want lumber to their appropriate lumber-room. It caters neither for the goose nor for the rat, but for creatures who are trying to be human. The desire to know more, the desire to feel more, and, accompanying these but not strangling them, the desire to

[1] They hit it in 1944.

313

help others : here, briefly, is the human aim, and the Library exists to further it.

So much for its seriousness. Its good sense is equally remarkable. For it would be possible to have these admirable ideals, but to render them unacceptable through red-tape. That is the great snag in institutionalism. There may be fine intention and noble provision, but they often get spoiled by the belief that the public cannot be trusted, that it is careless, dishonest, grubby, clumsy, that it must on no account be ‘ allowed access ’ to the shelves, and is best served from behind a wire netting. The London Library, though an institution, will have nothing to do with this fallacy. It takes the risks. Its members can go all over its book-stores. There is a price to be paid ; books do get stolen, or taken out without being entered or taken out in unauthorised quantities, or kept out too long, or dogs-eared, or annotated in the margin by cultivated scribes who should know better ; but it is worth it, it is worth treating the creatures as if they were grown up, the gain to the humanities outweighs the financial loss. Moreover, it is the tradition of the library to help the student rather than to snub, and this promotes a decent reaction at once. And ‘ help ’ is indeed too feeble a word ; the officials there possess not only good-will, but wide and accurate knowledge, which is instantly placed at the enquirer’s disposal.

The library owes its origin to the spleen and to the nobility of Thomas Carlyle. The spleen came first ; Carlyle needed books of reference while he was writing his *Cromwell*, he could not afford to buy them all, and the journey from Chelsea to the British Museum Library was a vexatious one. Besides, when he got to the British Museum he found other people reading there too, which gave him the feeling of a crowd, and it is impossible to work in a crowd : ‘ add discomfort, perturbation, headache, waste of health.’ Grumbling and growling at his miserable fate, he betook himself to the drawing-room of Lady Stanley of Alderley in Dover Street, and burst forth there ; even in Iceland, he said, the peasants could borrow books, and take them away to read in their huts during the Arctic night ; only in London was there this ‘ shameful anomaly.’ The company tried to soothe him or to change the subject, but his growls continued ; books, books, one ought to be able to borrow books. And before long, he effected one of his junctions between private peevishness and public welfare, and persuaded other men of distinction to combine with him in launching a library. Gladstone, Hallam, Grote, Monckton Milnes joined him. A meeting was held at the Freeman's Tavern to promote a scheme for ' a supply of good books in all departments of knowledge.' Lord Eliot was in the chair, and Carlyle made a fine speech. It is said to be his only speech. Here are some sentences from it :

A book is a kind of thing which requires a man to be self-collected. He must be alone with it. A good book is the purest essence of the human soul. . . . The good of a book is not the facts that can be got out of it, but the kind of resonance that it awakes in our own minds. A book may strike out a thousand things, may make us know a thousand things which it does not know itself. . . . The founding of a Library is one of the greatest things we can do with regard to results. It is one of the quietest of things ; but there is nothing that I know of at bottom more important. Everyone able to read a good book becomes a wiser man. He becomes a similar centre of light and order, and just insight into the things around him. A collection of good books contains all the nobleness and wisdom of the world before us. Every heroic and victorious soul has left his stamp upon it. A collection of books is the best of all Universities ; for the University only teaches us to read the book : you must go to the book itself for what it is. I call it a Church also—which every devout soul may enter—a Church but with no quarrelling, no Church-rates. . . .

At this point, Carlyle was interrupted by laughter and cheers, and sat down good-temperedly. His speech is too optimistic, in view of our present information ; also too subjective in its emphasis on the ' resonance ' from books ; also too little aware of the power of concentration possessed by many readers, which enables them to-day to continue through an air-raid. But it is a noble utterance. It recalls us to the importance of seriousness, and to the preciousness and the destructibility of knowledge. Knowledge will perish if we do not stand up for it, and testify. It is never safe, never harvested. It has to be protected not only against the gangster but against a much more charming and seductive foe : the crowd. ' I know what I like and I know what I want,' says the crowd, ' and I don't want all these shelves and shelves of books. Scrap them.'

The Library started in two rooms at 49 Pall Mall, with five hundred members, and three thousand books. Conditions were Spartan ; no ink or paper was provided, and for a time there was no clock. In 1845 it moved into St. James's Square, and now it has a membership of four thousand, and about four hundred and seventy thousand books, together with various luxuries, including a comfortable reading-room. Its rise is largely due to a great librarian, Sir Charles Hagberg Wright, who died last year. Hagberg Wright had a European connection, and a European outlook. He was free from the insularity which has such a numbing effect on the collecting of books, and it is largely thanks to him that one feels the library to be not English but civilised. For the moment it has one overwhelming problem before it : that of not getting smashed and not getting burnt. But if normality returns it will have the task of getting into touch with the thought and literature of the Continent, however repellent the mental state of the Continent may be. And—a more congenial task—it will have to get up to date on America. It has never admitted, and it must never admit, the idea of exclusion ; in Hagberg Wright's wise little pamphlet, *The Soul's Dispensary*, there are some pertinent remarks on this, and a curious account of the war which he had to wage after the last war with various government departments before he could regain liberty for the reimportation of foreign literature.

[1941]

PLACES

A Letter to Madan Blanchard[1]

The London Library,
St. James's Square,
London.

April, 1931.

MY DEAR MADAN,

Captain Wilson keeps telling me about you, and I feel I should
like to write you a line. I shall send it by air mail to Paris, but
from Paris to Genoa in a pre-war express. At Genoa the confusion will begin. Owing to the infancy of Mussolini the steam-
packet will not start on time, and will frequently put in for
repairs. So slow is the progress that the Suez Canal may close
before it can be opened, and my letter be constrained to cross
Egypt by the overland route. Suez is full of white sails. One
of them, tacking southward, will make India at last, another
bring tidings of Napoleonic wars on a following breeze. Smaller
boats, duskier crews. Brighter dawns? Quieter nights anyhow. The world is unwinding. What of Macao, where no
news follows at all? What of the final transhipment? The
last little vessel scarcely moves as she touches the Pelews, the

---

[1] My correspondent is not imaginary. See *An Account of the Pelew Islands,
situated in the western part of the Pacific Ocean. Composed from the journals and
communications of Captain Henry Wilson and some of his officers, who in August
1783 were there shipwrecked in The Antelope, a packet belonging to the Hon. East
India Company*, by George Keate, Esq., F.R.S. and S.A. (Dublin, Luke
White, 1788.)

See also India Office, *Marine Records, 570a and 570c*, where his name is
spelt Blanshard.

See furthermore Rupack Street, Rotherhithe, London, S.E.

waves scarcely break, just one tiny ripple survives to float my
envelope into your hand. As the tide turns, I reach you. You
open my letter a hundred and fifty years before it is written, and
you read the words My dear Madan.

Before I forget, there are messages. Don't lose the compass
you asked for. Maintain the pinnace and her tackle in proper
repair. Help the natives to work any iron they recover from
the wreck, and look after the arms and ammunition for them.
£23 8s. 3d. wages are still due to you—do you want them ?
Above all Captain Wilson asks me to ' request Blanchard he will
never go naked, like the natives, as by preserving the form of
dress his countrymen have appeared in, he will always support
a superiority of character ; that he may be better enabled to
follow this advice, he was furnished with all the clothes we could
spare, and directed, when these were worn out, to make himself
trowsers with a mat.' He hopes that all this has been done, and
that you have not forgotten your Sundays. You may follow
Pelew customs in other ways. He sees no objection to two wives,
since Abba Thulle offered them, indeed a refusal might well cause
offence, but Sunday stands apart. Knot a string to remind yourself of it, or count coral insects, or something. Prince Lee Boo
saw the importance of Sunday as soon as he landed in England,
and has indeed gone so far as to be buried in Rotherhithe Church.
How about baptizing your Cockilla and Cockathey ?—though
this is my suggestion, not the Captain's. He says that I am not
to plague you with niceties, especially as you can't read, and
indeed wants me to draw a picture of a church and a pair of
trousers, and leave it at that. But I'm writing, because there's
just a chance that, on the turn of the tide, the answer to my
question may float back to me.

I want to know why you stopped behind when the others
went.

At the present moment I'm stuffed in between books, and old
ladies with worried faces are making notes in long arm-chairs, so
I feel it natural enough you should stop. The ends of the earth,
the depths of the sea, the darkness of time, you have chosen all
three. But when you chose them you were stuffed in somewhere or other yourself, latitude 6° 25′ N., longitude 136° E.,
date November 12th, 1783, so what were your grounds for
deciding ? Did it start as a joke ? Your mates never took you
seriously, and Wilson talks of your dry sense of humour. You

helped them to the very last to build the sloop, you even came aboard as she was moving to show where a sail had been stowed, then you took leave without the least regret, 'as if they were only sailing from London to Gravesend, and were to return by the next tide.' They couldn't believe their eyes when you went and sat down with the savages and the canoes, it seemed like a dream. Even Prince Lee Boo was amazed. He pointed to you as the canoes fell astern, and then he pointed to himself and said, ' I go with his people, he stop with mine. But I go with wise English, he stop with the savage Pelew. I go to visit King George and God, he only visit King Abba Thulle my father. Oh mystery ! How curious ! ' Captain Wilson then invited him to dine, after which he started being sick.

That ramshackle craft got safely to China, looking more like a packing-case than a sloop, with every sort of rag flapping, and the black and white magic stuff still showing round the stern. The John Company officials at Canton were not too pleased with the vision. They had sent out the *Antelope*, you see, one of their best vessels, and this was what came back, and they questioned Wilson pretty straightly over what had happened. I suspect—owing to my knowledge of history—that the *Antelope* had been despatched to annex the Pelew Islands for Great Britain, instead of which the Pelews have annexed the *Antelope*, and she now forms part of the coral reef at Oroora. Wilson had to explain this away as well as he could, also the disappearance of the stores, the death of Quarter-Master Godfrey Minks (drowned through swimming ashore with two suits of clothes on), the mortality among the Chinese crew (occurring no one remembered when) and the absence of two dogs and yourself. On the other hand, he could point to Prince Lee Boo, and this certainly calmed the officials. Lee Boo was a hostage, though the word was never used, he ensured the good behaviour of his father. The Company's plan was to educate him in England, and send him back to rule the islands for us ; he was to take with him horses, dogs, cows, pigs, goats, seeds, clothes, rum, and all that makes life bearable ; he was to oust Qui Bill from the succession, conquer the Artingalls with musket-fire, and reign over corpses and coco-nuts in a gold-laced suit. The small-pox had something to say to all that, and there will be no more talk of annexation yet awhile. You may rest in peace, my dear Madan, if rest is what you want, and your king Abba Thulle has saved his kingdom at the moment he lost his son. Such an amiable youth, and so intelligent. First he was puzzled by houses, then he called everything a house ; at Portsmouth he was ' put into a little house which was run away with by horses, most agreeable, the trees and fields went the other way,' and so reached London, which was ' all fine country, fine house upon house up to sky,' and skipped about half the night in a four-poster bed, peeping between the curtains, and crying, ' in England a house for everything. How wise ! ' He must have been charming. But I am more intrigued by you, about whom I know nothing except that you preferred the ends of the earth, the depths of the sea. Answer this letter if you can —there are various methods—and let me know why you went native, and how you are.

I meant to break the Prince's death to you gradually, but the news is already out, besides, I don't see why you should mind. I enclose his picture—it will amuse you, and you will hardly recognise who it is. You saw him going on board man-naked, with masses of wild fruit in his arms. Well, in a week they taught him to wear clothes like these, in a fortnight he wouldn't take even a waistcoat off except in the dark, and a year later you might have seen him in Mrs. Wilson's dining-room at Rotherhithe, offering her, with exquisite grace, three small cherries in a spoon. He had offered them in his hand at first, whereat the old lady had smiled slightly—you too may not know, but cherries are never handed in the hand. Observing her smile, he resorted to a spoon, and ' a blush actually forced itself through his dusky complexion.' Nothing was too refined for him, or too moral ; he embraced civilisation with the grace of a courtier and the integrity of a curate. He admired all Englishmen. He adored all Englishwomen ; he called the old ones ' mother '—the young ones—we shall never know. I wish he hadn't died—he must have been a dear. He seems to have loved his country. He was always talking about it, and collecting rubbish to sow there when he got back. His chief treasure was two little barrels of blue glass on stands, which an official gave him in Canton. His chief pleasure : driving in St. James's Park, close to where I am writing to you now. The Wilsons would not take him about much, for fear of infection. He went to see Lunardi go up in a balloon, but failed to mistake the balloon for a house, so was bored. Most days he was at school—an

Academy for young gentlemen close by, and many a merry tale did he bring back, but never an unkind prank. The Wilsons were devoted to him—he and young Harry used to practise javelin-throwing for hours in the attic—and there is no doubt that he came to his end among friends. You can tell this or not tell it to Abba Thulle as you like. Probably you had better not tell it, for the noblest of savages is apt to be deranged by the death of a son, and whatever else this letter does I do not want it to do you harm.

> Though the good CAPTAIN and his household strove
> Each other to excel in deeds of love,
> Will this, when told thy father (noble chief !),
> Stop the strong current of resistless grief ?
> Has not imagination, in alarms,
> Portray'd his son return'd with arts and arms,
> To bless his kingdom with a lasting race
> Of warriors all, and all in love with peace ?
> Shall he, regardless of each social tie,
> Calmly resign LEE BOO without a sigh ?
> And will unmoved thy generous uncles stand
> To hear thou died'st regretted in our land ?
> Ah no ! . . .

This is from an anonymous poem which someone sent Wilson after the funeral. I, too, feel ' Ah no ! ' If the generous uncles realise that we have, with the best intentions, committed murder, they will not be unmoved, and when they see you alone among them, and you're just his age—well, perhaps, they'll make you their king instead, but I wouldn't risk it. I would watch Abba Thulle tying a knot in a string at every full moon until his son comes back with the wise English, and I would say nothing.

What about your own relatives ? I don't even know whether you're English or French. I find you signed on to the *Antelope* at Falmouth, but that means anything, and the books in the library here make their usual imbecile noises when I mention your name. Here are *Metamorphoses, mœurs et instincts des insectes*, by Emile Blanchard. Would this attract you as a connection ? Or Samuel Laman Blanchard's *Collected Poems*. May I send them you ? Or a letter from Pierre Blanchard, *Sur les questions qui divisent l'Eglise gallicane*. Or Edward Blanchard's *Descriptive Guide to the Great Western Railway*. Or Frank Nelson Blanchard's

A revision of the king snakes : genus Lampropeltis. This is what is termed research. The Madans offer even wider scope to the earnest student, but I shall not pursue it beyond *Thelyphthora, a Treatise on Female Ruin.* This helpful work was composed by one Martin Madan, only three years before the *Antelope* struck, and him, if anyone, I assign to you as uncle. I haven't any news about your mates either—they scattered and got other jobs— Nick Tyacke, little Will Cobbledick, and all. Young Mr. Devis stopped in India, to paint portraits there, the rest of the party proceeding to England as aforesaid, via St. Helena. The two arrow wounds he got on your expedition still hurt him in the jaw. Do you remember when Mr. Devis drew Abba Thulle's wives, and they were so frightened—Ludee in particular, that very pretty one? Are your Cockilla and Cockathey very pretty too? I suggested to Wilson that they might be, which would explain your vagaries, and he answered yes, they very well might be, but no one knew, since they had not arrived from the interior by the time the sloop sailed. He also said that you were known to have formed 'no special attachments on the island '—it seems rather to have been a general feeling, something connected with the Artingall wars. It was in a canoe among savages and Englishmen mixed, coming back from the second war, that you said ' I mean to live here for ever.' Wilson was irritated, for he had noticed nothing remarkable about you ; you were like any other seaman at £2 a month, good tempered, inoffensive, quiet, enjoyed fighting—the usual thing : he took it for insolence when you stuck to it, and perhaps still isn't quite sure. ' Did you ever want to stop on there yourself, sir ? ' I asked him. He sighed, ' Ah well, ah well,' and looked at his wrist. The bone with which Abba Thulle invested him still encircles his wrist, he won't have it removed, and polishes it every evening to keep his luck, as he was told. ' This denotes that I am a Rupack, or noble, of the first rank,' he continued, smiling, ' and it was conferred on me by the natives in front of one of their public assembly halls or " Pyes." Dr. Keate says the bone belongs to a whale, but in my judgment it is a merman's, for they are not uncommon in the China seas.' I questioned him more on the Pyes, and he said, ' Ah well, the Pyes, most remarkable, most.' I like to hear him sigh ' Ah well.' It runs under so much of his talk. He will never forget the three months he spent on the island, or the Apples of Paradise they brought him the morning he sailed, or the canoes escorting him over the reef while they cried, 'Come again to us, good Englishman, come!' The English will not come again—at least I hope not. Your island has swung away from ours into what we choose to call darkness, and into what I can't help calling life.

Look at Lee Boo! Think how it ended, in spite of all the care they took. Mr. Sharpe (your late surgeon) never let him out of his sight, and as soon as the first trace of infection appeared they sent for Doctor Carmichael Smith too. Doctor Smith examined him, and told the Wilsons at once that he must die. A few days later he knew it himself. He was walking across the room, saw himself in the glass, and was disgusted—shook his head, and said that his father and mother, thousands of miles away, were grieving. To Mr. Sharpe he said : ' Good friend, when you go back to Pelew tell Abba Thulle that Lee Boo take much drink to make small-pox go away, but he die ; Captain Wilson, Mother Wilson, very kind—all English very good men —much sorry he could not speak to the King the number of fine things the English had got—he do all they tell him, but he die.' The little barrels of blue glass were to be given to the king. As long as Doctor Smith was with him, he complained of his symptoms in case he could be cured, but at other times he thought only of his friends. To add to their misery, old Mrs. Wilson lay ill in the next room, and he kept calling out to her ' Lee Boo do well, mother,' to comfort her, or tried to visit her, and had to be stopped. Hot baths, blistered back and legs —the boy endured it all, sensible, unselfish, ultra-civilised to the last. What he really thought, no one knew or has dared to guess. He managed to pass away without distressing the Christians or disappointing the philosophers, and he has a tablet in Rotherhithe churchyard consequently. John Company paid for it, and for the funeral, too, though the Wilsons would gladly have settled it all themselves. All Rotherhithe attended—the two little painted figures upon the alms houses couldn't ever have looked down on so vast a concourse—officials from London, all the young people from the Academy, although it was their Christmas holiday. The stone was put up after a year, which gives enough time for all flesh to decay.

To the Memory
of Prince LEE BOO,
A native of the PELEW, or PALOS Islands:
and Son to ABBA THULLE, Rupack or King
of the Island COOROORAA ;
who departed this Life on the 27th of December,
1784
aged 20 years ;
This Stone is inscribed
by the Honourable United EAST INDIA COMPANY,
as a testimony of Esteem for the humane and
kind Treatment afforded by HIS FATHER to the
Crew of their Ship the ANTELOPE,
Captain WILSON, which was
wrecked off that Island in
the Night of the 9th of August, 1783.

Stop, Reader, stop !—let NATURE claim a Tear
—A prince of *Mine*, LEE BOO, lies bury'd here.

I almost shed a tear, but not quite ; he was rather too harmless
a blackamoor—such a puppet, he always did as he was bid, and
people like that don't seem quite real. The people who touch
my imagination are obstinate suddenly—they do break step, and
I always hope they'll get by without the sergeant punishing them.
It was so like poor Lee Boo that he loved above all things to see
the Guards drilling in the Park. They are drilling there still, so
are the ladies in the long chairs in this library, so are the books
in the shelves. If it isn't one set of rules it's another, even for
heroism. I ought to feel free myself, as I've health, strength,
and am middle-aged, yet I can't keep my hat on in a church, for
instance, even if no one's looking, and if I'm fighting never
manage to hit below the belt. While not getting fussed over
this, I can't but remember the people who managed better, and
it's in order to meet them in the flesh that I study history. Here
and there, as I rake between the importancies, I come across them
—the people who carried whimsicality into action, the salt of
my earth. Not the professional whimsies—their drill's dearer
than anyone's—but the solid fellows who suddenly jib. The
queer thing is we all admire them—even when we're hard-bitten
disciplinarians like old Wilson. They've got hold of something
which we know is there, but have never dared to grasp in our

hands. A sort of stinging nettle. I went down to the tomb the other day, and thought ' No, he isn't quite good enough, he was stung when he wasn't looking, which happens to anyone.' I took down a lot of notes about Rotherhithe church, the neighbourhood, Shad Thames, etc., thinking they would interest you, but if they interested you, you'd have come back to them, so I tore the notes up and wandered about feeling rather tired and out of place, then I got across the river to Stepney, and through in at Aldgate and out at Newgate, back to this part, where I live now.

Well, that concludes my news, and now it's your turn. I will enclose you one more poem, and then I'm done :

> O'er the mighty Pacific whose soft swelling wave
> A thousand bright regions eternally lave,
> 'Mid rocks red with coral and shellfish abounding,
> The note of the parrot and pigeon resounding :
> Crowned with groves of banana and taper bamboo
> Rise the gay sunny shores of the Isles of *Pelew.*

This is how a Miss Heisch, before she married a Mr. Hookey, imagined your present home. I laughed the first time I read her poem, but the second time I found myself sighing ' Ah well ! ' Write to me if you possibly can—I suppose on the bark of some tree. Lower it one evening as the tide turns, and watch it drift out through the coral reefs. The monsoons will hurry it westward, and the spray begin whispering ' Progress ' against it. Swifter boats, paler crews, and an intelligent interest among savants as it is raised aboard in a dredge off, let us say, Réunion. ' C'est bien une lettre ? ' Pourquoi pas ? It is addressed ? Apparently ! Then forward it onward to England. The waves are rising, the world's winding up, but King George is still on his throne, so's God. Boom ! Before the last echo of 1815 dies away, 1914 strikes, and here we are. Your letter now takes to the air. Heavily surcharged, liable to customs duty, enterable under income tax, subject to quarantine, notifiable, censorable confiscatable, it crashes through the library window, and explodes in my hand. None of the old ladies notice it—they are still researching. I wait until the envelope of smoke has vanished, I find my right spectacles, and I decipher a hundred and fifty years after it was written, the single word ' aaa.'

What can ' aaa ' mean ? Perhaps you have forgotten your

English. I will send for a Pelew dictionary. While it is coming I have one more thing to say to you.

Once I used to come across an Irish clergyman—an unusual fellow, I never liked him much, he died before your time. He invented a group of islands to relieve his feelings on, and oddly enough placed some of them south-east of Formosa—that's to say, more or less where you actually are. One of these islands contained very small men, another very large ones, a third was inhabited by horses, and the fourth flew. The clergyman was too bad tempered to take much notice of what he was doing : I mean whether the men were big or little they were intended to make men of his own size look small, and so with his horses : he didn't care for horses but he hated people, and used horses for saying so. Well, in one of the islands he imagined men living for ever. It sounded like Paradise, but of course there was a catch—I will not tell you what, but it is a terrifying one, and nothing he has ever said to me has upset me more. If he is right on the subject of eternal youth in the Southern seas, don't answer this letter, in fact you won't want to. But if I am right, send the answer that tells everything, the answer I have imagined, 'aaa' (Pelew for Yes).[1]

Yours ever,

E. M. Forster.

[1] My letter was never delivered. An explanation for this can be found in *A Supplement to the Account of the Pelew Islands ; compiled from the journals of the Panther and Endeavour, two vessels sent by the Honourable East India Company to those Islands in the year* 1790, by the Reverend John Pearce Hockin, of Exeter College, Oxford, M.A. London, printed for Captain Henry Wilson by W. Bulmer and Co., Cleveland Row. 1803.

[1931]

India Again

I

It was a dull, cold Friday morning in October 1945 when I left England. Two days later, on the Sunday afternoon, I was in India. Below me lay the desert of Rajputana, baked by the sun and blotched with the shadows of clouds. The 'plane came down for half an hour near the dragon-shaped fort of Jodhpur, then took off again, and it was Delhi. I felt dazed. And we had travelled so fast that we were ahead of schedule, and had no one to meet us. Suddenly very slow, instead of very quick, we jogged in a tonga through the Delhi bazaars, our luggage in front, our legs hanging down behind, the dust rising, the sun setting, the smoke drifting out of the little shops. It became dark and the sky was covered with stars. Were we lost? No. An unknown host, an Indian, received us, and next day I stood on the high platform of the Great Mosque, one of the noblest buildings in India and the world. Profound thankfulness filled me. The sky was now intensely blue, the kites circled round and round the pearl-grey domes and the red frontispiece of sandstone, sounds drifted up from Delhi city, the pavement struck warm through the soles of my socks ; I was back in the country I loved, after an absence of twenty-five years.

I was bound for a conference of Indian writers. The All-India centre of the P.E.N. Club had invited us. The people I was to meet were nearly all Indians, of the professional classes —doctors, lawyers, public servants, professors at the university, business men. Many of them were old friends or the sons of old friends. They were what is termed ' intellectuals ' and they lived in towns. I did not see much of the countryside nor of the industrial conditions. I met a few Englishmen but not many, and have often looked round a crowded room and observed that I was the only westerner in it. Such are my credentials, or, if you prefer, such are my limitations.

The big change I noticed was the increased interest in politics. You cannot understand the modern Indians unless you realise that politics occupy them passionately and constantly, that artistic problems, and even social problems—yes and even economic problems—are subsidiary. Their attitude is ' first we must find the correct political solution, and then we can deal with other matters.' I think the attitude is unsound, and used to say so ; still, there it is, and they hold it much more vehemently than they did a quarter of a century ago. When I spoke about the necessity of form in literature and the importance of the individual vision, their attention wandered, although they listened politely. Literature, in their view, should expound or inspire a political creed.

Externally the place has not changed. It looks much as it did from the train. Outside the carriage windows (the rather dirty windows) it unrolls as before—monotonous, enigmatic, and at moments sinister. And in some long motor drives which I took through the Deccan there were the same combinations of hill, rock, bushes, ruins, dusty people and occasional yellow flowers which I encountered when I walked on the soil in my youth. There is still poverty, and, since I am older to-day and more thoughtful, it is the poverty, the malnutrition, which persists like a ground-swell beneath the pleasant froth of my immediate experience. I do not know what political solution is correct. But I do know that people ought not to be so poor and to look so ill, and that rats ought not to run about them as I saw them doing in a labour camp at Bombay. Industrialism has increased, though it does not dominate the landscape yet as it does in the west. You can see the chimneys of the cotton mills at Ahmedabad, but you can see its mosques too. You can see little factories near Calcutta, but they are tucked away amongst bananas and palms, and the one I have in mind has an enormous tree overhanging it, in whose branches a witch is said to sit, and from whose branches huge fruit occasionally fall and hit the corrugated iron roofs with a bang, so that the factory hands jump. No—externally India has not changed. And this changelessness in her is called by some observers ' the real India.' I don't myself like the phrase ' the real India.' I suspect it. It always makes me prick up my ears. But you can use it if you want to, either for the changes in her or for the unchanged. ' Real ' is at the service of all schools of thought.

It is when you leave the country, or the streets of the town, and go into the private houses, that you begin to notice a second great alteration, second only to politics—namely, the lifting of purdah, the increasing emancipation of women. It struck me particularly in cities which are largely Moslem, such as Lahore and Hyderabad, where women once kept rigidly behind the veil. I have been in my life three times to Hyderabad, some of my happiest Indian days were spent there, so I have been able to trace this change. My first visit was in 1912 and then I saw scarcely any Indian women. My second visit was in 1921, when I was admitted into some family circles and saw a good deal of what may be called ' semi-purdah '—ladies coming out into company, but not coming avowedly, and retiring at any moment behind the veil if they felt disposed to do so. To-day, purdah has broken down at Hyderabad, except amongst the most conservative, and at the receptions to which I went the women sometimes outnumbered the men. Since they kept to their lovely Indian saris, the effect was exquisite ; it was a delight to look round at so much gracefulness and graciousness, at so many and such well-chosen colours. I don't know how far into society this lifting of the veil has extended. But I imagine that sooner or later the change will extend to the villages and transform the Indian social fabric from top to bottom. Our world does not go back, though whether it progresses God alone knows, and in India, as in the west, women will shortly have the same opportunities as men for good and for evil.

The receptions I have been mentioning usually took the form of buffet dinners—they are an innovation since my time. Long tables are loaded with Indian food, and sometimes one table is labelled ' vegetarian ' and the other ' non-vegetarian.' You help yourself, or are helped. I take away pleasant memories of these buffet dinners, memories of Indians moving elegantly through well-filled rooms, with well-filled plates in their hands, and miraculously conveying food to their mouths in the folds of a chapatti. There is rationing, but its workings are mysterious and I did not grasp them or suffer from them. For the well-to-do, life is much easier in India than in England. The shops are full of tinned delicacies for those who can afford them— butter, cheese, even plum puddings. For the poor, life is much harder there than here.

The Indians I met mostly talked English. Some of them spoke very well, and one or two of them write in our language with great distinction. But English, though more widely spoken than on my last visit, is worse spoken, more mistakes are made

in it, and the pronunciation is deteriorating. ' Perpéndicule '
for ' perpendicular '. ' Pip ' into my office for ' pop.' Here
are two tiny slips which I noted in a couple of minutes, and both
of them made by well-educated men. The explanation, I think,
is that Indians at the schools and universities are now learning
their English from other Indians, instead of from English teachers
as in the past. Furthermore, they have little occasion to meet
our people socially and so brush it up ; intercourse is official and
at a minimum, and even where there are mixed clubs the two
communities in them keep apart. So it is not surprising that
their English is poor. They have learnt it from Indians and
practise it on Indians.

Why talk English at all ? This question was hotly debated at
the P.E.N. conference of All-India writers. Writers from central
or upper India were in favour of Urdu or Hindi as a common language for the whole peninsula. Writers from Bengal
favoured Bengali, and it has great claims from the literary point
of view. Writers from the south, on the other hand, preferred
English. The debate, if I may say so, continues, and into it, as
into everything, come politics. I mention it to indicate the
trend of events, the change in emphasis. Meanwhile, in this
uneasy interregnum, English does get talked and gets interlarded
in the oddest way with the Indian vernacular. I was travelling
one day to Baroda in a crowded second-class carriage. Indians,
my luggage, their luggage, myself and a number of loose oranges
were piled up together in confusion, and the Indians were
arguing. Their language was Gujarati, but they used so many
English words that I followed what they were saying. They
were arguing about religion and free-thought. I intervened and
was welcomed into the conversation, which was now carried on
entirely in English out of courtesy to me. I did not follow it
the better for that, but they peeled me an orange and we parted
friends. Indeed, it is difficult to conclude an Indian railway
journey on any other note. Their response to ordinary civility
is immediate. I don't think they are particularly friendly in the
street—if you ask them the way they are suspicious. But
squashed in a railway carriage they seem to expand. And my
reason for wanting English to be the common language for
India is a purely selfish reason : I like these chance encounters,
I value far more the relationships of years, and if Indians had not
spoken English my own life would have been infinitely poorer.

My visit ended all too soon. On a Friday afternoon in December—it was again a Friday—I was walking about in the sunshine of Karachi. And on the Sunday evening I was in London. Our train was icy cold, it arrived at Waterloo two hours late, midnight, thick fog, refreshment-rooms closed, waiting-rooms closed, local trains gone, no taxi could leave the station. The grumpy railway policeman to whom we appealed was glad we were uncomfortable, and said so, while a poster on the wall exhorted us to practise even greater austerity, since it was peace time. It was not much of a return, it was not like the arrival in Delhi, and as the policeman's sulky bulky back disappeared into the gloom I found it understandable that not everybody should care for England.

2

The conference I had attended was held at Jaipur. A thousand people, nearly all of them Indians, were assembled in the great town hall. It is a magnificent apartment. At one end was a platform, on which sat Mrs. Naidu, the President of the conference, the Prime Minister of Jaipur, and other notables. At the lower end five big arches opened on to the outer world. The arches were hung with straw curtains through which could be seen the tops of trees and the roofs of the Maharajah's palace, sweltering in the October sunshine. Above the arches, high on the wall, ran a lattice and behind it every now and then shadowy gracious figures passed, just discernible against the brightness. Silent as ghosts, colourless though not formless, they were the figures of ladies going to their purdah galleries to watch our deliberations. Or perhaps they were coming away from their purdah galleries because we had bored them. I don't know. But that sort of cloud-movement high up in the thickness of the wall, that ethereal shuttle playing left to right, or right to left behind the lattice, went on all the time, and gave a sense of spaciousness and of strangeness. We might be the future, but we were observed by the past.

Down in the hall we plodded away at our agenda. We had come to discuss literature as a unifying force, the future of the Indian languages, the Indian copyright act, a scheme for an encyclopedia, and so on. Fascinating to me, though I knew nothing of the subjects, was the symposium on the Indian languages. Twenty minutes were allotted to each. There were sixteen languages in all, and so writers from all parts of the peninsula could learn what was being done elsewhere, and could contact their colleagues, perhaps for the first time. A sense of enlargement and of complexity stole over the audience as they discussed whether, despite all these languages and perhaps through them, India could not be one. In fact we slid towards politics. Everything out there does. But we did not go over the edge. It remained a conference of writers and the organisation which convened it is pledged to be non-political.

Out of school we amused ourselves. We rode on elephants —though I myself find such a ride elevating rather than amusing. We looked at the curious pink city of Jaipur—an early example of town planning—and went to the romantic ancient capital of the state which lies above it in a crack of the hills, and is said to have as its neighbour a fabulous hoard of jewels. We entered a Hindu temple—a rare experience in these days for the non-Hindu ; twenty-five years ago, if my memory serves, entry was not so difficult. We attended a political demonstration. We ran over a cobra. But the conference dominated, and I would like to refer, before leaving it, to the moving address made by the Prime Minister of Jaipur, Sir Mirza Ismail. He described the atmosphere in which all modern writers must function, and held it to be their duty to keep in touch with the world, but not as politicians. Not much of the oratory was of his high order or struck his international note. But his concern with moral issues was typical of other speakers, and typical, too, his indifference to art for art's sake. Listening to him and to others, I felt that India had indeed changed. The Jaipur conference would have been impossible twenty-five years back.

When it was over, I travelled about, meeting many writers, and acquiring a good many books. These last are following after me in a boat and have not yet arrived. When I have digested them I shall have a better general notion of the Indian literary scene. Here meanwhile are a few notes. Book production : very active, though the authors are miserably paid. Short stories are popular : I read some excellent ones in Bengal. Poetry often echoes T. S. Eliot or Auden. Drama is not prominent. Criticism weak. Indians have a marked capacity for worship, or for denunciation, but not much critical sense, as criticism is understood in the west. As for great writers, there is no one alive to-day of the stature of Tagore, or of Iqbal. I have had the honour of meeting each of these great men once. Both are dead now, and their disappearance has impoverished the scene.

The cinema. Since my last visit to India, a film industry has sprung up. I believe it is the second largest in the world. It has its headquarters in Bombay. Its results are evident, and in the cities advertisements brighten the walls or hang from the lamp-posts. They often take the form of a youth and a maiden. The maiden gazes before her at the traffic, the youth gazes down the nape of the maiden's neck ; and thousands of passers-by see them and go in the evening for more. I went twice myself, but had no luck. My first film was crude anti-Japanese propaganda. It was shown in a remote Indian State, in an excellent little modern cinema ; you could not have wanted a better designed house—very simple, with a royal box at the back. The hero was a police inspector, who sang a good deal, and the heroine, who also sang, tricked some fifth columnists. No money had been spent on it, and there was no talent in it. The other Indian film I saw was at Delhi : an ambitious historical film on the subject of the Emperor Humayun. This was much better—decent photography and acting—but I could not agree with my ardent young host who declared it was far superior to our ' King Henry V.' That remark, though I did not tell him so, was an example of the Indian uncritical spirit. The production of ' Humayun ' was fussy and the camera was always on the move. But though I was not fortunate with my two pictures, I am certain that a great future awaits the Indian film industry. There is the climate, there is the scenery ; for subjects there is the dramatic history, and the varied contemporary life ; and Indians have an innate power of acting naturally and of looking graceful. So I wish that youth and maiden on the advertisements well, even when they warble a duet.

Of modern architecture, the chief example I saw was the great new university at Hyderabad. This is an interesting innovation. It is built in the American fashion on a Campus, a wide open space several miles from the centre of the city, in beautiful country, among flowering shrubs. And it attempts to blend two styles of architecture which occur in the Hyderabad state—

one style being Mohammedan, and the other derived from the famous Buddhist caves of Ajanta. It is an ambitious work and there is nothing comparable with it over here ; you could put dear little Cambridge down in the middle of it. And another achievement—this time in engineering—is the titanic steel bridge over the Hoogli at Calcutta. It connects the squalid railway station with the tousled city, and the contrast between it and both of them is overwhelming.

Painting and sculpture : are they progressing ? A good deal may be heard about them in the future. For painting, Bengal is the chief centre. I went to several studios in Calcutta, and I also visited Santaneketan—the home and the creation of Tagore. Santaneketan, about eighty miles from Calcutta, is an impressive little place, a sort of cultural and humanistic university. I spent a night there, and understood why it has exercised a mystic influence on many of its sons. You will either know a great deal about Santaneketan or else you will never have heard of it. It is that kind of place. Its name means ' The Home of Peace.' The painters whom it has nurtured tend to the religious, the gentle, the ethereal. Down in Calcutta, on the other hand, are pictures which are definite, robust, and based on the Folk Art of Bengal. Folk Art there has a genuine existence among the people—I saw, for instance, a delightful collection of dolls which had been made in the villages. Each doll was a joy and sometimes a terror, too—dolls can be both at once. And the art of the best-known Calcutta painter, Jamini Roy, came out of the villages and is based on the earth. I went to Mr. Roy's studio. Many small white rooms were filled with his work, for he is prolific. Although a Hindu, he once made an imaginative approach to Christianity, and his ' Christian ' pictures, particularly of the Last Supper, have great poignancy. I met other excellent painters too—younger men, who call themselves the Calcutta Group, and there has been an exhibition of Bengal Art at Government House under the auspices of the Governor's wife, Mrs. Casey, and the Calcutta Group has helped her with it.

To the tragic problem of India's political future I can contribute no solution. And perhaps you may think that there was not much justification for allowing a person of my type to go out at a moment of crisis. If you think that, you will agree with a chorus of indignant colonels at Delhi who were overheard exclaiming ' What next ! Fancy sending out old gentlemen who fall ill and can do no possible good.' As regards myself, the colonels were not accurate. Old I am, gentleman I may or may not be, ill I was not. I have never felt better. And did I do any good? Yes, I did. I wanted to be with Indians, and was, and that is a very little step in the right direction.

And turning from myself to people who are far more important than I am, namely to the young, I do pray that young English people who like Indians and want to be with them will be encouraged to go to their country. Goodwill is not enough. Of that I am too sadly convinced. In fact, at the present moment goodwill out there is no use at all. The reactions to it are instantly cynical. The only thing that cuts a little ice is affection or the possibility of affection. Whatever the political solution, that can surely do no harm. But it must be genuine affection and liking. It must not be exercised with any ulterior motive. It must be an expression of the common humanity which in India and England and all the world over has been so thwarted of late, and so despised.

[1946]

Luncheon at Pretoria

I have only been to Pretoria once, but it was a great success. It happened back in the twenties. I was staying with some acquaintances at Jo'burg—thus we called it—and the idea was that we should go to lunch with some acquaintances of theirs over at Pretoria. We were to drive over and see the sights, and, after lunch, attend an official reception at Union Buildings.

This idea was carried out with good humour. The drive was, to be sure, not a remarkable one. The boundless spaces of South Africa were in a measured mood, they rolled inadequately, and every now and then a label was stuck in them to show that we were passing the entrance of private property. The dust was like any other dust, and there was a good deal of it, and the trees were greyish and lanky. But Pretoria turned out to be a dear little place, with the touch of two civilisations upon it. Down below were the straight streets of quiet modest Dutch houses, and the statue of Oom Paul by the railway station. Up on the hill was a fine Imperial effort : Union Buildings, with its pavilions, its long terraces, its two domes. An agreeable morning was spent, the sights were indicated and viewed with complaisance, and then it was time for lunch.

The Pretoria acquaintances of my Jo'burg acquaintances were bankers. They lived in a very good class suburb. The husband was away on business, so his wife, a dignified handsome and civil lady, had to do the honours. She welcomed us to her cool marblified house, which had a commodious drawing-room, a dining-room, a hall, and (as I was to discover later) the usual offices. There were eight or ten guests all going on to the government reception, like ourselves. They behaved as guests do, or did, behave. We went into the drawing-room and talked a little, and then we went into the dining-room and talked a little more and ate and drank a little. It would be unjust to call us a set of dull dogs. We were not dogs, we were not even dull. We were not amusing or bored or critical or cross or anything. We were just a collection of well-fed people who did not know one another well and did not want to. This sort

336

of entertainment used to go on—and pray why not?—all over the padded portions of the globe. The acquaintances gather and goggle, their mouths fall open, food goes into the mouths and noises come out, neither at the call of necessity, and never simultaneously. (Belching is confined to the Tribes without the Law.) Sometimes the mouths open sideways to express deference, benignity, or repletion. Wearing a blue serge suit which had cost, when new, eleven pounds, I performed these antics with my peers, I too simpered pleasantly.

Then came the dish which transformed our lives.

It was a chicken fricassee.

It was a fricassee of the moister persuasion. The birds lay low in the water and the various vegetable adjuncts scarcely broke its steaming surface. The mixture swished and trembled upon an enormous oval platter, which no doubt was of silver, having regard to the status of the house. The house-boy carried it round, inclining towards each guest with deference but without intimacy, and each guest, without looking at the house-boy, swayed both hands leftward, and removed a moderate portion to the plate. When he came to me, he tilted the platter a little, to convenience me further. A piece of chicken dragged its moorings and slid to the edge, another followed, and then the gravy gathered in a great tidal wave, gathering strength as it moved, and rolling little onions in its depths. I was busy simpering, and had no conception of what was upon me. Something stung my wrist. The platter had overbalanced, and the entire fricassee poured over me and splashed on to the carpet. ' Sah, sorry sah, sorry,' said the house-boy, waving his foot which had been scalded. I answered with a shriek of laughter. Why is laughter so difficult to describe? I hooted, I yelled, I shrieked. I saw a merrythought perching on my waistcoat and went all faint. An onion bumped, I thought I should have died. Up jumped our hostess, flung away her napkin, took hold of me where I was dry, and led me to a suitable apartment. She too was weak with laughter. The guests jumped up, waving their arms and spluttering, more negroes came running to the cries, the children's Scotch Nanny appeared with a bottle of ammonia from the nursery. Not a moment was to be lost if I were to be got right for the government reception. ' Sah, sah, sorry,' repeated the house-boy. He had lost his head, but without animation. I gave him my trousers—in some ways our gravest

problem. He dropped them upon the tessellated pavement of
the hall, and they were there, a lamentable concertina, when
other guests arrived. Our hostess lent me her husband's sky
blue Japanese dressing-gown. Though not of the best period,
it was a sumptuous garment, and clad in it I hopped round the
house like a tropical bird, now taking a sip of coffee in the dining-
room, now putting in some work at the pantry sink. ' He likes
to look like that,' she wailed, indicating me to the newer arrivals.
' He always looks like that. He likes to.'

Afterwards, rationalising the incident, she praised me without
stint, she interpreted my hysteria as a deliberate piece of good
manners, designed to save her lunch party. It is true that most
bankers would not have laughed. Their sense of value is too
sound. And King Edward VII is said to have ill-brooked the
arrival of a tureen of anchovy sauce upon his shirt front, at a
moment when he was cementing the entente cordiale. But it
was not true that I had behaved well. I could not help myself ;
except in the severely scientific sense, I was not behaving at all.
' You were wonderful, quite marvellous,' she insisted. Pleasant
it was to walk by her side into Union Buildings, and in my blue
serge suit too. Miracles had been wrought upon it by the Nanny
and negroes, and for a short time I did not look so bad. Towards
the end of the reception some ominous clouds appeared, and the
drive back to Jo'burg was altogether too searching. I arrived
with every grease-spot stencilled in African dust.

So next day it went to the cleaners, and was back in time to
be packed for my journey northward. It came out for a mayoral
tea in Rhodesia. The noted pattern reappeared, faint at first,
then unmistakable. I had it seen to again on the boat, and
wore it for a lunch at Mombasa. Three days of the red soil of
Uganda finished it off, and by Egypt it was clear that it could
not be worn again. So when I got home, I claimed from the
insurance people and told them the whole story. They forked
out four pounds, but not graciously. They said that the under-
writers had expressed surprise.

[1940]

The United States

America is rather like life. You can usually find in it what you look for. If you look for skyscrapers or cowboys or cocktail parties or gangsters or business connections or political problems or women's clubs, they will certainly be there. You can be very hot there or very cold. You can explore the America of your choice by plane or train, by hitch-hike or on foot. It will probably be interesting, and it is sure to be large.

I went there for the first time at the age of sixty-eight. By sixty-eight one is so to speak a pilgrim grandfather who knows very clearly what to look for when he disembarks. I had no doubt as to what I wanted to discover in America. It was to provide me with scenery and individuals. The scenery was to be of two sorts—gigantic and homely. The individuals were not to be representative—I never could get on with representative individuals—but people who existed on their own account and with whom it might therefore be possible to be friends. That is the America I looked for and was to find. My visit was a complete success from my own point of view.

After a respectful glance at New York, I went a hundred miles north into the Berkshires. It was April. The trees were leafless—thousands and thousands of birch trees, their trunks whiter than the birch trees here, milk white, ghost white in the sharp sunshine, covering the sides of the valley and the crests of the hills ; and among the birches pushed pine and hemlock—which is like a not very dark green yew. Was I in England ? Almost, but not quite. That was again and again to be my sensation, and in the Arizona Desert I was to feel I was almost but not quite in India, and in the Yosemite Valley that it was not quite Switzerland. America is always throwing out these old-world hints, and then withdrawing them in favour of America. To return to the Berkshires : after a few days' quiet the snow descended and silence became absolute. The country became primeval and polar—endless purity, underspreading motionless trees. I can never be grateful enough for those opening days of silence and snow. They imposed proportion. They made me

realise that America is not all town : such a generalisation would
be truer of England. It is country—controlled no doubt by
mechanised gadgets, still it is country. I was glad I had not
gaped too long at the New York skyscrapers. Exciting as they
are, they mislead. They do not epitomise what lies behind
them. Presently the snow melted. Where it had lain appeared
dark brown earth and occasional pale lilac hepaticas, and the
spring began—in double quick time compared to our spring.

The Berkshires are homely scenery. Gigantic scenery is more
difficult to describe, but I will make an attempt. Suppose yourself walking on a Surrey common near Bagshot. There are a
good many fir trees about, the soil is sandy, and the prospect
rather dull. Suddenly the common stops, and you are standing
without any warning on the brink of a precipice which is one
mile deep. One mile into the tortured earth it goes, the other
side of the chasm is miles away, and the chasm is filled with
unbelievable deposits of rock which resemble sphinxes draped
in crimson shawls. That, as far as I can get it into a single
sentence, gives you my first impression of the Grand Canyon of
the Colorado River, but the Grand Canyon would need many
sentences to describe and many books. It is the most astounding
natural object I have ever seen. It frightens. There are many
colours in it besides crimson—strata of black and of white, and
rocks of ochre and pale lilac. And the Colorado River itself
is, when one gets down to it, still more sinister, for it is muddy
white and very swift, and it rages like an infuriated maggot
between precipices of granite, gnawing at them and cutting the
Canyon deeper. It was strange after two days amongst these
marvels, and terrors, to return to the surface of the earth, and go
bowling away in a 'bus between little fir trees.

The second item I sought in America was the human, the
individual. My work lay mainly in universities, and there and
elsewhere I found the individuals I sought. I had expected
generosity and hospitality. I had not expected so much tact,
charm and sensitiveness ; here was the delightful surprise.
Wherever I went I found delicate understanding of our troubles
in Britain over food and clothing, and a desire to help that was
never patronising. This was not confined to the highly educated
classes. I recall a cheap eating-house in Nevada where some
strangers came up and asked what they could send. I remember
the chambermaid in the hotel at Salt Lake City who when I

offered her a tip replied, ' I don't like to take your money, brother, you need it more than I do.' That is the sort of remark which comes from the heart and goes to the heart, and in the light of it and the warmth of it I found difficulty in examining the defects of the American character. The defects are, I suspect, lack of discrimination, emotionalism, and a tendency to narrow the idea of freedom into freedom to make money. ' What else have we fought the war for ? ' a business acquaintance enquired. But I cannot feel these defects are basic. My friends reassure me against this, and not only my friends ; the faces of strangers lighting up everywhere, compassionate, respectful, anxious to help. The individuals I met were mostly of Anglo-Saxon stock ; I also knew some Swedish and some Italian farming people, made some Oriental contacts, and had one or two Mexican friends. I did not have the good fortune to get to know any Negroes. On the whole I saw as much of the human landscape as an elderly traveller may reasonably expect, and I liked it.

But now comes a qualification. Although the Americans I encountered were full of charitable feelings towards Great Britain, I cannot say that they showed much interest in us otherwise. I have often been asked since my return home : ' What do they think about us over there ? ' Indeed, it is often the only thing English people want to know. The answer, not very flattering to our pride, is that the Americans scarcely think about us at all. They are curious about our Royal Family, they are grateful and appreciative towards Mr. Churchill, they are—or were—enthusiastic over British films. That is all. They do not discuss our Empire. India, over which they have been so critical in the past, is now scarcely in the news and seems to bore them. Even Palestine was seldom mentioned. An explanation of this indifference is that they concentrate, as we all do, on home affairs, and that when they do think of foreign affairs they think of Russia. China to some extent, but mostly Russia. Russia is always weighing on their minds. They are afraid of war, or that their standard of life may be lowered. I shall never forget a dinner party, supposedly given in my honour, at which one of the guests, a journalist, urged that atomic bombs should be dropped upon the Soviet Union without notice, and quoted with approval a remark which he inaccurately ascribed to Oliver Cromwell : ' Stone dead hath no fellow.' ' That's good, isn't it, Tom?' he called to another journalist. 'Stone dead hath no fellow.' Tom agreed that it was very good, and they shouted: 'Stone dead hath no fellow' in unison or antiphonically for the rest of the evening. They were cultivated men, but as soon as the idea of Russia occurred to them, their faces became blood red; they ceased to be human. No one seemed appalled by the display but myself, no one was surprised, and our hostess congratulated herself afterwards on the success of her party. This obsession over Russia should be realised by all who would understand America, and it explains in part her lack of interest in us.

I did not encounter such hysteria elsewhere, and maybe did not frequent the circles where it is likeliest to occur. Most of the people I was with were not influential or highly placed: many of them were teachers, and some of them were young— students, or they practised music or painting or acting or the ballet, or they were doing small commercial jobs or working on the land. My general impression was of good temper and good-will and hopefulness. I could darken the picture, no doubt. I do not take the Statue of Liberty in New York harbour as seriously as she takes herself. And I did encounter hints of oppression and of violence, and of snobbery. But the main verdict is favourable, and I do beg anyone who happens to have fallen into the habit of nagging at America to drop it. Nagging is so insidious. It often resides not in what is said but in the tone of voice. It proceeds not from considered criticism but from envy and from discontent—and, of course, life out there is far more comfortable for the average man than it is here. The food is nicer, if dearer, the clothes are nicer and cheaper, the cold drinks are not lukewarm, and the railway carriages are not dirty. But these advantages over ourselves should not embitter us against the people who enjoy them. Nor should we charge it against all Americans that their politicians do what our politicians tell them, and tell us, they ought not to do.

I chanced to end my three months' visit in the same district of the Berkshires where it had begun. Now it was high summer. The little spring from which I fetched water every day had already begun to flag. The meadows were full of flowers— ox-eye daisies, black-eyed susans, orchids, and an under-carpet of creeping jenny; the meadows sloped down to a brook where the farm hands bathed. There were swallow-tail butterflies and fritillaries, and the bobolink, a very agreeable bird, skipped from post to post carolling, and another bird, the phoebe, repeated ' phoebe, phoebe, phoebe,' whence its name. At night there were fireflies to remind us that this was in the latitude of Madrid. Thunderstorms did not disconcert them, and I would watch their flash vanish in the superior brilliancy of lightning, and reappear. Some of them flew at the level of the grass, others across the curtain of birch trees. They were extraordinarily bright ; it was a good year for fireflies, and the memory of them sparking in the warm rain and the thunder is the latest of my American impressions, and the loveliest.

[1947]

Two hundred years ago, Anne Lee, a Quaker of Manchester, England, went to New England and became a Shaker. She founded a sect. The early records of the Shakers are curious and show fantastic elements which have disappeared. There was an attempt to rectify Christianity in the interests of the female—an attempt also made by Mariolatry in the Middle Ages. Mother Anne made a half-hearted bid for equality with Christ, and there are hymns—not sung to-day—in which homage is paid to them both as the co-regents of the universe, and Adam celebrated as bisexual. This had to be dropped. The sect did not take the intransigent route of Mormonism, it dug up no plates of gold, and commended itself to its neighbours by hard work, good if dull craftsmanship, satisfactory bank-balances, honesty, and celibacy—recruiting its ranks from orphanages. It became a quiet community of men and women—simple folk who liked to feel a little different : even the simplest have this weakness. Meetings were held where sometimes they were seized by the Spirit and shook : otherwise nothing remarkable occurred.

The sect to-day has almost died out, for its industry has been superseded by industrialism, and orphans have something better to do. But a few settlements of aged people survive or recently survived, and the friends with whom I was stopping in Massachusetts in 1947 were in touch with the most considerable of these settlements : Mount Lebanon, where Mother Anne herself had once dwelt. It was arranged that we should call at Mount Lebanon. We had with us a pleasant journalist from the *New Yorker* who had been commissioned to write the Shakers up, though I never saw his article—only what he wrote up on me. It was a twelve hours' expedition. The month was April but the weather wintry and myriads of birch trees were bare and sharp against the sky. We ascended to a broad pass with a view over sub-Alpine scenery, half covered with snow. The settlement was down hill, below the high-raised modern road. Life had shrunk into one enormous house, a huge wooden box measuring a hundred and eighty feet long and fifty feet thick, and it was five or six storeys high. We knocked at the door and an old lady peeped out and greeted us in a dazed fashion. This was Elderess Theresa. Further down the box another door opened and another old lady peeped out. This was Sister Susan and she was bidden to retire. They seemed a bit dishevelled, and it was agreed we should go away for lunch and come back again : they wished they could have entertained us. My friends were in great excitement. The experience was more romantic for them than it was for me, and the idea of home-made chairs hanging from pegs on a wall filled them with nostalgia. It was part of the ' dream that got bogged,' the dream of an America which should be in direct touch with the elemental and the simple. America has chosen the power that comes through machinery but she never forgets her dream. I have seen several instances of it. The most grotesque was the handicraft fair in Greenwich Village, where pieces of copper, wood and wool, which had been bothered into ugly shapes at home, were offered for sale at high prices. Another instance is the yearning for Mexico, whose peasants were drunk and dirty, but they did sing. And another instance was these Shakers, to whom, having had our lunch at a drug store, we returned.

They had smartened themselves up no end. Elderess Theresa wore a dove-coloured cape and Sister Susan's hair had been combed. Sisters Ellen, Ada, Maimie and Ruth also appeared —the first-named sensible and companionable and evidently running the place. Each had plenty of room in the vast building since the community had shrunk : it was like an almshouse where the inmates are not crowded and need not quarrel, and they seemed happy. I had a touching talk with the Elderess, now ninety-one, who had come from England, and dimly remembered a baker's shop in the Waterloo Road, and the voyage in a sailing ship away from it. She did not regret the days when Mount Lebanon had eighty inmates. ' It is much better like this,' she said. Her room was full of mess and mementoes, all of which she misdescribed as Shaker-made. It was nothing to the mess in the apartment of Sisters Ada and Maimie, who kept kneeling without obvious reason on the carpet and crackling toilet paper at the parrot to make him dance. On their wall ticked a clock which had the face of a cat, and a cat's tail for pendulum. Up and down the enormous passages Sister Susan stalked, her raven locks flying, and gesticulating with approval on the presence of so many men. We saw the dining-room, where a place was laid, a little humorously, for Christ. We saw the communal meeting-room. Did they —er—shake ever ? No—nobody shook now. Did they—er—meet here for prayer ? No, said the Elderess complacently. We used to meet once a month. Now we never meet. They were in fact bone idle and did not even know it. I found myself wishing that other groups, the Oxford for instance, would imitate them.

While the New Yorker questioned them, I went out and looked at the five or six other houses which completed the original Mount Lebanon colony (Shaker houses are always in little colonies). They were empty except for ponderous wooden machinery. The ground still sloped into a view, and bright streams and pools of water twinkled at every corner. The sun shone, the snow melted, the planks steamed. The simplicity of the buildings was impressive but not interesting. I went back into the main building to meet Brother Curtis. For the sisters above described only occupied half the huge house. On each floor in the longitudinal central passage was a door, which was locked or supposed to be locked, and beyond the doors, all alone in the other half, dwelt the enigmatical brother Curtis. He could also be reached by walking along outside. He was a healthy elderly man in overalls, very stupid from the New Yorker point of view, though probably not from his own. Much time was spent in trying to make him say something characteristic : he was understood to have different ideas on carrying in logs from the Sisters' ideas, but since he carried in the logs his ideas prevailed. Perhaps he had been interviewed before. He had a roguish twinkle. Then we took our leave. One of our party found a tin dust-pan in the attic, and was allowed to purchase it ; and I myself became an object of envy because the Elderess presented me with a ruler. It is an ordinary wooden ruler, it is eighteen inches long, it rules, but little more can be said of it. We waved good-bye—Sister Susan again bursting out of her special door—and that is the last I saw of these gentle harmless people, though the New Yorker returned on the following day to consolidate his investigations. To me, the Shakers were interesting because they interested. My companions were moved by them to a degree which I could not share ; they were a symbol of something which America supposes herself to have missed, they were the dream that got bogged. Mount Lebanon has, I believe, now been closed down.

[1951]

Ferney

Cultivated monkeys, Charles and I clung to the iron palings
of the park. Froggy as well as monkey, he appreciated better
than I did what we saw, but even to me the sight was an exciting
one. For this was Ferney. So this was Ferney ! This was the
house that Voltaire built, those were the trees he planted, here
his niece, Madame Denis, and others whom I read about afterwards in *La Vie Intime de Voltaire*, by Perey and Maugras, a very
entertaining book—here Madame Denis, anyhow, lived, as shape-
less as my sentence, but generally liked. With a heart like a
warming pan and a figure like a dumpling, Madame Denis
queened it here and reigned it, acted it and reacted it, danced it,
reasoned it, unreasoned it, she drove in from Geneva to take
possession covered with diamonds, she flounced away to Paris
in a pet, she sneaked back. Voltaire was pleased when she
arrived, thankful when she left, delighted when she returned.
However, that is enough about Madame Denis for the moment.
She is all in the book. We are clinging to the park railings.

Our feet slithered upon the uncomfortable parapet. We
wished they were more prehensile. Craning our noses to the
left, we could see the chapel. It was a small and simple structure,
and it looked a trifle *moisi*. I cannot think of the right English
equivalent of ' moisi.' ' Mouldy ' will not do. ' Moisi ' must
stand. After all, we are in France. That always was the
advantage of Ferney—it was just in France, and Voltaire, who
preferred a pop-hole to a moat, could be over the border into
Switzerland if he felt nervous, and back again if his nerves
relaxed or reversed. The chapel ranked with the *loca senta situ*
of which Virgil speaks, it had acquired the art of neglect with
dignity, and had no wish to look trim. On its frontal was the
famous inscription, ' Deo erexit VOLTAIRE,' and we saw with
delight that the lettering of the Voltaire was twice the size of
the Deity's. Proportion had been observed. Listen, while you
look at this, to what they sang to him in the October of 1767,
on the occasion of the feast of St. Francis of Assisi. They had
begun the day by going to Mass, at two o'clock they had dined

in state, a vast concourse of people, at six o'clock they attended a performance of two plays at his private theatre, and when this was over the actors and actresses, including Madame Denis, came forward in their brilliant dresses and grouped themselves around him and sang :

> L'Eglise, dans ce jour, fait à tous ses dévots
> Célébrer les vertus d'un pénitent austère.
> Si l'Eglise a ses saints, le Pinde a ses héros,
> Et nous fêtons ici le grand nom de Voltaire.

Then came fireworks, then an enormous supper, and then a ball at which Voltaire, who was over seventy, danced until midnight. Yes ; the chapel has done well to observe proportion.

Straight ahead of us lay the chateau. It was quiet enough now, no singing, no guests, no work, the shutters were closed, the doors locked, and a man in an apron was sweeping up the leaves of 1939—not many of them, for our year was still at its June. Tourists were not admitted, and we were, we knew, almost the last of our sinewy tribe. Soon we should have to skedaddle for our tram. Lucky, happy we, to get this last peep at one of the symbols of European civilisation. Civilisation. Humanity. Enjoyment. That was what the agreeable white building said to us, that was what we carried away. It was not a large building and that has been part of the disaster. It was too small to cope with the modern world. A Ferney to-day would have to be enormous, with rolling staircases and microphones, if it was to function proportionately, and if it was enormous could it be Ferney ? Even Voltaire felt that he saw too many people, and that the universe, though fortunately bounded by Russia, was upon too cumbrous a scale. He could just illuminate it, but only just, and he died without knowing that he was the last man who would ever perform such a feat, and that Goethe would die asking for more light. On the crest of a wave Ferney sparkled. The boundaries of the universe were to extend bewilderingly, the common people were to neglect the pursuit of agriculture, and, worst of all, the human make-up was to reveal deadnesses and depths which no acuteness could penetrate and no benignity heal.

His end was actually at Paris, and technically not happy. ' Count no man happy until he is dead,' saith the spirit of dullness. Happiness up to one's final collapse is the better criterion, and this Voltaire achieved. The pains and fears of his last

moments (which most of us are doomed to share) altered the
sum of his life but inappreciably. The death-bed or death-
tumble or death-jumble, death-battle, death-rattle, death-splinter,
death-squirt, appalling as it will be to each deserted and dying
individual, is a transition, not an epitome. It has no retrospective
force. It does not taint (except in a gleam of diseased memory)
any of the triumphs that have gone before. Against that over-
emphasis, that priestly organisation of the death-moment, Voltaire
had himself protested, it was part of the infamous thing he had
tried to crush. His real end was Ferney, and there we saw him
that afternoon, as a house and trees.

Suppose he had come out as a person, and seen our snouts,
what would he have done? He would probably have gone in
again. But he would possibly have been very kind, and with a
twentieth century kindness, for he had an up-to-date heart.
When his secretary's children pestered him with questions which
the eighteenth century deemed foolish, he would answer the
questions seriously, and put aside his work to do so. When a
waiter was nice to him at Maintz, he insisted on stopping at the
hotel kept by the waiter's father at Strasburg. It turned out to
be a dreadful doss-house, but he would not leave it, although he
was at the height of his fame, for the reason that he had made a
friendly compact with the Maintz waiter. Humanity to him
was not a platform gesture. He got down to brass tacks over
it. Humanity meant saving the Calas family, or being respectful
to his secretary's children, or to an unimportant little domestic.
'Oh, but that is not the whole story,' saith the spirit of dullness,
looking up from its ledger; 'he was also a capricious, shifty,
cruel, litigious, indecent, panicky capitalist; I have it all down.'
And that exercise of a summing-up goes on, summing up an
achievement which is a pattern, not a sum, and a pattern so
intricate that the eye rests with the most conviction upon the
spots of gold. Whether he would have greeted us is doubtful.
Madame Denis, ever too sensitive to externals, would have
recoiled with a *moue*, I fear. But they would certainly have
caught sight of us. I want to make that plain, for it brings out
the restricted character of the site. It was more of a packet than
a park. We and the chateau and the man sweeping leaves and
the chapel and the porter's lodge were all bunched up together
among residential greenery. There was nothing august or wide-
sweeping in the demesne, though two hundred years ago, before

the trees grew up, there must have been views of the lake. Oddly enough, I catch a parallel with Max Gate as I try to reconstruct. A nest made by a celebrated literary man, going a little untidy. But whereas Hardy belonged to the soil, the soil belonged to Voltaire, and one has not, when visiting Ferney, any poignant sense of locality. Here is merely a place which he happened to buy and make his own, after Cirey and Potsdam and Les Délices had failed, and it is appropriate that he should have failed to die in it, and that his corpse should have been bandied about in revolutions, and perhaps got mixed up with Rousseau's.

But one cannot cling for ever to an alien pale, or peep for ever at a scene with which curiosity and hope are one's only links. Monkeys must let go. 'I am content to have seen Ferney,' remarked Charles, as he dusted his paws. I popped the object into my pouch for future use. One never knows, and I had no idea how precious it would become to me in a year's time, nor how I should take it out, and discover that it had turned faintly radio-active. We caught the tram back to Geneva all right, crossed the almost unguarded frontier, and then we departed to our respective cages, which were closed and locked not long after we entered them.

[1940]

Clouds Hill

I used to stop at Clouds Hill in the old days with T. E.—I can't ever think of him as Colonel Lawrence. It's not exactly a show place, there's not much to see, only a tiny four-roomed cottage hidden away in a four-acre dell of rhododendrons in the Dorsetshire heath-land. But it's charming and it's unusual, indeed there's something magical about it.

I first went there back in 1924. T. E. was then a private in the Tank Corps at Bovington Camp. We met down in a pub to talk over the *Seven Pillars*, the early version of which he had allowed me to see. We scarcely knew one another, and the talk was decidedly sticky. Then he said, in a casual, diffident way, that there was an old cottage where he and his fellow soldiers sometimes went when they were off duty, to get a little peace and quiet or to play the gramophone : would I care to come up and see it ? He took me up through the bleak, ungracious desert of Bovington Camp by a straight road which mounts slightly, and then falls over into a little dip into peacefulness and wildness. There was Clouds Hill. I liked the place at once. His friends were friendly, I felt easy, and to feel easy was, in T. E.'s eyes, a great recommendation. Two Greek words are over the door. He carved them himself. *Ou phrontis*—meaning roughly : ' I don't care.' They came, he told us, out of a story in Herodotus, a story about a young man who was going to marry a king's daughter, but unfortunately during the dinner party he got drunk, stood on his head on the table and began dancing with his legs in the air. The king was shocked at such conduct in a prospective son-in-law, and said to him severely : ' You have danced away your bride.' But the young man didn't care. He replied : *Ou phrontis*, ' I don't care,' and continued to wave his legs in the air. That is the motto T. E. chose for Clouds Hill. We weren't to care, as soon as we were inside ; we were to feel easy, and not worry about the world and its standards.

In those days the two bottom rooms were full of firewood and lumber. We lived upstairs, and the sitting-room there looks now much as it did then, though the gramophone and the books have gone, and the fender with its bent ironwork has been remodelled. It was, and it is, a brownish room—wooden beams and ceiling, leather covered settee. Here we talked, played Beethoven's symphonies, ate and drank. We drank water only, or tea—no alcohol ever entered Clouds Hill, in spite of the story from Herodotus. We drank out of pretty cups of black pottery. And we ate out of tins. T. E. always laid in a stock of tinned dainties for his guests. There were no fixed hours for meals and no one sat down. If you felt hungry you opened a tin and drifted about with it. It's a grand way to feed : the drawback is that you may lose count of how much you are eating. That didn't matter to T. E., who scarcely ate at all, but the rest of us sometimes went too far. You always know a place better when you've been ill in it, and I've been quite ill at Clouds Hill, from overeating out of those treacherous tins.

When I stopped there, I used to sleep in the little room opposite—it is nattily fitted up to-day with a bunk and drawers, it has a porthole and looks like a ship's cabin, but then it was all anyhow. T. E. slept in camp, coming out when he could during the day, as did the rest of the troops. It was fine being alone in Clouds Hill at night : so silent—and those were the times when there still was silence. Silence scarcely exists now—it is a lost luxury. One night the silence was disturbed by a night-jar, which perched on the roof above my head and churred and churred —the sort of fantastic thing that would happen at Clouds Hill. It's annoying to be kept awake by a bird even when it's a night-jar, so I went into the garden and shouted at the thing. It kept on churring. Finally I threw a stone. This missed the night-jar, as I had intended, but smashed a tile, which I hadn't intended. T. E. was delighted when he heard of the mishap. He liked his visitors to leave these little evidences of their presence behind them. He declared that the whole affair was an extremely good omen, he refused to have the tile replaced, and it is still broken to-day.

I don't know whether these trivial remarks convey the atmosphere of the place—the happy casualness of it, and the feeling that no one particularly owned it. T. E. had the power of distributing the sense of possession among all the friends who came there. When Thomas Hardy turned up, for instance, as he did one sunny afternoon, he seemed to come on a visit to us all, and not specially to see his host. Thomas Hardy and Mrs. Hardy came up the narrow stairway into the little brown room and there they were—the guests of us all. To think of Clouds Hill as T. E.'s home is to get the wrong idea of it. It was rather his *pied-à-terre*, the place where his feet touched the earth for a moment, and found rest. I was to have stopped there yet again in May, 1935, the date of his tragedy. I have been down there since, with thoughts which were necessarily sad, and there came into my mind an inscription which I once saw on a gateway in India : ' Jesus—on whom be peace—said : The world is a bridge : pass over it, but build no house on it.' Clouds Hill is not so much a house as a point where T. E.'s feet tarried for a little on their all too swift passage through this world.

The ground floor has no memories for me—except that there are a couple of twisted candlesticks, which used to be upstairs. The big lower room was fitted up by him in later years to sleep in, and for his books. He had a good collection, of modern stuff specially. For instance there was Bernard Shaw's *St. Joan*, inscribed ' To Private Shaw from Public Shaw.' And there was a copy of Hardy's *Dynasts* with two inscriptions : the first ' Colonel Lawrence from Thomas Hardy,' and the second ' To T. E. Shaw for his comfort in camp from Lawrence.' He, as it were, passed the book on from one of his personalities to another ! All these treasures have gone, and in the empty shelves has been arranged an exhibit of photographs. Some of these are from negatives which he himself took when he was out East, others are photographs of him : there are illustrations to the *Seven Pillars* and to *Crusaders' Castles*, and a couple of photographs of the rooms as they used to be, and so on. The little room opposite—that's now a bathroom containing a snowy and hygienic bath. Nothing of the sort in my time. I remember one of our party retiring into a corner with a coin, tossing it, and muttering to himself : ' Heads I wash, tails I don't. Tails. I've won.' And that represented our general attitude to washing. We did not allow it to win too easily. But—if I may mention so unheroic an article—a hot bottle did figure. T. E.'s kindness and consideration over trifles were endless, and after he had returned to camp one would find a hot bottle in the bed, which he put there in case his precious visitor's feet should be cold. That was so like him. The harder he lived himself, the more anxious he was that others should fall soft. He would take any amount of trouble to save them.

Clouds Hill 355

There's a little piece of grass outside the house, also ' The Nook,' a pleasant semicircle of rising terraces which he contrived. And a visit should end in a climb through the rhododendrons behind to the upper lip of the dell. There you get a surprising and a noble view, right away down to the sea, and incidentally a new idea of rhododendrons. They don't seem like ornamental bushes any more, they become part of the landscape. We used to pull the dead wood out of them for fires, and it burnt splendidly. Clouds Hill, viewed from above its rhododendrons, shrinks into a tiny box. You get instead the vast expanses of the purple heath surrounding it, where gentians can be found, and sundew. T. E. cared intensely for the English countryside ; he was hoping to explore it quietly upon a push-bike when the end came.

[1938]

Cambridge

It is difficult to meditate on one's dear old university without falling either into snobbery or priggishness. I am a prig, and Mr. Steegman sometimes disconcerts me. For instance, when he says in his book :

> The poor man from the elementary school really does not get very much out of Cambridge. He is not likely to make friends, and will almost certainly remain a fish out of water. He would be much wiser to go to one of the newer universities where he will feel less discontented with his lot. Discouraging though it may be for the social reformer, the man from the elementary school is unquestionably excluded from everything that makes Cambridge worth while.

Oh dear. As we push off in our punt, Mr. Steegman doing all the work and doing it with efficiency and grace, as we glide under Clare Bridge and through the Gate of Honour and down the Combination Room of John's, this little quotation worries me, like a pea under the cushions, and I ask myself what is wrong with it, or if nothing, what is wrong with me. The prig tries to get down to brass tacks in fact. What am I prepared to bequeath the place which I have loved for forty years, and where I have made my best friends ? Do I really want the whole of its architecture to be remodelled into bed-sitting-rooms ? Do I want its courts to be asphalted, and its lavatories to plunge and roar with municipal self-righteousness ? Lavatories were few and far once. They belonged to the Silent Service, and were called Fourths because one of them was rumoured to lurk in the fourth court of Trinity. Ivy peeped. To go to one was an expedition only rivalled by the taking of a bath. Those hardships are vanishing. Hardship is vanishing, but so is style, and the two are more closely connected than the present generation supposes. The food that arrived on heads from the kitchens —lukewarm but from the kitchens—will soon arrive no more. The punt drifts on, floating away from the cafeteria and cash register down the broadening stream. Here is the Pitt Press,

charming, the freshman's first chapel. If we rise up a certain
staircase in Caius, we can see the far-away tower of the Pitt
Press through the whole breadth of the Senate House, shimmer-
ing and bending behind two thicknesses of glass. This is my
private discovery. I announce it half asleep. And now the
Campanile of the University Library is mercifully concealed
behind the Chestnuts of Jesus, and now we bob in the Market
Piazza, where a fine new building, the Guildhall, has arisen in
the nick of time. How happy am I that Mr. Steegman should
praise the new Guildhall ! The centre of the town will never
go smartiboots now, and never become a civic centre. What a
lot my guide knows ! How deftly he steers ! I drowse. A
cushion falls into the Pem. And then again that disquieting pea.
This time the pea is feminine in gender.

While the various parliamentary reforms can be defended as
well as attacked, it is unusual to find anyone defending Girton
and Newnham. . . . Cambridge owes a great deal to the
munificence of such women as the Lady Clare, the Countess
of Pembroke, Queen Margaret, the Lady Margaret, and the
Countess of Sussex. But these pious foundresses founded
their colleges for men and the argument is pointless. . . . The
most serious indictment of the women students, apart from
the fearsomeness of the women which these students almost
always become unless they marry quickly, is the complete
pointlessness of their being there.

So women, like elementary schoolmen, must be banned from
our precinct, because they cannot enter properly into its social
life. Does not the rest of the educational world lie open, hood
upon hood, gown upon skirt, mortar-board upon corduroy, until
the appointments-board creaks ? O spare Cambridge ! Is not
the city a little one ? Is she not unparalleled ? Oxford, her
swollen sister, is so distended by endowments as to be unrecognisable, and her old Gothic ornaments hang around her neck
like a broken locket which she may at any moment swop.
Cambridge still keeps her antique shape. No idealistic million-
aire has yet raped her. The dons at her High Tables still rise
into civilised conversation out of tired grunts. O leave her
where she is and as she is, leave her to her peculiar destiny. She,
Edinburgh and Bath are the only towns in Great Britain to
retain any style, and she is unique, because to style she adds

intellect and the power to mould a certain type of male. So keep off, you women, elementary and otherwise ; you shall gain nothing from the Cam, not even a degree—that was the little trick it played you, ha ha ! Horny-handed miners, meagre-faced technicians, high-collared clerks—go where you will feel less discontented, and where your fellow students will not decline to be your friends. Indians, be so good as to remain at Patna. Americans, have you not Carolina for your portion ?

> In North Carolina the poets are fewer,
> We never were much at literature.

The phantoms fly as I sing. So varied, but all so unsuitable, they fly and educate themselves where and how they will, and our punt drifts on, and Mr. Steegman and myself are soon engaged in a passionate dispute on the subject of the Chimney at Jesus. What ! He would destroy the Chimney ? What ! He calls it a ' depressing flagged path between high walls ' ? I cannot contain my rage, and utter a series of little Cambridge shrieks. For the Chimney, to me, is part of a delicate dramatic effect ; at the end of its calculated dullness rises Alcock's rich Gate Tower, promising a different world—a promise faithfully fulfilled. I like, too, to think that Coleridge stole down it when he ran away to enlist in the Dragoons, and that Malthus paced up it as he planned how to decrease the human race and, incident-ally, our troubles. I do not know its date—perhaps it did not exist in their day. All the same, hands off !

This is my major architectural quarrel with Mr. Steegman so it may be gathered how fully, in this department, I accept him. He might perhaps have mentioned the court of Emmanuel which lies across Emmanuel Street—I always like it, although it did destroy a group of picturesque cottages. And he might have mentioned—nobody does—the carving on the wooden west door of the chapel of King's. Still, unlike the Chimney, these are no matters for a blood feud. On we drift, and as each noted build-ing appears and reappears I am delighted by the comments of a learned and courageous mind. The work of the young Wren, of Gibbs, Wilkins and Cockerell, is focused with that of the anonymous medieval builders, until we see our Alma Mater advancing physically down the centuries, not always logically or gracefully, but to the measure that fascinated her sons,

So that if at night, far out at sea, over the tumbling waves, one saw a haze on the waters, a city illuminated, a whiteness even in the sky, such as that now over the Hall of Trinity, where they're still dining, or washing up plates,—that would be the light burning there—the light of Cambridge.

How splendidly these words express our faith ! How unlucky that they should have been written by a woman !

The book is a guide to Cambridge, in the fuller sense of the word Guide. Three parts. Cambridge as it was—historical ; as it is—architectural ; and modern Cambridge—mainly social, with surmises on what is to come.

> The Fellows went into Chapel on Monday before noon ; after prayers and sacrament they began to vote. Thus they continued, scrutinising and walking about, eating and sleeping, some of them smoking . . . at two in the morning there never was a more diverting or more curious spectacle. Some wrapped in blankets, erect in their stalls like mummies ; others asleep on cushions, like so many Gothic tombs. Here a red cap over a wig, there a face lost in a rug. One blowing a chafing-dish with a surplice sleeve, another warming a little negus.

This is from the historical section. We have backed into the eighteenth century, and are assisting at the election of a Provost of King's. The eighteenth century is an appropriate landing-stage, our punt moors, and I get out on the steps of the Whig-Conservative Club. Prig's feelings are mixed. He has enjoyed his conducted tour, and found himself more of a snob than he intended. The selective Cambridge he loved cannot possibly survive, except as a museum piece. But the Cambridge-open-to-all, the in-accordance-with-national-needs-Cambridge will only be a technical finishing school, an educational crammery, a degree-monger, not a University at all. I dislike Mr. Steegman's hopes, but I share his fears, and in this dilemma I proffer a third solution—that of razing the whole sacred area to the ground. The dons and other portable valuables could first be transplanted to a safer spot, and Hitler would do the rest free of charge. She would survive as a memory then. And a memory can do more than either a mummy or a travesty towards civilising the world.

But if it came to a vote, I am against my Guide. I know so

many elementary schoolmen who ought to have gone up twenty or thirty years ago, and who would have given as well as gained. And I know so many women who have retained their learning in spite of marriage, and their charm in spite of spinsterhood. He will say that these are exceptions, and will also point out that he holds no brief for rank or wealth. This is true, but his conception of Cambridge lacks generosity, he is always scrutinising the entrance lists, he will risk nothing which is not familiar to him socially ; and if generosity is excluded the idea of a University becomes meaningless.

I have been drawn to think rather of the tens who have failed than of the units who have succeeded, and of the ore that lies buried in our social strata rather than of the bright coins that circulate from hand to hand. If a field of coal or of some other material lies unworked and unused, yet it is always there. It may be kept for some future age when its wealth will be more needed, and posterity will bless the prescience and parsimony of their ancestors who refrained from using it. But the human mind is born and lives and perishes. If it is unenlightened, it passes away into its native darkness.

This is generosity, this is the warmth without which all education is senseless, and it is not to be laughed away by dubbing it Social Reform.

(Writing as I am on an academic theme, I had better give authority for my quotations throughout. The first two are from Mr. Steegman's *Cambridge*, the third was imported from America by Lowes Dickinson, the fourth is from Virginia Woolf's *Jacob's Room*, the fifth is quoted by Mr. Steegman from Cooper's *Annals of Cambridge*, and the final one is from Oscar Browning.)

[1941]

London is a Muddle

London is a muddle, and not always an unpleasant one. At the present time the muddle is being hidden away, as far as possible, for this is Coronation Year, but it remains, and it will re-emerge. If you want an example, look out of your bedroom window, even if the bedroom is in an hotel. Your view is sure to be 'spoilt' by something vulgar or shabby, but it may be redeemed by something charming, entertaining, antiquated. Anyhow, it will not be all of a piece.

Or go for a walk. You need not even leave the main thoroughfares, you need only look sideways from them with a little attentiveness, and you will see to right or to left the casualness and the confusion which are the Spirit of London. Stand, for example, at the city end of London Bridge. What do you see at the first glance? An enormous building called Adelaide House. Built in an Egyptian style, it towers into the sky, it plunges into the depths; in its vast cube are accommodated hundreds of business men with their clerks, typewriters, and anxieties all complete, all making money as hard as they can for the sake of the Empire, and upon its roof, which is flat, are a garden, an orchard, and a putting-green, where the anxieties of the business men can take another form. Adelaide House attempts to set the pace. It is pompous and practical; it suggests that London is a mart, a hub, a focus, a last word on something or other; it bullies the visitor as he approaches from the Surrey side. Wait a minute, though. What is that narrow chasm beneath, and what is that building down in the chasm, nestling against Adelaide's flank? Descending by a ponderous and grimy stairway, you reach Lower Thames Street. Here quite another pace is set and quite another language spoken. Fish and their retainers from Billingsgate throng it in the early morning, lorries and drays rumble at all times. London Bridge is high above, and higher still—nearly two hundred feet in the air—the business men are 'phoning or putting. And the building crouched in the chasm? What is that? Oh, that is only a third London—that is only one of Sir Christopher Wren's best churches,

St. Magnus the Martyr. It is crouched between the grubbiness
and the hygienic tiles, indifferent to both, still leading its own
life, and letting the waves of traffic and business roar over its
head. Notice the passage going through its tower and leading
to a blank wall. A hundred and fifty years ago that passage was
the footway of old London Bridge ; people went by it to go
over the river. The city has piled itself up, like a geological
series, and, perhaps, the process will continue until a skin of
unsmashable glass is stretched over her, as in H. G. Wells's
dream.

This Adelaide-Billingsgate-Magnus combination is typical of
London, which is an untidy city, and ought not to be tidied
up.

Though attempts have been made to tidy her. Wren himself
made one of them, and drew up a town-planning scheme after
the Great Fire. The present Bishop of London, on the other
hand, thinks that it is Wren who needs tidying, and he pulls
down a City church whenever he can. St. Magnus the Martyr
has eluded him hitherto, but he has recently scored a success
in the demolition of All Hallows, Lombard Street. Another
attempt at tidying was made over a hundred years ago by Nash,
in the West End. It was a good attempt. Nash planned to
connect Carlton House, where the Prince Regent lived, with
Regent's Park. His plan to-day is unrecognisable, but it made
some progress, and I am old enough to remember what his
Regent Street looked like while it was still untouched. I wish
it was there to-day, for a bad muddle, instead of a good one,
has superseded it. It was not great architecture, but it knew
what it was doing and where it was going ; it was reasonable
and refined. Of course, it had to be scrapped. Greed moulds
the landscape of London, as of other great cities, and the Regent
Street frontages were too valuable to be occupied by such lowly
piles. Besides, they belong to the Crown, and the Crown seems
even greedier and more unaesthetic than most landlords. So
Nash went, and the present insipid mixture took his place.

If you want a muddle, look around you as you walk from
Piccadilly Circus to Oxford Circus. Here are ornaments that
do not adorn, features that feature nothing, flatness, meanness,
uniformity without harmony, bigness without size. Even when
the shops are built at the same moment and by architects of
equal fatuity, they manage to contradict one another. Here is

the heart of the Empire, and the best it can do. Regent Street exhibits, in its most depressing aspect, the Spirit of London.

However, you can easily escape. Go, for a change, up the Caledonian Road, and lean over the bridge which crosses the canal. A much pleasanter muddle awaits you. A queer smell hangs about, sweetish and not disagreeable, and seems to rise from the water. The surroundings are grubby and cheerful, the colouring quiet, as is usual with London colouring, the district poor. The smell comes from the locust beans which are used for making cattle food in an adjoining factory, and the little boys of the district go bathing at suitable times and steal the locusts. Yes, they pinch them. Almost like John the Baptist, though not quite, they tie them up in handkerchiefs, and push them before them through the savoury waters of Jordan, devouring them as soon as they reach shore. This, too, is London—a London undreamt of in Regent Street—nor is it the only vision to be gained from this particular bridge. Turn the other way and you will have a little surprise. For the canal disappears into the side of a hill. Pitch darkness, no lamps, no towpath. It has vanished under the heights of Pentonville. It keeps its course for over half a mile, absolutely straight, so that when the tunnel is empty the swimmers can see a tiny spot of daylight at its further end. Occasionally a string of barges passes through behind a tug, on its way to the docks.

They are typical, these surprises, these oddnesses. No doubt, all cities which are large and old contain them—they are certainly to be found in Paris. But London has a deceptive air of dullness. One does not expect her to indulge in irregularities and pranks. The business men inside Adelaide House, the shops of Regent Street—these seem, at the first sight, to set the pace. Only when one prowls about and loiters and wastes time do the competitors become visible ; the church of St. Magnus hiding in Lower Thames Street, the canal hiding in the depths of Pentonville, the little boys pushing their cargoes across the canal. There is something more in the City than the getting of money and the spending of it ; there is even something which escapes the denunciations of Blake.

> I wander thro' each charter'd street,
> Near where the charter'd Thames does flow,
> And mark in every face I meet
> Marks of weakness, marks of woe.

Blake is on the right lines, but he goes too far on them. London is full of injustice, joylessness, and smugness, but there is good temper and rebelliousness in her, too.

Dickens realised this, and so did another great novelist, whose name is not quoted in this connection as often as it should be : Daniel Defoe. Defoe's *Moll Flanders* is the apotheosis of the Cockney ; not criminal, not law abiding, not respectable, warm-hearted. Next time you go down the little passage which leads to St. Bartholomew's, Smithfield, give a thought to Moll Flanders, for it was here that she robbed of a gold necklace a little girl who was coming back from a dancing class. She thought of killing the little girl, too, but desisted, and, conscious of the risk the child had run, she became indignant with the parents for ' leaving the poor little lamb to come home by itself, and it would teach them to take more care of it another time.' Give a thought to her when you are stifled with cant, for she is the goods. I used to loathe London when I was young. Living an immense distance away (to be precise, in Hertfordshire), I used to denounce her for her pomp and vanity, and her inhabitants for their un-manliness and for their unhealthy skins. Like Blake, I went too far. Time has tamed me, and though it is not practicable to love such a place (one could as easily embrace both volumes of the Telephone Directory at once), one can love bits of it and become interested in the rest. She does not pay for being smartened up, and these Coronation arrangements, with their false splendour and false orderliness, do her wrong. She can be casual and gentle. Leave Regent Street for ever. Walk instead through the unsmart squares which lie east of the King's Cross Road—the group which begins with Percy Circus and ends in Arnold Bennett's Riceyman Steps. Or walk as close as you dare to the south bank of the river from Blackfriars Bridge to Tower Bridge—an excellent expedition, including possibilities of trespass and the best available view of St. Paul's. Or go up the river to Battersea Church, where Blake was married, or down it to Rotherhithe Church, where Prince Lee Boo lies buried— he who once was prince of the Pelew Islands. And then return to where you first started from—that is to say, to the City end of London Bridge. Lean over the chasm by Adelaide House again, and allow a few words of one of our living poets to slide through your mind :

> O city, city, I can sometimes hear
> Beside a public bar in Lower Thames Street,
> The pleasant whining of a mandoline
> And a clatter and a chatter from within
> Where fishmen lounge at noon : where the walls
> Of Magnus Martyr hold
> Inexplicable splendour of Ionian white and gold.

T. S. Eliot has felt and has well expressed the muddle of London—the muddle which need not be unpleasant.

[1937]

The Last of Abinger

Written in a Surrey not free from worry, these notes are unlikely to please the nature-lover. Nor are they documentary enough to interest the historian. Most of them come from a common-place book. The date of the final entry (which is partly a dream) is Monday, July 27th, 1946.

EVENING WALK round by the yew-wood on the Pilgrims Way that I have kidded myself into thinking terrifying. It isn't. The junipers looked like men, the yew-roots were silvery in the last light, and resembled skeletons or snakes, a ghostly little plant or two waved at the entrance of the great warm cave. . . . Yet it isn't, it isn't. And a rabbit moving suddenly in the dark as I came down—it isn't either. The really terrifying things are bacteria or the small trefoil that spoils my rockery. I have not time to see or feel this. I waddle on under a ruck-sack of traditional nature-emotions, and try to find something important in the English countryside—man-made, easily alterable by man. George Meredith, my predecessor on these downs, could upset himself with a better conscience.

HONEYSUCKLE BOTTOM. The path is blocked by trees that have fallen in the snow. Wild, wild, wilder than the genuine forests that survive in the South of Sweden. I excite myself by learning the names of the woods on the Ordnance Map, by hearing a wry-neck, and by seeing a swallow and a bat—all these pleasures early. Think I will learn the names of all the fields in the parish. Wish I had talked to old men.

BLIND OAK GATE. The soil of our parish consists of green-sand and of chalk, and is unpropitious to earthquakes. Since the days of King John, who once behaved very badly indeed near Paddington Farm, tragedy has averted her face. The Tillingbourne is too shallow to get drowned in, the banks of the Smugglers' Lane too sloping to be leapt off fatally, and though there are wells, millponds, quarries, a tower upon Leith Hill and several high Wellingtonias, these may not rank as natural dangers ;

they are artificial death-traps which have been constructed by man for his own destruction, often unsuccessfully. Similarly with the mechanically-propelled vehicles which certainly do rush along at lethal speeds ; they have always gathered impetus outside the parish boundaries, and similarly with the aeroplanes. Left to itself, there is not a safer place in England than Abinger.

Yet if not a bang, there is a whimper. Here and there, in this ten-mile ribbon of fluffy Surrey, comes a rumble of occurrences below. One of these rumbles is at Holmbury Camp, where the brow of the heathland is furrowed by neolithic frowns. The other, better known to me, is at Blind Oak Gate.

Blind Oak Gate lies at the extreme north. The tracks leading up to it from the south climb up the clean chalk of the downs, and the sun shines into their ruts. Then begins a brash of bushes —hawthorn, sloe, bramble, heightening into holly and ash, and the sunlight gets frittered away. The ridge of the downs is crossed inadvertently, and after a hundred yards the traveller— for he has become a traveller—reaches this queer clearing. It slopes and slides, descending to the quarter of the north. It has no special shape. Eight or ten paths converge on it—some so unobtrusive that they fail to get counted. It is surrounded by trees, some of which are big, and many of which are undamaged. Tucked away at the top of it is a pond. The pond is small and shallow, and pretty ranunculus cover it in June. But what is it doing up hill ? Like the paths, it is trying to hide itself. It is the centre of the whole affair, if affair there be. When the traveller has passed, the pond rises on its elbow and looks around it. When he returns, it lies back, and only a dribble through silver-weed reveals its dubious bed.

Many years ago, at Cairo, I encountered as a traveller the ruinous Mosque of Amr. The neighbourhood was deserted, the sunlight violent. I stood outside the enclosure and peeped. There was nothing particular to look at—only old stones—but peace and happiness seemed to flow out and fill me. Islam means peace. Whatever the creed may have done, the name means Peace, and its buildings can give a sense of arrival, which is unattainable in any Christian church. The tombs at Bidar give it, the Gol Gumbaz at Bijapur, the Shalimar Gardens at Lahore, the garden-houses at Aurangabad. But it came strongest from the Mosque of Amr, and I learnt afterwards, with super-stitious joy, that others, besides myself, had noticed this ; that the Mosque had been in early days the resort of the Companions of the Prophet ; that the sanctity of their lives had perfumed it ; that the perfume had never faded away. Anyhow, I remember the feeling and am grateful for it, and it is the exact opposite of the feeling I get at Blind Oak Gate. No peace here. Only a sense of something vaguely sinister, which would do harm if it could, but which cannot, this being Surrey ; of something muffled up and recalcitrant ; of something which rises upon its elbow when no one is present and looks down the converging paths. Anyone who knows the novels of Forrest Reid will realise what I am trying to say. He, better than any living author, can convey this atmosphere of baffled malevolence, this sense of trees which are not quite healthy and of water which is not quite clear. Yes—something is amiss. Our parish ingredients have been wrongly combined for once, and I can't honestly say I am sorry.

The Blind Oak and the Gate, which lent their names to the clearing, are both gone. The oak goodness knows when. The gate was pulled up for a lark by a boy who is now a middle-aged butcher. He and some other boys set to work and dragged it over the crest of the downs to the great chalk pit on the southern slope, where they crashed it. The place, deserted by its sponsors, has been left to its very own self, and who knows what it is up to during autumn nights ? Not I. But I have sometimes stood there of a late afternoon, and flirted with the shadow of the shadow of evil. When I can go there no longer, I shall still remember it : it will remain as a faint blur opposite the calm cleansing sunlight of the Mosque of Amr. And when its trees are cut down and its pond emptied and its levels altered, it will not exist anywhere except in my memory. Cursing feebly, Blind Oak Gate will have been cleaned up for ever, and I can't honestly say I shall be glad.

THE OLD CRAB TREE near the second chalk-pit on the downs has been blown down this spring, but is flowering as in other years. Neither sad nor glad that this should be, yet my heart beats to its importance. My head and deepest being said, ' We approve of your heart—*it* is important—but why exercise it over nonsense ? Only those who want, and work for, a civilisation of grass-grown lanes and fallen crab-trees have the right to feel them so deeply.' Most people who feel as I do take refuge in

the ' Nature Reserve ' argument, so tastelessly championed by
H. G. Wells. The moment nature is ' reserved ' her spirit has
departed for me, she is an open-air annex of the school, and only
the semi-educated will be deceived by her. The sort of poetry
I seek resides in objects Man *can't* touch—like England's grass
network of lanes a hundred years ago, but to-day he can destroy
them. The sea is more intractable, but it too passes under human
sway. Peace has been lost on the earth, and only lives outside
it, where my imagination has not been trained to follow, and I
am inclined to agree with Gerald Heard that those who do follow
will abandon literature, which has committed itself too deeply
to the worship of vegetation. To substitute the worship of
motor pumps is unsatisfactory, because it is mere assertiveness,
and can never rise out of the advertisement-catalogue atmosphere. The man who says, ' Look what I'm doing ! ' is merely
reassuring himself that he has done it. Hence the quantity of
empty noises in Walt Whitman.

FALLEN ELMS. Have seen so many of them in the past week
that I ought to be able to describe them in a few vivid words.
All the black outer twigs are crashed and stamped into the earth
and stain it like the ghost of a tree. The wood, where it splits,
suggests commonness, where it is sawn and shows ruddy-choco-
late surrounded by white, distinction. Reggie B. showed me the
sawn top of a great one used as a table ; the old fellow what
walks on two sticks says they were put to many uses when he
was young, only coffins now. Three fell across the garden,
seventeen in Hackhurst Lane, one a double elm or cuckold, which
broke the steps, one of the pair by the drive gate has shown a
surround of cracks as if it will heel over into the field, one leans
across the public path into the wood and rests on three ashes.
The flesh of fallen ashes is beautifully pink here and there where
sawn, and smells different to the elms, though here again I can't
describe or even remember the difference.

CAT IN WOOD washing its face on the grand new oak stump
with amphitheatre of hollies behind it. After a time turned and
saw me—cat I knew slightly but not in that place. We stared,
motionless, but it gradually lowered its head after a bit. I
guessed what was up—it wouldn't take its eyes off mine, yet

wanted to get them down to a place where they couldn't be on them. A frond of fern was enough, and cat bolted.

SANDY FIELD, between Deer Leap and the Railway. Here, a few years ago, three black cinerary urns of the 1st century A.D. were found, the most perfect of which was given to the B.M. by Mrs. E., now herself dead. I saw it there, proffered by a polite colonel, and to-day went to the field. There is a pond, large but difficult to find, and no doubt of the Silent Pool type, for it lies under the down. This was crammed with carp, and when it was cleared out some of them stocked Paddington. Ernest R. told me all this. Up in Deer Leap is a tumulus, spiky with trees, and the field called ' Great Slaughter Field ' is on the other side. (Great Sloe Tree Field really). Peaceful feeling after turning out this tiny pocket of history. Pond lies on watershed and drains towards Mole.

BUNCH OF SENSATIONS. Listening in the late dusk to gramophone records I did not know ; smoking ; the quarter moon shone as the light faded, and brought out sections of my books ; motors coming down the Felday road shone through the window and flung the tulip-tree and pane shadows on the wallpaper near the fireplace. When the music stopped I felt something had arrived in the room ; the sense of a world that asks to be noticed rather than explained was again upon me.

PADDINGTON. Gently and happily relate the evening. In some sort of poetry if it is was mine after the vexatious little prosaic day. I go down to Paddington, old Empson fishing there, and chubb, dace, bream, pike, perch, gudgeon are all mentioned as being in the pond. Seldom caught because they find so much in the mud, and their fins break the surface like tiny sea-serpents or float like sticks. There was a woman once nearly drowned bathing—she had been making a film of the Clock House, and bathed. The ropes flayed her arms. The fish moved, the trees regrouped, the lovely summer night came on. I did not want fun or wit or lust, sat on a rail by a young couple and heard old Empson talk. Did not want anything else, or think of my approaching expulsion from unexplored paradises. One gentle fact after another hit me—as that a pigeon's nest is close. Teeth of the pike, dorsal fin of the perch, they hurt, the fin is poison. Old Empson and I are old and moderate friends, he regrets I am going but did not say, he wanted to talk about fish. The loveliness of indifference ! The restfulness ! The happiness not mystic or intense ! Nothing hanging on it.— Now it is 1.0 a.m. I lie down on my pond, but first will read what I have written.—Have done so.—My hour at Paddington has not come through. I have not the vocabulary, my mind is not sufficiently equable. Yet I still see the fishes' tails breaking the water and the small white float which they never approached. —I am sleepy, I should like the kindly meaninglessness in my dreams. I must go to my pond, to its depths which are not deep only a couple of feet, but out of sight.